DICKENS
AND THE
INVISIBLE
WORLD

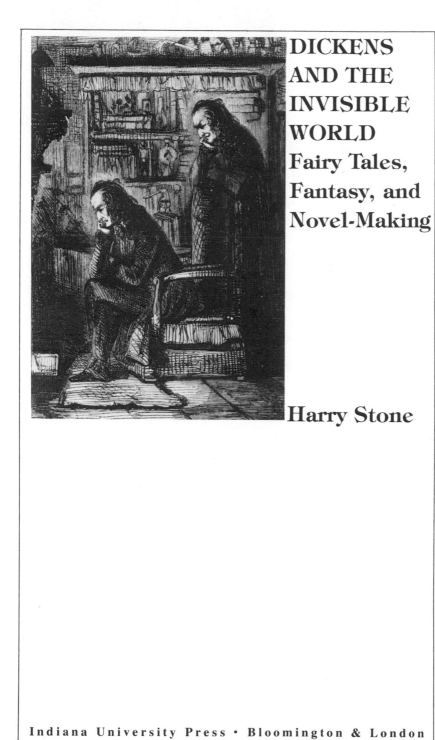

DICKENS AND THE INVISIBLE WORLD

Fairy Tales, Fantasy, and Novel-Making

Harry Stone

Indiana University Press • Bloomington & London

Manufactured in the United States of America

Library of Congress Cataloging in Publication Data

Stone, Harry, 1926–
   Dickens and the invisible world.

   Bibliography: p.
   Includes index.
   1. Dickens, Charles, 1812–1870—Criticism and interpretation. 2. Fairy tales—
History and criticism. 3. Fantasy in literature. 4. Children's literature—History and
criticism. I. Title.
PR4588.S75   823'.8   78–20281
ISBN 0–253–18366–9   1 2 3 4 5 83 82 81 80 79

For *JONATHAN* and *ANN*

Life was . . . a great fairy story, which I was just about to begin to read.

David Copperfield

Contents

Preface

I have sought in this book to study the ways in which fairy tales—and by fairy tales I mean not simply fairy stories, but folklore, myths, legends, enchantments, dreams, signs, recurrences, correspondences, indeed all the mysterious murmurings of the invisible world—entered Dickens' imagination and shaped his art. This development is closely related to one of the fundamental characteristics of his art: the impulse toward fantasy, transformation, and transcendence. That crucial impulse has never been examined in a comprehensive way. This is surprising, for the fairy-tale focus of Dickens' creativity is so basic and pervasive, so entwined with his most primary meanings, that it seems to cry out for analysis. Forster, in his wise and indispensable biography, drew attention, in passing, to Dickens' indebtedness to fairy stories, and many subsequent commentators—also usually in passing—have repeated Forster's insight. But for the most part these acknowledgments have served to preempt the subject rather than examine it. The subject is not an easy one. Dickens' debt to the invisible world is deceptive. For one thing, his storybook effects are usually part of a captivating and compelling realism. Like a master magician—and Dickens was an accomplished magician—he conceals in order to reveal. In any case, a study of Dickens' commerce with the invisible world can take us to the very heart of his creative vision, and can, as I hope this book demonstrates, provide major new insights into his achievement.

I have attempted to deal with every important aspect of Dickens' traffic with fantasy—the historical background, the personal conditioning, the emotional commitment, the evolving use, the mature mastery. I have tried, however, to be representative rather than exhaustive. Dickens' use of enchantment changed and evolved through the first half of his *oeuvre*. I have traced that evolution through *The Pickwick Papers, Oliver Twist, Nicholas Nickleby, The Old Curiosity Shop, Barnaby Rudge, Martin Chuzzlewit,* and the Christmas books. With *Dombey and Son,* Dickens arrived at his mature, but not yet fully refined, fairy-tale method, and I have looked closely at this major advance. *David Copperfield* is the first consummate rendering of that new method—the prototype, in terms of perfected storybook technique, of all the novels that came thereafter—and I have studied *Copperfield* at length as the exemplar of Dickens' mastery of his fairy-tale art. I have touched on the other novels in passing, but I have given special attention to *Great Expectations*. My reasons for this concentration are simple. First, *Great Expectations* provides a late example of Dickens' storybook method; second, it allows me to trace one or two patterns not illustrated in the other novels; and third, it permits me to study the genesis, evolution, and fulfillment of one of Dickens' most beautiful designs—to demonstrate how Dickens translated ordinary encounters and everyday circumstances into rich fairy-tale fabling.

This book has been supported by a Guggenheim Fellowship, a National Endowment for the Humanities Fellowship, and grants from California State University, Northridge. I am deeply grateful for this aid.

HARRY STONE
Los Angeles
April, 1979

DICKENS
AND THE
INVISIBLE
WORLD

1 | Dickens, Cruikshank, and the Sanctity of Fairy Tales
A Prologue

In JULY 1853 Dickens was summering in Boulogne. He had come there about the middle of June, and except for a few days in London in September, he remained there until the middle of October. When he arrived in Boulogne he was badly overworked. He had been chained to *Bleak House* for a year and a half, still had four monthly parts to write, but in addition (and as usual) had simultaneously been caught up in enough activities to fill the days and nights of several ordinary men. He was, for example, deeply engaged in every aspect of Angela Burdett-Coutts' home for fallen women; he was also writing the insistent installments of *A Child's History of England,* supervising theatrical benefits, overseeing the weekly issues of his magazine, *Household Words,* and whirling through the comings and goings of his frenetic social life.

Boulogne proved to be an ideal prescription. Dickens had never summered there before, but he soon found that the situation, the town, and the routine suited him perfectly. He had rented a charming villa on a wooded hillside. The grounds included beautiful terraced gardens dense with thousands of roses and lush with a myriad other flowers. From his perch high in the hills he could see the picturesque jumble of Boulogne spreading down the slopes before him. The walk to the post office was ten minutes; to the sea, fifteen. In these surroundings Dickens quickly threw off his "hypochondriacal whisperings."[1] A day or two after arriving in Boulogne he found that he was able to return to his writing with "great ease";[2] two weeks later he had finished Part XVII of *Bleak House.* By 24 July he had finished Part XVIII, and on 1 August he began work on the double number that concluded the novel.

Dickens fell gratefully into the slowed rhythm of his pastoral life, and

1

he luxuriated in his lightened responsibilities. Day followed day in ordered measure. The end of *Bleak House* was now fast approaching. London enticements and London duties were a world away. Yet he still had much to occupy his time. His chief ongoing responsibility was *Household Words,* and he contrived, insofar as *Bleak House* and distance would allow him, to maintain his usual surveillance over that periodical—settling makeup, suggesting subjects for essays, titling articles, rewriting papers, correcting proofs, writing his own contributions, and so on. He managed this long-distance feat by having his subeditor, William Henry Wills, send him early proofs of each forthcoming issue. Dickens then went over the tentative number and returned it with his advice, corrections, rearrangements, vetoes, or whatever. Wills also sent on Dickens' customary newspapers and magazines and any items that required his personal attention.

Among the periodicals that Dickens received each week was the *Examiner,* edited by his close friend and confidant John Forster. In the *Examiner* for 23 July 1853, Forster had reviewed George Cruikshank's latest production, an edition of *Hop-o'-my-Thumb* rewritten and illustrated by the "illustrious George." *Hop-o'-my-Thumb* was to be the first pamphlet in a series of similar redactions by Cruikshank, the entire series to bear the title, *George Cruikshank's Fairy Library*. In his review of *Hop-o'-my-Thumb*, Forster lauded Cruikshank's designs, pointed out that he had interpolated social doctrines into the story, concluded that this was perhaps good, and urged readers to support the series. Dickens read Forster's review in Boulogne, and it gave him an idea for *Household Words*. "I have . . . thought," he wrote Wills on 27 July 1853, of an article "to be called Frauds upon the Fairies—*apropos* of George Cruikshank's editing." Then he went on:

> Half playfully and half seriously, I mean to protest most strongly against alteration—for any purpose—of the beautiful little stories which are so tenderly and humanly useful to us in these times when the world is too much with us, early and late; and then to re-write Cinderella according to Total-abstinence, Peace Society, and Bloomer principles, and expressly for their propagation.
>
> I shall want his book of Hop o' My Thumb (Forster noticed it in the last Examiner) and the most simple and popular version of Cinderella you can get me. I shall not be able to do it until after finishing Bleak House, but I shall do it the more easily for having the books by me. So send them, if convenient, in your next parcel.

Dickens' idea and the consequences that flowed from it not only put an end to his long friendship with Cruikshank—already seriously strained—but served to epitomize (and in part to generate) some of his most deeply held beliefs concerning art and life.

When Dickens told Wills his idea for "Frauds on the Fairies," he was probably only dimly aware of how deep his feelings on the subject were. His initial response to Cruikshank's editing seems to have been a mixture of amused incredulity and lingering irritation. But more was at stake. All unwittingly, Cruikshank had challenged some of Dickens' formative childhood experiences, some of his fundamental concerns and credos. Dickens was convinced that the literature he read as a child had been crucial to his imagination. He was equally certain that the literature he read as a youth had prevented him from perishing. The literature of childhood was the source of all his "early imaginations"; the literature of youth "kept alive my fancy, and my hope of something beyond that place and time."[3] At the center of the latter period was the blacking warehouse, and Dickens literally believed that reading, and the imagination nurtured by that reading, allowed him—but only barely allowed him—to survive. Dickens came to these conclusions much later as he looked back on his early years. As we shall see in the succeeding chapters, his books reflect these judgments and these commitments. But more than that—and this too we shall see—his writings are profoundly shaped by that early reading and imagining, a shaping that has the fairy tale as its matrix.

His writings are also rich with nostalgic allusions to the childhood literature that soothed and sustained him. By the time of the autobiographical *David Copperfield* (1849–1850), he was so certain of the benign influence of that early reading that he made his own reading experiences a central feature of young David's survival and development. About this time too he turned his own experiences into articles of faith. In a period of early desolation (so his syllogism ran), literature, especially childhood literature, had saved him; in an iron time, literature could help save others. He came increasingly to enunciate this principle. In March 1850, in the manifesto which inaugurated *Household Words*, he reaffirmed this childhood-engendered belief. In that manifesto he asserted his faith in literature as salvation. *Household Words* would "teach the hardest workers at this whirling wheel of toil, that their lot is not necessarily a moody, brutal fact, excluded from the sympathies and graces of imagination." And Dickens ended his declaration by alluding to an "old fairy story" and promising that he would "Go on!"[4]

By 1850, then, Dickens strongly and consciously associated the literature of childhood with the greatest of public ends. The literature of childhood nursed the imagination and softened dehumanizing toil. What Dickens most valued in that literature was its ability to nurture the imagination. Without imagination (or "fancy," as Dickens often called it) human beings could not be truly human. He therefore set his face against any attempt to make literature serve narrow, anti-

imaginative ends. Here again he remembered the lessons of his childhood. For there was a deadly as well as a saving literature of childhood.
The deadly literature of childhood was a dreary counterbalance to the
childhood literature that had helped save him. His writings are sprinkled with disparaging references to this "other" literature, the
off-putting literature of his early years. He abhorred his childhood
arithmetic books with their "cool impertinent inquiries"; rejected his
spelling books as productive of "weariness, languor, and distaste";
turned away from those "horrible" tracts "which commenced business with the poor child by asking him . . . why he was going to Perdition"; commiserated with students who "abandoned hope half through
the Latin grammar"; and despised the kind of literature that "didacti-
cally improved all sorts of occasions, from the consumption of a plate
of cherries to the contemplation of a starlight night."[5] This stultifying
childhood literature was so distasteful to Dickens that it darkened everything associated with it. Even a name could become tainted by
spelling-book connotations. From childhood on, Dickens would always
associate "Philip" with direful didacticism. "Philip" would forever
sound "like a moral boy out of the spelling-book, who was so lazy that
he fell into a pond, or so fat that he couldn't see out of his eyes, or so
avaricious that he locked up his cake till the mice ate it, or so determined to go a bird's-nesting that he got himself eaten by bears who
lived handy in the neighbourhood."[6] The virtuous counterpart of Philip
was equally obnoxious. Dickens abhorred "Little Margery, who resided in the village cottage by the mill; severely reproved and morally
squashed the miller, when she was five and he was fifty; divided her
porridge with singing birds; denied herself a new nankeen bonnet, on
the ground that the turnips did not wear nankeen bonnets, neither did
the sheep who ate them," and so on.[7] On the other hand, he surrounded the pictures in his childhood geography book with fanciful
imaginings, reveled in the wit and ingenuity of *Aesop's Fables,* and
associated all that was unforgettable or marvelous in *The Arabian
Nights, The Tales of the Genii, Robinson Crusoe,* and similar works,
with the comings and goings and responses of his everyday life. The
test in all such matters was very simple. He attacked all childhood
literature that was given over to dour prosing; he exalted all childhood
literature that was wild or fanciful or free.

    The literary quintessence of that wild freedom was the fairy story.
More and more through the 1840s and the early 1850s Dickens was
coming to regard the fairy tale and its correlatives—fantasy, enchantment, legends, signs, and correspondences, indeed all the thronging
manifestations of the invisible world—as potent instruments and incarnations of imaginative truth. The fairy tale was the most important
of those incarnations. It transformed mysterious correspondences and

veiled manifestations into ministering art. The fairy story was an emblem, at once rudimentary and pure, of what contemporary society needed and what it increasingly lacked. The fairy story was also inextricably associated with childhood; it shaped the very character of future generations. In Dickens' lexicon the fairy tale was becoming a shorthand way of emphasizing a contemporary danger and suggesting an essential solution. The lesson, Dickens felt, was clear. In an age when men were becoming machines, fairy stories must be cherished and must be allowed to do their beneficent work of nurturing man's birthright of feeling and fancy.

So Dickens had come to believe when, in July 1853, in his rose-begirt villa high above Boulogne, he leafed through the pages of the *Examiner* and lighted upon Forster's review of Cruikshank's *Hop-o'-my-Thumb*. Given Dickens' attitude toward childhood literature, his response was predictable. The review evoked a powerful array of active and slumbering feelings. His childhood memories of fairy stories, his conviction that he had been succored by early imaginative reading, his hatred of didactic children's literature, his sense of the importance and sanctity of fairy tales—all these elements contributed to his response. But there were other factors as well. Dickens had been Cruikshank's friend and companion for almost twenty years, and the tangled history of their personal friendship added powerful point to what Dickens soon after did.

Dickens and Cruikshank first met on 17 November 1835, shortly after John Macrone, Dickens' publisher, arranged to have Cruikshank illustrate the forthcoming *Sketches by Boz*, Dickens' first book. At the time Dickens was twenty-three and virtually unknown; Cruikshank was forty-three and the preeminent graphic artist of the day. In the circumstances one might have expected the younger man to defer, in artistic matters at least, to his famous illustrator. But Dickens soon made clear that his view of their professional relationship was that Cruikshank should illustrate what he had written. In the case of *Sketches by Boz* First Series (1836), virtually everything that Cruikshank was to illustrate had already been published before Cruikshank set to work—so precluding any possibility of interference—but in later works that was not the case. Soon there was intermittent friction between the rising young author and the established illustrator. In part the friction had to do with haste and pressure—late copy, delayed plates, clashing schedules, and the like; in part it had to do with differences over the suitability of subjects for illustration. But these were difficulties more or less common to such collaborations; they were irritants rather than confrontations. Within months, however, there was a more serious opposition.

When Dickens heard from Macrone that Cruikshank had expressed a desire to see the manuscript of *Sketches by Boz* Second Series (1836) in order to suggest "any little alteration to suit the Pencil," he exploded scornfully (?19 October 1836):

> I have long believed Cruikshank to be mad; and his letter therefore, surprises me, not a jot. If you have any further communication with him, you will greatly oblige me by saying *from me* that I am very much amused at the notion of his altering my Manuscript, and that had it fallen into his hands, I should have preserved his emendations as "curiosities of Literature". Most decidedly am I of opinion that he may just go to the Devil; and so far as I have any interest in the book, I positively object to his touching it.

Dickens went on to suggest that perhaps the Second Series should dispense with illustrations altogether, or if it were illustrated, that Hablot Knight Browne ("Phiz") should be the artist. Macrone finally managed to calm Dickens down, but two years later, when *Oliver Twist* (1837–1838)[8] was coming to an end, another confrontation—the culmination of a series of conflicts—took place. Dickens was so upset by the poor quality (as he saw it) of several of the concluding illustrations for *Oliver Twist* that he asked that two of the plates be withdrawn at once, even though the book was already being printed. He finally modified this demand, and wrote directly to Cruikshank suggesting that Cruikshank cancel the "Fireside" plate (the worst offender) and replace it with a new design.[9] Cruikshank tried to save the plate by improving it, but Dickens found the improvement unacceptable, and Cruikshank finally replaced the illustration with the equally insipid "Church" plate.[10]

Dickens must have vowed at this time never again to collaborate with Cruikshank on a major project. In the next year or two there was some talk of such projects, and Cruikshank was eager for them, but as Dickens' plans became realities, he invariably turned elsewhere for illustrators.[11]

By 1841, the two men had ceased to collaborate even in minor ways.

Strangely, during all these vicissitudes, Dickens' friendship with Cruikshank waxed. When the two men met in 1835, they were immediately attracted to one another, and this attraction grew despite some early impediments. It overcame their twenty-year disparity in age, survived their differences concerning *Sketches by Boz* and *Oliver Twist,* and triumphed over their divergent personalities. Cruikshank was gradually captivated by the geniality and high spirits of the young author, who soon proved to have a steadiness and acumen equal to his energy and genius. Dickens, on the other hand, was delighted with

Cruikshank's warmhearted zeal, and with his eccentricity and whimsicality as well. Though middle-aged and often crotchety, Cruikshank had preserved a childlike openness and vitality that appealed to Dickens. As their friendship grew, the traditional roles of youth and age seemed to be reversed, Dickens acting the prudent mentor to Cruikshank's wayward exuberance.

The friendship flourished through the late 1830s and early 1840s. Beginning with notes and calls, it progressed to visits and dinners, and culminated with parties, excursions, amateur theatricals, and nights on the town. Paradoxically—or perhaps significantly—the friendship seems to have been closest and the meetings most frequent at the very time in 1842 and 1843 when the two had ceased to work together professionally. If there had been any lingering asperities, they seem to have vanished by then. Dickens regarded Cruikshank as a delightful fellow, someone who could liven a dull party or transfigure a listless evening. Cruikshank, for his part, came to Dickens for advice and aid and comfort, as well as for companionship.

Cruikshank often needed the advice, and he needed the aid as well. He loved the convivial, carousing life, but he drank too much. Dickens was not offended by his friend's drinking. He regarded Cruikshank's inebriated escapades as part of his eccentricity. After a night on the town, Cruikshank would sometimes appear on Dickens' doorstep, boozy and disheveled. Dickens would then nurse him through his morning-long bouts of remorse and finally conduct him to a shamefaced reunion with his family.[12] Cruikshank seemed content with this wayward life, but his wild escapades concealed a guilty conscience. He was profoundly disturbed by his drinking. His father had died of drink. Cruikshank felt that a similar fate was gradually engulfing him. His fear and self-revulsion finally propelled him to change. By 1847 he had committed himself to the temperance movement; by the end of that year he had become a total abstainer. He soon developed into a fanatical crusader for abstinence. His conversion to teetotalism gave a new impetus to his life. In private homes and at public banquets, in etchings, pamphlets, letters, speeches, testimonials, and exhortations, he tirelessly preached the fatal consequences of drink. His extremism and his single-mindedness often offended those about him and lost him many friends. On one occasion, at Dickens' house, he enraged Dickens by snatching a glass of wine from a fellow guest and attempting to dash it to the floor.[13] Dickens intervened and reproved Cruikshank, but he did not allow the episode to rupture their friendship. After an interval, Dickens would shrug such scenes off as additional signs of Cruikshank's impetuous eccentricity.

But Cruikshank's artistic strategies were not so easy to shrug off. In 1847 Cruikshank had produced *The Bottle,* a direful drunkard's progress in eight plates. Dickens bought the series on the day of publication. He thought the scenes very powerful, and the last two plates, despite objections, "most admirable." No one living, he thought, could have done them so well.[14] But Cruikshank confused effects with causes. Drunkenness, Dickens thought, was not a primal evil, but a symptom of deeper pathologies. When, in July 1848, Cruikshank issued an eight-plate sequel to *The Bottle* entitled *The Drunkard's Children,* Dickens decided to speak out. On 8 July 1848, he reviewed the new series in the *Examiner,* using the occasion to discuss both works. Though again praising Cruikshank's "peculiar and remarkable power," his ability to create scenes and images that haunt "the remembrance, like an awful reality," he denied Cruikshank's social analysis. Drunkenness does not begin, as Cruikshank portrayed it as beginning in *The Bottle,* with an idle and motiveless drink. "It has a teeming and reproachful history anterior to that stage; and at the remediable evil in that history, it is the duty of the moralist, if he strikes at all, to strike deep and spare not." "Hogarth," Dickens continued, "avoided the Drunkard's Progress, we conceive, precisely because the causes of drunkenness among the poor were so numerous and widely spread, and lurked so sorrowfully deep and far down in all human misery, neglect, and despair, that even *his* pencil could not bring them fairly and justly into the light."[15] Yet Hogarth's art was infinitely deeper than Cruikshank's. Hogarth was not content to portray results. His art depicted the inception of evil, and his art was profoundly symbolic. Objects, persons, actions—all the details of his works—commented on the causes of the social disorder they also objectified. Cruikshank, on the other hand, neglected these considerations, and as a result his work was compromised and weakened.

Cruikshank must have been disturbed by Dickens' criticism, but the analysis did not change his ideas about teetotalism. In the next few years he redoubled his temperance agitations, and in the next few years the teetotal movement, which had started in the provinces, began to conquer the metropolis. In August 1851 there were giant temperance rallies in London. In these rallies Cruikshank played a prominent role. Dickens' response to the demonstrations and the agitation was an angry article in *Household Words*. On 23 August 1851, he published the piece, entitled "Whole Hogs," as the lead paper in his magazine.[16]

"Whole Hogs" attacked the fanaticism of the temperance movement, with special reference to its recent rallies and fêtes. Pointing out that most temperance enthusiasts were intemperate both in their proposals (which were for teetotalism rather than for temperance) and in their language, he dubbed such advocates "Whole Hog" fanatics— fanatics who insist that everyone act precisely and totally as they do. As Dickens put it figuratively in his article, such persons were not content to receive their own proper share of the hog and consume it in their own fashion, they insisted that everyone immoderately accede to their monomania and consume the Whole Hog, "sides, ribs, limbs, cheeks, face, trotters, snout, ears," and "tail," and "sinking none of the offal, but consenting to it all." Dickens went on to satirize temperance officials, temperance meetings, temperance demonstrations, and temperance pledges—especially those teetotal pledges extracted from children, who thereupon became members of "Juvenile Temperance Bands of Hope," the "Infantine Brigade of Regenerators of Mankind."

In addition to these criticisms, Dickens had another complaint. The temperance movement deflected interest from the great festering problems of society. All his life Dickens had concentrated on what he conceived to be the real and remedial causes of social pathology—ignorance, poverty, neglect, and despair. Those were the true enemies of mankind. Against those enemies, and against those movements which drew attention away from such problems, he would not stay his pen.

Thus matters stood in August 1851; and thus matters stood in July 1853, when Dickens came upon Forster's review of Cruikshank's *Hop-o'-my-Thumb*. What Dickens brought to that reading on the personal level was a conflicting tangle of emotions and opinions. He mingled positive interest in Cruikshank and admiration for his art with skepticism concerning his views and irritation at his tactics. Yet when he read Forster's review, his primary reaction was shaped not by years of Cruikshankian amiabilities and Cruikshankian crotchets—though these played their part—but by larger considerations. His reaction was dominated by his profound conviction (at the moment perhaps an intuition rather than a reasoned argument) that Cruikshank was once again tampering with fundamental matters, this time with the very sources of imagination and creativity.

This is corroborated not simply by what Dickens later wrote, but by the disparity between Forster's review and Dickens' immediate response. Forster's review was full of praise and acceptance. He hailed Cruikshank's entrance into fairyland. No artist living, he thought, was better equipped by temperament and skill to be "court painter to Oberon." He then went on to describe the illustrations in *Hop-o'-my-Thumb*. His enthusiasm was boundless. Words such as "delight," "charming," "exquisite," and "genius" sprinkle the page. The illustrations, he asserted, were among the best that Cruikshank had ever drawn. He went even further: "more perfectly illustrated such tales never have been, and never again are likely to be." He continued by pointing out that Cruikshank occasionally introduced his own moral precepts into the tale, but this, Forster felt, was no fault. Quite the contrary. Such editing "can . . . do no harm—for such morals are not here obtruded in any dull way—and in the opinion of many it may be very likely to do good."

Dickens took a far different tack. What caught his attention were the intruded morals, their incongruity and their subversiveness. Then and there he determined to protest "half playfully and half seriously" against Cruikshank's editing, and then and there he wrote, in the letter already quoted, for a copy of Cruikshank's *Hop-o'-my-Thumb* and for an ordinary version of *Cinderella,* so that he could prepare himself for his reply and write it as soon as *Bleak House* was completed. When Cruikshank's little booklet did arrive, it confirmed and intensified Dickens' fears and angers.

As chance would have it, even Cruikshank's cover (all unwittingly on Cruikshank's part, of course) touched sensitive areas of Dickens' inner life. The cover portrayed a fearsome ogre watching over two scenes of parental abandonment. These scenes, captioned respectively, "The Father proposes to lose the Children!!!" and "They Leave Hop 'o my Thumb and his Brothers in the Wood," depicted parents in the very act of plotting against and betraying their innocent children. Such a cover was calculated to arouse Dickens' most susceptible sympathies and fears. His feeling that his own parents had rejected and abandoned him was perhaps the most shaping emotion in his life. His works are filled with unnatural parents, tender references to *The Children in the Wood* (another fable of parental abandonment), and terrifying evocations of being lost and parentless in roaring streets. But more than this, the figure of the neglected or orphaned or outcast child—another projection of his overwhelming sense of childhood abandonment—recurs with obsessive power in his writings.

Cruikshank's cover was thus a call to Dickens' deepest feelings about the sanctity and violation of childhood, and the fairy tale Cruikshank was about to recount, and indeed all fairy tales, had long since become symbols to Dickens of that sanctity and that threat. More than this, all fairy stories stood for the saving grace of childhood imagination and childhood escape, and in a larger perspective, for the saving power of all imagination and art, a power that Dickens held to be sacred and inviolable. Cruikshank's text prostituted that power; Cruikshank, so it seemed to Dickens, manipulated the vulnerabilities of childhood and the privileges of art for narrow and fanatical ends. Cruikshank's marvelous illustrations captured the fears and fantasies and fulfillments of childhood. But the more wonderful the art, the greater the violation in making it serve purposes destructive of art itself.

In *Hop-o'-my-Thumb,* Cruikshank's art was a means of promulgating his text; for Dickens, that text was profoundly subversive.[17] First of all, Cruikshank played fast and loose with the fable. He eliminated the central episode of how Hop saved himself and his brothers by tricking the ogre into murdering his own daughters (an episode that had powerfully and fearfully impressed Dickens as a child), imported into *Hop* the "Fe Fi Fo Fum" of *Jack the Giant Killer* (another episode that had gripped Dickens' imagination), and tampered with a multitude of lesser matters. Alone, these changes would have evoked Dickens' dismay rather than his anger. But Cruikshank had also sprinkled the story with the most prosing moral precepts and examples, the kinds of intruded morals that Dickens had hated as a boy and inveighed against all his life. Nor had Cruikshank limited his advocacy to rules of conduct; he had dragged in pronouncements on religious instruction, popular education, and free trade. It was just the kind of pervasive didacticism that Dickens had always regarded as dreary and deadening, the antithesis of fancy and imagination. Cruikshank was constantly intruding remarks about "nasty tobacco," "betting and gambling," the virtue of "perseverance," and the need "to admit foreign grain" into domestic markets. Cruikshank was remorseless. Hop and his brothers learned to wash themselves "in cold water (which they did winter and summer, because it is most refreshing and healthy to do so)"; to forgo "much eating at supper"; and to avoid picking their teeth with a fork. They had also been taught by their "dear mother" to "go to bed early, which they all did, like good children, without any grumbling or crying." And every night good little Hop-o'-my-Thumb was always the first to say, "I'm ready to go to bed, mother."

From Dickens' point of view, Cruikshank's didacticism was doubly destructive. It intruded a pedestrian note that was totally alien to the spirit and tone of the fairy story. But more important, it imported into the world of the fairy tale the anti-fairy tale. Enticed by Cruikshank's compelling illustrations, the child would enter the storybook world only to find that it contained the same prosing precepts that nagged at him from the pages of his insufferable copybooks or his improving moral tracts. To Dickens, Cruikshank's text was a fraud. It would turn children away from the fount of fancy and imagination at the very source.

This was bad enough—in fact it was insupportable—but Cruikshank had gone further. He had infused *Hop-o'-my-Thumb* with an outrageous teetotalism. The ideology ran through the entire story. Drink was responsible for the poverty of Hop's father (who had been a rich Count before he turned to drink), for the deprivation of the family, for the abandonment of the children, and for most of the other sins and lapses in the story. Even the ogre's downfall was caused by drink. The ogre had imbibed so much on the night he had Hop and his brothers in his power that they were able to escape and ultimately to steal his seven-league boots. The story had a happy, teetotal ending. When Hop brought his father before the King, the King rewarded his old friend (for the King and the Count had been old companions) by making him Prime Minister. As Prime Minister, the erstwhile drunkard discovered that "strong drinks were hurtful to all." Accordingly he passed a law to "abolish the use of all intoxicating liquors; the effect of which law was, that in a short time there were very few, if any, criminals in the land; and the only paupers, or really poor, were those sick or aged persons who were unable to do any sort of work, for all the people in the land were industrious, and the country was rich."

This, Dickens thought, was Whole Hoggism with a vengeance. The entire notion would have been ludicrous had it not been aimed at children and had it not affronted Dickens' deepest beliefs. For in addition to violating Dickens' views concerning the crucial role of literature in childhood and the saving power of fairy stories, Cruikshank was intruding false notions concerning the causes of remediable social ills. He was now, to Dickens' way of thinking, introducing to the most sensitive areas of Dickens' belief the errors that Dickens had found in *The Bottle* and *The Drunkard's Children*. The origins of poverty and crime, the intricate gestation of neglectful or rejecting parents, the ravaging inception of ignorance, cruelty, and despair—all these and more, in the gospel of Cruikshank, were simply by-products of "strong drinks." Dickens' childhood experiences and his lifelong endeavors cried out against this notion. And Dickens' commitment to fancy and imagination cried out against transforming the child's bright birthright of fairy tales into dreary homilies and teetotal tracts.

With such feelings and such commitments impelling him, and with perhaps an occasional memory of the old Cruikshank amiably drunk or the new Cruikshank aggressively sober adding ironic relish to his purpose, Dickens sat down in September 1853, *Bleak House* now completed, to write "Frauds on the Fairies."[18] He had kind words for Cruikshank the artist. Cruikshank was a "man of genius" and "our own beloved friend." He should, Dickens continued, be the last to do violence to fairy stories because in his own art he understands fairy lore "so perfectly, and illustrates it so beautifully, so humorously, so wisely." But Cruikshank's text was another matter. "We have lately observed, with pain," wrote Dickens, "the intrusion of a Whole Hog of unwieldy dimensions into the fairy flower garden." The huge beast was there, "rooting . . . among the roses." Such an intrusion was neither an inconsequential nor a narrow matter. "In an utilitarian age, of all other times, it is a matter of grave importance that Fairy tales should be respected. . . . A nation without fancy, without some romance, never did, never can, never will, hold a great place under the sun." For fairy tales are the "nurseries of fancy." To preserve their usefulness they must be transmitted undisturbed. "Whosoever alters them to suit his own opinions, whatever they are, is guilty, to our thinking, of an act of presumption, and appropriates to himself what does not belong to him."

With his bow to Cruikshank and his manifesto of opposition out of the way, Dickens went on to retell *Cinderella* according to outrageous total abstinence principles, throwing in, for good measure, an abundance of quirky Cruikshankian-type asides on all sorts of social and political issues. The parody was hilarious and devastating. At the age of four, Cinderella, by her own desire, became a member of the Juvenile Bands of Hope ("Central district, number five hundred and twenty-seven"). Five years later her mother died, and Cinderella, accompanied by fifteen hundred members of the Juvenile Bands of Hope, "followed her to the grave, singing chorus Number forty-two, 'O come,' etc." The grave was located and regulated auspiciously. It was "outside the town, and under the direction of the Local Board of Health, which reported at certain stated intervals to the General Board of Health, Whitehall."

After a year Cinderella's father remarried. Unfortunately he married a very cross widow lady, but fortunately he did not have to abide her tyranny long. Owing to the fact that he had been "shamefully accustomed to shave with warm water instead of cold," his constitution was undermined and he died. Little orphan Cinderella then commenced her well-known odyssey (teetotal version). She culminated her adventures in the usual way by marrying the prince, but then undertook innovative measures. "Cinderella, being now a queen, applied herself to the government of the country on enlightened, liberal, and free principles. All the people who ate anything she did not eat, or who drank anything she did not drink, were imprisoned for life. All the newspaper offices from which any doctrine proceeded that was not her doctrine, were burnt down." And on and on with tyrannical fanaticism. Dickens concluded his essay with a Wordsworthian diagnosis and a personal prescription. "The world is too much with us, early and late," he wrote. "Leave this precious old escape from it, alone."

"Frauds on the Fairies" appeared on 1 October 1853, as the opening article in *Household Words*. When Cruikshank read the piece he was filled with resentment. Cuthbert Bede, who saw him shortly afterwards, described him as "smarting from the effects of Dickens's article."[19] Those effects included more than an assault on Cruikshank's beliefs and sensibilities, they included the possibility of damaging economic loss. *Hop-o'-my-Thumb* was the first story in a projected *Fairy Library* which would ultimately consist of a whole series of fairy tales rewritten and illustrated by Cruikshank. If Dickens' article damaged sales, the entire project might be jeopardized. Cruikshank was also about to launch a new monthly periodical entitled *George Cruikshank's Magazine*. This periodical and the *Fairy Library* were an attempt by Cruikshank—as it turned out his last really concerted attempt—to recapture his lost audience and his lost standing. The first issue of the new magazine appeared in January 1854, the second—and last—appeared the following month and contained "A Letter From Hop-O'-My-Thumb to Charles Dickens, Esq. Upon 'Frauds On The Fairies,' 'Whole Hogs,' Etc." Cruikshank's reply also contained a woodcut illustration showing Hop-o'-my-Thumb driving three enormous hogs—obviously gigantic Whole Hogs—back to *Household Words*.

Cruikshank's reply was rambling and discursive, at times defiant, combative, even abusive, at other times plaintive, humorous, even friendly. Cruikshank, writing in the guise of Hop-o'-my-Thumb, accused Dickens of going out of his way to find fault with him. Dickens was a man of "remarkable acuteness," but he had made a "great mistake" in allowing his "extraordinary seven-league boot imagination" to mislead him as to what the old fairy tales were. Dickens' article was "Much Ado About Nothing." For the text of a fairy story is not fixed, and to "insist upon preserving the entire integrity of a Fairy tale" is like "shearing one of your own 'whole hogs,' where there is 'great cry and little wool.'" Cruikshank's editing was essential and salutary. He had simply removed the immoral and depraved elements from *Hop-o'-my-Thumb*. As for the temperance coloring, Dickens had an "evident contempt, and even hatred, against that cause." "I take the liberty of telling you," Cruikshank went on, "that it is a question which you evidently do not understand." Cruikshank concluded with a request and a rejection. "I have therefore to beg, that in future you will not drive your 'whole hogs' against us, but take them to some other market, or keep them to yourself if you like; but we'll none of 'em, and therefore I take this opportunity of driving them back."

Cruikshank caused his magazine reply to be printed also as a separate penny pamphlet. When, about the same time, he came to publish the next of his rewritten fairy tales, *Jack and the Bean-Stalk,* he did not continue the controversy directly, though he did make the giant a depraved individual who drank himself tipsy every night and ravaged the countryside as a result. But in *Cinderella,* the third installment of the *Fairy Library,* also published in 1854, Cruikshank alluded directly to the controversy. In a note at the end entitled "To The Public," he admonished Harriet Beecher Stowe for describing him as "an old man, with grey hair"; reproved a reviewer for criticizing his setting of *Jack and the Bean-Stalk;* and advised would-be readers who might fall into "absurd mistakes" such as the aforesaid reviewer fell into or "such as my friend Charles Dickens has fallen into," to buy and read his penny-pamphlet reply to Dickens. (In later issues of this note, Cruikshank had his reference to Dickens reset so that "my friend Charles Dickens" became "Mr. Charles Dickens.")

As for the text of *Cinderella* itself, Cruikshank seemed bent on out-parodying Dickens' parody. When the King ordered fountains of wine in the street to celebrate Cinderella's marriage, Cinderella's godmother "begged that his Majesty would not carry out that part of the arrangements," for "drink leads also to quarrels, brutal fights, and violent deaths." When the King replied that such violence is only committed by those who take too much, the godmother replied that "the history of the use of strong drinks . . . is marked on every page by *excess, which follows, as a matter of course, from the very nature of their composition*, and are [sic] always accompanied by ill-health, misery, and crime." The godmother then launched upon a page-long disquisition which praised the beneficence of the Almighty in making harmful liquors intoxicating, admonished the King that "so long as your Majesty continues to take even half a glass of wine a-day, so long will the drinking customs of society be considered respectable," and advised the King to "look at Cinderella, who never has taken any in all her life, and who never will."

Cinderella brought the *Fairy Library* to an abrupt halt. Whether this was the result of poor sales, hostile reactions, or Cruikshank's own decision is not clear. What is clear is that *Puss in Boots*, the fourth and last fairy story that Cruikshank rewrote for his *Fairy Library*—one suspects that it was conceived like the last two in 1854—did not appear until 1864. In 1865 the four fairy tales were collected in a single volume, Cruikshank retaining most of his earlier addresses and announcements and reprinting a further justification of his editorial practices. The latter defense, originally published with *Puss in Boots* in 1864 and entitled, "To Parents, Guardians, And All Persons Intrusted With The Care Of Children," was based, for the most part, on the 1854 letter from Hop-o'-my-Thumb to Dickens. (The pamphlet version of that letter, Cruikshank explained, was now out of print.) Cruikshank, in effect, was making his controversy with Dickens a permanent part of his *Fairy Library*. His new reply contained few substantive changes. He reemphasized and reargued his position here and there, and he carefully pruned away all genial references to Dickens.

To all of this, both in 1854 and 1864, Dickens made no direct reply. Yet the aftereffects of his initial encounter with Cruikshank in 1853 were always with him. In that year "Frauds on the Fairies" had intensified and focused his lifelong feelings concerning the importance of fairy stories. The fairy tale now stood at the center of his imaginative and social beliefs; it was a shorthand way of referring to and dramatizing those beliefs. The fairy story was also a touchstone and an anodyne. When, immediately after writing "Frauds on the Fairies," Dickens suggested to Angela Burdett-Coutts that she read the piece, he added that he felt the essay would enlist her on his side—"which is for a little more fancy among children and a little less fact."[20] "More fancy . . . less fact" might stand as an epigraph for *Hard Times,* a book Dickens began a few months after writing "Frauds on the Fairies." And Sissy Jupe, it will be remembered, read all "about the Fairies . . . and the Dwarf, and the Hunchback, and the Genies," much to the consternation of the didactic Mr. Gradgrind.[21]

Dickens never tired of proclaiming the beneficence of fairy tales and imagination. In editorial policies, novels, essays, letters, and speeches, he illustrated and enunciated his belief. "In these times," he said in a speech in 1857, "when we have torn so many leaves out of our dear old nursery books, I hold it to be more than ever essential . . . that the imagination, with all its innumerable graces and charities, should be tenderly nourished."[22] The idea recurs insistently. In 1858, in another speech, he was again urging the doctrine, the doctrine of "Frauds on the Fairies," of *Hard Times,* of many additional writings, but above all, the doctrine of his inner life and his shaping imagination. "Let the child have its fables," he pleaded; "let the man or woman into which it changes, always remember these fables tenderly. Let numerous graces and ornaments that cannot be weighed and measured, and that seem at first sight idle enough, continue to have their places about us, be we never so wise."[23]

By the 1860s Dickens and Cruikshank were light-years apart. In 1864, when Cruikshank revised his original reply to "Frauds on the Fairies" for inclusion in *Puss in Boots,* he retained and even accentuated the wild, bewildered tone that reverberated intermittently through his initial reply. In his retouched climax, his sense of baffled injury increased rather than diminished:

> And what are these doctrines and opinions [introduced into the fairy tales]? Aye! What have I done? Where is the offence? Why, I have endeavoured to inculcate, at *the earliest age,* A HORROR OF DRUNKEN-NESS, and a recommendation of TOTAL ABSTINENCE from ALL IN-TOXICATING LIQUORS, which, if carried out universally, would not only do away with DRUNKENNESS ENTIRELY, but also with a large amount of POVERTY, MISERY, DISEASE, and DREADFUL CRIMES. also A DETESTATION OF GAMBLING, and A LOVE OF ALL THAT IS VIRTUOUS AND GOOD, and an endeavour to impress on every one the NECESSITY, IMPORTANCE, and JUSTICE of EVERY CHILD in the land receiving a USEFUL and RELIGIOUS EDUCATION. And I would here ask in fairness, what harm can possibly be done to Fairy literature by such re-writing or editing as this?

Cruikshank's question shows that even after ten years he was totally incapable of understanding Dickens' objections. He was so fixed on his own espousals and his own endeavors that everything else seemed inconsequential. It is not hard to understand why this was so. Dickens, in ridiculing teetotalism, had defied the center of Cruikshank's life; in a like manner, Cruikshank, by tampering with fairy tales, by "rooting . . . among the roses," had defied the center of Dickens' life. Artistically and imaginatively the two men had much in common. In certain areas of grotesque humor and satire, in certain ways of apprehending characters, streets, horrors, foibles, and eccentricities, in certain techniques of transforming the ordinary and animating the inanimate, in certain approaches to London and Londoners, they saw the world alike. But in life they had traveled a strangely erratic, collision-bound course. From the asperities of their early collaboration, they had moved on to friendship, then jovial companionship, only to drift gradually asunder, and finally to find themselves, all unwittingly, in mortal opposition.

That opposition was compounded of many impulses; it was composed of clashing ideas, diverging social worlds, conflicting wills, and abrading personalities. It was also forged from random happenings and innocent cross-purposes, from the push and pull of everyday circumstances: from such haphazard events as a sudden confrontation at a dinner party, a casually perused review in a London periodical, an evocative image starting up unexpectedly from an intricate cover illustration. But such diverse occurrences, occurrences conflated with feelings that range from antagonistic to admiring, complicate most human relationships. For Dickens the unforgivable offense at the heart of his controversy with Cruikshank, the offense that transformed intellectual opposition into fatal combat, grew out of something more central and more momentous than sudden anger, amused delight, or lingering irritation. It grew out of Cruikshank's subversion (to Dickens' way of thinking) of the realm of fairyland, a realm that Dickens had come to associate with nurture, succor, freedom, imagination, and humanity, a realm that Dickens intuitively perceived was coterminous with his innermost gifts and innermost commitments. Dickens' confrontation with Cruikshank, in other words, was a dramatic outward sign of a profound inward development.

How fairy tales and fairyland came to carry such surcharged meanings for Dickens, how they shaped the nature of his imagination—these tangled matters occupy the next two chapters.

2 | The Fairy-Tale Heritage
"All...as of Yore...Infinite Delights"

In 1812, the year of Dickens' birth, children's literature was in a sorry state. For the typical middle-class child growing up when Dickens did, children's literature consisted largely of regimented platoons of moral tales, religious tracts, didactic verses, edifying fables, and earnest pamphlets. The ancient heritage of English children, a motley budget of wonder and romance—fairy stories, folk tales, magical adventures, compendiums of superstitions, epic encounters—had been banished from respectable nurseries for well over a hundred years. How this came to be is something of a mystery. Possibly Puritan antagonism to what was felt to be a pagan and superstitious literature withered it in pious households and weakened it throughout the land. Perhaps also that opposition prevented such literature from establishing itself in respectable printed form. How else explain its dearth in the seventeenth century, an age when soaring literacy and surging book production would seem to have guaranteed both audience and means of dissemination? By the eighteenth century, when Puritan influence had waned, a new but equally antagonistic spirit took its place. This spirit—an ordered and prosing rationalism—regarded nurses' stories and miraculous tales as merest rubbish at best, and inimical ideology at worst. Lord Chesterfield, in typical eighteenth-century fashion, warned his natural son in 1740 and his godson in 1764 to avoid Mother Goose, fairy tales, romances, and stories about giants, enchantments, magicians, and all such fabulous matters.[1] Perhaps this interdiction contributed to Dickens' detestation of the Lord and his *Letters*. In *Barnaby Rudge*, Dickens pilloried Lord Chesterfield as Sir John Chester, a cynical and heartless villain. Sir John turns his natural son, Hugh, into little more than an animal. This is the destiny, Dickens seems to be saying, of human creatures unleavened by love and untouched by imagination.

When the rationalists sought to create a suitable literature for children, they wrote didactic tracts and improving novels which taught boys and girls (and their parents) how to act in a logical fashion or how to avoid the dire pitfalls of impulse and passion. For the most part these works, droning on in a flat, slack style, inculcated a materialistic ethic, rejected any notion of the nonrational, mistrusted the imagination, and ignored a child's capacities and sensibilities. The most popular of these books, well on through the nineteenth century, was *Sandford and Merton* (1783) by Thomas Day, a work that Dickens regarded as antithetical to fairy tales and subversive of all imagination. Mr. Barlow, the didact of *Sandford and Merton,* used every incident in the lives of manly Master Harry Sandford and spoiled Master Tommy Merton to teach a lesson or point a moral. Dickens remembered Mr. Barlow as one of the blighting miseries of his childhood:

> What right had [Mr. Barlow] to bore his way into my Arabian Nights? Yet he did. He was always hinting doubts of the veracity of Sindbad the Sailor. If he could have got hold of the Wonderful Lamp, I knew he would have trimmed it and lighted it, and delivered a lecture over it on the qualities of sperm-oil, with a glance at the whale fisheries. He would so soon have found out—on mechanical principles—the peg in the neck of the Enchanted Horse, and would have turned it the right way in so workman-like a manner, that the horse could never have got any height into the air, and the story couldn't have been. He would have proved, by map and compass, that there was no such kingdom as the delightful kingdom of Casgar, on the frontiers of Tartary. He would have caused that hypocritical young prig Harry to make an experiment,—with the aid of a temporary building in the garden and a dummy,—demonstrating that you couldn't let a choked hunchback down an Eastern chimney with a cord, and leave him upright on the hearth to terrify the sultan's purveyor.[2]

Mr. Barlow was bad enough, but the religious and quasi-religious tracts and the ferocious moral guides for children were even worse. Such works had a continuous and dreary history from the seventeenth century through Dickens' childhood and beyond. In the seventeenth century, Bunyan was the greatest exemplar of this dour tradition, not primarily with *The Pilgrim's Progress* (1678), written for adults, but soon read by children, and filled with a saving share of giants, monsters, castles, and imagination, but with grim warnings such as *A Book for Boys and Girls* (1686), written expressly to frighten children into the paths of righteousness. Bunyan was not alone in his endeavor. Earlier, in about 1671, James Janeway had published *A Token for Children; being an Exact Account of the Conversion, Holy and Exemplary Lives, and Joyful Deaths of Several Young Children,* an enormously influential book that referred to children as ''brands of Hell'' and that became a gloomy prototype for one strong stream of children's literature. In his ''Preface Containing Directions to Children,'' Janeway ministered to his young charges. ''Did you never hear of a little child that died?'' he asked. Then he continued: ''And if other children die, why may not you lie sick and die? And what will you do then, Child, if you should have no Grace in your Heart, and be found like other naughty children?''

In the ensuing centuries, the relentless denunciation of childish sin was continued by a host of additional writers. In the eighteenth century the formidable Mrs. Trimmer, an indefatigable opponent of fantasy, was the foremost castigator of infant vice. In the nineteenth century Mrs. Sherwood took her place. Her masterpiece, *The History of the Fairchild Family, being a Collection of Stories Calculated to Show the Importance and Effects of a Religious Education,* was published when Dickens was six. It went through endless editions right up to the end of the century, partly because of its narrative skill, but more importantly because parents regarded it as an effective warning to the young. Some notion of how these works approached the child may be gained in capsule form from the multitudes of deadly little pamphlets that were part of the same tradition. When Pip went to the Town Hall to be bound apprentice to Joe, one self-righteous individual ''of mild and benevolent aspect'' conceived that the innocent boy was so in need of correction that he gave him ''a tract ornamented with a woodcut of a malevolent young man fitted up with a perfect sausage-shop of fetters, and entitled, To be read in my Cell.''[3] Pip was not a special case. Arthur Clennam recalled

> the dreary Sunday of his childhood, when he sat with his hands before him, scared out of his senses by a horrible tract which commenced business with the poor child by asking him in its title, why he was going to Perdition?—a piece of curiosity that he really in a frock and drawers was not in a condition to satisfy—and which, for the further attraction of his infant mind, had a parenthesis in every other line with some such hiccupping reference as 2 Ep. Thess. c. iii. v. 6 &7.[4]

Dickens was not exaggerating in these vignettes. Here is an entire page from an early nineteenth-century booklet of cautionary tales, one woodcut illustration and one tale per page:

> The Brother's Grave. — A Gentleman walking through a church-yard, saw a little girl standing near a grave. He asked her whose grave it was. ''It is my brother's,'' she replied. ''He died because he would eat unripe fruit, unknown to father and mother; but he was very sorry for what he had done; and we are all sorry he is dead.'' ''It is a sad thing,'' said the gentleman, ''to do wrong, and then to add to it by concealing it.''

If once a little child offends,
How seldom there its error ends!

This devastating inversion of Wordsworth's "We are Seven" is accompanied by a woodcut which shows the gentleman and the little girl standing in the churchyard and viewing, not simply the brother's grave, but the wrapped and trussed corpse of the sinful child.

Not all the improving literature of Dickens' childhood was so implacable. Early in the eighteenth century Isaac Watts, a mild-mannered nonconformist clergyman, disturbed by the ferocity of most exemplary literature for children, determined to write a series of moral poems which would teach in a gentler fashion. The result, *Divine Songs, Attempted in Easy Language for the Use of Children* (1715), became the most popular collection of moral precepts for children during the eighteenth and nineteenth centuries. Watts' poems were overwhelmingly didactic and cautionary, but at their best they had a charm and a sensitivity to the capacities of children that made them infinitely better than anything of their kind. For more than a hundred years they occupied a middle ground between the harsh precepts of the moral tract and the dangerous literature of romance and marvels, and this fact, plus the intrinsic merits of some of the poems, probably account for their long hold on the middle class. Watts was a harbinger of things to come. In the middle of the eighteenth century John Newbery, and then one or two other publishers, began to issue works for children that juxtaposed didacticism and moral teaching with entertainment and pleasure. These works did not supplant the main staple of children's literature, grim regiments of cautionary tales, but the new works were respectable, and they made it possible for indulgent parents to brighten the nursery with occasional booklets that contained geniality as well as instruction. Beyond such fleeting diversions a child who craved imaginative reading had to fend for himself. Fortunately he had another resource.

All through the seventeenth and eighteenth centuries imaginative literature for children, along with ballads, almanacs, broadsides, criminal histories, and the like, had maintained a flourishing life in the little booklets and broadsheets that itinerant book-peddlers or chapmen hawked about the countryside and that stationers sold in shops. By the early nineteenth century this stream had swollen to a vast river of chapbooks, songsters, dream books, letter writers, fortune tellers, picture books, and much more. This turbid torrent was aimed at children, the untutored, and the naive. There were chapbooks for every taste. One could find condensed adventure stories, didactic works, bible tales, criminal histories, jest books, pornographic works, prophecies, sensation stories, and curiosities. One could also find fairy tales, nursery rhymes, alphabets, primers, fables, romances, and marvels. In the realm of imaginative children's stories this conglomeration of cheap popular literature included—to sketch a few typical categories— debased redactions of old histories and romances (*The Seven Champions of Christendom, Sir Bevis of Southampton, Robin Hood, Valentine and Orson*), brief versions of classic English folk tales (*Jack the Giant Killer, Tom Thumb, Jack and the Beanstalk, Dick Whittington*), attractive presentations of nursery stories and nursery rhymes (*The Children in the Wood, Cock Robin, The Cries of London, Mother Hubbard*), simplified retellings of the newly discovered continental fairy tales (*Cinderella, Beauty and the Beast, The Yellow Dwarf, Little Red Ridinghood, Sleeping Beauty*), and telescoped renditions, adapted for children, of adult literature (*Don Quixote, The Arabian Nights, Robinson Crusoe, Gulliver's Travels, George Barnwell, Philip Quarll*).

In Dickens' childhood these chapbooks varied in format from miniature booklets, usually of sixteen pages, to octavo pamphlets of twenty-four, thirty-two, or thirty-six pages. Occasionally the booklets had no wrappers, the first page serving as wrapper and title page, but more often they came with long printed titles on colored wrappers. Some of the chapbooks were adorned with woodcuts, sometimes as many as one per opening or even one per page. These designs varied in quality from crude slashes to dainty cameos. Some cuts were specially made for a text, others were used in chapbook after chapbook with little relevance to the story they were illustrating. Many of the octavo chapbooks contained no woodcuts in the text but had instead a folding frontispiece, boldly (and often crudely) colored in bright reds, greens, yellows, browns, and blues. The printing varied from passable to wretched; the design from engaging to nonexistent; the price from a halfpenny to sixpence. With a few exceptions, the entire operation was focused on cheapness and on an immediate appeal to the most rudimentary interest in entertainment, wonder, edification, curiosity, and sensation. Dickens, in the 1850s, passing an old-fashioned shop full of the chapbooks of his childhood, gives us a brief glimpse of that literature—its jumbled diversity and its lingering power:

Here, Dr. Faustus was still going down to very red and yellow perdition, under the superintendence of three green personages of a scaly humour, with excrescential serpents growing out of their blade-bones. Here, the Golden Dreamer, and the Norwood Fortune Teller, were still on sale at sixpence each, with instructions for making the dumb cake, and reading destinies in tea-cups, and with a picture of a young woman with a high waist lying on a sofa in an attitude so uncomfortable as almost to account for her dreaming at one and the same time of a conflagration, a shipwreck, an earthquake, a skeleton, a church-porch, lightning, funerals performed, and a young man in a bright blue coat and canary pantaloons. Here, were Little Warblers and Fairburn's Comic Songsters. Here, too, were ballads on the old ballad paper and in the old confusion of types; with an old man in a cocked hat, and an arm-chair, for the illustration to Will Watch the bold Smuggler; and the Friar of Orders Grey, represented by a little girl in a hoop, with a ship in the distance. All these as of yore, when they were infinite delights to me!⁵

One can understand concerned Georgian parents forbidding their children to enter this dense jungle of intertwined naiveté and exoticism, but given the desolate aridity of approved children's literature, one can also understand how exciting and liberating that forbidden jungle must have been to any imaginative child.

Central in that jungle was the fairy tale. Before Dickens' childhood, the fairy tale had begun to infiltrate slowly into respectable adult books and collections. From such respectable repositories, expensive and recondite, the fairy tale quickly migrated into the jungle. These developments (as far as England was concerned) had their origin on the Continent where a stirring of interest in fairy stories and then a vogue for collecting and retelling them swept through certain groups of French intellectuals. The first and most important of these collections, *Histoires ou Contes du temps passé; avec des Moralitez* (1697), by Charles Perrault, contained eight stories, including *Sleeping Beauty, Little Red Ridinghood, Bluebeard, Puss in Boots, Hop o' My Thumb,* and *Cinderella.* Though moralization looms large in the title, it does not loom large in the text. The frontispiece to the volume also contained the inscription *Contes de ma mère l'Oye*—which was repeated in the first English translation as *Mother Goose's Tales.* The other crucial collection, *Les Contes des Fées* (1698) by Madame d'Aulnoy, was translated into English in 1699 as *Tales of the Fairies.* Madame d'Aulnoy's stories were much more contrived than Perrault's. Though they contained some folk materials and some borrowings (especially from Italian collections), they were largely attempts to create longish literary equivalents of fairy tales, an outgrowth of the somewhat *précieuse* French vogue of telling fairy stories to one another. A few of Madame d'Aulnoy's stories—*The Yellow Dwarf, Fortunio, Goldylocks,* and *The White Cat*—passed into the accepted English fairy-tale tradition, but her chief importance, from an English point of view, rests in the almost immediate translation of her collection into English, and the early impetus she and her followers thereby gave to the dissemination in England of fairy stories and new attitudes toward fairy stories. One of her followers, Madame de Beaumont, was responsible for the version of *Beauty and the Beast* that finally became standard in English, and the impulse Madame d'Aulnoy helped engender also led to the vast *Le Cabinet des Fées* and to other series and periodicals that made use of fairy stories.

Perrault was not translated into English until 1729 (by Robert

Samber as *Histories, or Tales of Past Times*), but in the long run Perrault's collection was much more important to the English tradition than Madame d'Aulnoy's. Perrault's fairy tales were real fairy tales taken from a living oral tradition; the stories in his collection had a vitality and tenacity proved through long ages (*Cinderella,* for example, is at least a thousand years old). Furthermore, though he told his tales with great art, he sought through that art to preserve their authentic flavor. He wished to transmit the tales, not turn them into sophisticated literary constructions. Finally, Perrault had an unerring instinct for quality and power in a fairy story. All of the eight fairy tales he recorded have remained alive in English, and seven have remained among the dozen or so most popular in the language.

Soon after they were translated into English, Perrault's tales, as individual stories rather than as a collection, appeared in chapbook form, and in that guise became immensely popular and made their way into every village and hamlet in the British Isles. When Dickens was a boy, *Cinderella, Bluebeard,* and *Sleeping Beauty* were as well known and as "English" as *Jack the Giant Killer, Tom Thumb,* and *Jack and the Beanstalk.* This rapid assimilation was accomplished primarily through chapbooks and cheap literature; the fairy tale had scarcely touched the established tradition of respectable children's literature.

There were, however, several developments in the eighteenth century closely related to fairy stories and profoundly antagonistic to the dour mainstream of children's literature. The first of these developments was the publication of *Robinson Crusoe* (1719), a realistic tale of shipwreck, ingenuity, adventure, and suspense. *Robinson Crusoe* soon appeared in condensed and in chapbook form, and in these versions, if not in its original form, became one of the most widely read and widely imitated books of the eighteenth and nineteenth centuries. The second development was the publication of *Gulliver's Travels* in 1726. This narrative about little people, giants, talking animals, and fantastic lands had powerful affinities with fairy tales, and it, too, in simplified versions and chapbook abridgements (especially abridgements concerning Lilliput), became the province of children. However, by far the most important occurrence was not of native origin. This development, too, came through France, though it did not originate there. In 1704–1717, a French diplomat, Antoine Galland, translated *The Arabian Nights* into French. This translation was the first appearance of *The Arabian Nights* in a Western language. Galland's translation, in turn, was the basis for the first English version, a version that appeared almost simultaneously with its French counterpart. The first chapbook versions (mostly of individual stories) appeared while *The Arabian Nights* was still in the course of translation. Very soon *Ali Baba and the Forty Thieves, Sinbad the Sailor,* and

Aladdin and His Wonderful Lamp established themselves as the most popular stories from *The Arabian Nights* in chapbook form—and among the most popular of all chapbooks.

It would be difficult to exaggerate the enchantment that *The Arabian Nights* cast on the Georgians and the Victorians, or the revolutionary nature of its intrusion into English children's literature. Into the latter world, for the most part so literal and chilling, came magic lamps, all-powerful genies, fairy-tale palaces, incredible treasures, sinuous dancing girls, bold robbers, mythical kingdoms, veiled maidens, ingenious strategies, and magical transformations. Everything was exotic, yet somehow believable too, for the stories and all their trappings came out of a mysterious East where soft fountains and hanging gardens, harems and pleasure domes, sultans and scimitars, did most veritably exist. *The Arabian Nights* was alien and liberating. It was not simply that the stories evoked strange lands and customs: their fundamental ethos and purpose were light-years away from the smothering didacticism of *Primrose Prettyface* or *Little Goody Two-Shoes*. The Eastern tales were designed to entertain, to elicit amazement and wonder. The world of *The Arabian Nights* could be cruel, even savage, but in that world birds sang, lovers loved, and the most magical things were possible. This was no prosaic land of grey skies and stern teachings; no Mr. Barlows here.

It is hard to grasp how brilliant and visionary such a dreamworld must have appeared in 1820 to an imaginative boy suffocated by the droning drabness of *Sandford and Merton,* the church catechism, and Lindley Murray's *Grammar*. Dickens later gave many accounts of how that contrast appeared to him. The deadly opposition of Mr. Barlow and *The Arabian Nights* is one such account, but the far-off consequences of such oppositions, the many ways in which the unnatural separation of thought and imagination (or the repression of imagination) can lead to disaster, that awareness enters Dickens' writings in profoundly shaping ways. It enters, for example, the astonishing opening paragraph of *Edwin Drood,* written more than fifty years after Dickens' introduction to *The Arabian Nights*. In that paragraph the dull massive grey square tower of an ancient English cathedral and the rusty iron spike of a ramshackle bed in a miserable London opium den are contrasted with an alien and exotic vision: "Maybe, [the spike] is set up by the Sultan's orders for the impaling of a horde of Turkish robbers, one by one. It is so, for cymbals clash, and the Sultan goes by to his palace in long procession. Ten thousand scimitars flash in the sunlight, and thrice ten thousand dancing-girls strew flowers. Then, follow white elephants caparisoned in countless gorgeous colours, and infinite in number and attendants." Here is *The Arabian Nights* in all its menace and gorgeousness, still retaining its old associations, but transformed now by intricate art into a motif that will work through the entire novel and will undergird and enrich what Dickens has to say about monstrous repression and unnatural self-division in a quiet English cathedral town.

The lure of *The Arabian Nights* worked its magic on many before Dickens and on many besides him. The Eastern tale, in metrical and prose versions, became a familiar genre of Romantic writing, an almost archetypal way of rejecting the ordered strictness of neoclassicism and affirming the tempestuous exoticism of the Romantic imagination. Byron, Southey, and Moore, to name three poets with very different Romantic sensibilities, worked boldly in this vein. Their exotic tales—I am thinking of such fantasies as *The Giaour* (1813), *The Curse of Kehama* (1810), and *Lalla Rookh* (1817)—were strongly imbued with the color and atmosphere of *The Arabian Nights*. These indulgent caprices had their architectural counterpart in the Prince Regent's Pavilion, a domed and minaretted edifice that began to spring up in 1815 as startlingly and unexpectedly as Aladdin's palace—an *Arabian Nights* vision floating dreamlike near the grey marge of Brighton's shingled shore.

In prose *The Arabian Nights* exerted its influence on works such as Johnson's *Rasselas, Prince of Abyssinia* (1759), Beckford's *Vathek, An Arabian Tale* (1786), and James Ridley's *The Tales of the Genii* (1764). *The Tales of the Genii* is full of gorgeous processions, baleful enchanters, magical talismans, heaped jewels, fierce giants, nocturnal disguises, spell-induced slumbers, and human-to-animal transformations. To today's reader the book, despite its florid fabling, seems tedious and stillborn, the husk of *The Arabian Nights* rather than its beating heart. But for a hundred years Ridley's *Tales* remained vital and popular, especially in pantomimes and with children, a commentary perhaps upon the deadly dullness of most contemporary reading for children. As a child, Dickens read *The Arabian Nights* and *The Tales of the Genii* greedily.

The Arabian Nights is closely related to fairy tales: indeed it is, in essence, a collection of Eastern fairy tales. Many of its personages, plots, transformations, and fulfillments are cognate with Western fairy stories. This is not surprising, for many European fairy stories can be traced to ancient Eastern sources. This consanguinity between Western and Eastern fairy tales, the latter clothed for Western readers in a captivating exoticism, perhaps accounts for the quick ascendency of *The Arabian Nights* in the West. In any case, through most of the eighteenth and early nineteenth centuries, *The Arabian Nights* was a chief repository of fairy-tale literature for Western readers.

Despite the popularity of *The Arabian Nights,* however, fairy stories continued to be banished from most English nurseries. This was still true in 1823. In that year Dickens was eleven years old and drifting miserably in London, and in that year the next great event in the history of fairy tales in England occurred: a segment of *Grimm's Fairy Tales* was translated into English. The translation bore a title which emphasized the special nature and source of the stories, an emphasis which testified to a new Romantic sensibility that boded well for fairy tales: *German Popular Stories. Translated from the Kinder und Haus-Marchen. Collected by M. M.* [sic] *Grimm. From Oral Tradition.* This volume was an immediate success, calling forth several early reprintings, and by 1826 it was possible to add a second volume of translations from Grimm. The translator of *German Popular Stories,* Edgar Taylor, presented his collection to the English public as a remedy for a prevailing sickness. "The popular tales of England," he wrote, "have been too much neglected. They are nearly discarded from the libraries of childhood. Philosophy is made the companion of the nursery: we have lisping chemists and leading-string mathematicians: this is the age of reason, not of imagination; and the loveliest dreams of fairy innocence are considered as vain and frivolous."[6] Taylor then went on to affirm that "much might be urged against this rigid and philosophic (or rather unphilosophic) exclusion of works of fancy and fiction," for such works, and especially the fairy tales of childhood, sensitize the imagination and thus the ability to achieve pleasure and happiness throughout one's life.[7]

There had been earlier attempts in England to publish collections of fairy stories. About 1804, "Benjamin Tabart" began to issue a series of pamphlets with hand-colored plates under the general title, *Tabart's Popular Stories*. This series—some thirty-four titles—included most of Perrault, several stories from *The Arabian Nights,* and a number of traditional English stories, all told in a plain serviceable manner free from undue moralizing or didacticism. Tabart subsequently collected these tales in four volumes, and then in 1818, under his own proper name, Sir Richard Phillips, produced a one-volume edition called *Popular Fairy Tales; or, a Liliputian* [sic] *Library*. But these publications seem to have been regarded by readers as a species of elegant chapbooks and produced no special ripple in the public's consciousness. By the same token, though in a very different way, Thomas Crofton Croker's important three-volume *Fairy Legends and Traditions of the South of Ireland* (1825–1828), a collection similar in some of its motivations and methods to *German Popular Stories,* engaged antiquarians rather than children and did not succeed in touching the general consciousness.

The Grimms' collection was a different matter. Its stories, including such soon-to-be favorites as *Snow White, Rapunzel, Rumpelstiltskin,* and *Hansel and Gretel,* went directly into the nursery, and although the impact of the Grimm brothers on English attitudes toward imaginative children's literature did not reach its fullness until a generation or more later, the stories themselves soon became a part of the English heritage. This rapid acceptance was largely owing to the vigor of the tales themselves. Like those Perrault had assembled, the traditional stories the Grimms collected exhibited the winnowed strength and tenacity of a long oral tradition. In addition, the Grimms attempted to record the tales essentially as they heard them, thus preserving their unadulterated power as living dramatic narratives. The English edition was further enhanced by the illustrations of George Cruikshank. Cruikshank immersed himself in the spirit of the tales and then gave graphic form to their strange and powerful spell. His illustrations helped *Grimm's Fairy Tales* touch the imagination of a generation of readers.

There were many other signs of the new spirit. Between 1841 and 1849, for instance, "Felix Summerly" issued twelve booklets under the general title, *The Home Treasury*. These booklets, well illustrated and well printed, offered the best-known fairy tales—*Little Red Ridinghood, Beauty and the Beast, Jack and the Beanstalk,* and the like—as needful imaginative entertainment, a necessary antidote to the notion that children should subsist on an unadulterated diet of hard facts. The announced aim of the series was to "cultivate the Affections, Fancy, Imagination, and Taste of Children." Summerly's impulse in launching the series was thus similar to what Edgar Taylor's aim had been in translating *German Popular Stories* some eighteen years earlier. But Summerly's background and connections were very different from Taylor's. Felix Summerly was Sir Henry Cole, an active public official who was close to Prince Albert and who played an important role in founding such institutions as the Royal College of Music, Albert Hall, and the Victoria and Albert Museum. He was also a mover in educational planning, in organizing the Great Exhibition, and in developing Schools of Design.[8] The important point is that influential men such as Cole were beginning in the 1840s and 1850s to promote ideas concerning imagination, children's literature, and fairy tales that ran counter to the prevailing doctrines of the times.

There were many other writers and many other works that helped establish the new attitude toward fairy stories and imaginative children's literature. The 1840s saw the publication of J. O. Halliwell-Phillipps' *Nursery Rhymes* (1842) and *Popular Rhymes and Nursery Tales* (1849), Edward Lear's *A Book of Nonsense* (1846), Mark Lemon's *The Enchanted Doll* (1849), Dickens' five Christmas books (1843–1848), and the first translation of a group of Hans Christian Andersen's fairy tales, *Wonderful Stories for Children* (1846), the precursor of many additional works by Andersen. The 1850s included John Ruskin's *The King of the Golden River* (1851), Thackeray's *The*

Rose and the Ring (1855), and J. R. Planché's *Four and Twenty Fairy Tales* (1858, based on Madame d'Aulnoy). By 1865, when Lewis Carroll published *Alice's Adventures in Wonderland,* the centuries-long subservience of children's literature to moralizing, didacticism, and hell's fire was broken, though the old-style literature was produced and read in great quantities, and continued to be the sole diet of some children, right through the end of the century.

The victory of imagination and fantasy was epitomized by the popularity of Andersen and Carroll. Andersen was the first great modern writer for children. His success signalized the emergence in England of a market for original imaginative children's literature of substance and power, literature that made its first commitment to art and experience rather than to doctrine. Carroll's success marked the new importance of fantasy and nonsense, of delight for its own sake, and of irreverence toward the moral and cautionary shibboleths of the adult world and of the past.

This shift had taken place in little more than a generation. Yet during that generation the battle had been fierce. One gets a glimpse of the severity and restrictiveness of children's reading when one realizes that in 1802, in *The Guardian of Education,* Mrs. Trimmer, by no means an ogress, condemned *The Babes in the Wood* as "absolutely unfit for the perusal of children."[9] By contrast, this tender tale of innocent children betrayed by callous adults moved Dickens profoundly. He identified closely with the story as a child, and he continued to feel its pull all his life. In *The Old Curiosity Shop,* innocent Nell, asleep in death like the innocent babes, rests, as they did, on a leaf-strewn bier; in *Hard Times* Mr. Sleary's circus troupe—a correlative for imagination and warmth—gives equestrian performances of *The Children in the Wood;* and in 1854, Dickens thought of writing a dramatic version of *The Children in the Wood* for his own children to perform.[10] These examples could be multiplied manyfold. Dickens obviously regarded the story as an epitome of compassionate feeling.

The disparity of response between Mrs. Trimmer and Dickens is instructive. Mrs. Trimmer, championing a narrow didacticism and a rigid morality, sees the little fable as weakening the authority of adults, as teaching children that those placed over them can be calculating and murderous, unworthy of obedience. Dickens, on the other hand, champions the power of imaginative sympathy. He sees the story as a means of melting hardened' (or hardening) hearts, as a way of evoking the power of sympathetic response that slumbers within each person. That power—the power of imaginative sympathy—humanizes and saves. Mrs. Trimmer places her reliance on prescription, Dickens on imagination. These opposed positions were widely held, though it was a rare adherent of either camp who examined the grounds of his belief.

Nevertheless, the issue was joined. It is not too much to say that in this conflict two attitudes toward life were battling for children's minds.

Yet, if one looks back on the development of imaginative children's literature, one can see that the winds of change had begun to blow very early and that the evolution of that literature was part of a much larger process. That larger process was the Romantic revolution, a revolution that was heralded, insofar as children's literature was concerned, by parallel developments in general literature. It was prefigured, for example, by the new interest in popular literature, antiquarian lore, primitive survivals, and vestiges of the past—an interest represented equally by William Collins' "Ode on the Popular Superstitions of the Highlands" (1749), Bishop Percy's *Reliques of Ancient English Poetry* (1764), and Sir Walter Scott's *Minstrelsy of the Scottish Border* (1802–1803). The latter two works, collections of folk literature, mainly ballads, look forward to the Grimms' collections of folk literature, mainly fairy tales. The revolution was presaged also by the new interest in dialect literature and by the strong strain of folklore, superstition, and supernaturalism in such literature, in the work of Robert Burns, for instance. It was heralded as well by the immense popularity of *The Arabian Nights,* by the vogue of the Eastern tale, and by the explosion of Gothic literature toward the end of the eighteenth and the beginning of the nineteenth centuries—the latter literature replete with ghosts, dungeons, giants, spells, curses, magical signs, distressed maidens, devilish villains, and much more.

The Romantic revolution was heralded, too, by the developing cult of the child, by a growing tendency to see the child not as a miniature adult, full of sin and wickedness, but as a blessed innocent, close to divinity, shaped by his earliest experiences, and shaping out of those experiences all his adult being. Such an emissary of God does not require instruction and admonition as though he were a "brand of Hell" (he is not corrupt, it is the world that corrupts him), but rather can teach the corrupted adult out of his own intuitive wisdom. Such ideas are latent in Blake's "little Lamb" (kin to child and God), Wordsworth's "best philosopher," and Dickens' orphaned Oliver, the latter representing the "principle of Good surviving through every adverse circumstance."[11] What this innocent child needs is "fair seedtime" for his soul, a nurturing interval before worldliness, an interval in which he can grow and unfold the capabilities of his still-uncorrupted spirit. In children's literature fair seedtime means delight and imagination and freedom, not the prison house of fear, fact, and restriction.

These were some of the doctrines that were beginning to infiltrate the middle-class consciousness when Dickens was a child. Yet, at that time, these ideas were still very advanced, still vaguely and inconsistently held by those who held them, and still largely unformulated in public positions and public statements. Even the chief literary advocates of the new sensibility, the leading Romantics, some of whom believed that fairy stories and wild romances were a child's saving birthright, articulated these views mostly in private. In 1797 Samuel Taylor Coleridge wrote to a friend that "from my early reading of Faery Tales, & Genii &c&c—my mind had been habituated *to the Vast.*" Then he asked and answered a question: "Should children be permitted to read Romances, & Relations of Giants & Magicians, & Genii?—I know all that has been said against it; but I have formed my faith in the affirmative.—I know no other way of giving the mind a love of 'the Great', & 'the Whole.'"[12] A few years later, in 1802, Charles Lamb wrote to Coleridge taking the same position, but on less lofty grounds. After complaining that Mrs. Barbauld's "stuff" and Mrs. Trimmer's "nonsense" had "banished all the old classics of the nursery," he went on to affirm the "beautiful Interest in wild tales which made the child a man, while all the time he suspected himself to be no bigger than a child." After explaining that science had supplanted poetry, he continued:

> Is there no possibility of averting this sore evil? Think what you would have been now, if instead of being fed with Tales and old wives' fables in childhood, you had been crammed with geography and natural history?
> Damn them!—I mean the cursed Barbauld Crew, those Blights and Blasts of all that is Human in man and child.[13]

Here the new Romantic view is stated succinctly, the enemy clearly labeled. Yet Lamb's ideas, like Coleridge's, are confined to a private letter; they constitute a prescient ripple of inward opposition in a sea of outward conformity. Dickens' good fortune and ill luck was to be born at a time when standard children's literature was stultifying, imaginative children's literature chaotic but liberating, and ideas about children's literature in a state of flux. That flux began to take defined form in quiet and largely unregarded ways. The seemingly monolithic adherence to smothering morality and overpowering didacticism was about to give way to the accumulating pressure of new ideas and new literature. Dickens was to be shaped by those new ideas, but later he was also to have a part in shaping them. He was also to be influenced by some of the very doctrines he would reject—moral teaching, for instance, albeit deepened and transformed, was always to have an important place in his writings. But Dickens' attitude toward children's literature, and to literature and imagination in general, was not simply a function of the historical movements and historical developments that impinged upon his life. Those inescapable outward forces were modulated by inner experiences of transcendent importance, experiences that helped transform a sensitive and precocious, but not really unique confluence of reading, seeing, and imagining, into something quite extraordinary.

3 | Dickens' Fabling Mind
"A Mist of Fancy
over Well-Remembered Facts"

$\mathbf{B}$EFORE DICKENS could read, he was introduced to the magical world of fairy tales. He heard fairy stories countless times from the lips of his nursemaid, Mary Weller, and he heard them also from his paternal grandmother, Elizabeth Ball Dickens, who had long been famous at Crewe Hall as an "inimitable" teller of fairy tales.[1] Dickens became acquainted with fairy stories, therefore, in the age-old way of the folk. He heard fairy tales over and over again; they were part of a living oral tradition, and they were part of his life. To imbibe fairy stories as part of his daily life was formative enough, but to imbibe them from two such virtuosi as Elizabeth Dickens and Mary Weller was something special. His grandmother's exceptional storytelling talents are attested to by others, but Mary Weller's unusual gifts are certified by Dickens himself.

Mary Weller came to work for the Dickenses in Chatham when Dickens was five, and she stayed with them until the family moved to London, when Dickens was almost eleven.[2] Though she was young (only twelve or thirteen when she began to work for the Dickenses), she was given the task of supervising the children, and she seems to have managed her job reasonably well. She helped them play and perform, took them on neighborhood visits, comforted them in their tribulations, and sometimes sang them to sleep.[3] She was no paragon, though, and Dickens' later references to her reflect hostility as well as love. She apparently had a ghoulish interest in lyings-in and layings-out, and she had a remarkable flair for the macabre and the horrific.[4] When she came to the Dickenses she brought with her a fantastic budget of weird stories and country superstitions, and she also brought with her a baleful imagination that embroidered and personalized everything that she related. Dickens proved an ideal audience, and Mary Weller practiced on him endlessly. She told and retold him stories of supernatural tomcats, ghostly hauntings, bloody murders, and cannibalistic rituals. Horror-stricken, yet fascinated, too, Dickens would tremble and listen, anticipating and magnifying each all-too-familiar touch of terror. One of Mary Weller's favorite stories—a story that exerted a lifelong influence on Dickens—was "Captain Murderer."

"Captain Murderer" recounts the history of a well-bred man who married young women in order to eat them. His procedure was invariable. A month after each marriage, he would have his teeth, which were pointed, ground razor sharp, and he would command his bride to prepare an enormous pie shell. Then he would tell her that she would serve as meat for the pie, and while she watched in the mirror, he would cut off her head. He would then chop her up, put her in the pie shell, season her, have her baked, and feast on her. Captain Murderer devoured bride after bride until he married and ate a fair-haired girl who had a dark-haired twin sister. The dark-haired twin, after peeping through the window and divining that her sister had been murdered and eaten, married the Captain, and in due time was chopped up, baked, and eaten too. But before being murdered, the dark twin took a virulent poison, and her poisoned flesh caused the Captain to die most horribly.

One can imagine the effect such a bedtime story, sadistically elaborated and emphasized, would have on a child. Dickens described how it affected him:

> Hundreds of times did I hear this legend of Captain Murderer, in my early youth, and added hundreds of times was there a mental compulsion upon me in bed, to peep in at his window as the dark twin peeped, and to revisit his horrible house, and look at him in his blue and spotty and screaming stage, as he reached from floor to ceiling and from wall to wall. The young woman who brought me acquainted with Captain Murderer had a fiendish enjoyment of my terrors, and used to begin, I remember—as a sort of introductory overture—by clawing the air with both hands, and uttering a long low hollow groan. So acutely did I suffer from this ceremony in combination with this infernal Captain, that I sometimes used to plead I thought I was hardly strong enough and old enough to hear the story again just yet. But, she never spared me one word of it, and indeed commended the awful chalice to my lips as the only preservative known to science against "The Black Cat"—a weird and glaring-eyed supernatural Tom, who was reputed to prowl about the world by night, sucking the breath of infancy, and who was endowed with a special thirst (as I was given to understand) for mine.[5]

This savage story is only one of many similar tales that Dickens heard from Mary Weller's lips. Another story, "Chips and the Devil," concerned a shipwright named Chips who made a compact with the devil for an iron pot, a bushel of tenpenny nails, half a ton of copper, and a rat that could speak. Chips was soon inundated by rats. There were rats in his pockets, rats in his hat, rats in his coat, and rats in his bed; rats crawled up his legs when he worked and sat on his tools as he used them. Most horrible of all, Chips knew what all the rats were saying. He also knew what they were doing—nibbling at larders, sniffing at sleeping babies, gnawing on corpses in graveyards. Chips, in a torment, did everything he could to kill the speaking rat: plunging him into burning pitch, thrusting him into fiery furnaces, but the rat always emerged saying:

> A Lemon has pips,
> And a Yard has ships,
> And *I*'ll have Chips!

At last Chips put out to sea, but the rats pursued him, slowly gnawed through the rotting hull (Chips could hear them chewing, chewing), and finally, one midnight, sank the ship. When Chips' corpse washed up on shore, a fat, laughing rat slithered off his half-eaten body. "And there was a deal of seaweed on the remains. And if you get thirteen bits of seaweed, and dry them and burn them in the fire, they will go off like in these thirteen words as plain as plain can be:

> A Lemon has pips,
> And a Yard has ships,
> And *I*'ve got Chips!"[6]

There were additional tales: of strange death-foreboding animals that appeared menacingly in nearby streets; of dead persons materializing as weird apparitions and then haunting and admonishing the living (distant forerunners of Marley's ghost); of an innkeeper who cut the throats of innocent visitors, boiled his erstwhile guests in huge coppers, and baked their remains into pies; of a one-eared burglar who sought to punish his disfigurer by marrying her and then murdering her (the latter stories vary the "Captain Murderer" theme); and of dark-visaged men, blood-steeped sheets, choppers, sacks, spades, and a parrot that screamed, "Blood, blood! Wipe up the blood!"[7] It is no wonder that Dickens called nursemaids "the most dreary and uncomfortable people" and often associated them with terrorizing storytelling and cannibalistic imagery. It is no wonder, too, that he held them accountable for deep and encompassing traumas: "If we all knew our own minds (in a more enlarged sense than the popular acceptation of that phrase), I suspect we should find our nurses responsible for most of the dark corners we are forced to go back to, against our wills."[8]

Dickens' statement demonstrates that he recognized the profound significance of this early storytelling. He felt that it did more than shape his imagination, crucial as such an influence was; it shaped the very core of his personality, his most hidden sensitivities and obsessions. Dickens tells us that he heard all these stories before he was six. The stories themselves are virtual compendiums of fairy-tale motifs and techniques. Brief summaries of their action fail to convey their rich reliance on storybook devices. "Captain Murderer" contains such age-old folklore elements as warning names that do not warn, grisly hints and jokes, telltale signs (sharp teeth, milk-white horses that develop one red spot), recurrent numbers and recurrent spans of time, supernatural happenings, fabulous objects and implements (golden rolling pins, silver pie boards), predictive mirrors, paired personages (fair and dark twins), hidden watchers, clairvoyant responses, cosmic retributions, and an overwhelming array of repetitive phrases, sentences, formulas, and actions. "Chips and the Devil" displays a similar range of fairy-tale attributes: infernal compacts, speaking animals, telltale signs (sparks of blue fire, clattering metal), charmed lives (the unkillable rat), supernatural gifts, recurring objects, uncanny powers (ability to read thoughts, awareness of distant happenings), sinister affinities (Chips' inundation by rats), repeated rhymes, unheeded warnings, infallible prophecies, poetic retributions, magical numbers (thirteen words, thirteen bits of seaweed), and again an overwhelming array of repetitive phrases, formulas, names, rhymes, and events. In short, both stories, like many others that Dickens heard and reheard in these early years, exploit the traditional subject matter and technique of fairy tales.

This matter and manner burned into Dickens' consciousness as deeply as the stories themselves. Aided by unforgettable storytelling, the spirit and ambiance of fairy tales touched the primal regions of Dickens' nature. Given his preternatural sensitivity, it is no wonder that this was so. "Captain Murderer" and "Chips and the Devil," like their many counterparts, body forth universal fears and fantasies. Such tales distill the primary conflicts of life. They convey and often resolve those conflicts through the strange dreamlike poetry of symbolism and magic. Many children are unconsciously shaped by the fabling power of fairy stories. Dickens' distinction lies not in responding to that power, but in responding to it so fully and so lastingly. In this he owed much to his natural gifts, but he also owed a great deal, as we shall see, to the fast-gathering impositions of chance and circumstance.

Fairy tales shimmer with signatures. In fairy stories, objects, places, persons, acts—all the familiar realities of everyday life—display their secret significances. The solid ordinary world, mundane and incomprehensible, dissolves into wild distortions and derangements, and emerges, paradoxically, ordered and interconnected. In the enchanted region of fairy tales names convey significance, numbers recur and have magical import, mirrors limn the future, horses mete out retribution, rats speak, objects cry out, persons become monsters and monsters persons, phrases and actions repeat and return in compound circles of accreting meaning. This strange world, at once so familiar and so fantastic, beguiled Dickens. The potencies and transformations of fairy stories became part of his vision of life and part of his way of conveying that vision.

In "Captain Murderer" and "Chips and the Devil," Dickens is concentrating on one strand—the savage and Gothic strand—in Mary Weller's storytelling. But he remembered her as a comforter as well as a ghoul, and she undoubtedly told him milder and brighter stories too. But whether Mary Weller or his grandmother or some other persons inducted him into the sunnier regions of fairyland, his later remarks show that he knew those regions well and connected them with the blessed enchantment of childhood imaginings. Indeed his extended allusions to all but the darkest and most frightening fairy tales usually glow with a rhapsodic sense of wonder and delight. Even fairy stories containing powerfully frightening elements shine brightly in his memory. Dickens has no difficulty connecting such tales with Christmas, childhood delights, nobility, and love. When he thinks of the Christmases and Christmas trees of childhood, he remembers, quite typically, *Jack and the Beanstalk* and *Jack the Giant Killer,* and then drifts into a characteristic reverie:

> But, now, the very tree itself changes, and becomes a bean-stalk—the marvellous bean-stalk up which Jack climbed to the Giant's house! And now, those dreadfully interesting, double-headed giants, with their clubs over their shoulders, begin to stride along the boughs in a perfect throng, dragging knights and ladies home for dinner by the hair of their heads. And Jack—how noble, with his sword of sharpness, and his shoes of swiftness! . . . I debate within myself whether there was more than one Jack (which I am loth to believe possible), or only one genuine original admirable Jack, who achieved all the recorded exploits.[9]

The reminiscence itself takes on the attributes of a fairy tale, transforming, dissolving, and blending with magical freedom and swiftness. As usual, delight and admiration overwhelm the darker strain, but the darker strain is there too, and it emerges—as so often in Dickens' references to fairy stories and childhood literature—as an allusion to cannibalism or eating human flesh, a tribute perhaps to Mary Weller's storytelling. This conjunction repeats itself a moment later when Dickens connects *Little Red Ridinghood* with his childhood Christmas trees:

Good for Christmas-time is the ruddy colour of the cloak, in which—the
tree making a forest of itself for her to trip through, with her basket—
Little Red Riding-Hood comes to me one Christmas Eve to give me infor-
mation of the cruelty and treachery of that dissembling Wolf who ate her
grandmother, without making any impression on his appetite, and then ate
her, after making that ferocious joke about his teeth. She was my first love.
I felt that if I could have married Little Red Riding-Hood, I should have
known perfect bliss.[10]

The allusions to *Little Red Ridinghood* begin in wondrous recollection
and end in love and bliss, but the ferocious joke and horrible feasting
are there too, though softened and distanced by humor. Dickens' writings are filled with similar references to the childhood fairy stories that
delighted and frightened him. There are scores upon scores of allusions
to grisly or distressing tales such as *Bluebeard, Jack the Giant Killer,*
and *The Yellow Dwarf,* to disturbing yet ultimately reassuring stories
such as *Beauty and the Beast, Jack and the Beanstalk,* and *Sleeping
Beauty,* to more benign tales such as *Cinderella, Whittington and His
Cat,* and *Fortunatus,* and to stories that had a special pathos for Dickens, such as *The Children in the Wood, Hop o' my Thumb,* and later
Hansel and Gretel. There are scores of references to other fairy tales as
well; Dickens mentions virtually all of the fairy stories that were well
known in his childhood.

In most of these multifarious references, despite their differences of
conception, despite their diversities of application and context, two
chords emerge and persist. The first chord is compounded of wonder,
delight, innocence, and freedom, though it sometimes takes on nostalgic harmonies of yearning and loss. It is coterminous with imagination
and goodness, often with liberation and salvation. It surrounds the
beneficent fairy tales or the more beneficent parts of fairy tales. The
second chord is compounded of horror, fear, and loathing, often
strongly counterpointed by the attraction of repulsion. This chord is
sometimes softened by obliqueness, adult skepticism, circumlocution,
or humor, but its fundamental threat reverberates unmistakably. It
surrounds the violent, gruesome, nightmarish portions of fairy stories.
It is coterminous with aggression and evil, often with obsession and
aberration. Of course, not all Dickens' references to fairy stories exhibit these characteristics. In between the polarities of his typical responses are briefer, more neutral references to isolated details and
images. Yet in the longer passages, the characteristic tonalities are
almost always present: sometimes the bright chord dominates, sometimes the somber one, sometimes the two blend and combine in strange
harmonies and dissonances.

It is hard to know which came first, Dickens' interest in fairy tales or
his conditioning by them. Did his needs and idiosyncrasies produce his

wonderful sensitivity to the storytelling of his childhood, or did that singular storytelling engender his needs and idiosyncrasies? Probably the process was simultaneous and reciprocal: the storytelling served his sensibility, but also shaped it. In any case, by the time he was six, storytelling and sensibility were powerfully reinforcing one another—a concurrence that had far-reaching results. For the pattern that one sees emerging so unmistakably in this early response and imagining runs like a dominant leitmotif in all his subsequent writings. Those writings partake of the matter and manner of fairy tales. The happy endings, the fairy godmothers, the beautiful princesses (whether appreciated or neglected), the unblemished princes, the dazzling transformations, the blissful sanctuaries, the redeeming tasks, the perfecting quests, the benign disguises, the fortunate coincidences, the propitious signs, the responsive environment, the fulfilled wishes—all are allied to that amiable fairy-tale realm of bright hopes, unfading summers, and limitless possibilities, the realm that Dickens first met in the fanciful stories of his childhood, and that he later idealized as the incarnation of imagination and freedom. The wicked stepmothers, the mistreated children, the horrible witches, the leering devils, the rapacious (often cannibalistic) monsters, the baleful enchantments, the dreadful hauntings, the maleficent transformations, the terrifying dreams, the loathsome appetites, the noisome dens, the imprisoned innocents, the sinister omens, the dire recurrences, the cosmic retributions—all are allied to that nightmare fairy-tale realm of wild fears, hopeless suffering, and dark destruction, the realm that Dickens also first met in the fanciful stories of his childhood, and that he later distilled into the essence of evil and malignancy.

Mr. Dorrit's accession to riches in *Little Dorrit,* Miss Betsey's godmotherly interventions in *David Copperfield,* Nicholas' magical exorcism of Dotheboys Hall in *Nicholas Nickleby,* Scrooge's wonderful transformation in *A Christmas Carol,* little Nell's soothing influence in *The Old Curiosity Shop,* Florence's charmed sanctuary in *Dombey and Son,* Mr. Boffin's benign disguise in *Our Mutual Friend,* Pip's equivocal gift in *Great Expectations*—these and their multitudinous analogues are latter-day extensions of the reassuring component in the storybook world of Dickens' childhood. Fagin's dark den in *Oliver Twist,* Quilp's leering demonism in *The Old Curiosity Shop,* Jonas Chuzzlewit's hallucinated murder-journey in *Martin Chuzzlewit,* David's terror-filled wanderings in *David Copperfield,* Richard Carstone's baleful enchantment in *Bleak House,* Magwitch's graveyard materialization in *Great Expectations,* Mrs. Clennam's haunted house in *Little Dorrit,* Mr. Vholes' ghoulish feeding in *Bleak House*—all these and their myriad counterparts are marvelously transmuted evocations of the nightmare component in the fairy-tale world of Dickens' childhood. It is as though Dickens was held in thrall by the storytelling of his childhood, yet in an enriching rather than a stultifying way. When he came to engage in his own elaborate storytelling, he preserved that childhood vision, but he also transformed it. He fashioned it into a deep-grappling fusion with the realities of everyday life.

That childhood vision was more than a reflection of the inspired storytelling of Elizabeth Ball Dickens, Mary Weller, and others. One can see in retrospect that Dickens brought to that storytelling qualities of retentiveness, enlargement, and imaginative realization that were truly special. He seems to have captured images, phrases, and impressions as in an unfading photograph—he later compared his mind to "a sort of capitally prepared and highly sensitive [photographic] plate."[11] Or to use another of his later formulations, suggested in many of his writings, but set forth definitively in an essay entitled "Where We Stopped Growing," certain powerful impressions of his childhood fixed themselves indelibly in his mind; his growth, insofar as such impressions are concerned, stopped at the moment of encounter. This is why (according to his theory) the stories, pictures, and reading of his early years continue to exert their old power over him. The chance impingements and distortions of childhood, so he insists, are with him still.

This assertion is borne out by the evidence of his writings. *Sleeping Beauty* for Dickens is more than an idea or fable, it is a series of precise, highly visualized images and actions, and these impressions are likely to recur whenever he invokes that fairy tale. The aspect of *Sleeping Beauty* that impressed him most—that caused him to stop growing—was the century-long enchantment that froze all motion and activity in Sleeping Beauty's palace. This idea recurs throughout his writings in ever-fresh yet reiterated ways. He will refer to "a tawdry fancy ball in the Sleeping Beauty's palace during the hundred years of enchantment," or to the "sleeping beauties, whom the Knight will wake one day, when all the stopped spits in the kitchen shall begin to turn prodigiously!"[12] One catches a glimpse of how fixed yet imaginatively free this image was when one meets the same detail in a totally transformed context. When Dickens conjured up an image of organ-grinders with hands poised on the handles of their instruments, he immediately fused the image with the motionless spits in *Sleeping Beauty,* and had his character speak of organ-grinders stopped "with their handles half-turned fixed like the Sleeping Ugly—for I cannot say Beauty."[13] The imaginative force that lies behind these reiterated details controls more than images and figures. The stopped time and stopped spits of *Sleeping Beauty* enter characters, strategies, and conceptions. Characters such as Miss Havisham and Mrs. Clennam are, in

Dickens' evocative phrase, Sleeping Uglies. He conceives such personages and presents them to us (in one aspect at least) as veritable denizens of fairyland, as tormented beings imprisoned by baleful spells. Room-bound, fixed, obsessed, they are characters who have been frozen into hate-filled immobility by the deadly enchantment of the intolerable past.

Dickens retained a host of images and scenes from his early introduction to literature. This, in itself, is not unique. What is remarkable is the vividness, the fullness, and the imaginative richness of what he remembered. What is also remarkable is the shaping role those childhood images and conceptions continued to play in his everyday life and in the creative vision of his maturity. And what is true of *Sleeping Beauty* is even more true of such favorites as *Bluebeard, Jack the Giant Killer, Robinson Crusoe,* and *The Arabian Nights.* These stories, many additional works, and many early images and phrases, became forever fixed and yet forever vital for Dickens in their primordial form. Two examples can stand for innumerable instances.

Dickens probably was given *The Dandies' Ball; or, High Life in the City* in 1819, the year it was published, for he called it his first picture book.[14] *The Dandies' Ball* was an offspring of *The Butterfly's Ball* (1807), one of the first works for children to make pure fancy and entertainment its sole purpose. *The Dandies' Ball* had an amusing colored illustration by Robert Cruikshank on the top of each page and a six-line stanza of indifferent but engaging verse on the bottom. This charming booklet told the story of how a group of effete dandies—this was the heyday of the Prince Regent—overcame such dire obstacles as holes in their stockings, tight lacing, and over-fatigue from dressing, and finally made it to a ball in Great Camomile Street given by Mr. Pillblister and his sister Betsey. In an essay written in the 1850s, Dickens describes the illustrations, retells the story, and quotes two stanzas—all in a context that combines humor, gentle satire, and nostalgia. Dickens' memory of the pamphlet, more than thirty years after he read it as a seven-year-old boy, is astonishingly full, detailed, and exact. Yet slight inaccuracies in the text of the stanzas show that he was quoting from memory, and indeed *The Dandies' Ball* would have disappeared from the Dickens household at least thirty years earlier, that is before the blacking-warehouse and Marshalsea disasters. But the most interesting part of Dickens' reminiscence is his claim that when he came to live in London (most likely at Christmas time in 1822), he "rejected the Tower, Westminster Abbey, Saint Paul's, and the Monument, and entreated to be immediately taken to Great Camomile Street."[15] It is the kind of claim that he often made. He made it, for example, in relation to Colman's *Broad Grins,* saying that when he first came to London he sought out Covent Garden and King Street and thought of them (because of their associations with *Broad Grins*) as the very essence of romance.[16] One need not take the remarks about Great Camomile Street and Covent Garden to be literally true (though they might well be), but the impulse behind the remarks is profoundly true. That impulse affirms that the early stories Dickens heard and read were so real and so important to him that they dimmed the traditional wonders of the world and made them give way before the brighter charms of the imagination.

This ability to make what he saw or read real, and more than real, and then to preserve it as an undimmed icon, is exhibited also in his references to *Cock Robin*. Those references often have a striking visualness. In the poem, the bell-pulling stanza is simply:

> Who'll toll the bell?
> I, said the Bull,
> Because I can pull,
> I'll toll the bell.

Yet in *Dombey and Son* Dickens describes a man ringing a church bell "like the bull in Cock Robin, with his foot in a stirrup"; and in *Great Expectations,* he has another man "pulling a lock of hair in the middle of his forehead, like the Bull in Cock Robin pulling at the bell-rope."[17] Obviously, Dickens is not simply remembering the stanza, but the picture-book illustration that accompanied the stanza. Early nineteenth-century illustrations of the scene usually depicted the bull pulling at the bell rope, often with his foot in a stirrup. Dickens is again recalling an image directly out of childhood, and the image, characteristically, is intensely visualized and intensely real. It is also completely assimilated. It has become a living part of his everyday life, flashing into his mind as naturally as the real objects he sees on his desk or the real scenes he glimpses out his window.

The Dandies' Ball and *Cock Robin* were picture books (or perhaps in the latter case a chapbook). There were many other picture books that Dickens remembered from this period. "I dreamed," he wrote in 1860, "I was in Russia—the identical serf out of a picture-book I had, before I could read it for myself."[18] There are other references to precise images drawn from these early books, references to grotesque fortune tellers, to Bamfylde Moore Carew, King of the Beggars, to Mother Shipton, a shriveled, prophesying witch, and to the gaunt skeleton, Death—the latter image coming from Holbein's *Dance of Death,* a work that haunted Dickens' consciousness.[19]

Dickens recognized that a childhood image or association could help color and form one's life. He gave the infant David Copperfield a legacy of shaping sense impressions and imaginings, a legacy much like his own. David had a favorite picture book about crocodiles and alligators that Peggotty often read him. From this slight filament, Dickens spins a complicated web. He uses the intricate associations surrounding the crocodile book (much as Proust uses the associations surrounding the madeleine dipped in tea) to link David to characters, places, and feelings throughout the novel. In much the same way, in Dickens' own life, a lock of hair, a color, a texture might at any moment evoke its picture-book counterpart. "A shaft of light in this perspective" could remind him, as it reminded Clennam, of "the child's old picture-book, where similar rays were the witnesses of Abel's murder."[20] But picture books were primarily reminders of fairy-tale wonder and enchantment. They were "all about scimitars and slippers and turbans, and dwarfs and giants and genii and fairies, and blue-beards and bean-stalks and riches and caverns and forests and Valentines and Orsons: and all new and all true."[21]

Dickens also recalled another kind of picture book, the alphabets and primers of his childhood, and here again his recollections display a striking intensity of image and feeling. These early books and pictures live in his consciousness with their original visual, tactile, and emotional associations. His alphabets and primers were thin books with "deliciously smooth covers of bright red or green."[22] His mother helped him with those books: "I faintly remember her teaching me the alphabet; and when I look upon the fat black letters in the primer, the puzzling novelty of their shapes, and the easy good nature of O and S, always seem to present themselves before me as they used to do."[23] In these alphabets, which married woodcut and letter to text, it is easy to see how "O" who "was an oyster girl, who went about town," and "S" who "was a sailor, who spent all he got" could become, in Dickens' mind, prompted by the accompanying illustrations, easy and good-natured letters. But while the woodcuts and the inscriptions may have influenced Dickens' feelings about certain letters, they do not explain the force or duration of that influence. Many persons have learned the alphabet in picture-book primers, but few recall the substance of the experience as an adult, and fewer still (even assuming the initial responsiveness) remember how strange and puzzling the shapes of the letters seemed at first or how each letter had its own secret life and character. And finally—again assuming the initial hypersensitivity—how many reexperience that long-dead response each time they look at a primer?

The fact is that Dickens demonstrates a wondrous sensitivity in the earliest responses of which we have knowledge. Or to put the matter in a different perspective, in his earliest perceptions and reactions he shows the rudiments of the artist's sensibility and the artist's gifts. No one could have recognized this at that time or indeed for many years after, but in retrospect one can see that an artistic potential was already manifesting itself, though whether that potential would reach fruition, and what color and character it might take, were other matters altogether. In the slow growth toward that fruition, a growth so infinitely intricate and mysterious, the traits and influences I have been tracing played powerful roles. Dickens' preternatural sensitivity guaranteed that the great imaginative forces of these early years—the extraordinary storytelling, the astonishing picture books, the liberating reading—would form and shape and endow his fabling mind.

The influences I have been describing were overlapping and cumulative. The puissant godmothers, talking animals, fearsome ogres, and magical transformations that he had met in the fairy tales told by Elizabeth Ball Dickens and Mary Weller, he met again in his picture books, and once more in his earliest reading. And when he began reading independently (a development that took place very early), he entered the whole wild world of chapbook literature. There he again found the powerful enchanters and strange creatures of fairyland. In those chapbooks he could peruse all of Perrault, the best of Madame d'Aulnoy, the gleanings of other collections, the best-known stories from *The Arabian Nights,* the native English fairy tales, and the dark terrifying nightmares of Gothic horror.

That Dickens' parents allowed, even encouraged, this storytelling and reading—surely they must have given him some of those picture books and some of those multitudes of thin volumes with the "deliciously smooth covers of bright red or green"—places them among that minority (steadily growing in numbers) who felt that children required entertainment and imaginative nourishment as well as morality and lessons. It seems likely that this liberality was partly the result of conscious policy, partly the consequence of neglect, or at least of distraction. There are many indications that during this period Dickens' mother was often preoccupied with younger children, dunning tradesmen, and strategies for survival, while his father was busy with pay-office duties, convivial gatherings, and making orotund requests for money. Indeed, when Dickens thought of his early imaginative reading, he thought of himself as "a very small and not over-particularly-taken-care-of-boy."[24] It is likely, then, that he was often left to his own devices in this reading, and that he read much—especially in chapbooks—that his parents would not have chosen for him. In any case, the terrific storytelling of his earliest childhood was reinforced by the terrific reading of his next few years, and both these chance influences (which simultaneously fed and engendered his tastes) shaped his sensibility and his imagination. This was a haphazard process. Yet one can see how all these circumstances—his innate gifts, his times, his nursemaid, his parents, and his situation—were already conspiring to produce the special amalgam that made his achievement possible. Dickens understood this. Speaking of the strange chances and dark turnings of his early life, he said, "I know how all these things have worked together to make me what I am."[25]

Among the things that made him what he was were childhood recitations. Here his parents, especially his father, certainly encouraged him strongly. The elocutionary arts flourished during the Regency; recitations were a familiar part of creative middle-class life. The Dickens family reveled in such performances. Dickens, prompted by his father, was reciting and declaiming at a very early age. Mary Weller remembered Dickens' recitations vividly. She recalled that Dickens used to declaim Dr. Watts' "The Sluggard" "with great effect, and with *such* action and *such attitudes*."[26] Voice piping, arms gesticulating, Dickens would begin:

> 'Tis the voice of the sluggard; I heard him complain,
> You have wak'd me too soon, I must slumber again.

There were other pieces from Watts in Dickens' repertory:

> Let dogs delight to bark and bite,
> For God hath made them so;
> Let bears and lions growl and fight,
> For 'tis their nature too.
>
> But, children, you should never let
> Such angry passions rise;
> Your little hands were never made
> To tear each other's eyes.

Dozens of echoes of Watts, mostly humorous or satiric, reverberate through Dickens' writings. But there were recitations from other authors as well. Most likely some of Dickens' favorite passages from Shakespeare, Pope, Gray, Milton, and Johnson were first learned in this way, though in most instances it is impossible to tell whether a repeated allusion goes back initially to declamations, reading, or the theater. References drawn from Milton's *Comus* almost certainly go back to childhood recitations, and so do passages from Home's *Douglas*. The latter was a declamation favorite, and Dickens' writings are sprinkled with allusions to the most familiar lines of the recitation passage:

> My name is Norval; on the Grampian hills
> My father feeds his flocks; a frugal swain,
> Whose constant cares were to increase his store,
> And keep his only son, myself, at home.

Dickens sometimes has his young boy characters, encouraged by their fathers, recite from the declamation repertory of his youth. In "The Boots," little Harry Walmer's father "never tired of hearing him say my name is Norval."[27] There are many additional echoes of those far-off recitations. In *David Copperfield,* Wilkins Micawber (who is largely based on Dickens' father) is a veritable walking encyclopedia of declamation literature, and he rarely lets an opportunity go by without some sounding quotations from his histrionic store. Mr. Micawber is also a devotee of the convivial song, and his son, Master Wilkins, early gains a modest fame and preferment through his ability to render a song. In this Master Wilkins was like Dickens himself, for Dickens became an accomplished singer and performer while still a very young child.

During this period, Dickens was frequently performing. Dickens Senior often took his little boy to the nearby Mitre Inn in Chatham, perched him on table tops, and there watched him sing and declaim.[28] One such performance included a duet with his sister Fanny. The duet was entitled "Long Time I've Courted You, Miss"; Dickens began, then Fanny replied, and so they continued:

> Long time I've courted you, miss,
>   And now I'm come from sea;
> We'll make no more ado, miss,
>   But quickly married be.
>   Sing fal de ral, etc.

> I ne'er will wed a tar, sir,
>   Deceitful as yourself;
> 'Tis very plain you are, sir,
>   A good-for-nothing elf.
>   Sing fal de ral, etc.

—and so on, until the two are reconciled.[29]

Dickens' specialty was comic songs, and if one looks at the comic songs of his childhood, one finds an astonishingly Dickensian world. Here are prototypes of many of Dickens' early characters, episodes, sentiments, and jokes—Wellerian cockneys, blind-shooting Winkles, Gampish harridans, cowardly duelists, child-quelling beadles—frequently elaborated with those details of patter and oddity that Dickens later made his own. While still scarcely more than an infant, he found himself elevated on tables or chairs, singing in a clear treble voice "The Cat's Meat Man," with its chorus of

> Down in the street cries the cats'-meat-man,
> Fango dango, with his barrow and can,[30]

or "Guy Fawkes," with its chorus of

> Bow, wow, wow,
> Fol de rol de iddy, iddy, bow, wow, wow![31]

These comic songs—the specialty but by no means the bulk of his repertory—ran the gamut from rollicking to broad to sinister humor. The songs themselves, whether about orphans, beadles, sailors, or cockneys, were delivered with gestures, accents, and other dramatic effects. Years later Dickens could still recall the shrill tones of his childhood voice, and he blushed when he thought of the nuisance he must have been to many a suffering adult.[32] But perhaps he judged these early performances too harshly; he remained a skilled singer all his life, and he made the great popular world reflected in those songs—a subliterary world that he knew partly from life, partly from the songs, and partly from other popular genres—a vital resource for his own creation.

Dickens' elaborate childhood recitation and singing bore rich fruit. One could easily trace the imprint of those performances on his writings, not only in hundreds upon hundreds of references, but in a whole range of subjects, attitudes, and techniques. Certainly some of Dickens' taste for the inflated, the dramatic, the humorous, and the popular goes back to this early conditioning. Certainly, too, there were connections between the recitation and singing and the simultaneous storytelling and reading. Mary Weller's melodramatic storytelling, replete with frightening gestures and frightening sounds, had its counterpart in Dickens' histrionic declamations, abounding with "*such* action and *such attitudes*"; the heroic posture of Jack the Giant Killer and Hop o' my Thumb was not too far removed from the lordly stance of Cato and Norval; the amusing difficulties of dandies on their way to a ball were no different from the mishaps of scores of characters in dozens of comic songs; the crude woodcuts and the jumbled typography of legions of chapbooks were close relatives to the stark pictures and staring types of multitudes of ballads—indeed both species of productions came from the same publishers, used the same resources, and were sold by the same shops and hawkers. The imaginative world of Dickens' childhood was growing and coalescing: magic was becoming strangely entangled with the ordinary, horror with the comic, nobility with the popular.

The recitation and the singing helped bring other crucial elements into the developing pattern. Both these activities were performances; they were associated with drama, acting, audiences, applause, and approval. It is not farfetched to see, in the little boy perched on a table, captivating an appreciative audience, the embryo of the man, standing on a platform, enthralling a much larger audience. Certainly at an early age Dickens came to know the power of the word, the gesture, the cadence; and he also came to know the sweet thrill of appreciative response. But whatever the far-off consequences, one thing is certain: from the very outset literature, imagination, and make-believe became entwined for Dickens with power, praise, and status.

Dickens' histrionic singing and recitation were types of dramatic performances. But the theater and the theatrical entered his life in other, more direct ways. At a very early age, Dickens was introduced to the drama proper. By the time he was seven, he was acting out scenes from plays, and not long after that, he was reading and rereading Mrs. Inchbald's collection of *Farces and Other Afterpieces,* a seven-volume set containing dozens of plays.[33] But he was also taken to the theater as a small boy. When only seven, and then again when eight, he was brought up to London to see the great pantomime clown, Grimaldi, perform.[34] These visits were special treats, but they only confirmed and heightened Chatham pleasures. At Chatham he had watched his relatives by marriage, the Lamerts, get up private theatricals at the Ordnance Hospital.[35] As he savored the preparations, the rehearsals, and then the performances, he was tasting joys that would later become his own special delight. During this period, too, at the local theater, the Theatre Royal, Rochester, he was seeing everything from Shakespeare to farces to pantomimes. At the Theatre Royal he first saw *Richard III,* and he remembered how Richard "had made my heart leap with terror by backing up against the stage-box in which I was posted, while struggling for life against the virtuous Richmond."[36] Here, too, he first saw *Macbeth* and noticed that the witches later doubled as thanes, and that good King Duncan was resurrected for other uses after his sanguinary death.[37] It was here also that he first met the bluff stage Englishman of noble principles who would "crunch up his little hat and throw it on the ground, and pull off his coat, saying, 'Dom thee, squire, coom on with thy fistes then!' "[38]

Dickens could remember his childhood theater with amusement, laughing at its threadbare resources and contrivances, but its impact upon him was stunning. Here was a world that translated much of his reading, reciting, and imagining into veritable reality. In the literary degeneracy but theatrical gorgeousness of the early nineteenth-century theater, in its spectacle, farce, harlequinade, fantastic color, and fooling, he found the same liberating transcendence he also found in his reading. The note he strikes again and again when recalling the meaning of those early experiences is of a bright magical untrammeled world that is superior to life.

An evening at the theater often meant not simply a drama but a one-act farce and a pantomime as well. The pantomime especially was an extension of the fairy tale. This was true not simply because many of the pantomimes, particularly around Christmas time, were dramatizations of familiar fairy stories, but because they all (even those not based on fairy tales) had transformation scenes, magical happenings, and dire enchantments that made them close blood relations of fairy tales. Here the very essence of fairyland took on form and substance and motion. Dickens' reactions to the pantomime clearly indicate this relationship. For him the pantomime was the closest tangible realization of that limitless inner world of fairy stories and imagination. Dickens' descriptions of the pantomime of his childhood are lyric and rhapsodic:

> Comes swift to comfort me, the Pantomime—stupendous Phenomenon!—when clowns are shot from loaded mortars into the great chandelier, bright constellation that it is; when Harlequins, covered all over with scales of pure gold, twist and sparkle, like amazing fish; when Pantaloon (whom I deem it no irreverence to compare in my own mind to my grandfather) puts red-hot pokers in his pocket, and cries 'Here's somebody coming!' or taxes the Clown with petty larceny, by saying, 'Now, I sawed you do it!' when Everything is capable, with the greatest ease, of being changed into Anything; and 'Nothing is, but thinking makes it so.' Now, too, I perceive my first experience of the dreary sensation—often to return in after-life—of being unable, next day, to get back to the dull, settled world; of wanting to live for ever in the bright atmosphere I have quitted; of doting on the little Fairy, with the wand like a celestial Barber's Pole, and pining for a Fairy immortality along with her.[39]

One sees immediately what Dickens longed for and what he found in the pantomime: comfort, magic, spectacle, fun, fairy-tale transformation ("when Everything is capable, with the greatest ease, of being changed into Anything"), fairy-tale wish fulfillment ("'Nothing is, but thinking makes it so'"), and fairy-tale transcendence ("pining for a Fairy immortality along with her").

The pantomime gave outward visibility and additional shape to Dickens' inward fairy-tale vision. A few years later, another form of the drama helped Dickens translate that vision still further. That other form was the toy theater or juvenile drama, a phenomenon that had its beginnings about the time of Dickens' birth, reached its heyday in the twenties when he was most engrossed by it, and had already begun to decline when he began to publish.[40] In its ascendency it was extremely popular, a source of recreation and pleasure for thousands upon thousands of middle-class children. The toy theater consisted of miniature cardboard copies of actual theaters complete with curtains, footlights, drop scenes, and all the machinery of the legitimate stage. For this theater one bought sheets of characters—penny plain, twopence colored—which one carefully cut out (and colored, if plain), mounted on cardboard, and placed on long sticks or wires for manipulation. The characters were always portrayed in full costume and in theatrical poses, faithful reflections, usually, of real actors and real productions. One bought several sheets of characters in order to assemble a complete cast in a variety of attitudes, bought the requisite sheets of backdrops, scenery, and props, and finally acquired the "book" (at first full-length versions of the play, but later cut and rewritten to suit the needs of the toy theater). All these, plus powders that burned in vivid colors and made spectacular effects, and preparations that would explode and make a grand finale of noise, glare, and smoke, could be bought at the premises of the toy-theater publishers as well as at local stationery stores and toyshops.

The result was a miniature theater that mirrored the theater of the day and that reproduced, in brilliant color and melodramatic gesture, most of the plays and dramatizations of the period. They were virtually all there: Shakespeare and Scott; tragedies and comedies; burlesques, ballets, spectacles, pantomimes, and much more. There was some skewing toward the tastes of the juvenile audience, toward the melodramatic, the Gothic, the exotic, and the fanciful (especially toward the pantomime and the fairy tale), but the whole was still a remarkable reflection of the contemporary theater and a remarkable splash of life and color to brighten the sparse imaginative fare available in most respectable middle-class homes.

Many respectable homes banned the toy theater, just as they banned romances, chapbooks, and fairy stories. The Dickens home, however, welcomed the juvenile drama. The introduction took place in 1823, a most crucial time for Dickens, as we shall shortly see. In that year, James Lamert, a cousin by marriage, eight or ten years older than Dickens, helped the boy construct, paint, and launch a toy theater. Later, from about 1824 to 1826, when Dickens was at the Wellington House Academy, there were more toy-theater presentations, got up now most gorgeously with the aid of classmates and presented to other schoolmates. Thus from the time when he was ten or eleven, and for a number of years thereafter, Dickens took part, first mostly on his own, and later as the leader of a group, in choosing, learning, producing, and performing dramatic productions from the literature of the juvenile drama.

That literature reiterated and reinforced all the fairy stories, chapbooks, recitations, and pantomimes—all the imaginative conjunctions—of his earlier and his present years. Here were *Richard III* and *Macbeth,* even as in the earliest theatergoing of his Chatham days; here were *Cato* and *Comus* and *Douglas* as in his childish declamations; here were *Ali Baba and the Forty Thieves, Tom Thumb, The Children in the Wood, Aladdin and His Wonderful Lamp, Mother Bunch,* and *The Devil and Dr. Faustus* as in those chapbooks of yore that were "infinite delights" to him; here were *Sleeping Beauty, Bluebeard, Jack and the Beanstalk, Jack the Giant Killer,* and *Beauty and the Beast* as in his earliest fairy tales; here were *Harlequin Sinbad, Harlequin Fortunio, Harlequin Gulliver, Harlequin Whittington,* and *Harlequin Robin Hood* as in his beloved pantomimes—the latter productions with all the necessary tricks, scene changes, and transformations. Here, in short, was another version of what had fed and shaped his imagination.

The toy theater reinforced Dickens' long-standing delight in creative performance—in storytelling, reciting, and singing. Here, in the juvenile drama, controlling and breathing life into its brilliantly colored pasteboard figures, speaking for them, feeling for them, passionately responding and imagining for them, he was doing the very things he would later do for his own creations. The toy theater of his childhood, so fixed and paltry, would metamorphose into the limitless theater of his fiction.

II.

During his years in Chatham and for some time thereafter, Dickens was small and sickly. The exact nature of his sickliness is not clear. Forster, referring to these years, speaks variously of "attacks of violent spasm which disabled him for any active exertion," of "continual attacks of illness," and of "another attack of fever."[41] The spasms were in his side and appear to have been a form of acute kidney colic with strong psychosomatic overtones. The attacks seem to have occurred frequently during the Chatham years, several times during the blacking-warehouse months, then to have tapered off, but to have flared up from time to time when he was overwrought (as with Mary Hogarth's death in 1837) or overworked (as in Geneva in 1846). In any case, these spasms plus the mysterious fevers, plus a component of nervous susceptibility, often kept Dickens apart from the strenuous activities of childhood. In place of these activities, he immersed himself in reading and imagining. The picture one gets from scores of glimpses scattered through his letters, reminiscences, and writings is of a sensitive boy often cut off from the life about him, watching that life from a distance, his head filled with dreams and romances engendered by omnivorous reading.

Reading was his great resource. Dickens himself testified to its constancy and importance. While others sported, he read. He liked to watch other boys at their games, but he was always at a distance, "reading while they played."[42] This distance and separateness was an affliction. Yet as in a fairy story, where a curse often metamorphoses into a gift, Dickens' ill fortune, as we shall see, had its compensations.

Dickens was no invalid. The games and parties and entertainments that also belong to this period show that he was a lively and outgoing child. But for weeks and months on end he was a child set apart, his head full of Captain Murderer, seven-league boots, Robinson Crusoe, and Arabian palaces. When he thought of this time and this reading, he thought of a summer evening, the boys at play in a churchyard visible from his window, and he sitting on his bed, "reading as if for life."[43] The phrase was more than a metaphor. Though he had no way of knowing it at the time, he was already reading in order to survive.

Dickens goes on to say that he invested the churchyard and the surrounding countryside with the personages and events of his reading. We have here, I think, the beginning of a profoundly important Dickensian stance. His sickliness, withdrawal, reading, and imagining, and his concomitant habit of sympathetic yet distant observation, are the onset of his being both participant and observer, insider and outsider, native and alien. This simultaneous closeness and distance, this being a member of the group and yet divorced from it, is crucial to many artists, and certainly to Dickens. It was a creative tension, a double vision, that was to be intensified and extended, again in intimate conjunction with his reading, when he moved to London. It was a habit of mind that was to remain with him all his life. Some observers caught glimpses of this dark alienation deep in the brightness of Dickens' personality. Carlyle, perhaps, expressed this perception most dramatically. Beneath Dickens' "bright and joyful sympathy with everything around him," he wrote, there were "deeper than all, if one has the eye to see deep enough, dark, fateful, silent elements, tragical to look upon, and hiding, amid dazzling radiances as of the sun, the elements of death itself."[44]

This profound division in Dickens' response to life appears in work after work. Oliver Twist is well-born hero and pursued thief; little Nell is adored angel and hunted quarry; Florence Dombey is rich heiress and unloved daughter; David Copperfield is pampered son and wayworn waif; Mr. Dorrit is society darling and prison parasite; Pip is stylish gentleman and blacksmith's apprentice; Bradley Headstone is respectable schoolmaster and calculating murderer; Mr. Jasper is melodious choirman and opium-dreaming aggressor. All these characters seem to be one thing and yet are another thing; they belong and yet do not belong. Perhaps *George Silverman's Explanation,* Dickens' last completed story, most succinctly dramatizes this recurrent duality and disinheritance. George Silverman, eternal candidate for acceptance, who thereby assures that he will become an eternal victim of rejection, is both sympathetic observer and lonely alien. Like George Silverman, and like so many of his other latter-day surrogates, like Sydney Carton or Arthur Clennam, say, Dickens, in one repeated vision, saw himself—the matured product of those early years of isolated reading and watching—as "always in the peaceful shade"; and again like George Silverman, he felt himself alienated and alone. "I can see others in the sunlight; I can see our boats' crews and our athletic young men on the glistening water, or speckled with the moving lights of sunlit leaves; but I myself am always in the shadow looking on. Not unsympathetically,—God forbid!—but looking on alone."[45]

Dickens' preoccupation with separation and deprivation was lifelong. Given the origin of that preoccupation—probably in his mother's sudden turning from him to care for a steady procession of younger brothers and sisters—and given the intimate mingling of those feelings of separation and deprivation with his childhood sickliness and his compensatory reading, it is not hard to understand why that reading became so crucial to him. For that reading not only occupied his time when the days and weeks of enforced idleness stretched out empty before him, it wooed him from his sickness and mitigated his alienation. The giants and talking animals, the dream books and fortune tellers, the shipwrecked sailors and bejeweled sultans plunged him into a realm where everything was possible. In that realm troubles vanished and mortal limitations fell away. But his reading did more than provide an escape. It fed his extraordinary imagination, and in so doing, gave richness and transcendence to his everyday life. That transcendence became part of his daily habit. He invested chairs and tables, streets and houses, with the magic and radiance of fairyland. He fused the dull workaday world with the numinous fairy-tale world and produced his characteristic vision, a vision of minute realism transfigured by fancy. Singing and reciting had won him praise and status; reading and imagining brought him solace and delight; both gave him power: the power to sway others, the power to re-create his world, and the power to comfort himself. In the long dislocation of his childhood, reading, performing, and imagining succored and protected him. Both that dislocation and that succoring shaped his art.

Another type of reading also shaped his art. Very early, as early as seven or eight (perhaps earlier), coincident with his sickliness, and coincident with his reading in those other realms, he immersed himself in a whole new range of imaginative literature, a range that included some of the great classics of prose fiction. Many parents would have regarded this literature as unsuitable for a child—or even for an adult.

But Dickens was allowed to explore this literature without restriction.

The good fiction was part of the household. The story of how his father bought a cheap reissue of prose-fiction classics and placed the set in a garret room adjoining Dickens' room is well known; so is the story of what that little collection meant to Dickens. Dickens himself (in a passage that he transcribed word for word from his fragmentary autobiography[46]) tells the tale in *David Copperfield:*

> My father had left a small collection of books in a little room upstairs, to which I had access (for it adjoined my own) and which nobody else in our house ever troubled. From that blessed little room, Roderick Random, Peregrine Pickle, Humphrey [*sic*] Clinker, Tom Jones, the Vicar of Wakefield, Don Quixote, Gil Blas, and Robinson Crusoe, came out, a glorious host, to keep me company. They kept alive my fancy, and my hope of something beyond that place and time,—they, and the Arabian Nights, and the Tales of the Genii,—and did me no harm; for whatever harm was in some of them was not there for me; *I* knew nothing of it. It is astonishing to me now, how I found time, in the midst of my porings and blunderings over heavier themes, to read those books as I did. It is curious to me how I could ever have consoled myself under my small troubles (which were great troubles to me), by impersonating my favourite characters in them—as I did . . . I have been Tom Jones (a child's Tom Jones, a harmless creature) for a week together. I have sustained my own idea of Roderick Random for a month at a stretch, I verily believe. I had a greedy relish for a few volumes of Voyages and Travels—I forget what, now—that were on those shelves; and for days and days I can remember to have gone about my region of our house, armed with the centre-piece out of an old set of boot-trees—the perfect realisation of Captain Somebody, of the Royal British Navy, in danger of being beset by savages, and resolved to sell his life at a great price.[47]

The language Dickens uses is fervent and grateful. He calls the book-holding garret "that blessed little room"; he labels the characters who emerged from those books "a glorious host"; he assures us that those wonderful creatures served "to keep [him] company." Nevertheless, he feels obliged to affirm twice that he took no taint from any harm that might have been in the books. Apparently in 1850, thirty years after his own induction to imaginative fiction, it was still necessary to counter the argument that such works were harmful for children. For Dickens, however, it was not a matter of harm but of survival. The ability to live intensely in this imaginative world, to *be* Tom Jones or Roderick Random for "a month at a stretch," helped him transcend his sickliness, his isolation, his lost mothering, and his London neglect. As Dickens put it, reading "kept alive my fancy, and my hope of something beyond that place and time."

Dickens goes on, underlining the compensatory, creative quality of his reading:

> [My reading] was my only and my constant comfort. When I think of it, the picture always rises in my mind, of a summer evening, the boys at play in the churchyard, and I sitting on my bed, reading as if for life. Every barn in the neighbourhood, every stone in the church, and every foot of the churchyard, had some association of its own, in my mind, connected with these books, and stood for some locality made famous in them. I have seen Tom Pipes go climbing up the church-steeple; I have watched Strap, with the knapsack on his back, stopping to rest himself upon the wicket-gate; and I *know* that Commodore Trunnion held that club with Mr. Pickle, in the parlour of our little village ale-house.[48]

Before Dickens left Chatham, he had read all the books in "that blessed little room." He had read them "not for the first, the second, or the third time" but "over and over" again. "They were a host of friends when he had no single friend."[49] But his Chatham and early London reading (that is, the reading he did before he was twelve) included many works not mentioned in *Copperfield*. It included, to cite some notable examples, *Gulliver's Travels, The Scottish Chiefs, The Pilgrim's Progress, The Life of Baron Frederic Trenck, Philip Quarll*, books by Sterne and Washington Irving, and Mrs. Inchbald's *Collection of Farces and Other Afterpieces*. It also included the periodical essays of Addison, Steele, Johnson, and Goldsmith, especially the *Tatler*, the *Spectator*, the *Idler*, the *Citizen of the World*, and the *Bee*.[50] These books, too, Dickens read over and over again.

It would be hard to exaggerate the contribution this reading made to Dickens' writing, especially his early writing. *Pickwick*, for example, with its traveling group, its visit to Bath, its man-hungry women, its sojourn in debtor's prison, its idealistic knight-errant, and its loyal Sancho Panza, is deeply indebted to Cervantes, Goldsmith, Fielding, and Smollett (especially *Humphry Clinker*), and in his early novels Dickens consciously tried to work in the tradition of his great prose-fiction predecessors.[51] But much more important than such borrowings is the imaginative habit that this reading helped shape. Dickens merged himself with his reading. "My only and my constant comfort" he called it. He lived in his reading world for days and weeks on end, acting out its adventures, becoming its personages, breathing its atmospheres, living its problems. He transfigured his daily living with the glorified vision of his reading: the local town hall became Aladdin's palace; the village alehouse blossomed into a haunt from *Peregrine Pickle;* and his baby brother Augustus became Moses from the *Vicar of Wakefield* (and from Augustus' mispronunciation of "Moses" as "Boses," which was

then further changed and shortened, came Dickens' pen name, Boz).[52]
This projective ability, combined with his psychological need, is central to everything that Dickens later wrote. Perhaps more than any
other author, he submerged himself in his creations, laughing and
weeping as he wrote, living as totally in his created world as in the real
world.

Of all the books that Dickens read before he was twelve, the most
important was probably *The Arabian Nights*. There are more references in his writings to this Eastern collection of fairy tales than to any
other imaginative work. As with his other favorites, he continued to
read and reread *The Arabian Nights* all his life—constantly taking it
down from his library shelves, buying a cheap copy to read on a railway journey, or bringing a volume with him for a country weekend.[53]
He was, he confessed, "one of the most constant and delighted readers
of those Arabian Entertainments . . . that they have ever had."[54] This
loyalty to *The Arabian Nights* is duplicated in his response to other
groups of fairy tales. On his first trip to America he immersed himself in
another multivolumed gathering of fairy stories, *The Child's Fairy Library*, "a charming collection . . . in which I had great delight."[55]
These and many similar remarks attest to Dickens' awareness that fairy
tales were more than inconsequential diversions for the young. They
were, as he very well knew, at the heart of what had saved him as a
child and shaped him as an adult.[56]

In Dickens' writings only deprived or depraved children—the waifs,
the Bitzers, the young Smallweeds—are cut off from fairy stories and
imaginative reading. This deprivation is part of what perverts such
children. Even Scrooge, a lonely and neglected child, had read *Robinson Crusoe, Valentine and Orson,* and *The Arabian Nights* as a boy.
That early reading, that core of warmth and fancy in his childhood, was
a portion of what made Scrooge redeemable. Dickens, in turning back
to *The Arabian Nights* and the other fairy stories of his childhood, was
turning back to his earliest sustenance, to his creative beginnings. If
early reading was his only and his constant comfort, fairy tales were
the quintessence of that comfort; if early reading helped him transcend
the afflictions and disappointments of life, fairy tales were the essence
of such transcendence; if early reading was a matrix of his art, fairy
tales were the very form and shape of that matrix. In fairy tales all
objects were transformed or transformable. That transforming power,
which soon became a part of his own habit and vision, and later a
hallmark of his own creation, he first found in fairy stories.

He never forgot that introduction or its meaning. He intuitively recognized that fairy tales were coeval with his creative power—
"nurseries of fancy," he later called them.[57] This feeling often strongly
colors his longer references to fairy stories. It colored, for instance, the

four lengthy paragraphs in "A Christmas Tree" devoted to *The Arabian Nights*. After lovingly calling up the onset of "the bright Arabian Nights," he goes on to fuse the real and the magical in a rush of rhapsodic evocation:

> Oh, now all common things become uncommon and enchanted to me. All lamps are wonderful; all rings are talismans. Common flower-pots are full of treasure, with a little earth scattered on the top; trees are for Ali Baba to hide in; beef-steaks are to throw down into the Valley of Diamonds, that the precious stones may stick to them, and be carried by the eagles to their nests, whence the traders, with loud cries, will scare them. Tarts are made, according to the recipe of the Vizier's son of Bussorah, who turned pastrycook after he was set down in his drawers at the gate of Damascus; cobblers are all Mustaphas, and in the habit of sewing up people cut into four pieces, to whom they are taken blindfold.[58]

The torrent continues, rushing on and on, transforming iron rings, dates, olives, apples, dogs, rice, rocking horses, and "awful ladies"— ladies akin to the ghoul who feasted nightly in the burial place. The enchantment that produces these transformations is always the same. "On every object" remembered from the realms of childhood, "I see this fairy light!" It bathes each item, scene, and feeling in its magical glow. It is there during the day, and it is there at night; it is there too "when I wake in bed, at daybreak, on the cold, dark, winter mornings, the white snow dimly beheld, outside, through the frost on the window-pane."[59]

This enchantment pervades his vision from that time forth. The diminutive Rochester town hall, imposing to his childish eyes, turns into the model on which the Genie of the Lamp built Aladdin's palace.[60] Unfamiliar London, exotic in his boyish gaze, becomes interfused with Sinbad the Sailor, Rocs' eggs, caravans, bazaars, Bagdad, and "a veiled lady from the Sultan's harem, riding on a donkey."[61] One smiles at such naive transmutations. But in later life this fairy-tale commerce with reality continues, no longer now the result of childish ignorance and awe, but of a habit of mind that freshly sees the magical in the mundane.

But the days of Dickens' untrammeled reading and imagining were coming to a close. Late in 1822 the family moved from Chatham to London, apparently leaving Dickens in Chatham to complete the school term. Shortly thereafter, that is probably around Christmas 1822 (six weeks before his eleventh birthday), he rejoined his family in London. For most of the ensuing year the Dickenses lived in a small house on Bayham Street in Camden Town, moving on 23 September to larger quarters on Gower Street, the latter relocation part of an ill-conceived plan to recoup their sinking fortunes by opening a school. The Gower move was disruptive enough, but for Dickens it was the earlier move that marked the end of an epoch. That earlier move, the move from Chatham to London, devastated his life. The green lanes and flowery fields of the countryside suddenly gave way to the drab streets and brick buildings of the city, and the young boy, expecting to go back to school, fell instead into loneliness and neglect.

The last year or so in Chatham had been beset by difficulties. John Dickens, expansive and openhanded, was spending more than he earned. For the Dickens family, crisis and retrenchment had become a way of life. But in Chatham Dickens had friends, had Mary Weller, had his sister Fanny (his constant companion), had a school, and had William Giles, a young and enlightened schoolmaster. In London all was changed. He had no friends, Mary Weller was gone, Fanny was living and learning at the Royal Academy of Music, and there was no school. The latter omission dumbfounded him. Fanny was at school, why not he? He waited for some sign from his parents, but none came. His bewilderment and resentment grew. "[My father]," he later wrote, "appeared to have utterly lost at this time the idea of educating me at all, and to have utterly put from him the notion that I had any claim upon him, in that regard, whatever. So I degenerated into cleaning his boots of a morning, and my own; and making myself useful in the work of the little house; and looking after my younger brothers and sisters (we were now six in all); and going on such poor errands as arose out of our poor way of living."[62] In *David Copperfield,* Dickens gives us a glimpse of how he must have felt during this period. "All this time," David writes, speaking of the withering interval when he was put aside but not yet put to work, "I was so conscious of the waste of any promise I had given, and of my being utterly neglected, that I should have been perfectly miserable, I have no doubt, but for the old books. They were my only comfort; and I was as true to them as they were to me, and read them over and over I don't know how many times more."[63]

This state of affairs continued for about a year, slowly and then more rapidly degenerating as John Dickens declined into debt. Dunning tradesmen now grew more numerous and more insistent; badgered relatives became less approachable and less generous; saving schemes poured forth in increasing numbers—all unrealistic and self-deluding. Dickens' parents were worried and distracted. He was left to his household duties and his own devices. All too soon he took his beloved books, his "host of friends when he had no single friend," to a tipsy bookseller in Hampstead Road.[64] A little later he carried the household treasures one by one to a local pawnbroker. As Christmas 1823 approached, the large beleaguered house on Gower Street, so recklessly rented, grew bleak and empty. The end for Dickens came on Monday 9 February 1824, two days after his twelfth birthday. On that winter morning he began work at the blacking warehouse. Eleven days later his father was arrested for debt, and on 23 February John Dickens entered the Marshalsea. The Dickens family struggled on for a month longer, selling the last remnants of their middle-class respectability to the local pawnbroker, and then, on the twenty-fifth of March, they all—except for Dickens—joined John Dickens in the Marshalsea. Dickens was sent to lodge with a reduced old lady. He worked from eight in the morning till eight at night, and saw his family only on Sundays.

The Chatham period had had its sickliness, isolation, and disorder, but nothing like this. Seen through the somber dusk of his first year in London, his Chatham childhood seemed serene and idyllic—appareled in that "fairy light." Seen through the dark shadow of the blacking warehouse, it took on the radiance of paradise itself. Even before the blacking warehouse, it seemed to Dickens that he had fallen from grace. Chatham had been the source of "all my early readings and early imaginations"; in leaving Chatham he felt that he had left that blessed heritage behind.[65]

There were two mitigations in that first desultory London year. One was the fact that many of the Chatham books, "that glorious host," had been brought to London. The other was that James Lamert had helped him set up a toy theater. Confronted by a cold uncaring world, he sought to preserve a secret life of the imagination. In between running errands, blacking boots, and tending younger brothers and sisters, he concentrated on his toy theater and on reading and writing. He was attempting to maintain a continuity with a vanished past. His first effort at authorship, composed in Chatham a year or two earlier, had been *Misnar, the Sultan of India,* based upon *The Tales of the Genii,* a volume of pseudo-Oriental fairy stories in his father's collection. He now took as his model *Gil Blas,* another book that had been in "that blessed little room" at Chatham, and sought to become the contemporary Le Sage of his current London life. The attempt was modest enough. In Bayham Street, Dickens' family was waited on by a deaf old woman who made delicate hashes out of walnut ketchup. Using the canon's housekeeper in *Gil Blas* as his guide, he drew a vignette of this deaf old servant. He thought his sketch "extremely clever," but lacked the courage to show it to anyone.[66] Another sketch, this time of a cantankerous old barber, dates from the same period. Dickens had often seen this odd character shaving his Uncle Thomas. The barber was full of contentious ideas about the Napoleonic wars, Napoleon's errors, and Napoleon's life. Dickens described the old man and all his mannerisms, but this vignette, like its companion, languished unread by others.[67]

When Dickens went into the blacking warehouse, the last disintegrating links with his earlier imaginative life—his reading (already drastically diminished), his toy-theater acting, and his fledgling writing—were abruptly severed. He soon sank into the deadening routine of the warehouse, a "small Cain," a "labouring hind," cut off from family and friends, drudging six days a week from morn till night with rough boys and men.[68]

Yet even during the blacking-warehouse period there were a few frail connections to Chatham and the life of the imagination. While a very young boy at Chatham, Dickens had exhibited a special talent for storytelling. Perhaps he was emulating the unforgettable example of his grandmother, or Mary Weller, or both; perhaps he had inherited the former's gift. In any case, while still a little child "he told a story offhand so well . . . that he used to be elevated on chairs and tables, both at home and abroad" in order to display this talent better.[69] Storytelling had thus long ago become for Dickens, like comic singing and recitation, a means of creative self-expression and a way of gaining recognition and respect. Cut off in the blacking warehouse from books, toy theaters, and all the creative sources of his past, he turned to storytelling as a remnant of what he had lost. Dickens describes how he used to entertain the men and boys in the blacking warehouse with stories remembered from his old Chatham reading, but then he adds that this reading was "fast perishing out of my mind."[70] The latter realization, a despairing realization of what reading and imagination meant to him and what he was likely to become without them, occurs over and over again in the autobiographical fragment. He speaks in the fragment of the anguish and grief he felt when he realized that "day by day, what I had learned, and thought, and delighted in, and raised my fancy and my emulation up by, was passing away from me, never to be brought back any more."[71]

After a month or two of this isolation and despair, Dickens begged his father to allow him to lodge closer to the Marshalsea so that he might breakfast with the family each morning before setting off to work and sup with them each evening after getting through. His father agreed, a back attic was found for him on Lant Street in the Borough, and early each morning he lounged near London Bridge waiting for the prison gates to open. There he sometimes met the young maid-of-all-work who served the Dickens family, and who also waited for the gates to open. She was an orphan from the Chatham workhouse who had come up with them to London, and who later served as a model for that fairy-tale character, the Marchioness, the Cinderella of *The Old*

Curiosity Shop. As this workhouse waif and Dickens waited for the gates to open, he would tell her wild stories about the wharves and the Tower of London—stories replete (if one may take Dickens' usual associations with these places and Dick Swiveller's stories to the Marchioness as a guide) with airy fantasies, rats, entombed prisoners, mysteries, severed heads, ghosts, magical happenings, and fanciful legends: a potpourri of Mary Weller's Gothic storytelling, sensational chapbooks, and wish-fulfilling fairy tales. Dickens adds, speaking of these stories, "But I hope I believed them myself."[72]

What strikes one in these accounts is the importance Dickens attaches to storytelling. In view of the crushing events he is describing, one would not expect something as trivial as storytelling to be mentioned at all. Obviously for Dickens it was not trivial. It was a last bright link to an imaginative world that was "fast perishing" from his mind. Storytelling was a gift he could still wield; it made it possible for him to delight and move others as of old; it made him important and special. That Dickens' blacking-warehouse storytelling served these purposes is confirmed not only by the role he allotted it in the autobiographical fragment, but by the role he gave it in *David Copperfield.*

Before David is sent to Murdstone and Grinby's warehouse, he spends a year or two at Salem House. He comes to this school in disgrace, being sent there after biting Mr. Murdstone, and being required when he reaches the school to wear a sign on his back saying, *"Take care of him. He bites."* David arrives at Salem House in the middle of the holidays, and when the boys return, they find this strange small helpless creature with the degrading sign on his back. In other words, David enters the school in as low and powerless a position as one can imagine. He gains status and power by attaching himself to Steerforth. Steerforth condescends to this arrangement out of vanity, cupidity (he commandeers David's resources), and delight. The delight stems from Steerforth's discovery that David is a marvelous storyteller, and this discovery—or rather David's talent—soon makes David famous throughout the school. Steerforth's discovery had come about as a result of David's casual remark that an aspect of their life at school was like something in *Peregrine Pickle,* a kind of identification, of course, that had become a habit of Dickens' childhood. When David reveals that he knows much more than *Peregrine Pickle,* that he knows all the other books lodged in that "blessed little room," and that he knows them well enough to reproduce them in detail, Steerforth has David undertake the entire repertory, allowing him, like Scheherazade in *The Arabian Nights* (Dickens himself makes the comparison), to tell a fragment of story each morning and a fragment each night.[73]

David has "profound faith" in the stories.[74] His faith is rewarded. In the enclosed hierarchical universe of Salem House, his storytelling brings him special aids and special treats. Steerforth helps David with his hard school exercises and gives him periodic sips of cowslip wine to "wet [his] whistle" while he is storytelling. David drinks the wine gratefully and is "very sensible" of Steerforth's attention.[75] David continues to narrate *Peregrine Pickle* for months, the interest of his audience never flagging, and then he goes on to *Gil Blas*. David analyzes what flowed from this precocious storytelling. ["I was,"] he writes, "cherished as a kind of plaything in my room, and the consciousness that this accomplishment of mine was bruited about among the boys, and attracted a good deal of notice to me though I was the youngest there, stimulated me to exertion."[76] There were other consequences: "Whatever I had within me that was romantic and dreamy, was encouraged by so much story-telling in the dark."[77] David's assessment of what storytelling did for him is very clear. It gave him status, imbued him with a desire to excel, and encouraged his innate romanticism and dreaminess. When David is consigned to the wine warehouse, he continues his storytelling, now to the men and boys he works with, and when he runs away from the warehouse, he spends his first night in a haystack in back of his old school, comforted in his misery by being so near "the bedroom where I used to tell the stories."[78]

David Copperfield is simply another rendering (insofar as Dickens' storytelling is concerned) of what also emerges from letters, contemporary accounts, other fictions, and the autobiographical fragment. What all these sources convey is that storytelling, always an important activity in Dickens' life, became crucial during the blacking-warehouse period, that storytelling then became a desperate and despairing focus of the central imaginative development of his mind, a development that had gone on intricately for twelve years, but now seemed about to perish in neglect. In retrospect, Dickens made storytelling a token of his deprivation and a correlative of his solace. In an interval when he might have perished, storytelling (so he came to believe) had helped him survive. Storytelling stood for all that he had created and delighted in, and all that he had lost. The conviction that storytelling and all that lay behind it had succored and saved him became a mainstay of his belief. It became a foundation of his faith in literature, a source of his championing literature (and all imagination) as essential to human survival. Seen in this light, and seen in the context of the symbolic role that storytelling took on in the blacking-warehouse period, it is not hard to understand why it looms so special in his accounts of those dark days.

But storytelling had another and perhaps even deeper value for the mature Dickens. Storytelling had shaped his earliest fancies (witness the storytelling of Mary Weller and his grandmother), brightened his

Chatham childhood (witness his table-perched storytelling), and succored his stressful youth (witness his blacking-warehouse storytelling). Now in manhood storytelling had become the center of his life. For what was he now if not an elaborate and consummate storyteller? Storytelling was the destiny that had molded and finally fulfilled him.

There were a few additional sources of imagination glimmering fitfully in the prevailing blacking-warehouse darkness. One source, strange and impoverished, had a lasting impact on the isolated boy.

Dickens was paid at the blacking warehouse on Saturday, and on his way home on Saturday night, he began to buy some of the cheap weekly periodicals that came out at the end of the week. One of these magazines was the *Portfolio of Entertaining and Instructive Varieties in History, Science, Literature, the Fine Arts, &c.*[79] This double-columned sixteen-page octavo-sized periodical cost twopence and had a crude black woodcut on the front page of each issue. The magazine contained, as its title implied, instructive articles on geography, nature, popular history, cooking, science, and the like. It also contained poetry, humorous verse, epigrams, anecdotes, fiction, and occasional pieces on Margate excursions, London neighborhoods, and the kind of city vignette that Dickens later made his mark with in *Sketches by Boz*. But the specialty of the *Portfolio* was something quite different. There were scores of articles on murders, executions, dying words, disasters, escapes, dreams, superstitions, visions, and ghosts, and the woodcut on the front page often dramatized one of these sensational events. Shortly after leaving the blacking warehouse, Dickens began to buy other penny and Saturday magazines, including the *Terrific Register; or, Record of Crimes, Judgments, Providences, and Calamities.*[80] This periodical, like the *Portfolio,* was octavo in size and sixteen pages in length and carried a staring woodcut on the front page of each issue. It also contained a sprinkling of historical and didactic pieces and some serial fiction (including Dickens' beloved *Baron Trenck*), but the *Terrific Register* lacked the *Portfolio*'s interest in useful knowledge and instruction, and emphasized instead macabre histories and bloody horrors. The woodcuts mirrored this emphasis and depicted, in the most graphic detail, a veritable inferno of enormities. There were pictures of barbaric rites, horrible tortures, sanguinary executions, ferocious assaults, brutal massacres, ghostly hauntings, miraculous resuscitations, calamitous shipwrecks, gruesome impalements, and cannibalistic feastings. Dickens later described how this habitual commerce with the horrific affected him: "I used . . . to take in the *Terrific Register,* making myself unspeakably miserable, and frightening my very wits out of my head, for the small charge of a penny weekly; which considering that there was an illustration to every number, in which there was always a pool of blood, and at least one body, was cheap.''[81]

The *Portfolio* and the *Terrific Register* demonstrate that during the blacking-warehouse period, and during the difficult months that followed, Dickens maintained a second continuity with his imaginative past. The first continuity had grown out of his storytelling. His storytelling had kept alive the ''glorious host'' of his blessed Chatham reading. The second continuity grew out of the *Portfolio* and the *Terrific Register*. Such periodicals magnified the wonder and darkness that were part of Dickens' earliest imaginative heritage. He had long been an initiate of that chaotic realm, a realm of awe, fear, disturbance, and dread. ''Captain Murderer'' with its cannibalism, ferocious executions, and terrific revenge, and ''Chips and the Devil'' with its infernal compact, shipwreck, and eating of human flesh—to cite these stories and these themes only—are prototypes of motifs and proclivities that recur in profusion in the *Portfolio* and the *Terrific Register*. When one adds to these continuities such additional recurrences as rampant supernaturalism, weird happenings, strange transformations, human grotesques, notorious histories, and all the other prodigies one finds in these periodicals, one sees that this weekly reading perpetuated in the days of Dickens' imaginative deprivation one strong focus of his early imaginative bent. For the world of fancy, wildness, and horror—the world of fairy tales, Mary Weller's storytelling, and luridly colored chapbooks—is continued in these periodicals on a weightier but still undisciplined and elemental level. Here, then, the wild fancifulness of fairy stories and the dark attraction of repulsion, both nurtured in childhood, are confirmed in adolescence. And here the nightmare strain in Dickens' imagination is reinforced and given the somber coloration of his blacking-warehouse and Wellington House Academy emotions. One can trace this strain in all Dickens' works: the gargoyle characters, maleficent atmospheres, and Gothic actions, the sinister animisms, haunted murderers, and recurrent cannibalism. It is a strain that produces some of Dickens' weaknesses and some of his greatest strengths. It is a strain that increasingly infuses his writings, but that does so, as we shall see, in ever more subtle and domesticated ways.

Storytelling and reading cheap periodicals were crucial to Dickens' imaginative development in the blacking-warehouse period, but another outgrowth of those long tedious days and empty nights was even more important. As he labored ten-and-a-half hours each day over the blacking pots, as he went into the streets during the dinner hour or at teatime, as he walked to and from work, he came more and more to spin his own stories about the places he frequented and the persons he saw. ''I fitted my old books,'' Dickens has David Copperfield say, speaking of this time, "to my altered life, and made stories for myself, out of the streets, and out of men and women."[82] This was not a totally new development. In Chatham Dickens had married the real world to the world of his imaginative reading, and in London he had seen a real servant as a character from *Gil Blas* or a real barber as fit subject for an imaginative sketch. But in those days, even in the desultory London days, there was much else that he could do, indeed was required to do. Now for the most part he had no other resources. With minor exceptions there was no reading, no recreation, no studies, no relief, no companionship—only work. Re-creating the world imaginatively became the habit and chief recourse of his mind. The wharves and the Tower of London (real objects that he saw in front of him even as he talked on London Bridge to his companion, the orphan from the Chatham workhouse) became the objects of "astonishing fictions" that "I hope I believed . . . myself."[83] The shops, the teeming streets, the prison precincts, the waiters, workmen, and prisoners—all became part of a giant kaleidoscopic pantomime that he embroidered with coruscations of fantasy and romance. Everything remained real, eidetically, almost hallucinatively so, but at the same time everything was intensified, magnified, and transformed by imagination. It is clear that Dickens quickly came to see the rich color and drama in the variegated life swarming about him. Or perhaps it would be more accurate to say that he increasingly viewed that life with a certain detachment and penetration even in the midst of his passionate involvement, that he increasingly developed the artist's eye and the artist's fabling mind. The strategy begun in Chatham had become the mainstay of his life in London.

It is easy to see that this is so. In the autobiographical fragment, his descriptions of the dirty debtor and his common-law wife, the public-house landlord and his wife, the dancing coal heavers, and many similar scenes show that he was already observing such persons and places, in part at least, as a detached self-aware creative recorder. One might assume that this quality is something Dickens much later threw over such events, and there is no doubt that memory intensified what he subsequently wrote, but it is easy to demonstrate that the essence of the special vision I am talking about is not a later evolution, but an emanation of his immediate perception of the experiences themselves.

This can be seen if one examines the episode in which John Dickens presided over the signing of a Marshalsea petition. The actual petition, as the autobiographical fragment makes clear, requested that the king grant a bounty to the prisoners to enable them to drink the king's health on his forthcoming birthday.[84] The entire scene was incorporated in *David Copperfield* virtually *in toto,* though in the novel the request was changed to praying for abolition of imprisonment for debt. The details of the original scene—the description of how John Dickens listened modestly but approvingly to his own phrases, the account of how Captain Porter gave a luscious roll to certain words—seem to indicate that Dickens saw the scene and marked its details, even at the time, as an artist would have observed it; that is, he was seeing the daily life about him with an artist's eye, translating the ordinary and the mundane into patterns rich with meaning. Dickens himself assures us that this was so:

> Whatever was comical in this scene, and whatever was pathetic, I sincerely believe I perceived in my corner, whether I demonstrated or not, quite as well as I should perceive it now. I made out my own little character and story for every man who put his name to the sheet of paper. I might be able to do that now, more truly: not more earnestly, or with a closer interest. Their different peculiarities of dress, of face, of gait, of manner, were written indelibly upon my memory. I would rather have seen it than the best play ever played; and I thought about it afterwards, over the pots of paste-blacking, often and often.[85]

Three of Dickens' assertions are especially striking: first, that he invented a character and a story for each petitioner; second, that he would rather have watched the scene than "the best play ever played"; and third, that he filled his drudging hours with reenactments of what he had witnessed. Here is direct evidence that Dickens was already habitually taking ordinary life and transforming it, that he looked upon ordinary life as a remarkable drama to be observed and at the same time embroidered, and that these imaginative preoccupations—essentially translating life into art—gave meaning and comfort to his empty hours.

There is one other item in this account that makes it certain that Dickens was truly relating what he felt and did at that time. This is the revelation that he got excused from the blacking warehouse—the only known occasion on which he sought or received such a respite—to witness the petition signing. "When I heard of this approaching ceremony," he tells us, "I got leave of absence on purpose, and established myself in a corner, near the petition."[86] This can only mean that at the time, and before the fact, Dickens was so self-consciously aware of the drama and richness inherent in this scene, that he took special pains to witness it. This sense of the import and fascination of ordinary life (of tawdry, commonplace life at that), this notion of its being the stuff of imagination, better than any play, is not something that one musters up for an isolated occasion, but something that one brings to all the countless impulses that batter and bombard one.

It was not prison ceremonies, however, but the constant dramas of the swarming streets that now became the imaginative center of his solitary life. In the blacking-warehouse period, and especially before he moved near the Marshalsea, his only relief from the warehouse or his room was the streets. He would walk to work through the streets in the early morning, go out into them again for an hour at dinnertime and a half hour at teatime, and then make his way home through the night streets after work. The streets were inimical and terrifying, but they were also endlessly fascinating, and they were a relief from the deadening drudgery of work or from the "miserable blank" of the lonely hours in his prisonlike room.[87] During the two breaks in his workday, he usually wandered about the tangle of nearby streets, stopping at coffeerooms and pudding shops, walking through Covent Garden Market, playing on dusty coal barges, ducking through the Adelphi arches, sitting on public-house benches, or sauntering near the river.[88] Little of this was fun. The streets offered badly needed relief and diversion, but they proclaimed his disinheritance. They were alien and threatening, symbols of danger and neglect: "I know that I have lounged about the streets, insufficiently and unsatisfactorily fed. I know that, but for the mercy of God, I might easily have been, for any care that was taken of me, a little robber or a little vagabond."[89] These feelings were deeply, even bitterly felt, but never expressed. Through everything he kept his own counsel, and through everything he kept himself apart. He was "solitary and self-dependent," and he was ever watchful and observant.[90]

For part of this period he must have risen in the dark and gone out into the dark morning streets; for most of the period he went home in the dark. On the other hand, the areas in which he worked (near the Strand and Charing Cross) and his different ways home at different times (including Tottenham Court Road and Blackfriars Bridge) were amongst the busiest and the best lighted in London. These streets were crowded with workers, shoppers, hawkers, loungers, street arabs, tavern customers, theatergoers, and much more. The streets bustled and stirred through all the day and much of the night. They were busy when Dickens entered them in the morning, when he returned to them during the day, and long after he walked home through them at night. They were a magic lantern, and in a time when he had been deprived of virtually all his reading, all his reciting, and all his old imaginative reliefs, the streets became the source of his new imaginings. The streets and their thronging crowds, the darkness and the flaring gas, were now the substance of his own fairy tales, his own *Arabian Nights,* his own transformations, his own storytelling, his own Gothic fancies, and his own nightmare imaginings. The streets, in other words, and his banishment to them, were the cause and source of his new

creativity—the creativity that would feed his art as richly as his childhood fairy stories and childhood reading. Indeed he reshaped the
streets in the images of that reading and imagining.

The streets, though photographically seen and indelibly remembered, remembered in all their wretchedness and all their teeming bustle, would then and ever after be transmuted into something magical
and strange. The streets would always remain preternaturally real,
minutely and uncannily identifiable, but they would also be preternaturally expressionistic, the streets of dreams and fairy tales. Houses
would lean toward one another, gossip and groan; cobblestones would
cry out, "don't go home"; doors would frown, door knockers take on
life, windows stare, chimney pots get drunk. The streets would be filled
with portents and omens. They would fall under baleful spells, flourish
in benign enchantments, echo to invisible feet. They would contain
lofty castles, fairy-tale palaces, rude huts, and malignant hovels. The
streets would become dense dark forests in which ogres and monsters
lurked, in which one could easily become lost and perish. The streets
would teem with the veritable regiments of fairyland: witches, giants,
godmothers, dwarfs, princesses, stepmothers, gnomes, ghosts, and
dragons. Out of the darkness, pain, and drudgery, out of the mean
streets and low experiences of that time, and out of the fairy stories and
imaginings of an earlier time, came the needs and fulfillments that
shaped his later fictions. Dickens knew this very well. "When my
thoughts go back now," he had David write of the petitioning episode,
"to that slow agony of my youth, I wonder how much of the histories I
invented for [the petitioners] hangs like a mist of fancy over well-
remembered facts! When I tread the old ground, I do not wonder that I
seem to see and pity, going on before me, an innocent romantic boy,
making his imaginative world out of such strange experiences and sordid things."[91]

In retrospect one can see, as Dickens put it, "how all these things
. . . worked together to make me what I am."[92] A seemingly unpropitious combination of history, sensibility, and happenstance determined
the form and bent of his genius. Born in an age dominated by dour
notions concerning imagination and children's literature, he yet found
his way into the realms of fancy—realms made all the more precious to
him by the vast desert of opposition. Born in an age when fairy tales
were considered rubbish and wild stories pernicious, he had a grandmother who excelled in one and a nursemaid who excelled in the other.
Childhood sickliness isolated and encumbered him, but it also forced
him to find comfort and recompense in the life of the imagination.
Parental neglect wounded him profoundly, but it also left him free to fill
his mind with "Captain Murderer," *Jack the Giant Killer, The Golden*

Dreamer, and the *Terrific Register,* a world at once popular and esoteric, natural and supernatural, comic and sinister—a crude, colorful microcosm of the world he would later create. The storytelling, comic singing, declamation, and toy-theater production caused him to crave notice, response, applause, but the same experiences also taught him to project himself into characters and situations, to sway audiences, and to feel the exhilaration and power of creation.

Yet all these strange intersections and reinforcements, embryo premonitions of what was to be, seem fragments of a larger pattern. That pattern consists of a wonderfully sensitive child responding to the stimulation of early imaginings and then enlarging those imaginings. Imagining soon became paramount. On the one hand it became Dickens' chief source of power and status, on the other his chief means of transcending sickness and disorder. By the time he moved to London, imagination itself was threatened, yet it still saved him: first by providing some continuity with the imaginative resources of the past, and second by allowing him to translate the intolerable present into the realm of make-believe and art. This is a bald and reductive way of summarizing something that was infinitely more mysterious and complex. After all, who can plumb the unfathomable chemistry of mind and circumstance? Yet the chief contours of Dickens' imaginative development seem clear enough, and in that development the free and the fanciful were all-important.

The quintessence of the free and the fanciful for Dickens was the fairy story. This was true not only because fairy tales had first brought him into the realm of imagination, but because fairy tales were the source and embodiment of untrammeled imagination, "nurseries of fancy," he called them. In fairy stories all things were possible; in fairy stories the universe became interconnected and numinous. Dickens' art may be seen as a most consummate melding of reality and fairy tales, a melding that intensifies and distorts reality in order to be more profoundly true to it. For through the magic and technique of fairy tales, Dickens found that he could convey life in its exactitude while at the same time dramatizing and commenting on that deceptive exactitude and depicting its intricate mystery.

Seen in this light, all Dickens' books are fairy stories, and all make use of fairy stories. Yet the relationship is more a matter of vision and belief, one might almost say of conditioning, than of conscious emulation—though the latter often enters the equation too. By the time Dickens emerged from the blacking warehouse, he could no more extract the magical from his vision of the world than he could divorce his eyes from seeing or his ears from hearing. Both his need to see in his special way and his habit of doing so had been enforced by years of cumulative, unexpungeable experience. Furthermore, by the time he left the blacking warehouse the essential habit of his creativity had been formed. At the center of that habit was the fanciful transformation of life, a transformation that was not simply a by-product of his creativity but indistinguishable from it. There was much more that would enter into his creativity, and there would be many other experiences that would continue to shape and change him. But his habit of vision was already fixed, and his habit of vision was all-important.

Everything he wrote filtered through that fanciful vision. How could it be otherwise? That was the way he saw the world: real and yet transformed, mundane and yet transfigured. Each novel would bear that fairy-tale imprint, yet each would be unique. The fairy-tale vision would always be present, but in different configurations, different emphases, different densities. And the manner in which Dickens would use the fairy story would change also. The manner would evolve with his evolving technique. The fairy story, and all its rich legacy of metamorphosis and enchantment, would become a crucial reflex of his growing mastery and growing insight.

4 | From *Pickwick* to *Chuzzlewit*
Fairy Tales and the Apprentice Novels

IN SCENE, texture, and allusion, *The Pickwick Papers* is the least indebted to fairy stories of all Dickens' novels. Page after page goes by without a hint of magical influence. The main current of the story, despite its strong idealizing and caricaturing tendency, is workaday and prosaic. Many contemporary readers found the book vulgar and low. *The Pickwick Papers* deals with bustling inns, drafty country houses, lumbering coaches, and unfashionable flats; it depicts eccentric servants, obfuscating lawyers, insinuating sharpers, and rowdy journalists. Dickens seems intent on describing realms he knows well, and then investing those realms with confrontations and japes drawn from eighteenth-century novels, early nineteenth-century plays, and rollicking comic songs. His purpose is to entertain and enlighten the reader with a rapid series of adventures depicting the variety, humor, pretensions, mishaps, and comforts of everyday life. The emphasis is upon this world, upon sparkling mornings, corrupt institutions, hilarious imbroglios, steaming meals, predatory tricksters, and large-hearted camaraderie. The fairy tale is not purposely excluded from these scenes. Dickens is simply so immersed in the tangible, so enthralled, at times so overwhelmed, by his first large-scale opportunity to record the limitless sights and contrivances of an intoxicating universe, that he is content to celebrate the ordinary—a celebration that contains wonder enough.

Yet there are two important exceptions to these generalizations. For one thing, the latter portion of the overall design of *Pickwick* has strong storybook elements. In the beginning Mr. Pickwick is a butt, and it is clear that Dickens originally intended him to be a pompous fool who would constantly fall victim to his obtuse self-importance. But Mr.

Pickwick grew under Dickens' hand, evolving, almost independently, it would seem, into an amiable innocent who embodied goodness and genial fellow feeling. As this transformation occurs, the book increasingly polarizes, with the forces of good rallying again and again to defeat or cauterize the forces of evil. For the most part (with the exception of the Fleet episodes) these contests take place on the ordinary levels of life. The evil takes the shape of chicanery, imposture, ignorance, sharp dealings, and the like. We watch the Jingles, Job Trotters, George Nupkins, Justice Stareleighs, Serjeant Buzfuzes, and Dodson and Foggs of life take their toll, but their impositions are not fatal, and in *Pickwick* the evil they do is undone or contained or at the very least mitigated. This mitigation is effected by the forces of good, which, with the notable setback of the Fleet, wax stronger and stronger as the book progresses, and center increasingly about the person of Mr. Pickwick. As the book draws to a close, Mr. Pickwick takes on the unmistakable role of a fairy godfather, summoning, reproving, transforming, rewarding, and blessing. But his metamorphosis begins much earlier. Hundreds of pages before he enters the Fleet, we recognize his invincible goodness. We have long since come to understand that no matter what his ineptitude, his mistakes, his drunkenness, or his credulity, he will emerge unscathed and ever innocent. In the Fleet, his sternest trial, where he must confront devastating poverty and ubiquitous evil, his response is characteristic: he meliorates what he can, and from the rest he sorrowfully turns away, immuring himself at last from its painful sights and insidious contagions.

What he accomplishes before he turns away is sorcery enough. He transforms seasoned con artists and hardened rogues with a wave of his magic wand. Here is how he refashions those lifelong predators, Jingle and Job:

> "Come here, sir," said Mr. Pickwick, trying to look stern, with four large tears running down his waistcoat. "Take that, sir."
> Take what? In the ordinary acceptation of such language, it should have been a blow. As the world runs, it ought to have been a sound, hearty cuff; for Mr. Pickwick had been duped, deceived, and wronged by the destitute outcast who was now wholly in his power. Must we tell the truth? It was something from Mr. Pickwick's waistcoat pocket, which chinked as it was given into Job's hand, and the giving of which, somehow or other, imparted a sparkle to the eye, and a swelling to the heart, of our excellent old friend, as he hurried away.[1]

The gift moves Mr. Pickwick, but it transforms Jingle and Job. They give up their predatory ways and accede to Mr. Pickwick's authority. Their transformation is magical. With a gesture Mr. Pickwick has changed them from beasts of prey into civilized men.

Mr. Pickwick's magical power is benevolence, his magical instrument is money. In Dickens' later novels, money will take on strange mercurial properties; it will often prove a deceptive or treacherous gift; but here, and in most of the early novels, money has a simpler function. It speeds one to perdition, or helps one to felicity. Dickens' fairy godmothers and godfathers, especially in the early novels, and especially toward the end of such novels, use the magic wand of money to transform, reverse, and save. With the aid of that potent wand, they redeem the redeemable, lift up the fallen, and permit the pure of heart to live happily ever after. Mr. Pickwick's exit from prison is a fairy tale pure and simple: he takes with him his entire entourage—Jingle, Job, Mrs. Bardell, and Sam—enemies and persecutors as well as friends. Dickens is projecting his childhood daydream of rescuing his father, releasing his father's friends, and pardoning his father's persecutors; he is triumphing vicariously over the past.

After the Pickwickians emerge from the Fleet, the book concludes with a rush of fairy-tale activities. Mr. Pickwick is involved in a host of godfatherly works—uniting, blessing, freeing, enriching, sponsoring, and entertaining. Under his benign aegis Mr. Jingle and Job Trotter are sent to the West Indies where they become "worthy members of society"; Emily Wardle is married to Mr. Snodgrass and Mary to Sam Weller; Tony Weller has his savings invested and they grow to a "handsome independence to retire on"; and innumerable babies are godfathered.[2] Our final glimpse of Mr. Pickwick is of a genial godfather radiating contentment and living happily ever after:

> And in the midst of all this, stood Mr. Pickwick, his countenance lighted up with smiles, which the heart of no man, woman, or child, could resist: himself the happiest of the group: shaking hands, over and over again with the same people, and when his own hands were not so employed, rubbing them with pleasure: turning round in a different direction at every fresh expression of gratification or curiosity, and inspiring everybody with his looks of gladness and delight.[3]

We leave Mr. Pickwick and the Pickwickians as the "sunshine of the world is blazing full upon them."[4] Mr. Pickwick is a being of light; he is, as Sam Weller tells us, an "angel in tights and gaiters."[5]

This loose overarching thrust of *The Pickwick Papers* in the direction of fairy tales, especially toward the end, is one exception to the paucity of fantasy elements in the novel. The other exception is the interpolated tales. The point has often been made that the interpolated tales are dark and Gothic, while the main narrative is sunny and sane. But this is hardly accurate. A number of the stories are not dark, and a number are not Gothic. As for the bright main narrative, it descends unhesitatingly into the gloomy squalor of the Fleet. The interpolated stories do have something in common, however. What all nine tales possess—and this similarity has not been noticed before—is a debt, in most cases an overwhelming debt, to fairy stories.

The interpolated pieces are striking emanations of Dickens' fairy-tale imagination. The strength of that debt to fantasy varies. Some stories, such as "The Stroller's Tale" and "The Story of the Convict's Return," reveal their indebtedness mainly toward the end. The narrator of the "Stroller's Tale" begins by assuring us that "there is nothing of the marvellous in what I am going to relate," a disclaimer that alerts us to the suprarational.[6] The tale is about a wretched actor dying of drink. He is terrified and demon-ridden. He stares about him with an "unearthly air of wild anxiety," and accuses his mild wife of being "an evil spirit—a devil."[7] Emaciated and grotesque, he is, the narrator assures us, more ghastly than the spectral figures in Holbein's *Dance of Death*.[8] This haunted actor goes to his death hallucinating a demonic vision as phantasmagoric and horrible as anything Mary Weller ever dreamed up: "There were insects too, hideous crawling things with eyes that stared upon him, and filled the very air around: glistening horribly amidst the thick darkness of the place. The walls and ceiling were alive with reptiles—the vault expanded to an enormous size—frightful figures flitted to and fro—and the faces of men he knew, rendered hideous by gibing and mouthing, peered out from among them."[9]

The "Convict's Return" contains no wild hallucinating, but it has a nightmare ending nevertheless. A convict, returning to his native village after seventeen years, finds that he has no place there, and he lies down despairingly in a meadow. Lying not far off is an old man from the workhouse who turns out, as fate (or fairy story) would have it, to be his father. His father had been drunken, abusive, and neglectful; he was, in effect, responsible for the convict's wasted life. The convict calls the old man "Father—devil," grasps him by the throat, but then drops his hands. Justice is miraculously meted out, however. The old man utters a "loud yell . . . like the howl of an evil spirit."[10] His face turns black, gore rushes from his mouth and nose; he staggers back, and dies.

In most of the interpolated tales the storybook elements are more central than this and govern more of the fable. Jack Bamber, the narrator of "The Old Man's Tale About the Queer Client," prefaces his principal story with several macabre spirit-haunted tales. Only after this ghost-laden introduction does he launch his main story of Heyling's pathological revenge. In that story the surreal elements cluster at the center. Heyling has two elaborate nightmarish dreams. These long, magical dreams prefigure the ending of the story, one in direct fashion, the other in symbolic guise.

It might seem from these three stories that the fantasy component in the interpolated narratives is a function of hallucination and pathological emotion, but this is emphatically not the case. "The Parish Clerk: A Tale of True Love" is a satiric story of everyday life, a story of flirtatious girls, misjudged affections, and farcically duped hopes—all very much in the manner of similar vignettes in *Sketches by Boz*. But while the events are ordinary and realistic, the mode of narration is another matter: it quickly guides the reader into the realm of fairyland. Here is the opening sentence of "The Parish Clerk": "Once upon a time in a very small country town, at a considerable distance from London, there lived a little man named Nathaniel Pipkin, who was the parish clerk of the little town, and lived in a little house in the little High Street, within ten minutes' walk of the little church; and who was to be found every day from nine till four, teaching a little learning to the little boys."[11] This storybook style is maintained throughout the tale, which ends, despite the farcical imbroglios, with everyone living happily ever after.

The remaining five interpolated stories are also indebted to fairy tales. "The Bagman's Story" tells how Tom Smart found himself one stormy night at a snug inn owned by an attractive widow. After drinking tumbler upon tumbler of delicious hot punch, he goes to his room and stares in fascination at a strange, old, fantastically carved chair:

> Tom gazed at the chair; and, suddenly as he looked at it, a most extraordinary change seemed to come over it. The carving of the back gradually assumed the lineaments and expression of an old shrivelled human face; the damask cushion became an antique, flapped waistcoat; the round knobs grew into a couple of feet, encased in red cloth slippers; and the old chair looked like a very ugly old man, of the previous century, with his arms a-kimbo. Tom sat up in bed, and rubbed his eyes to dispel the illusion. No. The chair was an ugly old gentleman; and what was more, he was winking at Tom Smart.[12]

Soon Tom and the chair are deep in conversation. Dickens handles the scene with marvelous skill, giving the chair an appropriate character and ringing delightful changes on an ingenious series of correspondences between an old chair and an old man. The chair turns out to have supernatural knowledge of everything going on at the inn. It tells Tom how to win the widow and how to dispose of her present suitor—the latter gentleman is already married and proof of this fact is in a nearby clothespress. Tom falls asleep. When he awakes in the morning the chair, though fantastic, is just a chair; "it must have been a remarkably ingenious and lively imagination, that could have discovered any resemblance between it and an old man."[13] Nevertheless, Tom checks the press, finds the letter, disposes of the suitor, marries the widow, and lives in everlasting contentment. The story ends with a repetition of details evoked in the opening and sounded, fairy-tale style, throughout the sketch. Dickens, of course, possessed that "remarkably ingenious and lively imagination" he gently mocks—an imagination that had fed since boyhood on magical correspondences and storybook transformations.

Toward the end of *Pickwick* the Bagman tells another tale, and it, too, is filled with weird transformations. The Bagman specializes in such stories; he is a master of enchantment. When we come upon him the second time he is "relating some tale of wonder" to the landlord.[14] The Bagman's present story is a tale of wonder too. It is about his uncle, Jack Martin. That worthy, after drinking in Edinburgh at the house of a friend, takes his way homeward one wild gusty night, but pauses at an enclosure of old worn-out mail coaches. Being a great lover of old coaches, he climbs over the palings and sits quietly contemplating the dozen or so derelicts, all ragged skeletons of their former glory. As he contemplates the chilly scene, he thinks of the departed people who used to ride in the coaches. He falls into a doze, but is awakened by a church bell striking two. Then he jumps up in astonishment. For as the bell ceases to vibrate, the coaches are restored and the scene springs to life with all the bustle, noise, and activity of the last century. A moment later he is getting into a coach with bewigged ladies and gentlemen. He then takes part in an extravagant romantic adventure, an adventure complete with evil courtiers, a beautiful lady in distress, and much dreamlike distortion. After many strange happenings, the adventure climaxes when Jack rescues the beautiful lady and drives off with her in a coach, only to be pursued by a madly galloping and steadily gaining pack of ruffians. Jack stamps wildly on the boot and wakes up. It is grey morning. He is sitting on the box of an old Edinburgh mail, shivering with cold, and stamping his feet to warm them. In this wise Jack Martin discovered "that the ghosts of mail-coaches and horses, guards, coachmen, and passengers, were in the habit of making journeys regularly every night."[15]

Both of the Bagman's stories, but especially the first, are examples of what Dickens could do marvelously well, that is, translate the everyday into the realm of untrammeled fancy. He did much the same in "Meditations in Monmouth Street," a sketch written and published at virtually the same time as the first of the Bagman's stories and then collected three months later in the second series of *Sketches by Boz* (1836). But these early efforts are short and self-contained; it would be years before he could make his characteristic fusion of reality and fantasy support an entire novel. Nevertheless, these endeavors are signs of the strength and multiplicity of Dickens' fairy-tale vision, a vision that also dominated the remaining interpolated stories of *Pickwick*.

In "The True Legend of Prince Bladud," Dickens exploits an entirely different storybook genre. "Prince Bladud" is a legendary history; in this case a satirical account of how Bath was founded. Actually there are two accounts, the first a devastating lampoon in the mode of the beast fable, the second a gentler satire in the mode of the romance. How Dickens combines satire with these versions of fairy tale the two legends are full of magical happenings, talking animals, prisons in "lofty turrets," and elaborate allusions to mythical personages (such as King Cole)—may be seen in the ending of the second account of the founding of Bath. Prince Bladud, crossed in love by a tyrannical father (a combination of King Cole and an outraged Victorian paterfamilias), wanders weeping to the site now occupied by Bath where, overcome by his beautiful surroundings, he prays that his tears "might flow in peace for ever!"[16] The legend then rapidly concludes:

> The wish was heard. It was in the time of the heathen deities, who used occasionally to take people at their words, with a promptness, in some cases extremely awkward. The ground opened beneath the Prince's feet; he sunk into the chasm; and instantaneously it closed upon his head for ever, save where his hot tears welled up through the earth, and where they have continued to gush forth ever since.[17]

Very different again from these legend fairy stories is the demon-filled fantasy of "A Madman's Manuscript." The protagonist of this first-person tale, fearing the onset of hereditary madness, is tormented nightly by horrible dreams. "Large dusky forms with sly and jeering faces crouched in the corners of the room, and bent over my bed at night, tempting me to madness."[18] When he does go mad, no one realizes what has happened. In a nightmare scene, he drives his wife to insanity and death, and later is on the point of killing her brother when he is surprised and forced to flee. He escapes but is surrounded by "strange beings" that flock around him. Then he is "borne upon the arms of demons who swept along upon the wind, and bore down bank and hedge before them, and spun me round and round with a rustle and a speed that made my head swim, until at last they threw me from them with a violent shock, and I fell heavily upon the earth."[19] He awakes in his madman's cell. He is beset there, too. All night, every night, the specter of his wife haunts him. She stands motionless in a corner of his cell, her face very pale, her eyes "glassy bright," her hair stirred by "no earthly wind."[20]

The most important of these interpolated stories, and the one I have left for last, is an example of yet another variety of fairy tale, the goblin story. This tale, entitled "The Story of the Goblins Who Stole a Sexton" (for easier reference I shall call the piece "Gabriel Grub"), appeared at the end of Number X (December 1836), the number in which the Pickwickians celebrate Christmas with Mr. Wardle at Dingley Dell. Along with the rest of the number, the story is a celebration of Yuletide, a seasonal garnish for the Christmas fireside. Both the celebration and the story owe a good deal to Washington Irving (as do some of the other interpolated tales), but the chief significance of the story lies elsewhere. "Gabriel Grub" is a prototype of *A Christmas Carol* and the other Christmas books, a prototype, therefore (as we shall see in the next chapter), of a development of great consequence in Dickens' use of fairy tales and in the growth of his art.

In one of those curious confluences of creativity, Dickens not only took the technique of *A Christmas Carol* from that Christmas number of *Pickwick,* but the name as well. For immediately before Mr. Wardle tells "Gabriel Grub," he sings a song celebrating Christmas—we are given all five stanzas and forty lines of it. The song, written by Dickens, is titled "A Christmas Carol," and that name appears in big bold black Gothic type at the head of the poem. When Dickens came to write *A Christmas Carol* seven years later, again for Christmas firesides, and when he chose (whether consciously or not) to follow the pattern of "Gabriel Grub," the title of the song, connected so closely with that earlier story, must have come, full of warm associations, strongly into his mind. In any case, the title and a prototype of *A Christmas Carol* are there in the tenth number of *Pickwick.*

The connections between "Gabriel Grub" and *A Christmas Carol* are strong and manifold. The interpolated story tells the tale of Gabriel Grub, a morose, surly, solitary sexton and gravedigger. Like Scrooge in *A Christmas Carol,* Gabriel is ill-humored, offended by geniality, and outraged by Christmas celebrations. He responds to cheerful greetings with "a short, sullen growl."[21] Again like Scrooge, Gabriel has his adventure on Christmas Eve. Rather than join in Christmas festivities, he proceeds to the graveyard in order to dig a grave, an activity congenial to his gloomy soul. On the way he meets a boy singing a carol and raps him over the head with his lantern five or six times. Thus refreshed, he enters the churchyard, works diligently at the grave for an hour or so, and then pauses to drink and make a macabre joke. "A coffin at Christmas!" he says. "A Christmas Box. Ho! ho! ho!"[22]

At this instant a voice behind him echoes his laughter, and Gabriel, like Scrooge after him, begins to be visited by spirits who torment and teach him. Gabriel turns to see "a strange unearthly figure," a goblin, seated on a tombstone next to him. The goblin—he is, in fact, the King of the Goblins—reprimands Gabriel for his meanness and misanthropy. A moment later, a brilliant light appears in the church, the organ peals forth, and troops of goblins swarm into the churchyard and commence to play leapfrog amongst the tombstones. Suddenly the goblin king grasps Gabriel and drops through the earth with him. Gabriel is now in a large cavern surrounded by crowds of goblins who sit in judgment on him. Then, like Scrooge, Gabriel is shown a series of scenes that slowly teaches him the lessons he must learn. When he has learned these lessons, the goblins begin to disappear one by one, and Gabriel sinks into sleep. When he awakens, it is day, and he is lying on a flat gravestone with an empty liquor bottle beside him. "But he was an altered man."[23] He immediately walks off, abandoning his lantern, spade, and bottle, and leaves the town—hence the legend that he was stolen by goblins. Ten years later he returns, "a ragged, contented, rheumatic old man."[24] He then tells his story, and "in course of time it began to be received, as a matter of history, in which form it has continued down to this very day."[25]

This bald summary does not do justice to Dickens' art. Here, and in the other stories, I have had to sacrifice his slow building of supernatural moods, his wild transformations, his portentous atmospheres in order to isolate the magical core of each. But even thus stripped and condensed, the strength and fecundity of their fairy-tale origins are clear. The best parts of these stories are generated and leavened by storybook energies. Such energies interfuse, indeed they are one with, the wildness or satire or banter that lift the stories above the ordinary, though some of the tales, low in such energies, are unsatisfactory and even feeble. The tales of revenge, for example, however interesting autobiographically, and however transmuted here and there by inspired touches, are not good art; they strain for grand effects (effects that fascinated Dickens) and quickly degenerate into hackneyed fustian.

None of these successes or failures, however, can obscure the central fact concerning the relationship of these stories to the main body of *Pickwick.* That fact is that Dickens turned away from fairy tales in the main body of *Pickwick,* and then embraced them overwhelmingly in the interpolated stories. Some commentators have attempted to elucidate an intricate relationship of theme and design between the stories and the basic text. Such critics have sought to show that the stories elaborately undergird the central patterns of *Pickwick;* that Dickens used the stories as cunning reinforcements of his grand design. Such arguments are ingenious rather than convincing. They impose rather than reveal meaning. The strategy of the interpolated stories, improvised like much of *Pickwick,* was very simple, I think. Dickens wanted to provide his readers with variety—variety of pace, interest, tone, and subject matter. He saw the interpolated stories primarily as instruments of diversity rather than theme. Indeed the discontinuity of the interpolated stories is so great that some critics have wrongly assumed that Dickens wrote them before *Pickwick* and desperately introduced them as filler when he was sorely pressed for time. The sketchy evidence of the fragmentary manuscript and of occasional letters disproves this theory. The stories are an indication of plenitude, not of desperation. A tale of Gothic horror added a missing and unexpected dimension to the farcical wanderings of the Pickwickians; an episode of fairy-tale transformation provided a perfect foil to the worldly traffic of courts and inns; a Christmas goblin story added a strange but satisfying chord to the Yuletide harmony at Dingley Dell. The stories were pauses, moments of intensification, relief, or diversion. Dickens was simply putting into effect his "streaky bacon" theory of literary construction, a theory he enunciated half humorously in *Oliver Twist* while *Pickwick* was still in the course of publication, and a theory that calls for varying layers (that is, chapters) of comedy and tragedy, bustle and calm.[26] In *Pickwick,* where the main narrative is essentially all of a piece, the interpolated stories provide the streaky variety.

What is so extraordinary is that through all the range and diversity of the interpolated stories, the fairy tale enters and dominates. It is as though Dickens, having excluded the fairy story from the ordinary exploits of the Pickwickians, felt that he must make up for that absence in the interpolated tales. It is as though he believed that strangeness, unbridled imagination, and nightmare hauntings—all the transforming fancies and phantoms of the invisible world—while inappropriate to his main narrative, were too important to exclude from the larger sweep of his novel. Or perhaps these elements crept into his work willy-nilly. Dickens' imagination may have been too attuned to fairy stories and too accustomed to fairy-tale effects to do without them for long. If this is true, fairy tales dominate the interpolated stories because when Dickens decided to allow a certain kind of fanciful counterpoint into *Pickwick,* he could not keep the fairy tale out.

Yet in either case, there was a profound difficulty for Dickens. His fundamental tendency was to combine the everyday and the fanciful, not to keep them apart. It is probably no coincidence that as *Pickwick* moves towards its close and the fairy-tale influence becomes more pronounced in the main narrative, the interpolated stories decrease. There are seven interpolated stories in the first half of the novel, only two in the remainder. There is one interpolated story in the last twenty-one chapters, none in the last eight. No doubt some of this diminution resulted from Dickens' increasing control over his narrative, from the lessening need to rely on interpolation and improvisation. No doubt, too, some of that diminution came from his attempt to draw the novel together as it approached its conclusion. But then

again, an important part of that drawing together—the satisfying ceremony of summonings, pledges, blessings, rewards, releases, transformations, and so on—was taken directly from the fairy tale.

Nevertheless, it is true that the real and the surreal are more segregated in *Pickwick* than in any other Dickens novel. Dickens himself
was aware of this segregation and usually sought to accentuate it. That
this is so can be seen in "A Madman's Manuscript." That macabre
story, with its dusky forms, pursuing demons, and pale revenants, ends
when Mr. Pickwick finishes reading its last words and his candle suddenly goes out. Mr. Pickwick, terrified, glances around fearfully, and
hastily scrambles into bed. The very next words—they begin a new
paragraph but are otherwise without break or pause—are as follows:
"The sun was shining brilliantly into his chamber when he awoke, and
the morning was far advanced. The gloom which had oppressed him on
the previous night, had disappeared with the dark shadows which
shrouded the landscape, and his thoughts and feelings were as light and
gay as the morning itself. After a hearty breakfast, the four gentlemen
sallied forth to walk to Gravesend."[27] The magical world of *Pickwick,*
the world of ghosts, talking chairs, and grotesque goblins, is banished
abruptly to the realms of night, and the customary world of *Pickwick,*
the world of brilliant sunshine and hearty breakfasts, resumes its more
habitual sway.

The sudden, almost bridgeless, transition from "A Madman's Manuscript" to the familiar everyday world of *Pickwick* is typical rather than
unusual. In *Pickwick* Dickens sought to introduce the fairy story and
cordon it off from its antithesis. Yet he found this an unsatisfactory way
of bringing the magic of fairy tales into his writings. This can be seen
not only from his curtailment of the interpolated story in the latter
portions of *Pickwick* and his complete abandonment of the technique
soon after, but from his constant attempts in all his subsequent works
to bring the wonder and fancy of fairy tales into his main narrative. As
a matter of fact, in his early writings Dickens tried over and over again
to find a form that would accommodate the ordinary and the marvelous. I do not mean by this that Dickens was consciously setting himself
the task in each new novel of fusing the everyday and the fantastic. I
mean that he was attempting to give satisfactory and harmonious expression to the two great generative nodes of his imagination—the
realistic and the fanciful.

That satisfactory and harmonious expression did not come about
until *Dombey.* But *Dombey* was a long way off. In the novels before
Dombey, Dickens' triumphs and difficulties as he sought to fuse the
magical and the mundane form a fascinating and instructive history.

After *Pickwick,* and before *Dombey,* Dickens wrote five novels: *Oliver Twist* (1837–1838), *Nicholas Nickleby* (1838–1839), *The Old Curiosity Shop* (1840–1841), *Barnaby Rudge* (1841), and *Martin Chuzzlewit* (1843–1844). I will discuss *Oliver Twist* and *The Old Curiosity Shop* at the end of the chapter, for they differ somewhat in their reliance on enchantment from the other three novels in question. The latter novels—*Nickleby, Barnaby,* and *Chuzzlewit*—repeat the pattern of fairy-tale use set in *Pickwick,* though with important modifications in centrality and emphasis. In these novels, as in *Pickwick,* Dickens concentrates the storybook energies in the overall structures. In the case of *Nickleby,* he also interrupts the main narrative and inserts two self-contained fairy stories, "The Five Sisters" and "The Baron of Grogzwig," but this reversion to the segregating technique of *Pickwick* occurs very early in *Nickleby*—in the sixth chapter—and it constitutes Dickens' last use of this strategy. Despite this early abandonment of the interpolated fairy story, *Nickleby* owes more to fairy tales than *Pickwick.* Even the wrapper for the monthly parts displays that indebtedness. The design, among other fanciful details, features a troop of goblins shining lanterns on a discomfited man.

The opening chapter of *Nickleby* reinforces the promise of the wrapper. The chapter relates the history of the Nickleby family down to the death of Nicholas' father, and it recounts that history in a storybook style, though with a sophisticated distance and humor. Here is the first sentence of *Nickleby*: "There once lived, in a sequestered part of the county of Devonshire, one Mr. Godfrey Nickleby: a worthy gentleman, who, taking it into his head rather late in life that he must get married, and not being young enough or rich enough to aspire to the hand of a lady of fortune, had wedded an old flame out of mere attachment, who in her turn had taken him for the same reason." This fairy-tale style gives way in the second chapter to a more realistic mode of narration, but the folk-tale flavor is perpetuated by the central fable. That fable tells an ancient story. Mrs. Nickleby, a silly widow of diminished fortune, comes to the large city to seek help from the rich uncle of her children, but slowly discovers that he is a monster who lays snares for them. This storybook *donnée* is buttressed by all sorts of tributary conceptions that have a similar character. Nicholas, for example, is soon off to Dotheboys Hall, a grotesque dungeon wretchedly populated by deformed and emaciated brimstone-eating urchins of unsurpassed ugliness, and presided over by Squeers, a brutal one-eyed monster. Squeers holds these goblin-boys in his baleful spell until he is defeated and exiled by the forces of good. At this point Mrs. Squeers, the witch of the establishment, loses her power as well, and is made to kneel in obeisance and swallow penitential doses of brimstone and treacle. Moments after this scene, the boys vanish and the school is empty.[28]

The boys vanish, but they survive. They are victims who escape. But Smike, the holy innocent of the novel, bereft of his wits by the power of evil (as Barnaby Rudge will be after him), cannot preserve himself. Though, like Oliver, he escapes and is retaken and escapes again, he cannot, like Oliver, be restored by the forces of good. The spell of evil is too great. He dies in freedom, but he dies a victim still, the helpless prey of that lingering thralldom.

These themes and structures, cognate with age-old folk tales, are combined with sentiment, melodrama, and magic in ever-varying permutations. Many other motifs and characters reveal a similar folklore heritage. Madeline Bray is the princess in disguise. Though she appears meekly before the world as the poor daughter of a wretched debtor, she is actually the heir to a large property, a property concealed by a monstrous old miser, Arthur Gride. As in countless fairy tales and pantomimes, Madeline agrees to marry this disgusting creature if he will grant some boon—in this instance pay her father's debts. She is saved from this unnatural marriage by a magical series of last-moment deaths, interventions, and discoveries. Restored to her proper fortune, she marries Nicholas and lives happily ever after.

Ralph Nickleby is also shaped in a storybook mold. He is the crafty uncle of fairy tales and folklore, rich and wicked. At the end, his plottings foiled, his persecutions turned back on himself, he commits suicide in the very chamber associated with his most grievous sin. His suicide is a self-judgment. It is the punishment he metes out to himself for his archetypal crime, a crime that echoes endlessly in fable and romance. He has murdered his son. In destroying the unrecognized Smike, he has, unwittingly, destroyed himself.

Ralph lifts his own hand in judgment against himself, but his fate is sealed by the triumph of the forces of good. In all Dickens' novels, but most emphatically and unambiguously in his early ones, the forces of good rally toward the end and assert their primacy. In the early novels that contest between good and evil is conceived in out-and-out fairy-tale terms. The devils and demons of darkness, the dynamic Fagins and Quilps, are defeated by their pallid opponents, the angelic Brownlows and Garlands. Darkness teems with energy but is somehow no match for the magical ascendency of light. In *Nickleby* the demons and goblins and monsters of life, the Squeers and Grides and Ralph Nicklebys, despite their seemingly invincible power, are overcome by the naive yeomen, godfathers, and heroes of this world, the Browdies and Cheerybles and Nicholas Nicklebys—a magical victory indeed.

How redolent of fairy tales all this is may be seen with the twin

Cheeryble brothers. They are the fairy godfathers of *Nickleby,* Mr. Pickwick shorn of all but his benevolence and his money and then doubled. They preside over the victories of righteousness in *Nickleby* as magically and protectively as the good fairy in a benign fairy story. Their sole role in the novel is to aid, save, reward, and reconcile. They dispense opportunity and largesse to half the good characters in *Nickleby*—to Madeline Bray, Tim Linkinwater, Mrs. Nickleby, Kate Nickleby, Frank Cheeryble, Miss La Creevy, and many more. They literally pluck the needy Nicholas off the streets, give him a job, and help save his mother and sister. Eyes twinkling, faces smiling, double chins dimpling, they are beneficent elves, godfathers in gaiters and broad-brimmed hats.

The brothers Cheeryble joyously wield their magic wand, and again it is made of money. Their joy is so unalloyed, their benefactions so great, their power so omnipotent that readers understood them at once: they were instruments of wish fulfillment, creatures created to transcend life, to wave away the disasters and failures and frustrations that confront one in everyday existence. The Cheerybles fulfilled the same fantasies as the latter-day Mr. Pickwick, the benevolent Mr. Brownlow, the kindly Garlands. Then Dickens made a mistake. He authenticated his and his readers' fantasies. In the preface to *Nickleby* he wrote that the Cheerybles were "drawn from life."[29] He had never been asked to forward appeals to Mr. Pickwick, Mr. Brownlow, or the Garlands, but now he was inundated with so many applications for "loans, gifts, and offices of profit" to forward to the brothers Cheeryble, that to satisfy them would have "exhausted the combined patronage of all the Lord Chancellors since the accession of the House of Brunswick, and would have broken the rest of the Bank of England."[30]

This disparity between the dream of felicity and its actuality points up the role of the fairy story in *Nickleby.* As in *Pickwick, Barnaby,* and *Chuzzlewit,* the fairy tale resides mainly in the broad structures and motifs of the work. It confirms, intensifies, and reassures. It does not interfuse the page-by-page texture of the novel, and it rarely deepens vision or meaning. When Dickens testified that the Cheerybles were real, he invested a reassuring conception of storybook wish fulfillment with the possibility of tangible help. The fusion of fairy tales and reality—a fusion that Dickens ultimately achieved—was not to come from insisting upon the reality of fairy stories, but from using the profound insights and resonances of fairy tales to undergird and enlarge meaning.

On occasion Dickens does this in *Nickleby.* For the most part Ralph Nickleby is the wicked uncle of folklore, a two-dimensional character who enacts a stereotyped role. But when he is about to die, he takes on a new dimension and a new life.[31] Ralph's last journey and suicide are full of folk-tale specters and folk-tale portents. He seems to be followed by "one black gloomy mass" like a "shadowy funeral train"; he must pass a "mean burial-ground," a "rank, unwholesome, rotten spot," containing the body of a man who had cut his own throat; he watches a little, drunken, wizened, humpbacked man, "a grotesque fantastic figure," begin to dance; he remembers that when he was a child, he had been obsessed by the figure of a goblin he had once seen chalked on a door; he is disturbed by "a loud knocking at the door below"; and he hears a deep bell toll.[32] These thronging signs from within and without fuse the moral and the psychological with the physical world. They testify to Ralph's disturbance; at the same time they objectify the preternatural world that he has disturbed. As in *Macbeth,* where invisible daggers, indelible blood, and telltale ghosts—the hackneyed stuff of fairy tales—are more than fairy tales, and help us understand Macbeth and his lady (what they are, what they have done, and what they undergo), so in *Nickleby,* black clouds, weed-grown graveyards, and goblin figures help plumb the ravaged depths of Ralph's mind and turn a conventional ogre serving the plot into an anguished man. When Ralph becomes most imbued by magical forces, that is, when Dickens fuses him to the energy of fairy stories in this suggestive and integrated way, he also becomes most real. In the moment before he dies, and largely through fairy-tale means, Dickens gives him depth and complexity; we get our first real, probing glimpse of why he hates Nicholas, why he became what he is.

This episode—there is much more to it than I have indicated—is too obvious in places, and it is touched too much by melodramatic rhetoric, but it has real power, and it is similar in technique to many much longer and more elaborate scenes that become a hallmark of Dickens' later fairy-tale method. In *Nickleby,* however, this kind of fanciful enhancement is an exception rather than a rule. The scene unites with other scattered storybook touches that filter into the central realism of the novel, but by and large the fairy-tale energies of *Nickleby* are confined to the grand overarching outlines of plot and character. As with *Pickwick,* this separation sometimes creates problems, for the wand-waving that controls the grand design of the novel is often at odds with—at the very least out of phase with—the satirical realism, however stylized or caricatured, that dominates the main text. Such wand-waving belies the realism and struggle (self-deluding though such strivings may be) that motivate the Kenwigs, Lillyvicks, Crummles, Mantalinis, Linkinwaters, and La Creevys of the world—and even the Kate Nicklebys, John Browdies, and Madeline Brays in their more ordinary encounters with life. But despite these incongruities, *Nickleby* is more steadily controlled by fairy stories than *Pickwick,* and in this *Nickleby* is one with the other post-*Pickwick* novels.

Barnaby Rudge, for example, pivots on fairy-tale conceptions. At the center of *Barnaby* is the archetypal sin of murder, and much of the novel is devoted to showing how that sin haunts ever-widening circles of persons and actions. The term "haunts" is no metaphor, for Dickens largely conveys his theme through supernatural signs and agencies— through actual hauntings, and through ghosts, strange recurrences, irrational compulsions, devilish familiars, cosmic retributions, and deep-dyed bloodguilts.

The story opens on the nineteenth of March, the twenty-second anniversary of Reuben Haredale's murder at his manor house, the Warren. The murder was presumably done by the gardener, but actually by the steward, Barnaby's father. The gardener's unrecognizable body was discovered many months later clad in the steward's clothes and effects, so that all suspicion was cast upon the gardener, who was believed to have murdered Haredale and Rudge and then disappeared. The story of the murders is told in the opening chapter by Solomon Daisy. He tells the tale on the nineteenth of March at the Maypole Inn, Chigwell, and he fills his narrative with strange signs and predictions, and with ghostly trappings.

Barnaby was born the day after the murders. His father had come home all bloody on the night of the murders and sworn his horrified wife to silence. Barnaby, presumably as a result of that terrific encounter between his father and mother, and owing to the taint of bloodguilt, is born demented. He grows up wayward and witless. His physical appearance proclaims his inward deprivation. Owing to "the absence of the soul . . . far more terrible in a living man than in a dead one," Barnaby has a wild face, and he wears an "unearthly" expression.[33] Though innocent, he shares the burden of his father's guilt. He displays many signs of his paternal taint. He bears a bloody birthmark on his wrist—his father, in grasping the ruddy wrist of the murdered gardener, had literally as well as figuratively stained his hand with gore. Barnaby pays for that bloody deed. All his life, he has a pathological fear of blood: even a blood-red sky fills him with inexplicable dread. He is also unbearably restless. He wanders the earth like an unquiet spirit, a guiltless yet guilt-ridden Cain. His outward garb displays his inward disorder. He decorates himself in fantastic fashion with broken peacock feathers, colored ribbons, poor glass toys, and the steel hilt of a sword. These baubles are scattered over his person in fit reflection of his scattered wits. His speech is no less scattered: now acute, now disconnected, now aimlessly drifting. His words often have a prescience and an appropriateness, a wild poetic meaningfulness, that he cannot comprehend. Like Shakespeare's fools, out of madcap witlessness he conjures wit. But unlike Shakespeare's fools, he has no consciousness of wordplay or repartee. He is closer to the holy fool of folklore: bereft of wit, he displays a divine sensitivity that surpasses wisdom.

His imagination incorporates his curse and gift. It is aberrant and fanciful, a profound jumble of haunted disturbance and poetic felicity. Here is what he sees when he peeps out a back window:

> "Look down there," he said softly; "do you mark how they whisper in each other's ears; then dance and leap, to make believe they are in sport? Do you see how they stop for a moment, when they think there is no one looking, and mutter among themselves again; and then how they roll and gambol, delighted with the mischief they've been plotting? Look at 'em now. See how they whirl and plunge. And now they stop again, and whisper, cautiously together—little thinking, mind, how often I have lain upon the grass and watched them. I say—what is it that they plot and hatch? Do you know?"[34]

When Barnaby is told he has been looking at ordinary clothes, clothes hanging on lines to dry and fluttering in the wind, he is incredulous: "Clothes!" he says. "Ha ha! Why, how much better to be silly, than as wise as you! You don't see shadowy people there, like those that live in sleep—not you. Nor eyes in the knotted panes of glass, nor swift ghosts when it blows hard, nor do you hear voices in the air, nor see men stalking in the sky—not you! I lead a merrier life than you, with all your cleverness. You're the dull men. We're the bright ones."[35]

The imagination that Dickens gives Barnaby is magical and transforming. It resembles the incandescent fancy of Puck or Ariel; it is one with the transmuting imagination Dickens displays in "Meditations in Monmouth Street" or in "The Bagman's Story"; indeed it is Dickens' own imagination in its most fanciful and antic phase. But here the dazzling transformations are more than what they were in the past; they are more than a tour de force isolated in a vignette, as in *Sketches by Boz,* or encapsulated in a wild fairy tale, as in *Pickwick.* Here the magical metamorphoses both objectify and convey Barnaby's disordered mind and compensatory power; the metamorphoses are correlatives of his distorted vision, his demon-filled fears, his divine gifts. And these manifestations, in turn, are tied to motifs that recur throughout the novel. The transformations, in other words, are thematic and organic. Dickens has here brought the wildest sort of fancifulness into the realistic mainstream of his novel. He has, for the moment, fully domesticated the extravagant power of the fairy story.

He does much the same with Grip the raven. Grip is Barnaby's demon familiar, a sable emissary of darkness. But he is also comic and admirably realistic. Dickens' close observation of his own precocious ravens informs Grip's every croak and movement. Yet Grip's supernatural qualities are also evident. He is calculating and sly beyond the ken of birddom. As Gabriel Varden puts it, contemplating Barnaby and his pet, "The bird has all the wit."[36] Grip's wit is malign and devilish; his identity is self-proclaimed. "I'm a devil," he constantly insists. Dickens imbues Grip's limited repertory of mechanical phrases and fragments of phrases with magical meaning; in context Grip's rote interjections add pertinent punctuation to what is going on. In this Grip is like Barnaby, for Barnaby, too, speaks more tellingly than he knows. Indeed in some respects Grip is Barnaby's dark shadow, an objectification of the Satanic crimes that haunt and blight him. In other respects, Grip is Satan himself, albeit a rather comical and engaging Satan. Grip is immortal and irrepressible. He is 120 years old when the story takes place, approaching 200 when the narrator takes leave of him. The narrator assures us that Grip is talking more than ever in these latter-day times, and he implies that Grip will probably go on talking and living forever.[37]

Barnaby and his raven are fantastical. Though certain aspects of their conception are fused to the central realism of the novel, they are, by and large—and especially Barnaby—opposed to the realistic drift of the story. After all, what witless and deluded natural ever spoke and acted as Barnaby does? Barnaby is poetic rather than realistic; he is a fairy-tale figment given human form.

His father, Rudge, is a fairy-tale figment too, but much more Gothic in conception. Like Barnaby, he is a wanderer, a veritable Cain or Wandering Jew. He persecutes and haunts his family, a malign ghost from the violent past. He also haunts the scene of his crimes, an unquiet spirit drawn to the precincts of his bloody sins. These are not metaphorical interpretations but Dickens' own presentation of the character. When Rudge is occasionally glimpsed by the villagers as he drifts fleetingly through the night, he is thought of as the ghost of a dead man. This is not surprising. He is, after all, the veritable specter of his self-murdered self. When Solomon Daisy sees him one stormy night in the bell tower—the site of Haredale's murder—he cries out in terror, "The ghost! The ghost!"[38] Rudge is captured in that bell tower, and he is captured on the anniversary of his crime. He is as haunted as the persons and places he haunts. The murdered men torment his waking and sleeping consciousness.[39] He feels he is drawn to his fate and cannot escape it; he will be caught in the room where he did the deed.[40] When asked why he returned to the scene of his crime, he replies, "Why is blood red? I could no more help it, than I could live without breath. I struggled against the impulse, but I was drawn back, through every difficult and adverse circumstance, as by a mighty engine."[41] Later, when accused of betraying himself by these foolish visitations, he says: "The act was not mine. I did it, but it was not mine. I was forced at times to wander round, and round, and round that spot. If you had chained me up when the fit was on me, I should have broken away, and gone there. As truly as the loadstone draws iron towards it, so he, lying at the bottom of his grave, could draw me near him when he would."[42]

This haunted man and the son he bloodily tainted finally meet in prison. There the maleficent spell-like forces that guide and control them intensify and culminate. The fettered father reveals himself to his fettered son. As Barnaby embraces his dark progenitor, the devil Grip enacts a symbolic ritual: "Grip croaked loudly, and hopped about them, round and round, as if enclosing them in a magic circle, and invoking all the powers of mischief."[43]

The magic circle that encloses Barnaby and his father is the chief fairy-tale locus of the novel, but other elements of the book contribute to its supernatural aura. The Maypole Inn, in addition to its name and sign, both steeped in folklore, is presented initially as a snug sanctuary, a nonpareil of inns. On summer evenings the favored customers sit in the doorway under a porch and sometimes sing in their contentment. They dwell in a zone of enchantment. Year after year they lounged "on two grim-looking high-backed settles, which, like the twin dragons of some fairy tale, guarded the entrance to the mansion."[44] The inn itself warrants its storybook entrance. It is a region of wonderful transformations. Like the magical chair in *Pickwick,* the inn metamorphoses into a drowsy old man, front bulging out, sturdy timbers decayed like teeth, timeworn limbs wrapped in ivy—but now the transformation is part of the main story, not separated from it.[45] This comfortable inn, still hearty in its old age, is witness to many a magical tale and many a strange recurrence—the reverberations of the nineteenth of March repeatedly echo round its spacious chimney corner.[46] On the night Joe Willet leaves the inn for good, his entire chamber takes on enchanted life: chairs and tables become mysterious characters, portraits wink and doze, and leather screens frown like gaunt ghosts.[47] This magical inn and sanctuary, which under the aegis of the reactionary bully, John Willet, proves to be a preserve of privilege rather than a refuge of righteousness, is finally violated and reduced by the mob. The sanctuary is swept away along with John Willet's entrenched hegemony, but the dragon-guarded paradise of the opening pages is restored at the end of the novel under the beneficent sway of Joe Willet. The reopened Maypole is such a country inn as is rarely seen "in all England." As a matter of fact, "it is a great question whether there has ever been such another to this hour, or ever will be"—a fantasy inn indeed.[48]

Many other touches blend with these fairy-tale motifs. Hugh is the wild man of folklore. Unacknowledged son of a gentleman, savage brother to civilized Edward Chester, he plays a frightening latter-day Orson to the Chesters' well-mannered Valentine. Blind Stagg is an

all-seeing Mephistopheles; John Willet a selfish bully stricken witless in
divine exaggeration of his besetting sin—a favorite fulfillment in fairy
stories. Dolly is the coquette and tease who must learn to value true
love; Mrs. Varden is the termagant who needs taming and is tamed.
The rioters are wild demons. Their latent savagery is loosed by the
contagion of the pack. Gripped by that baleful enchantment, they
metamorphose into raging monsters. Heedless, thoughtless, exultant,
they gyrate in frenzied madness.

Yet the central difficulty present in the earlier novels is present here:
there is often a jarring dislocation between the fanciful and the real.
Though I have concentrated on the storybook aspects of *Barnaby
Rudge,* the fairy tale plays very little part in much of the novel. The
Varden household, the historical coloring, such characters as Miggs,
Tappertit, and Dennis, even much of the business at the Maypole or in
the Rudge family circle is innocent of preternatural effect. As a matter
of fact, in many places where the magical is introduced—the ghostly
appearances of Rudge, for example—the occult reverberations are
dampened by a rational explanation in the manner of Mrs. Radcliffe.
Dickens seems distrustful of his supernatural effects. He seems to be
aware that they war, on occasion, with the more realistic portions of
his novel. He is very comfortable with the transformations which grow
out of inner distortion or outward similitude—Joe Willet's last night at
the inn, the Maypole's anthropomorphic aging—but he often attempts
to rationalize or segregate the out-and-out supernatural.

Barnaby is a case in point, and here Dickens is both successful and
unsuccessful. In some respects Barnaby's antic manifestations are as
segregated as the sealed-off fairy stories of *Pickwick.* Yet Barnaby is
not separated from the main current of the novel. Dickens manages this
feat by virtue of Barnaby's madness—we understand that Barnaby
lives in a world of his own, and we accept, even on the realistic level,
that his world is magical and haunted. We can interpret his surreal
antics as the bizarre irrationality of insanity, while at the same time
translating their larger import. Barnaby's insanity is self-contained, yet
he himself participates in the main actions of the story. But the device
works only partially. Barnaby's insanity and bloodguilt are not
sufficiently related to the insanity and bloodguilt of the mob, though
Dickens obviously intended these structures to be parallel and mutually reinforcing. Rudge is even less successful. He is a two-dimensional
Gothic villain flitting in and out of the realistic narrative. Even the
Maypole reflects this antipodal confusion. In part the Maypole is a
storybook sanctuary that Dickens loves and believes in; in part it is an
inimical focus of smugness and stagnation. Dickens never resolves this
antithesis, though he destroys the stronghold of privilege (Chigwell, we

are supposed to see, is a provincial version of London) and restores the succoring paradise.

Barnaby Rudge depends massively and centrally on fairy tales. Yet, with some important exceptions, enchantment still controls the machinery rather than the texture of the novel. Fantasy and realism are often at odds. Or, to put the matter another way, *Barnaby Rudge* still relies too heavily on supernatural and Gothic effects that have not been fused with the novel's central realism. Nevertheless, the organization of *Barnaby* shows that Dickens was striving to harmonize the fanciful and the ordinary. He was seeking, in effect, to domesticate the supernatural. The unity of *Barnaby,* however, is more schematic than organic, more a matter of conception than execution.

Martin Chuzzlewit continues this pattern of incomplete fusion; yet, like *Barnaby Rudge,* it contains mythlike episodes and motifs that look forward to Dickens' later fairy-tale manner. At the center of *Chuzzlewit,* however, is an earlier and more primitive storybook device: the fairy godfather, familiar from *Pickwick* and *Nickleby,* who manipulates the plot and brings about a happy ending. In *Chuzzlewit* this crucial role is enacted by old Martin, a rich, eccentric, strong-willed man. But old Martin is a fairy godfather with a difference. Unlike Mr. Pickwick or the Cheeryble brothers, who are obvious founts of geniality and benevolence, old Martin is a witchlike figure whose suspicion, pride, and obstinacy encrust a loving heart. That loving heart induces him to enact a giant charade in which he assumes the role of gullible dotard in order to test the greedy hordes of relations and hangers-on (especially the archhypocrite, Pecksniff)—and the few true spirits—who cluster closely about him. In this he is like Mr. Boffin, the golden dustman of *Our Mutual Friend,* who assumes the role of miser in order to test and teach. Neither figure is believable as he plays out his elaborate deception; each is clearly a symbolic convenience, a shorthand device out of folklore and fairy story. Behind old Martin are Volpone and even Lear, while behind Pecksniff is Tartuffe; but behind all of these, and behind innumerable lesser renditions, are the age-old tales of gods and kings and powerful spirits (some maleficent and some benign) who disguise themselves in order to test, reward, and punish.

Old Martin in his charade, like Mr. Boffin in his, is not very believable, but Dickens was fascinated by the device and often used it with much greater finesse. Magwitch is a disguised tester and benefactor. And Miss Havisham, another dissembler (a witch disguised as a fairy godmother) is surrounded, like old Martin in the opening of *Chuzzlewit,* by a pack of ravenous relatives greedy for her death. In *Great Expectations,* however, these motifs are vastly enriched, and are fused, as we shall see, to the profound realism and the intricate fairy-tale texture of the entire novel. In *Chuzzlewit* old Martin is primarily a convenience, a magical *deus ex machina*. By means of this contrivance Dickens can manipulate his characters, resolve his plot, and affirm the triumph of good.

There are many signs of old Martin's godfatherhood. He is the secret preserver and benefactor of Tom and Ruth Pinch. Like a puissant enchanter in a fairy story, he suddenly, and through a disguise, provides Tom with a difficult task, a task that succors and saves him. With a wave of his magic wand (made of money, as usual), old Martin creates a jumbled mountain of books, encloses the huge mound in an isolated room, and requires that the books be sorted, repaired, ordered, and indexed. The library is as magical and the task as unbelievable as any heap of straw that must be spun into purest gold. But in the course of time, Tom faithfully reduces the heap to order, and thereby assures his golden future. The task, of course, is unreal; it is a piece of make-work concocted to support Tom and his sister, further prove Tom's worth, and above all, serve the plot.

The library also provides the special setting in which the ritualistic finale of the novel takes place, a finale of revelation, retribution, reconciliation, and reward. To that special setting are mysteriously summoned young and old, high and low, paragon and villain. Young Martin, Mark Tapley, Mrs. Lupin, Tom Pinch, Ruth Pinch, John Westlock, Mary Graham, Mrs. Gamp, Poll Sweedlepipe, young Bailey, and Mr. Pecksniff—all hasten to the library in obedience to old Martin's imperious behest or at the mysterious urging of some inner promptings. It was in this enchanted library that Tom had earlier discovered who his benefactor was. When old Martin revealed himself, Tom thought he was seeing "a spirit," so amazed was he, and so transformed was old Martin.[49] From apparent sickness and weakness, old Martin had sprung forth vigorous, resolute, and triumphant. Now, in the library, he shows his strength. He fells Pecksniff with his staff, banishes him from the bright regions of goodness, and watches him depart the library, made powerless by old Martin's power, and doomed thenceforth to dwindle into drunkenness and begging. Old Martin now turns his attention to other business. He reconciles himself and young Martin, admonishes Mrs. Gamp, instructs Mr. Sweedlepipe, and joyfully encourages a series of happy pairings. He soon presides over a rash of blithesome marriages. He oversees the union of young Martin and Mary Graham, John Westlock and Ruth Pinch, and Mark Tapley and Mrs. Lupin. All these blissful couples live happily ever after. Old Martin is now as melting and selfless as the transformed and beatified young Martin himself. All things bear witness to these astonishing transformations. Names as well as persons undergo magical changes.

The dragonish old Martin of the opening number, first seen at the Blue Dragon, becomes the jolly godfather of the closing number, last seen at the Jolly Tapley (or rather at a London improvisation of the Jolly Tapley)—Jolly Tapley being the new name of the Blue Dragon.[50] There are other wonderful changes and recurrences. Two good neighbors from the false Eden of America now miraculously turn up, "like their own ghosts," to occupy their rightful positions in the new Eden, the paradise of feasting and felicity that concludes the story.[51] Paradise beckons other characters as well. The final lines of the novel record the apotheosis of Tom and Ruth; the last words of the book assure us that those two ethereal creatures are uplifted "both to Heaven!"

The disguised storybook godfather who presides over *Chuzzlewit*, and the comforting storybook resolutions that conclude the novel, are complemented by many other fairy-tale elements. Some of these elements consist of allusions and comparisons—a kind of reference that unfailingly enters each of Dickens' novels. We are told that Mr. Pecksniff had "a Fortunatus's purse of good sentiments in his inside." We are further told that "in this particular he was like the girl in the fairy tale, except that if they were not actual diamonds which fell from his lips, they were the very brightest paste, and shone prodigiously."[52] Such allusions abound, as do characters who owe a good deal to fairy stories. Nadgett, the detective, is conceived as a secret and ghostly personage with innumerable identities. Like so many other characters in *Chuzzlewit* who are transformed or transform themselves, he changes in a twinkling. To the guilty Jonas Chuzzlewit, he is the inescapable embodiment of the "many shapes" and "phantom forms" of ineluctable truth. "This man, of all men in the world, a spy upon him; this man, changing his identity: casting off his shrinking, purblind, unobservant character, and springing up into a watchful enemy! The dead man might have come out of his grave, and not confounded and appalled him more."[53] Bailey, too, like some imp or hobgoblin, springs up from the dead. He is an immortal, a tenacious and irrepressible force. Jonas is a similar force, but sullenly cold and calculating. He is another version of the familiar ogre-miser, a redaction of Gride or Ralph Nickleby, but incomparably better done. Like Ralph Nickleby, when he journeys to death, he takes on his fullest and most extraordinary reality, and also, as we shall see, his fullest and most extraordinary fairy-tale coloring.

Sairey Gamp has her supernatural attributes too. She is a grotesque monster-goddess, presiding over life and death. She is majestic and evenhanded; she ministers with equal dispassion at lyings-in and layings-out. She is also godlike in her ability to create. She fashions full-fledged persons and intricate worlds—Mrs. Harrises, genuflecting hierarchies—out of her self-serving imagination. In her more worldly pursuits she dwindles into a lesser creature, but still puissant and awe-inspiring. When she and Betsey Prig dispute over a dying patient or a vanishing dram, she becomes, like her cohort and antagonist, a fearsome harpy and ghoul.

Many other women in *Chuzzlewit* have strong storybook attributes. Charity and Mercy Pecksniff, better known as Cherry and Merry, are like many folk-tale sisters, like the dissembling, selfish stepsisters of *Cinderella*, for example. Cherry is plain and formidable; Merry is pretty and foolish. Both are fraudulent. They fawn on the rich and powerful, and are haughty toward the weak and lowly. They patronize and mistreat poor Ruth Pinch, one of the Cinderellas of the story. In other respects they are like the plotting, striving daughters of a lesser king. They foolishly struggle to win their falsely glittering princes, but are discomfited and humiliated. Mary Graham and Ruth Pinch, on the other hand, are the rightful princesses, though dispossessed and unassuming. They have their fairy-tale rewards. Each marries a Prince Charming and lives happily ever after.

Montague Tigg is another storybook character. He is the devilish trickster of folklore who can assume a multitude of shapes and disguises. He is, at one and the same time, dirty, jaunty, bold, mean, swaggering, and slinking. He can turn himself upside down and inside out; he changes from Montague Tigg at the outset of the novel, to Tigg Montague at the end. Indeed he has no identity of his own; his destiny is to assume that shape which will allow him to prey on others. His whiskers typify and betray him. They are "the regular Satanic sort of thing."[54]

These folk-tale paradigms are not limited to characters. In some respects the whole trip to America and all the denizens of the United States are conceived in fairy-tale terms. The journey to America is a search for Eden, or rather for El Dorado, for Martin has come solely to find riches and to return with them to England. When Martin does reach Eden, it proves to be a hell rather than a paradise. Yet, ironically, in this poor Eden he finds, all unknowingly, what he should have been searching for all along. He finds no wealth, but he finds a reborn self. With the death of his old selfish self, and the birth of a new loving self, he has found his El Dorado: he will now flourish in life. All this takes place in a strange deceptive nightmarish land peopled by an incredible assortment of gnomes, goblins, monsters, dragons, and other grotesque creatures. Having sailed into this dangerous fairyland and almost met his death, Martin sails home bearing the secret of everlasting happiness.

These folklore analogues shape many of the structures and characters of *Chuzzlewit*. Yet most of what I have been concentrating on up to now has been schematic—perspectives from afar. But there are many other fairy-tale touches in *Chuzzlewit*. Dickens frequently fuses the supernatural with local scenes and strategies, often in totally transformed and transforming ways. The wind that opens the story proper is as magical and fanciful as any magical wind of fairyland, but at the same time it is as keenly and accurately observed as the most scientifically scrutinized phenomenon.[55] In a long virtuoso passage, Dickens brings the wind to life and then, as in a myth or fairy story, he gives it sentient roles to perform. The wind climaxes its performance by knocking Mr. Pecksniff down, an exact foreshadowing of his ultimate destiny. This is no metaphor. Mr. Pecksniff is knocked down by the wind when he first enters the book, and he is knocked down by old Martin when he finally leaves the book. The boisterous wind, whooshing through the village, teasing, chasing, and tormenting the dead leaves, not only allows us to comprehend the innermost nature and essence of wind, giving us new eyes and new understanding, but shows us that this airy energy is part of a numinous universe, a moral and sentient force. In other words, reality and transcendence are simultaneously served. The wind of *Chuzzlewit* is like the old clothes of "Monmouth Street," or the talking chair of *Pickwick,* or the ghostly Maypole furniture of *Barnaby Rudge,* but now worked on a greater scale, blended better into the texture of the whole, and made more thematic.

This growing ability to fuse the fanciful and the everyday and to achieve thereby a deeper sense of the *quidditas* and wonder of reality is marvelously demonstrated in the descriptions of Todgers's Boarding House, a magical place hidden in the forest of London. "Surely," Dickens writes, "there never was, in any other borough, city, or hamlet in the world, such a singular sort of a place as Todgers's."[56] Like some mythological palace, this unique little world is located in the heart of a dark labyrinth. Many an unfortunate searcher goes round and round for a weary time and never penetrates to Todgers's, even though its chimney pots are visible all the time.[57] This notion of a magical realm hidden in a maze or labyrinth is no invention of strained criticism. Dickens tells us in plain words that "Todgers's was in a labyrinth, whereof the mystery was known but to a chosen few."[58] The environs are as magical and mysterious as the center. The neighborhood contains "many a ghostly little churchyard," and cart horses in the vicinity rattle their halters "as disturbed spirits in tales of haunted houses are said to clank their chains."[59] The cellarage of Todgers's is rumored to be "full of wealth," and the vision from the rooftop is like "a very forest."[60]

This mythical edifice is part of a world in which all the inanimate objects take on life. Oranges fester, pumps hide themselves, trees feel caged, trucks lounge in narrow lanes, chimney pots whisper to each other. Yet this universal animism does not diminish the reality of each object but makes that reality more compelling. The objects, by taking on life, force their meaning and essence upon us: we cannot dismiss them with our usual unseeing recognition, a recognition that identifies but does not perceive. At the same time these superreal objects testify to the secret affinities and associations that lurk beneath the surface of things. This magical presence animates the world of Todgers's—a world of objects and persons—and reveals in a far more convincing way than old Martin or magic wands the arcane consanguinities of everyday life. Those consanguinities reside not only in objects and persons but in the relationship between objects and persons. On the rooftop of Todgers's, the insistent pressure of things exerts its baleful influence. The thingness of things soon becomes intolerable. The observer is assailed and battered by sheer physicality. "The hosts of objects" all around him seem "to thicken and expand a hundred-fold." The frightened spectator must retreat or plunge "into the street . . . headforemost."[61]

This potent relationship between persons and things is not limited to Todgers's. It occurs in other books; it is the chief feature of Tom Smart and the talking chair. It also occurs elsewhere in *Chuzzlewit;* it connects the wind (and thus nature) with Mr. Pecksniff's fall. It animates dozens of other pre-*Dombey* scenes. In the later novels, this magical relationship runs as a regular undertone or consistent counterpoint, enforcing and enlarging meaning. Todgers's is a virtuoso performance, but no different in impulse and vision from earlier, and lesser, examples, and from later, and more constant, achievements.

In a similar way, Jonas Chuzzlewit's murder of Montague Tigg is a tour de force, and it too goes beyond its earlier prototypes. There are many such prototypes. Murder, guilty flight, feelings when facing the penalty of death were subjects that Dickens turned to over and over again. Such fearful moments gripped his imagination; he felt their strangeness, their horror, their deep contradictions, and he sought to convey (and thus to understand) their nightmare reality. The condemned prisoner in *Sketches by Boz,* Sikes and Fagin and Oliver (the latter when pursued by the crowd) in *Oliver Twist,* self-sentenced Ralph Nickleby in *Nicholas Nickleby,* are a few pre-*Chuzzlewit* explorations of such experiences. These episodes are almost always conveyed with a compelling, almost hallucinatory, intensity, and with strong supernatural reverberations. Such scenes, especially in the early novels, start up from the text, propel stereotyped characters into sudden reality, and remain vividly in the memory when other portions of the novel are forgotten.

Ralph Nickleby, as we have seen, leaps into life as he hastens toward death. In a similar fashion Jonas Chuzzlewit is most fully realized, and emerges most convincingly as a complicated, self-divided, haunted man, when he embarks on murder. In both novels the scenes in question are richly freighted with magical energies. Through such energies Dickens conveys the psychological depths and cosmic significances of what is taking place.

Jonas Chuzzlewit is more intricate and individualized than Ralph Nickleby, and his journey toward death is more impressive. The greater sophistication of the later portrait is a measure of Dickens' growing artistry, a deepening artistry that is manifest in the fairy-tale aura as well. That aura presides over Jonas' direful journey and guides our awareness. The murderous journey is foreshadowed by an earlier journey that culminates in an abortive attempt to murder Tigg.[62] The earlier journey, dense with signs and portents, takes place during a terrific thunderstorm, and it ends with a premonitory vision. Tigg dreams of a locked door that is not locked, and he awakes to find Jonas hovering over him. The locked door, the hovering Jonas, and the unlocked entry will all soon figure in the actual murder.

When Jonas descends one evening into his unused back room, pleading exhaustion, and asking not to be disturbed day or night for two nights, the spectral embodiment of his darker self overwhelms him: "As the gloom of evening, deepening into night, came on, another dark shade emerging from within him seemed to overspread his face, and slowly change it. Slowly, slowly; darker and darker; more and more haggard; creeping over him by little and little; until it was black night within him and without."[63] This change, of course, is realistic and magical, literal and symbolic. The room is equally realistic, and equally magical: "It was a blotched, stained, mouldering room, like a vault; and there were water-pipes running through it, which at unexpected times in the night, when other things were quiet, clicked and gurgled suddenly, as if they were choking."[64] The room, like a magic glass, conveys what Jonas is feeling and prefigures his deed. The room is the inanimate counterpart of Jonas and speaks his dark message: "stain," "vault," "click," "gurgle," and "choke" are its watchwords. Jonas prepares to glide into the street, dressed in countryman's garb. He waits at the door. He listens to the clamoring church bells proclaim his presence (so he feels) to all the town; he hears two passersby talk of undiscovered murders.

As Jonas moves toward his deed, the whole universe shudders and quakes. When he passes by, people shrink, children see dark shadows in their sleep, dogs howl, and rats follow him.[65] His footsteps seem to leave a red mire, like Cain's; all nature appears to be watching him.[66] Tigg goes "down, down, down, into the dell," never to return, the red light of the setting sun on his face.[67] The forest where the murder takes place is marvelously described. The woods are totally and beautifully real and yet dreamily filled with the primordial symbolism of life and death. Dickens turns the dark magical woods of countless fairy stories into a subtle yet cosmic landscape.

The murder done, Jonas is obsessed not by the newly-burdened woods, but by his empty room. In concentrating on his empty room, supposedly filled with his ordinary self, he accentuates our understanding of his terrified self-division. As his murderous self speeds toward the supposedly slumbering ghost of his ordinary self, his awareness of his duality and danger grows. A knocking within the alehouse where he momentarily sits drinking makes him imagine someone knocking at the door of his empty room, and fills him with dread. Like the knocking on the gate in *Macbeth*, the sound presages a more fearful summons. Jonas is now terrified by the thought of his empty room:

> This [thought] made him, in a gloomy, murderous, mad way, not only fearful *for* himself but *of* himself; for being, as it were, a part of the room: a something supposed to be there, yet missing from it: he invested himself with its mysterious terrors; and when he pictured in his mind the ugly chamber, false and quiet, false and quiet, through the dark hours of two nights; and the tumbled bed, and he not in it, though believed to be; he became in a manner his own ghost and phantom, and was at once the haunting spirit and the haunted man.[68]

When he finally arrives at his room, he steals to the door "on tip-toe, as if he dreaded to disturb his own imaginary rest."[69]

In this wonderful episode, Dickens has brilliantly fused realism, symbolism, psychology, and the supernatural. The supernatural not only provides much of the framework of the episode, it identifies and magnifies meaning. It helps us comprehend the horror and aberration of murder, and it helps us appreciate its cosmic significance. I have woefully foreshortened the episode (which occupies two chapters) and concentrated on its storybook dimensions (and by doing so have made it appear more Gothic and more dependent upon the pathetic fallacy than it is), but even in such truncated form one can see how rich and powerful was the fairy-tale instrument that Dickens was fashioning.

Yet *Chuzzlewit* is not a fairy-tale whole. Dickens continues to use enchantment in intermittent and conflicting ways. Enchantment contributes to some of his most penetrating and powerful effects, and to some of his most unsatisfactory manipulations. Jonas and Tigg going down into the dell, Todgers's real yet surreal boarding house, the boisterously pursuing wind of the opening—these are specimens of consummate art, art that could not be what it is without the fairy tale. Such art, which makes the real more real by revealing everywhere its magical reverberations, contributes much to *Chuzzlewit* and much to Dickens' other apprenticeship novels, but it contributes even more to his subsequent works. In those later works, that seamless fusion of realism and fantasy becomes a central, integrating feature of his insight and his technique.

In the early novels, the fully realized fairy-tale episode is likely to rise fitfully out of the text, its life residing primarily within the episode. In *Chuzzlewit* such episodes are longer, more domesticated, better integrated, and more frequent than similar scenes in earlier novels, but they are still largely discontinuous. Furthermore, in *Chuzzlewit* there is much that is remote from this storybook enhancement, much that seems alien to it, and much that wars, as of old, with the gross wand-waving manipulations of the overall plot. Old Martin's impossible make-believe library, created especially for Tom Pinch, violates not only our sense of reality, but the deeper truth of Jonas' empty room, a true legendary room (at once real and magical) created by a haunting and haunted mind. In *Chuzzlewit*, the last of the apprenticeship novels, Dickens was moving toward a cohesion and a coherence that was still largely eluding him. In that advance toward a rich and diverse unity, enchantment was playing an increasing role: it was part of the forward movement, but also part of the drag.

Two of Dickens' six pre-*Dombey* novels—the second, *Oliver Twist*, and the fourth, *The Old Curiosity Shop*—are more dominated and integrated by enchantment than the others. Why this should be so is a question worth pursuing. I think there is an answer to this question, and I think that answer tells us a good deal about Dickens and his art.

The forces of darkness that control the greater part of *Oliver Twist* are deeply entwined with fairy tales. At the center of those forces is Fagin, and Fagin is a creature out of folklore and nightmare. He is in league with the devil; in part he is the "merry old gentleman" himself.[70] He carries with him the sinister aura of medieval legends, Renaissance plays, and terrifying nurses' stories. He is the infernal, frightening, miserly Jew, slaughterer of innocents, tempter and corrupter of childhood. He steals innocent children, gleefully entangles them in sin, and sends them to everlasting damnation. His appearance, surroundings, and accoutrements betray his Satanic lineage. He bears the stigmata of the stereotyped devil-Jew, familiar from stage and chapbook, but Dickens also endows him with a humor, vitality, and idiosyncrasy that are totally Dickensian. Fagin lives in no ordinary chambers but in a "den"—Dickens himself uses the term; and the walls and ceiling of this infernal den are "perfectly black."[71] Like the stage Jew and the Jew of caricature, Fagin is villainous looking, has matted red hair, and brandishes the instrument of his devilish office—a three-pronged toasting fork.[72] He hovers near his element, the blazing fire.[73] When Oliver enters, he ostentatiously draws the innocent boy near the fire.[74] He is polite, ceremonious, and mocking. He is also solicitous and menacing;

he constantly refers to Oliver and his other charges as "my dear." He is a Satanic father.

Fagin's first scene alone with Oliver combines stereotyped Jew, and folklore child-queller, with the most intense and magical vitality. Oliver, half sleeping, half waking, sees Fagin draw forth a secret casket, open it, and fondle its dazzling treasures: magnificent gold watches sparkling with jewels, glittering rings, shining heaps of brooches, bracelets, and trinkets.[75] Here is the miserly Jew of countless legends gloating over his storybook riches. Then Fagin sees that Oliver is awake. Their eyes meet "for the briefest space of time that can possibly be conceived," whereupon Fagin snatches up a bread knife and holds it quivering in the air. The instantaneous look of recognition and the weapon brandished over a helpless child recur constantly in Dickens. The instantaneous look is a sign of secret knowledge, of unuttered and indissoluble bonds. The look passes not only between Fagin and Oliver, but between Mrs. Pipchin and Paul, Carker and Edith, Magwitch and Pip, Jasper and Rosa, and many others. The brandished weapon is a sign of murderous adult aggression against defenseless childhood; it is Dickens' expressionistic way of conveying a victimized child's extremity, his powerlessness and terror. Fagin's gleaming blade quivers over innocent Oliver; Good Mrs. Brown's great scissors hovers over kidnapped Florence; Betsey Trotwood's upraised knife flashes over wayworn David. When Fagin darts his evil look and lifts his murderous hand, we witness an induction: Oliver's long London nightmare has begun. In the final chapters of *Oliver Twist,* the nightmare shifts from Oliver to Fagin. Fagin, folklore Jew and folklore devil, becomes another memorable Dickensian portrait of a condemned man confronting the inconceivable strangeness of death. As his end approaches, Fagin's magical energies shrivel into anguished mortality. Dickens now concentrates on the beleaguered inner consciousness of the tormented man.

Fagin traffics with underlings and cohorts who have their own supernatural attributes. His confederate Monks is a storybook villain with strong Gothic and melodramatic overtones. Dark-visaged and dark-clad, Monks slinks and scowls and skulks mysteriously through the novel. His name, Monks (adopted as a disguise), reverberates with directive associations. It calls up Monk Lewis' depraved protagonist in *The Monk,* and it conjures up the legions of villainous monks who throng the specter-haunted pages of Gothic romances. Monks hovers darkly in the background of Oliver's life, a malign force, a wicked fairy godfather who blasts and blights him. Monks' arsenal of weapons includes the age-old standbys of folklore, romance, and melodrama; disguised identities, hidden parentage, destroyed wills, treacherous witnesses, purloined rings, magical amulets, and the mysterious power to disappear without a trace. Monks turns out to be Oliver's wicked half-brother. He persecutes Oliver, enlisting the help of Fagin, because Oliver's inheritance is contingent, by will, on the provision that during his minority "he should never have stained his name with any public act of dishonour, meanness, cowardice, or wrong."[76] This fantastic provision, more akin to a fairy godmother's injunction than to a nineteenth-century will, is utterly unbelievable, but long before the bizarre clause is revealed at the end of the book, we have come to understand the true motivation of Monks and Fagin, and the true identity of Oliver. Monks and Fagin are unalloyed evil, Oliver unalloyed good. It is the nature of evil to pursue and destroy good; it is the nature of good to resist and overcome evil. We are in the realm of pure fairy-tale forces.

Another evil force, Sikes, is portrayed much more realistically, but from the murder of Nancy on he is surrounded by a strong spell-like penumbra. After the murder he is literally haunted by his crime. Like Jonas Chuzzlewit and old Rudge, he is driven and pulled by guilt and fear. He now suspects that people are staring at him, talking about him, shrinking from him, yet he cannot bear to be alone. He plunges into crowds, lingers near stagecoach stops, helps fight a great fire, but he cannot lose his identity or his knowledge. Nancy's staring eyes haunt his every step. Like the murderous madman in "A Madman's Manuscript," Sikes cowers and tries to hide, but he has no relief. Like the murderous Rudge, he is drawn back helplessly to the scene of his crime. Back in his old haunts, hunted, baited, Sikes is finally driven out of his unavailing hideaway and high up onto the roof. There Nancy's ghostly eyes startle him once more. Dazzled by those staring eyes, he staggers back, loses his balance, tumbles over the parapet, and inadvertently hangs himself.

This infernal ruffian, who betrays his ultimate destination with such expressions as "Burn my body!" is accompanied by an infernal dog—a familiar or alter ego. Bullseye, as the dog is called, is as villainous-looking as his master. He also exhibits his master's disposition: he growls and threatens and attacks. Bullseye is present at the murder of Nancy; "the very feet of the dog were bloody."[77] Bullseye and Sikes, in fact, are inseparable, but the dog proves more steadfast than the man. When Sikes tries to kill him, Bullseye runs off. He turns up, however, hours before Sikes, at Sikes' final hiding place—a fateful precursor and a telltale surrogate. Sikes' coming is heralded by a knocking on the door below, a Shakespearean knocking that recurs throughout the scene, but "it was the very ghost of Sikes" that entered the room.[78] Bullseye is on the rooftop when Sikes tumbles out into the void. He leaps for his master's shoulder but misses and dashes his brains out. Bullseye, like his counterpart and companion, meets his preordained end.

Taken out of context, Sikes' specter-haunted flight and his snarling familiar may seem perfervid and contrived. But these motifs of haunting and doubling are thoroughly fused to the realistic current of the story and to the psychological aberrations of a scarified mind. In the same manner, the surging mob that finally hunts Sikes down is totally convincing. The mob is both praiseworthy and evil, realistic and wildly suprarational. It is an instrument of law and order and a knot of raging bloodlust, a crowd of staring men and women and a writhing pack of demons. In all these scenes Dickens combines realism, psychological verity, and fairy-tale enlargement.

Fagin, Monks, and Sikes are only three inhabitants of the dark, claustrophobic underground of *Oliver Twist*. That nether world, a black tangle of dank dens and somber city labyrinths, yawns at every alley and every turning, and swallows up outcast, victim, and criminal alike. The innocents (Oliver), the officials (Magistrate Fang), the pawns (the Artful Dodger), the prostitutes (Nancy), the fences (Fagin), the informers (Noah Claypole), the thieves (Sikes), the functionaries (Mr. Bumble), the predators (Monks)—all dwell in or traffic with that nether realm, and only Oliver emerges with his soul alive. The nether realm is the realm of night. The transactions of that kingdom are usually conducted at night, or in black rooms where day never enters. Fagin slinks out at night; Noah Claypole overhears Nancy at night; Sikes murders at night; he meets his predestined death at night; Fagin suffers his last agony of torment at night. Black night engulfs all these characters in a stifling nightmare from which they are unable to awake.

The denizens of this nightmare world, seen through Oliver's frightened eyes, assume strange distorted storybook shapes. Fagin looms as a sinister leering devil, Sikes as a brutal rampaging monster, the youthful gang as a ravaging band of predatory gnomes. Menace, suffocation, and entrapment overwhelm Oliver. He seems to be under some evil spell or enchantment. He breaks away from his tormentors but is retaken and again placed in thrall. Even when he is freed, the dark power of Monks and Fagin haunts his waking and sleeping hours. It is only when these two evil spirits are utterly destroyed, and he can assume his true identity and destiny, that he emerges at last from their baleful spell.

This haunted atmosphere, these dark fantasies and feelings, surely have their profound origins in Dickens' blacking-warehouse months, in his own devastating experience of suffocation and entrapment. In part *Oliver Twist* is a metaphor of that experience. Oliver undergoes what Dickens underwent. The blacking-warehouse time was a period of walking city streets in the dark, becoming part of a band of rough men and boys, being inducted into a déclassé occupation (again involving great manual dexterity), and feeling that he would never escape. He even took the name of his archvillain—Fagin—from a boy who worked beside him.[79] Out of that period, too, comes the notion, so strong in Oliver, that an innocent life was being wasted and perverted, that, as Dickens put it in his own case, "but for the mercy of God, I might easily have been, for any care that was taken of me, a little robber or a little vagabond."[80] It is a symptom of Dickens' profound and still-lingering hurt that he should translate those months of drudging work into such expressionistic enlargements of anguish and fear, into devils and monsters, thieves and murderers, entrapment and nightmare.

Yet the forces of good, though pallid, prevail. They prevail because they possess magical powers stronger than the forces of evil. "Little Oliver," Dickens tells us in the preface of 1841, represents "the principle of Good surviving through every adverse circumstance, and triumphing at last."[81] Oliver, in other words, is immaculate; he is not subject to the stains and taints that shadow ordinary mortals. He is the prince in disguise, the noble scion in humble station, threatened and beleaguered by evil, but immune to it. He is also another of Dickens' favorite fairy-tale conceptions: he is the innocent child, bereft of parents, and cast into the dangerous forest of the city, where he must do battle with devils, monsters, gnomes, and ogres. These are not fanciful metaphors. The persons Oliver meets—the Fagins, Sikeses, Claypoles, and Bumbles—have these traits woven into their characterization. As for Oliver's princedom, his gentle manners and gentle speech—in his circumstances, supernatural attainments—attest to his anointment. But over and above such magical signs, he comes into his just inheritance at the end of the book. He proves to be of gentle birth, regains his stolen fortune, finds a loving relative, and is adopted by a rich and benevolent gentleman. Given these circumstances, it is no wonder that Oliver lives happily ever after.

The rich and benevolent gentleman, Mr. Brownlow, is the fairy godfather of the book and Oliver's surrogate father. He believes in Oliver and trusts him. He leads the forces of good—the Maylies, Bedwins, Losbernes, Grimwigs, and all the partisans of virtue—and helps them defeat the machinations of evil. He is tireless in ferreting out the *bona fides* of Oliver's identity—golden rings, secret lockets, hidden evidence, revelatory documents, and all the rest. He is also indefatigable in arranging meetings, finding witnesses, revealing plots, cowing villains, and helping the pure in heart. Like Mr. Pickwick and the Cheeryble brothers, his motivation is benevolence, his magic wand, money. He receives his reward. He retires to a little village, a rural paradise, and there becomes the leader of a perfect society. Oliver, Mrs. Maylie, Rose Maylie, Harry Maylie, Mrs. Bedwin, Dr. Losberne, Mr. Grimwig, Giles, Brittles, and others live there in harmony and fellowship, a blissful tribe. I am not exaggerating this storybook conclusion. Dickens tells us that this blessed band constituted "a little society, whose condition approached as nearly to one of perfect happiness as can ever be known in this changing world."[82]

This fairy-tale consummation is surrounded by a host of equally magical coincidences and relationships. The person randomly selected as the victim when Oliver tags along on his first pickpocket adventure turns out to be Mr. Brownlow. It is not enough that Mr. Brownlow will prove to be Oliver's fairy godfather, and eventually his adoptive father; he will also turn out to be the dear friend of Oliver's dead father and the secret admirer of Oliver's dead mother. In a similar way, when Oliver is forced to assist in his first robbery assignment, the home chosen by his compatriots is the Maylie residence. Rose Maylie, who soon becomes a sister to Oliver, eventually proves to be his aunt. Obviously Oliver is as magically predestined as any fated prince in fairy story or romance.

What are we to make of these potent amulets, perfect societies, and astonishing consanguinities? Clearly the forces of good in *Oliver Twist* are as exaggerated and fabulous as the forces of evil. And just as clearly, they, too, have their origins in the blacking-warehouse episode. The puissant fairy godfathers, gentlemanly ancestors, fortunate inheritances, blessed releases, and perfect societies are wishes come true, blacking-warehouse fantasies given new form in Dickens' fictions. As with the enlargement of evil in *Oliver Twist,* the enlargement of good testifies to Dickens' blacking-warehouse despair and longing for release. What Dickens yearned for is what Oliver is granted: a miraculous rescue, a perfect father, an assured status, a loving family, an angelic sister, a rich inheritance, and an inviolable paradise.

These fairy-tale energies—the hellish thieves' den and all that surrounds it on the one hand, and the perfect society and all that surrounds it on the other—confuse the central realism of the novel, not because of the starkness of the oppositions, but because of the differing nature of the truths to which we are asked to assent. One truth has to do with our realistic recognition of the shapes and ways and workings of the world, the other with our fervent longing for the bliss and peace and fulfillment of transcendence. In *Oliver Twist* Dickens often integrates these divergent impulses, more so than in most of his other early novels, but he also develops them in configurations that clash and weaken. We can accept—indeed we are forced to accept—the harshness of the workhouse environment and the depravity of Fagin's den, but given these acceptances, and knowing that Oliver is the product of these ferocious corruptions, how can we believe in his elegant purity of speech and thought? Or to turn the equation around, if we accept the miraculous nature of Oliver's purity and immunity, how can we take seriously the life-destroying threats that surround him? These difficulties are not limited to Oliver. There is a disparity between the whole unbelievable working of the plot and the intense realism of the London scenes.

Dickens often manages to avoid or disguise such oppositions, and he often fuses the real and the supernatural in ways that enhance rather than diminish meaning, but in *Oliver Twist* he sometimes blurs the real and the fantastic in a way very unusual for him. When Oliver is going with Mr. Losberne to visit Mr. Brownlow, he chances to see the Chertsey house he was taken to before the robbery. He and Mr. Losberne barge in excitedly, but everything is totally changed: the house is either the wrong house or it has been transformed as if by magic. But the house is tended by an "ugly hump-backed man"—Losberne calls him a "vampire," the narrator a "mis-shapen little demon"—who "set up a yell, and danced upon the ground, as if wild with rage."[83] Losberne says Oliver must have been mistaken, and he gives the hunchback some money, but the malicious looks and the wild actions of this avatar of Rumpelstiltskin seem to condemn him. In our last glimpse of this strange gnome we see him "beating his feet upon the ground, and tearing his hair, in transports of real or pretended rage."[84] This memorable scene, with its strong storybook overtones, is puzzling. It is not necessary, and it is not explained. We never know whether Oliver was mistaken, whether the gang transformed the house, or whether real fairy-tale magic was at work. Indeed we never hear anything more about the matter. In subsequent novels Dickens rarely left such loose ends, and I can think of no instance after *Oliver Twist* where he strongly encouraged a supernatural explanation of a realistic event.

In *Oliver Twist,* however, there is another, even more surprising scene of this kind. I have in mind the twilight episode in which Oliver, restored now and living with the Maylies in the country, falls into the same half-dreaming, half-waking state in which he saw Fagin gloating over his jewels.[85] Oliver feels the air grow close and confined, and with a glow of terror he dreams that he is back in Fagin's den. He awakens to find Monks and Fagin at the open window within touching distance of him. Oliver, in another of Dickens' magical meetings of eyes, suffers the fierce gaze of the intruders for "an instant, a glance, a flash," and then the two men vanish.[86] But "their look was as firmly impressed upon his memory, as if it had been deeply carved in stone, and set before him from his birth."[87] Oliver is transfixed. A moment later he calls for help and rushes into the garden. The help comes quickly, but the intruders have disappeared. The terrain is such that they could not vanish, but they have vanished. Indeed they have vanished without a trace, and this despite the fact that they have traversed ground—areas of long grass, ditches of damp clay, and the like—where they would have to leave footprints. Yet every inch of the surrounding terrain is pristine and untouched.[88] Harry Maylie suggests that Oliver must have been dreaming—which he certainly was, in part—but Oliver insists the men were real.

The scene is quite wonderfully wrought. Dickens suggests with great art that Oliver's mind is still filled with dark, fathomless fears, with dreams of claustrophobic entrapment and staring evil eyes; he suggests at the same time that Oliver is threatened by nightmare evil—he personifies that threat by limning a devilish childsnatcher and his dark cohort peering through a haunted window. He even suggests the transcendent power of that evil by giving it supernatural dimensions. But with the unmarked ground—surely an indication that Fagin and Monks are not simply metaphorical demons but real devils—he makes storybook enlargement subvert his central realism. On the realistic level Oliver must have been dreaming, for Fagin and Monks are not supernatural creatures who can vanish without leaving footsteps; they are ordinary men. Yet Dickens obviously wants us to believe that Fagin and Monks were really there; the scene is accompanied by an illustration that shows the two men gazing through the window at the sleeping boy. In his subsequent writings, Dickens often fused fantasy and reality—that fusion became a mainstay of his technique—but he always avoided a supernaturalism that could not be accommodated, however startlingly or coincidentally, by his fundamental realism. Dickens himself must have realized that he had introduced an anomaly. At the end of the book he has Mr. Brownlow tell the reader that Monks and Fagin had actually visited the house in the country; they had gone there "for the purpose of identifying" Oliver.[89] This lame explanation confirms that Oliver's terrified nightmare was more than a dream. Dickens leaves the pristine ground unexplained.

The scenes I have been discussing are remarkable and compelling; I have dwelt on them simply to emphasize that the disparity between the fanciful and the realistic, a disparity perhaps best exemplified by Oliver's fairy-tale role in a realistic world, also enters scenes that draw their chief energies from fairy stories. Yet *Oliver Twist* is more informed by fairy stories and more of a piece than any of the novels discussed so far. The question arises why this should be so. Why does Dickens' second novel owe so much more to fairy tales than his first or third or sixth, and why—since Dickens' overall development is toward more fantasy and more integration—do the magical energies of *Oliver* cohere more than those in the other early novels? The answer, I believe, lies in the nature of the impulses that helped feed *Oliver Twist.* Those impulses were linked to the most profound fears and hopes of Dickens' life. The fears were so intense and so appalling, they took on monstrous storybook shapes: they emerged as murderous devils with quivering knives, black dens in exitless labyrinths, fierce apparitions at haunted windows. Only nightmare images could convey such limitless danger and fear. A similar development occurred with Dickens' profound hopes. They were so intense and yearning that they too took on storybook shapes: they metamorphosed into benevolent godfathers who are all-powerful and all-good, hidden pedigrees that assure status and riches, loving societies that are sacrosanct and blissful. Only desperate longing could conjure up such solaceful and unrealistic beatitudes. Furthermore, in *Oliver Twist,* by virtue of the fable, these primordial fears and hopes were not limited to isolated scenes, but were attached to the great central movements of the novel. In other words, the pervasive fairy-tale force of *Oliver Twist* owes more to the conjunction of fable and life than to the evolution of technique.

This observation is borne out by *The Old Curiosity Shop,* the fourth of Dickens' six pre-*Dombey* novels. *The Old Curiosity Shop* shares with *Oliver* the distinction of being more dominated and integrated by enchantment than the other early novels. Again like *Oliver, The Old Curiosity Shop* owes a good deal of its preeminence in this respect to the special intersections of subject matter and life. At the same time the story is also a product of its initial conception and destination. Dickens conceived the work as a short story that would contrast dramatic opposites: youth and age, beauty and ugliness, country and city, life and death. Simultaneously, he also sought to contour the tale to the storybook atmosphere of *Master Humphrey's Clock,* the periodical in which it was to appear. *Master Humphrey's Clock* was designed to evoke some of the strangeness and wonder of fairy tales. The opening story in the periodical begins, "Once upon a time," an appropriate onset for a narrative that brings to life the Guildhall giants Gog and Magog. These giants tell their story, a spectral tale, the first of a promised series. The other stories woven into the periodical give additional weight to legends, curiosities, and supernatural happenings. *The Old Curiosity Shop* was to be an integral part of this fanciful scheme. When Dickens expanded *The Old Curiosity Shop* to a full-length novel—it eventually all but swallowed *Master Humphrey's Clock*—he elaborated rather than altered the vision that had originally controlled him. Furthermore, in *The Old Curiosity Shop* more than in any other novel, Dickens was dominated by feeling. Deep emotion, rather than a clearly perceived idea or sequence of actions, gave the work its innermost character. Forster testifies to this profound unconscious element in the genesis of the story. The novel, he writes, took "gradual form, with less direct consciousness of design on his own part than I can remember in any other instance throughout his career."[90] The controlling motifs that welled up so spontaneously had the attributes (and often the lineage) of fairy tales, fables, and allegories. The motifs themselves were not entirely new to Dickens. He had focused on some in earlier novels, and would return to others in later works, but never, before or again, with such single-minded concentration and centrality.

At the heart of *The Old Curiosity Shop* are several storybook conceptions. Foremost, perhaps, is that of the lonely and beleaguered child, wandering lost through the terrifying forests of the world, assailed by grotesque monsters and demons. Nell (the lost child of the novel) suffers from the onslaughts of these frightening creatures. Like Oliver, she cannot be sullied by their attacks; like Smike, however, she ultimately dies from the ravaging toll of the struggle. The injustice and evil of the world have destroyed her. Related to this idea is the motif of the sanctified child leading the corrupted father (an image of sinning man) through the threatening woods of life. Like the first motif, this conception, a sort of reverse *Children in the Wood,* is strongly connected to Dickens' childhood feelings of abandonment and danger, and to his sense of his parents' irresponsibility and insufficiency. The sacrificed and sanctified child is Dickens himself, but also, and increasingly as the novel progresses, his adored sister-in-law Mary Hogarth, dead three years before, at seventeen. Finally, on the most allegorical level, the story is conceived as the wanderings of two pilgrims through the dangers and temptations of life to a safe haven in death; the journey becomes a metaphor of life. This, like the first two motifs, is no imposition on the text but a design that Dickens wanted the reader to detect. He frequently refers to Nell and her grandfather as pilgrims, and when the two set out on their journey, he makes them speak of *The Pilgrim's Progress* and see themselves in the role of Christian.[91] Furthermore, immediately after finishing the novel, Dickens introduced into the first chapter of the first separate edition the idea of the whole story as an allegory. Nell, he interpolated, "seemed to exist in a kind of allegory."[92]

As in most of the early novels, these overall motifs are dramatized by a contest that pits good against evil. But in *The Old Curiosity Shop* that contest is more abstract and fablelike than in earlier or later novels. Central in this contest, and also profoundly allegorical in its presentation, is the Blakean contrast between city and countryside. The city, with its claustrophobic streets and predatory inhabitants, stands for

man-made evil; the countryside, with its green lanes and humble laborers, represents God-ordained wholesomeness. The city is a wen, the
countryside a balm. When Nell and her grandfather flee the city, they
have no destination; they are simply fleeing the diseased city, embrac-
ing the blessed country. Their destination is an idea: an unknown vale
of harmony and surcease. When, after long wandering, they find their
blessed refuge, it proves to be the vale of death.

The city is the abstract center of evil, but in individual terms, the
center and origin of evil is the sinister misshapen dwarf, Quilp. This
grotesque devil abounds in gleeful malice and demonic energy. His
fairy-tale attributes are everywhere apparent. Though a dwarf, his head
and face are "large enough for the body of a giant."[93] He has black
eyes, black stubble, and a "few discoloured fangs" for teeth.[94] His legs
are crooked, and his fingernails are "crooked, long, and yellow."[95] He
has the aspect of a "panting dog," and when he grins, he grins "like a
devil."[96] He is full of tricks and grimaces. At one instant he presents "a
horribly grotesque and distorted face with the tongue lolling out"; the
next moment he is perfectly bland and placid.[97] He performs monstrous feats. "He ate hard eggs, shell and all, devoured gigantic prawns
with the heads and tails on, chewed tobacco and water-cresses at the
same time and with extraordinary greediness, drank boiling tea without
winking, bit his fork and spoon till they bent again, and . . . performed
so many horrifying and uncommon acts that the women were nearly
frightened out of their wits and began to doubt if he were really a
human creature."[98]

This storybook goblin has a storybook residence. "Mr. and Mrs.
Quilp resided on Tower Hill; and in her bower on Tower Hill Mrs. Quilp
was left to pine the absence of her lord, when he quitted her."[99] The
bower also contains a dragon, Quilp's shrewish mother-in-law, Mrs.
Jiniwin, dubbed a dragon by Quilp. Quilp terrorizes his mild wife and
dragonish mother-in-law with equal zest. When his wife comes unbidden to his countinghouse, he cries, "How dare you approach the ogre's
castle, eh?"; and when she offends him, he threatens to bite her.[100]
The countinghouse itself is a fit fairy-tale office for its fairy-tale master.
It is depicted as "burrowing all awry in the dust as if it had fallen from
the clouds and ploughed into the ground."[101] Into this countinghouse
Quilp one day brings the figurehead of a ship. The figurehead reaches
from floor to ceiling and looks like "a goblin or hideous idol whom the
dwarf worshipped."[102] Quilp claims the figurehead resembles honest
Kit Nubbles, and he beats it savagely with a rusty iron bar. He batters
the figure until he is exhausted, and then he confesses to Sampson
Brass: "I've been screwing gimlets into him, and sticking forks in his
eyes, and cutting my name on him. I mean to burn him at last."[103]

Immediately after performing this primitive magic, Quilp refreshes himself. He raises a saucepan hot from the fire, puts it to his lips, and drinks off its contents: burning rum, "bubbling and hissing fiercely."[104]

This sadistic demon has other supernatural powers. He can appear out of nowhere, and he can vanish in a trice. On one occasion he vanishes so completely that everyone believes him to be dead. He can sleep with his eyes open, and he can hang head down from the ceiling. He often surrounds himself in clouds of dense smoke. He smokes so vigorously that nothing is "visible through the mist but a pair of red and highly inflamed eyes."[105] He can cast spells and work charms. Though grotesque and ugly, he has a pretty wife, and she confirms his irresistible power. "Quilp," she says, "has such a way with him when he likes, that the best-looking woman here couldn't refuse him if . . . he chose to make love to her."[106] Quilp, quite obviously, is a nightmare kin of Shakespeare's Richard III. Quilp's sexual potency hovers perversely over the immature, virginal Nell. He tells her he will make her "number two" when his wife dies, smacks his lips over her succulent budding ripeness, offers to sleep in her bed, does so, and then pursues her eagerly through the rest of the book.[107] This malignant gnome is often accompanied by his familiar, an "amphibious boy" who is always standing on his head, and who crouches "over the fire after the manner of a toad."[108]

Quilp's energy dominates and enlivens the book. His demonic vitality subdues and enslaves all who come within his reach. Only death can quench his irrepressible malice, and his death is as magical as his life. His death is heralded by "a knocking at the gate"—the Shakespearean overture to so many of the portentous deaths in Dickens' novels.[109] The atmosphere is equally portentous. It is night and a "thick cloud . . . rested upon the earth, and shrouded everything from view."[110] Quilp darts into this night "as if into the mouth of some dim, yawning cavern"; he calls the sinister darkness "a good, black, devil's night," and says he doesn't care if it is ever day again.[111] "As the word passed his lips, he staggered and fell—and next moment was fighting with the cold dark water!"[112] He hears the knocking at the gate again, but cannot save himself, and drowns struggling. His body washes up on a swamp, the red glare of his burning countinghouse flaming the sky and tingeing his face with an infernal glow.[113] He is buried like some fearsome monster or vampire "with a stake through his heart in the centre of four lonely roads."[114]

Quilp brilliantly blends human malignancy and sadism with fairy-tale powers and effects. But Nell, the disinherited fairy princess of the story, lacks Quilp's dynamic realism. She is a conception of goodness, surrounded by a storybook nimbus, but trammeled by her allegorical role. Dickens builds the legendary penumbra from the beginning. In the opening chapter we discover that Nell sleeps in "a little bed that a fairy might have slept in"; and later in the chapter we are told that she is "so very young, so spiritual, so slight and fairy-like."[115] But even without these labels we soon recognize that she is a creature from fairyland. She possesses perfect beauty, perfect goodness, perfect wisdom. She casts a spell on all but the wicked and depraved; the undefiled of the world feel drawn to her and worship her. Birds and animals that will not approach others come to her; the wildest of children cling to her and do her bidding. She leads her aged grandfather by the hand, his counselor and guide: wise youth leading childish age. Even the old man, wretched and half-demented, notes this strange reversal. "It is true," he says, "that in many respects I am the child, and she the grown person."[116] It is no wonder that travelers, observing Nell's gentle perfection and singular office, take her to be a changeling, a stolen princess: "Rumours had already got abroad that the little girl . . . was the child of great people who had been stolen from her parents in infancy . . . Opinion was divided whether she was the daughter of a prince, a duke, an earl, a viscount, or a baron."[117]

When these hints and signs are combined with her role as wandering seraph, her resemblance to the stolen and immured princesses of folklore becomes even more apparent. That resemblance is strengthened by the vassals who circle round her or later try to save her. Her haunted grandfather, his pilgrim's gear on his back and by his side, ends his days by her grave, existing vaguely in a dim world of ghosts and specters. Earlier he had dreamed of golden treasure, but this obsessed dream had only led to gambling and impoverishment. His mania had depleted his small treasure and increased the goblin gold of Quilp. Kit Nubbles, the simple swain, misunderstood and falsely accused, the loyal rustic retainer of countless folk tales and romances, serves Nell faithfully. His unadorned honesty has its storybook reward: it brings him love and prosperity. The Garlands, epitomes of goodness and benevolence, rally at the end to serve and save the princess. They are additional incarnations of sound middle-class rectitude; they stand beside the Wardles, Maylies, Vardens, and Browdies—serviceable vessels of hearty humanity. The single gentleman, rich granduncle of Nell, as it turns out, is the fairy godfather of the novel, disguised for a while, as old Martin was. His magic wand, as usual, is made of money. For once its magic potency does not avail: Nell dies before he can reach her. He persists in his fablelike mission, however. He spends his days traveling in the steps of the old man and the child, rewarding all those who had been kind to them.

These fairy-tale characters and actions are accompanied by many other fairy-tale patterns. The Garlands' cottage is an unmistakable storybook abode. It has "a thatched roof and little spires at the gable-ends, and pieces of stained glass in some of the windows."[118] Lest the reader fail to make the proper associations, when Kit first approaches this "beautiful little cottage," Dickens has him think about "giants' castles, and princesses tied up to pegs by the hair of their heads, and dragons bursting out from behind gates, and other incidents of the like nature."[119] By the same token, Dick Swiveller and the Marchioness, though very real, even sordid, dwell in an enchanted climate. The sordidness and the enchantment have a special significance: Dick and the Marchioness, but especially the Marchioness, are steeped in blacking-warehouse memories. Dick is a partial portrait of the youthful Dickens, the blacking warehouse behind him, sauntering in be-leaguered independence; the Marchioness is a redaction of the maid-of-all-work from the Chatham workhouse, the shrewd but kindly little orphan who listened raptly to Dickens' wild stories during the blacking-warehouse period.[120] Dickens propels both characters into felicity. They enact a version of *Cinderella*. Dick, boozy, impoverish-ed, and mildly disreputable, is a Prince Charming with real charm; the Marchioness, ignorant, abused, and ferretlike, a dweller in black cel-lars, is all the more a potential Cinderella. Dick by his humanity raises the Marchioness to grace. Then, by a compounding of the fairy tale, the Marchioness saves him: tending him through a dangerous illness. The end of the story combines *Cinderella* with *Beauty and the Beast*. Prince Charming marries the cinder girl (presciently called by him "Mar-chioness")—but only after further educating and transforming her. When the tiny drudge is nineteen, transformed by Dick's growing love into a "good-looking, clever, and good-humoured" woman, he weds her.[121] She proves "ever a most cheerful, affectionate, and prov-ident wife."[122] This storybook consummation is Dickens' latter-day gift to the strange little urchin who waited with him near London Bridge for the Marshalsea gates to open.

Dickens surrounds Dick and the Marchioness with other storybook associations. He entwines them with fairy-tale allusions and imagery. When Dick comes out of his delirium, he says: "It's an Arabian Night; that's what it is. . . . I'm in Damascus or Grand Cairo. The Marchio-ness is a Genie, and having had a wager with another Genie about who is the handsomest young man alive, and the worthiest to be the hus-band of the Princess of China, has brought me away, room and all, to compare us together. Perhaps . . . the Princess may be still—No, she's gone."[123] Such passages serve a triple purpose. They alert us to the underlying fairy-tale currents of the novel, emphasize the realism of the moment (Dick's half-lucid, half-hallucinating ramblings tell us he is still light-headed from his illness), and subtly point us to the future (the true

Princess really *is* there, after all). Other storybook passages work in analogous, yet different ways. After Dick has rented one of the Brasses' rooms to a strange gentleman, he muses: "This is a most remarkable and supernatural sort of house. . . . She-dragons in the business, conducting themselves like professional gentlemen; plain cooks of three feet high appearing mysteriously from underground; strangers walking in and going to bed without leave or licence in the middle of the day! If he should be one of the miraculous fellows that turn up now and then, and has gone to sleep for two years, I shall be in a pleasant situation."[124] This passage is exceptionally important (though it could be duplicated throughout the book). It shows us that even when Dickens presents fairy-tale conceptions without overtly identifying them as such—as in the original renderings of the happenings referred to above—he is aware of their storybook implications. The Brasses' house is a fairy-tale house by design, not by critical imposition.

In the preface to *The Old Curiosity Shop,* Dickens said, "I had it always in my fancy to surround the lonely figure of the child with grotesque and wild but not impossible companions, and to gather about her innocent face and pure intentions, associates as strange and uncongenial as the grim objects that are about her bed when her history is first foreshadowed."[125] This Dickens surely did. Nell asleep, surrounded by the grim clutter of the old curiosity shop, foreshadows Nell dead, surrounded by the solemn intricacy of her medieval haven. Both settings oppose the grotesque fixity of the encroaching past to the sad impermanence of an idealized present. Other contrasts enforce the same lesson or simply juxtapose goblin grotesquerie to innocent perfection. The chief embodiment of the contrast, of course, is the innocent child leading the corrupted old man by the hand—the central image of the novel. But other contrasts are no less strange and grotesque. Among the most successful are those enforced by means of the weird fairy-tale characters who cluster round Nell on the road. These wonderful characters are both real and utterly fantastic. I am not thinking of the gamblers, cardsharpers, and thugs—they are real and threatening enough, but sketchy and conventionalized. I am thinking of the long procession of itinerant showmen and their charges that Nell encounters and partly travels with. On the road she meets gaunt stiltwalking giants, outlandish images of Punch and Judy, strangely staring waxwork figures, amazing men who put leaden lozenges in their eyes and bring them out their mouths, sagacious dancing dogs, shaky weak-kneed giants, and astonishing ladies without arms or legs—an assortment of creatures as fantastic and bizarre as the wildest inventions in the most surreal fairy stories. These creatures surround and accompany Nell, a limitless *Alice in Wonderland* menagerie, a remarkable evocation of the gnomes and monsters of childhood storybooks, but all suddenly become overwhelmingly real. Nell watches tiny dogs, dressed as humans, bow and scrape and work and play; she sees towering giants lurch crazily out of the deceiving dusk; she observes miniature animals pop magically out of ordinary pockets. And she listens to the wonderful conversation of the showmen themselves:

> "Why, I remember" [says Mr. Vuffin] "the time when old Maunders as had three-and-twenty wans—I remember the time when old Maunders had in his cottage in Spa Fields in the winter time, when the season was over, eight male and female dwarfs setting down to dinner every day, who was waited on by eight old giants in green coats, red smalls, blue cotton stockings, and high-lows: and there was one dwarf as had grown elderly and wicious who whenever his giant wasn't quick enough to please him, used to stick pins in his legs, not being able to reach up any higher. I know that's a fact, for Maunders told it me himself."
>
> "What about the dwarfs when *they* get old?" inquired the landlord.
>
> "The older a dwarf is, the better worth he is," returned Mr. Vuffin; "a grey-headed dwarf, well wrinkled, is beyond all suspicion. But a giant weak in the legs and not standing upright!—keep him in the carawan, but never show him, never show him, for any persuasion that can be offered."[126]

In such scenes wild fairy-tale fancy combines with odd workaday realism to capture afresh the comedy and strangeness of life.

It is clear that fairy-tale energies contributed much to *The Old Curiosity Shop*. As in *Oliver Twist,* those energies helped produce a unity of effect; they helped imbue the center of the novel with a single, driving vision. Those energies also helped give the book an allegorical, fablelike force. That simplicity and singleness of force accounts, in part, for the novel's great appeal to the Victorians—it provided them with a myth that rationalized intolerable death. Finally those energies enhance the strength, realistic as well as fanciful, of Quilp, Swiveller, the Marchioness, the itinerant showmen, and much more.

Yet in other ways, those same energies weakened the novel. The allegory which added focus and force also produced abstraction. Quilp's pursuit of Nell, his persecution of Kit, his hounding of others are not motivated. The reasons alleged for these vindictive vendettas are not convincing; they will not bear the weight of psychological scrutiny. Yet we feel that Quilp's pursuit is fitting, almost inevitable. We feel this way because we realize that his pursuit goes beyond mere reason, that it is rooted in the allegorical need for evil to track down goodness. But while we can accept this need and the pursuit that follows, the realistic levels of the book suffer: we perceive that reality is being manipulated for the sake of the fable. In the same way, Nell's lingering decline and death move the book away from reality. Her slow descent into the grave becomes a masque in which gravediggers, tombs, gaping holes, churchly surroundings, and all the paraphernalia of death serve as props in a solemn shadowy ritual of extinction. Symbol and allegory substitute for deep-grappling reality.

How this abstraction weakens the novel may be glimpsed in one of its most memorable scenes, the scene in which Nell and her grandfather are allowed to sleep before the furnace fire.[127] Allegory gives the scene power, but lack of accompanying realism makes it schematic. The wanderers come into an industrial city, a harsh, inimical, self-centered place. The grandfather says, "Why did you bring me here? . . . I cannot bear these close eternal streets." The bleak city and its endless streets bring to Nell's mind a vision of their antithesis, a dream of the country, with "some good old tree, stretching out his green arms as if he loved us." Wandering through the desolate city, the old man and the child come upon a pale ghostlike creature begrimed with smoke. He proves to be the spirit of the industrial fire. Like his father before him, he has spent his whole life, from infancy on, tending and watching the fire. This genius of the fire brings them to the furnace room of a steel mill, an emblem of hell. The place is an inferno of fire, noise, hammering, and smoke. Shadowy figures, wielding great weapons, and laboring "like giants," move "like demons among the flame and smoke." Nell and her grandfather sleep "upon a heap of ashes." Their rest is as peaceful as if they had been in "a palace chamber." When the pilgrims awake, they prepare to go on. They are seeking some pastoral paradise away from the blear and smear of men, "some distant country place remote from towns or even other villages." The furnace watcher tells them the difficulties of the journey. They must take a path through "a strange black road" that is "lighted up by fires." Nell says they must go on. "Is there no turning back?" asks the furnace watcher. "There is none," cries Nell. They part, and the child continues "to lead her sacred charge farther from guilt and shame."

Taken in its entirety, the scene is unforgettable, but it is one-dimensional and contrived. It is there as a set piece. It contrasts the hellish fires of man-made industrialism to the bucolic sublimity of God-given nature. There is no reason why the wanderers should come to this city; there is no reason why they should meet the cindery genius of the industrial fire; there is no reason why they should travel on: no reason, that is, except the architectonic demands of the fable. Their destination is paradise, their quest a storybook search. The scene ends with an allusion to the legends and treasures chronicled on ancient tombs. That, in fact, is what the scene is: a legend or allegory, powerfully thematic, but lacking the dense, detailed texture of reality.

The same kind of debility weakens the role of Nell, especially toward the end of the novel. But here the abstraction and allegory are only part of the trouble: there is also a loss of emotional control. As Dickens approached the end of the book, he was haunted by the prospect of Nell's death, and as he neared the latter event, he increasingly associated it with Mary Hogarth's death. "All night," he wrote, "I have been pursued by the child; and this morning I am unrefreshed and miserable."[128] Several weeks later, speaking of Nell's impending demise, he continued the theme: "It casts the most horrible shadow upon me . . . I tremble to approach the place . . . Nobody will miss her like I shall. It is such a very painful thing to me, that I really cannot express my sorrow. Old wounds bleed afresh when I only think of the way of doing it: what the actual doing it will be, God knows. . . . Dear Mary died yesterday, when I think of this sad story."[129]

This emotion overwhelmed and engulfed him. The novel became a vehicle for expressing personal feeling; or to put the matter another way, personal emotion, undistanced and unleavened, controlled too much of the novel, especially with Nell, and especially toward the end. This emotion lacks compelling life. Paradoxically, what inhibits that deeper life is the emotion itself, an emotion that Dickens can only express through conventional feelings of loss and grief. This conventional grief, though profoundly believed in, substitutes for truer and more painful feelings and inhibits the deeper anger and anguish within. Dickens hints at this subversive paradox. In the same letter, indeed in the same passage, in which he said "old wounds bleed afresh," he also said: "I can't preach to myself the schoolmaster's consolation, though I try." The schoolmaster of *The Old Curiosity Shop* had a soothing message. He preached a doctrine designed to comfort man in the face of immutable death. "There is nothing," he said, "no, nothing innocent or good, that dies, and is forgotten. . . . There is not an angel added to the Host of Heaven but does its blessed work on earth in those that loved it here. Forgotten! oh, if the good deeds of human creatures could be traced to their source, how beautiful would even death appear; for how much charity, mercy, and purified affection, would be seen to have their growth in dusty graves!"[130] This was the consolatory message of *The Old Curiosity Shop,* a message that brought balm and inspiration to multitudes of bereaved Victorians. Nell's dissolution, understood in the context of the schoolmaster's consolation, meliorated the mystery of death; it turned cold finality into warm continuation.

But for Dickens, as he confessed, that doctrine did not work. The comfort he preached to others did not assuage his own outrage at the bitter finality of death. Dickens felt this, but in *The Old Curiosity Shop* he could not give that awareness meaningful fictional form. The solemn allegory of grief prevented him from getting beyond the schoolmaster's consolation, from loosing his innermost feelings, feelings that called into question the very doctrines he was purveying. It is as though Dickens immersed himself in grief to hide from himself. Grief became an end in itself, a substitute for belief. Hence the ill-assorted combination of carefully calculated effects and perfervid emotion that accompanies Nell's long decline and death, and hence Dickens' loss of balance and control. At the very heart of that contrivance and excess are doubt and self-deception. Dickens is convincing and indulging himself. Nell's death becomes a tour de force, a set piece rather than a profound comment on existence.

In *The Old Curiosity Shop,* allegory and wish-fulfilling manipulation combine with masking emotion to subvert reality. The central sweep of the novel, both fed and marred by fairy tales, lacks tragic life.

If one takes an overall look at the fantasy elements in Dickens' first six novels, one can see that there is a slow evolution toward a greater use of enchantment, both in controlling structures and subordinate parts. Mr. Pickwick's latter-day wand-waving gives way to old Martin's more pervasive storybook deception; the sealed-off fairy stories of *Pickwick* are replaced by the subtle fairy-tale enhancements of *Chuzzlewit*—by the vertiginous powers of Todgers's Boarding House or the cosmic reverberations of Tigg's murder. But this evolution is neither simple nor regular; it contains pauses, accelerations, and reversals. The evolution is a function of increasing mastery and maturing technique, but it is also a function of the peculiar, and in some respects arbitrary, entanglements of subject matter, emotion, and circumstance.

Yet there can be no doubt about the general tendency. In the six early novels, the storybook manipulations of plot, despite some irregularities, become more steady and more comprehensive (they do not, however, become more integrated with the surrounding realism). The introduction of fairy-tale touches into the main body of the story—into characters, settings, actions, and the like—grows, though not linearly, both in extent and in skill. Such touches become an increasing, and increasingly subtle, adjunct to theme and meaning. But this is too artificial and peripheral a way of putting the matter. The fairy-tale touches are more than touches, they are part of the very conception of the thing touched; they are part of Dickens' innermost perception of reality. Fagin or Todgers's or Quilp would simply not exist if their magical components were removed—an impossible task.

In his first six novels, Dickens uses virtually every fairy-tale device and technique that he will use in his later novels. Furthermore, in his early works one can find consummate examples of each use. What is lacking is integration: a steady, cohesive marshalling of the fantasy elements. What is needed is a satisfactory blending of the manipulative storybook plot and the realistic workings of the novel. What is needed, also, is a reciprocal and more consistent relationship between the fairy-tale plot and the many fairy-tale elements—the fairy-tale characters, places, and so on—already successfully imbedded in the central realism. This kind of unity had eluded Dickens. Yet he was very much aware of the sprawl and scatter of his early work. He soon came to wish that *Pickwick* had been "strung together on a stronger thread."[131] He kept reminding himself in *Nickleby* of the need to "spoil a number now and then, for the sake of the book."[132] And he said he had tried in *Chuzzlewit* to "keep a steadier eye upon the general purpose and design."[133] But it was not until *Dombey* that he really succeeded in integrating an entire novel. *Oliver Twist* and *The Old Curiosity Shop,* his two most unified works prior to *Dombey,* were misleading in this respect. Their imperfect unity was partly a reflex of mood and emotion and partly an outgrowth of the cohering fairy-tale energies that helped generate and sustain them. In each instance unity was a byproduct of adventitious conception, not a sign of structural mastery. The books that succeeded *Oliver* and *The Old Curiosity Shop* continued to sprawl and diverge.

I do not mean by what I have written to disparage the early novels. They are great works, full of genius. They are also brimming with achievements that have little to do with fairy stories. The trial scene in *Pickwick,* the Crummles troupe in *Nickleby,* the sublime hypocrisy of Pecksniff are just three examples of consummate art that does not spring from fairy tales. Nor do I mean to imply that Dickens' increasing mastery of structure, and his development of a more controlled and more richly ramifying art, is simply an outgrowth of his growing mastery of storybook motifs and devices. In part that growing mastery is one more reflection of a maturation that one sees developing everywhere in his work. In the more careful and unified novels of his middle and late periods one would expect the fantasy elements to be more careful and unified too. But in part, as we shall see, Dickens was helped to that later mastery by his growing use of fairy stories and by his conscious experimentation with them.

Dombey, when it began to appear almost four years after the onset of *Chuzzlewit,* displayed in most essentials the mastery that had eluded him in his first six novels, and it displayed also an analogous mastery of richly integrating enchantment. But in the more than five years between the beginning of *Chuzzlewit* and the completion of *Dombey,* Dickens had spent virtually all of his creative energies, when not working on those two novels, in experimenting with fairy-tale fiction. To that fairy-tale fiction, and to the results of that experimentation, we must now turn.

5 | The Christmas Books
"Giving Nursery Tales a Higher Form"

In THE interval between the beginning of *Martin Chuzzlewit* and the completion of *Dombey and Son,* Dickens wrote five Christmas books: *A Christmas Carol* (1843), *The Chimes* (1844), *The Cricket on the Hearth* (1845), *The Battle of Life* (1846), and *The Haunted Man* (1848).[1] *The Haunted Man,* the last of the Christmas books, straddles the later limits of this interval. *The Haunted Man* was conceived and partly written in the interval, but not finished until *Dombey* was completed.[2] With the exception of *The Battle of Life,* which depends for its central mechanism on a straightforward analogy between life and an ancient battlefield, the Christmas books rely on fairy-tale machinery to gain their characteristic effects. But this puts the matter too restrictively. The Christmas books draw their innermost energies from fairy tales: they exploit fairy-tale themes, fairy-tale happenings, and fairy-tale techniques. Indeed the Christmas books *are* fairy tales. As Dickens himself put it, he was here taking old nursery tales and "giving them a higher form."[3]

The pattern that Dickens traces in each of his Christmas books— always excepting *The Battle of Life*—is the pattern that he followed with "Gabriel Grub" in *Pickwick.* The design could hardly be simpler or more direct. A protagonist who is mistaken or displays false values is forced, through a series of extraordinary events, to see his errors. This familiar, almost pedestrian given is interfused with fairy-tale elements, a commingling that shapes and transfigures every aspect of the design. Storybook signs set the mood, herald the onset of the action, and enforce the moral lessons. Magical happenings dominate the story. The crucial action takes place in a dream or vision presided over by supernatural creatures who control what goes on. The resolution occurs when the happenings of the vision—a magically telescoped survey of the protagonist's life, and a masquelike representation of the consequences of his false attitudes—force him to reassess his views. In the fashion of most fairy stories, the moral is strongly reiterated at the end.

This structure was of immense value to Dickens. It gave him a framework that provided an aesthetic justification for the legerdemain which in his earlier works, especially in his finales, had usually appeared, not as fairy-tale felicities, but as arbitrary fairy-tale wrenchings. He could now show misery and horror and yet do so in a context of joyful affirmation. He could depict evil flourishing to its ultimate flowering and still deny that flowering. He could introduce the most disparate scenes, events, and visions without losing the reader's confidence. He could manipulate time with no need to obey the ordinary laws of chronology. He could make his characters and events real when he wished them real, magical when he wished them magical. He could effect overnight conversions which could be justified aesthetically. He could teach by parable rather than exhortation. And he could deal with life in terms of a storybook logic that underscored both the real and the ideal.

These potentialities, fundamental ingredients in Dickens' mature narrative method (but there thoroughly assimilated to the dominant realism), are exploited with varying degrees of success in all the Christmas books. In *A Christmas Carol,* to take the first of the Christmas books, Dickens adapts fairy-tale effects and fairy-tale techniques with marvelous skill. All readers are aware of the ghosts and spirits that manipulate the story, but these supernatural beings are only the most obvious signs of a pervasive indebtedness to fairy stories. Dickens himself emphasized that indebtedness. He subtitled his novelette *A Ghost Story of Christmas,* and he followed this spectral overture with other magical associations. In the preface to the *Carol* he told potential readers that he had endeavored "in this ghostly little book, to raise the Ghost of an Idea." Then he went on: "May it haunt their houses pleasantly and no one wish to lay it!"[4] The chapter headings continue this emphasis. Four of the five headings reinforce supernatural expectations: "Marley's Ghost," "The First of the Three Spirits," "The Second of the Three Spirits," and "The Last of the Spirits." With such signposts at the outset, we can expect the journey itself to be full of wondrous events. We are not disappointed, though the opening begins disarmingly enough. It insists on the deadness of Marley and then drifts into a long, facetious reference to the ghost of Hamlet's father. The narrator's attitude is worldly and commonsensical, but Marley's deadness and the ghost of Hamlet's father set the scene for the wild events that are about to take place.

Scrooge sets the scene too. He has much of the archetypal miser in him, but he is more of an ordinary man than his immediate prototypes, prototypes such as Gabriel Grub, Arthur Gride, Ralph Nickleby, and Jonas Chuzzlewit. Yet at the same time Scrooge is compassed round with supernatural attributes that cunningly suffuse his fundamental realism. One soon sees how this process works. The freezing cold that pervades his inner being frosts all his external features and outward mannerisms (nipped and pointed nose, shrivelled cheek, stiffened gait, red eyes, blue lips, grating voice), and this glacial iciness chills all the world without. "He carried his own low temperature always about with him; he iced his office in the dog-days; and didn't thaw it one degree at Christmas. . . . No warmth could warm, no wintry weather chill him."[5] In this respect Scrooge is a prototype of Mr. Dombey. That cold gentleman freezes and congeals his small universe with haughty frostiness.

The story proper of *A Christmas Carol* begins with the traditional "Once upon a time."[6] After this evocative opening Dickens quickly intensifies the storybook atmosphere. Scrooge lives in Marley's old chambers, and Marley died seven years ago on Christmas Eve, that is, seven years ago on the night the story opens. It is a foggy night. Nearby houses dwindle mysteriously into "mere phantoms"; ghostly forms loom dimly in the hazy mist.[7] Out of such details, out of cold, fog, and frost, and out of brief touches of contrasting warmth, Dickens builds an atmosphere dense with personification, animism, anthropomorphism, and the like. The inanimate world is alive and active; every structure, every object plays its percipient role in the unfolding drama. Buildings and gateways, bedposts and door knockers become sentient beings that conspire in a universal morality. Everything is connected by magical means to everything else. Scrooge's chambers are a case in point. The narrator tells us that they are in a lonely, isolated building that must have played hide-and-seek with other houses in its youth, run into a yard where it had no business to be, forgotten its way out again, and remained there ever since.[8] This lost, isolated, cutoff building, fit residence for a lost, isolated, cutoff man, has its own special weather and tutelary spirit. The fog and frost hang so heavy about the black old gateway of this building "that it seemed as if the Genius of the Weather sat in mournful meditation on the threshold."[9]

Given a universe so magical and responsive, we are hardly surprised when Scrooge momentarily sees Marley's face glowing faintly in his front-door knocker, its "ghostly spectacles turned up on its ghostly forehead."[10] When Scrooge sees an equally ghostly hearse on his staircase a few moments later, we know that he is in for a night of it. Thus we are fully prepared for Marley's ghost when it does appear, and we know how to interpret its every movement and accoutrement. Marley's ghost is a superb compound of social symbolism, wild imagination, realistic detail, and grisly humor. It moves in its own strange atmosphere, its hair and clothes stirring curiously, as though agitated by "the hot vapour from an oven"; it wears a bandage round its head, and when it removes this death cloth, its lower jaw drops down upon its breast.[11] Like Blake's city-pent Londoner, Marley's ghost drags and clanks its "mind-forg'd manacles," the chain it "forged in life" and girded on of its "own free will"; like the ghost of Hamlet's father, it is doomed to walk the night and wander restlessly abroad.[12] Scrooge is skeptical of this apparition, but he is no match for the ghost's supernatural power. Like the Ancient Mariner with the wedding guest, the ghost "hath his will." When Scrooge offers his last resistance, the ghost raises a frightful cry, shakes its chains appallingly, and takes the bandage from round its head. Scrooge falls on his knees and submits. Like the wedding guest, now Scrooge "cannot choose but hear." And as in the *Ancient Mariner,* where the wedding guest's struggle and reluctant submission help us suspend our disbelief, in *A Christmas Carol* Scrooge's struggle and submission help us to a like suspension. The ghost has accomplished its mission; the work of the three spirits, work that will culminate in Scrooge's redemption (and our enlightenment), can now begin.

The three spirits or ghosts (Dickens uses the terms interchangeably) are allegorical figures as well as supernatural agents. The Ghost of Christmas Past combines in his person and in his actions distance and closeness, childhood and age, forgetfulness and memory; in a similar fashion the Ghost of Christmas Present is a figure of ease, plenty, and joy—an embodiment of the meaning of Christmas; the Ghost of Christmas Yet to Come, on the other hand, a hooded and shrouded Death, bears implacable witness to the fatal course Scrooge has been pursuing. Each spirit, in other words, enacts a role and presides over scenes that befit its representation. But it is the scenes rather than the spirits that are all-important. The scenes embody Dickens' message in swift vignettes and unforgettable paradigms—Fezziwig's ball, the Cratchits' Christmas dinner, Scrooge's lonely grave. By means of the fairy-tale machinery Dickens can move instantaneously from magic-lantern picture to magic-lantern picture, juxtaposing, contrasting, commenting, and counterpointing, and he can do all this with absolute freedom and ease. He can evoke the crucial image, limn the archetypal scene, concentrate on the traumatic spot of time, with no need to sketch the valleys in between. Like Le Sage much earlier in *The Devil upon Two Sticks* (a boyhood favorite of Dickens), he can fly over the

unsuspecting city, lift its imperturbable rooftops, and reveal swift tableaus of pathos and passion; like Joyce much later in the opening pages
of *A Portrait of the Artist as a Young Man,* he can race through the
years, linger here and there, and provide brief glimpses of the unregarded moments that move and shape us. The overall effect, however,
is more like that of a richly colored Japanese screen. Amid swirling
mists and dense clouds one glimpses prototypical scenes of serenity
and turmoil, joy and nightmare horror.

Through Scrooge Dickens attempts to embody symbolic, social,
psychological, and mythic truth. Scrooge is an outrageous miser and
ogre, but he is also an emblem of more ordinary pathology: he is an
epitome of all selfish and self-regarding men. In his latter aspect, he
touches our lives. He allows us to see how self-interest—an impulse
that motivates each one of us—can swell to monster proportions. He
shows us how not to live, and then, at the end, he points us toward
salvation. That lesson has social as well as symbolic ramifications. We
are made to see that in grinding Bob Cratchit Scrooge grinds himself,
that in letting Tiny Tim perish he perishes alive himself. All society is
connected: individual actions are not self-contained and personal, they
have social consequences; social evils are not limited and discrete,
they taint the whole society. These ideas, of course, were not unique to
Dickens. They were being preached by many Victorians, by two such
different men—both friends of Dickens—as Douglas Jerrold and
Thomas Carlyle, for example. But Dickens presents these ideas in a
more seductive guise than any of his contemporaries. And he blends
teaching with much else.

For one thing, he merges symbolic paradigms and social doctrines
with psychological analysis. By means of a few swift childhood vignettes he gives us some notion of why Scrooge became what he is.
The first spirit shows Scrooge an image of his early self: "a solitary
child, neglected by his friends," and left alone in school at Christmas
time.[13] This scene of loneliness and neglect is mitigated by a single
relief: the boy's intense reading. The reading is not simply referred to,
it comes to life, a bright pageant of color and warmth in his drab
isolation. The exotic characters from that reading troop into the barren
room and enact their familiar adventures. Scenes from *The Arabian
Nights* flash before Scrooge, then images from *Valentine and Orson,*
then vignettes from *The Arabian Nights* again, then episodes from
Robinson Crusoe—all as of yore, all wonderfully thrilling and absorbing. Scrooge is beside himself with excitement. The long-forgotten
memory of his lonely self and of his succoring reading softens him: he
remembers what it was to be a child; he wishes that he had given
something to the boy who sang a Christmas carol at his door the night
before.[14] A moment later Scrooge is looking at a somewhat older image

of his former self, again alone in a school, again left behind at Christmas time. But now his sister Fan enters and tells him that he can come home at last, that father is kinder now and will permit him to return, that Scrooge is to be a man and "never to come back here" again.[15] These memories also soften Scrooge.

The memories, of course, are versions of Dickens' own experiences: the lonely boy "reading as if for life," and saved by that reading; the abandoned child, left in Chatham to finish the Christmas term, while the family goes off to London; the banished son (banished while Fanny remains free), exiled by his father to the blacking warehouse and then released by him at last. These wounding experiences, or rather the *Carol* version of them, help turn Scrooge (and here he is very different from the outward Dickens) into a lonely, isolated man intent on insulating himself from harm or hurt. In a subsequent vignette, a vignette between him and his fiancée, Scrooge chooses money over love. He is the victim of his earlier wound. He seeks through power and aggrandizement to gird himself against the vulnerability that had scarred his childhood. But in making himself invulnerable, he shuts out humanity as well. This happens to Scrooge because, paradoxically, in trying to triumph over his past, he has forgotten it; he has forgotten what it is to be a child, he has forgotten what it is to be lonely and friendless, to cry, laugh, imagine, yearn, and love. The first spirit, through memory, helps Scrooge recover his past, helps him recover the humanness (the responsiveness and fellow feeling) and the imagination (the reading and the visions) that were his birthright, that are every man's birthright.

All this, and much more, is done swiftly and economically with the aid of Dickens' fairy-tale format. The rapid shifts from scene to scene, the spirits' pointed questions and answers, the telescoping, blurring, and juxtaposition of time, the fusion of allegory, realism, psychology, and fancy—all are made possible, all are brought into order and believability, by Dickens' storybook atmosphere and storybook devices. *A Christmas Carol* has a greater unity of effect, a greater concentration of thematic purpose, a greater economy of means towards ends, and a greater sense of integration and cohesiveness than any previous work by Dickens.

A Christmas Carol is the finest of the Christmas books. This preeminence results from its consummate melding of the most archetypal losses, fears, and yearnings with the most lucid embodiment of such elements in characters and actions. No other Christmas book displays this perfect coming together of concept and vehicle. The result is a most powerful, almost mythic statement of widely held truths and aspirations. Scrooge represents every man who has hardened his heart, lost his ability to feel, separated himself from his fellow men, or sacrificed his life to ego, power, or accumulation. The symbolic force of

Scrooge's conversion is allied to the relief we feel (since we are all Scrooges, in part) in knowing that we too can change and be reborn. This is why we are moved by the reborn Scrooge's childlike exultation in his prosaic physical surroundings, by his glee at still having time to give and share. We too can exult in "Golden sunlight; Heavenly sky; sweet fresh air; merry bells"; we too can cry, "Oh, glorious. Glorious!"; we too can give and share.[16] Scrooge assures us that we can advance from the prison of self to the paradise of community. The *Carol*'s fairy-tale structure helps in that assurance. The structure evokes and objectifies the undefiled world of childhood and makes us feel that we, like Scrooge, can recapture it. Deep symbolic identifications such as these, identifications that stir us whether we are consciously aware of them or not, give *A Christmas Carol* its enduring grip on our culture. *A Christmas Carol* is a myth or fairy tale for our times, one that is still full of life and relevance. Its yearly resurrection in advertisement, cartoon, and television program, its reappearance in new versions (in Bergman's *Wild Strawberries,* to cite only one instance), testify to this.

Yet the vitality of *A Christmas Carol* raises other questions. Why is the *Carol,* which elaborates the central idea found in the Gabriel Grub story in *Pickwick,* so much better than its prototype? "Gabriel Grub" does not elicit the empathy of the *Carol.* This is so because Gabriel never ascends to universality; he is simply a mean man who is taught an idiosyncratic lesson. We see nothing of his childhood, of his development, of his future; we see nothing, in other words, of the shaping forces that would allow us to relate to his experiences. The story centers on his drunken vision; it scants his salvation and our enlightenment. Furthermore, "Gabriel Grub" lacks any rich social import. Unlike the *Carol,* there is virtually no intertwining of plot with social criticism: no ideas about ignorance and want, no anatomy of materialism, no criticism of relations between employer and employee, no effective demonstration of how to live. Misanthropy is simply presented and then punished. I am not suggesting that a work of art must have a social message. I am simply affirming that part of the *Carol*'s appeal comes from its powerful demonstration of how a man should live—live in society—if he is to save his soul, a kind of demonstration that is largely lacking in "Gabriel Grub."

By the same token, the supernatural machinery of "Gabriel Grub," despite successful local effects, is mechanical and abrupt. Unlike the *Carol,* where Marley's ghost is the culmination of many signs and actions, in "Gabriel Grub" the King of the Goblins appears with little preparation; again, unlike the *Carol,* where Marley's ghost is a prototype of Scrooge, and therefore deeply significant, in "Gabriel Grub" the King of the Goblins is simply an agency, a convenient manipulative device, a creature who has no relevance to Gabriel's life and habits (other, perhaps, than being an emanation of Gabriel's habitual drunkenness). Even the *Carol* equivalents to the King of the Goblins, the three spirits, have an allegorical pertinence that the King of the Goblins lacks. In part these differences in the two stories are owing to differences in length, but more importantly they are owing to differences in conception and execution. Obviously the preeminence of the *Carol,* its elevation to culture fable, comes not from the basic ingredients—they can be found in "Gabriel Grub"—but from the perfect blending of well-wrought theme and well-wrought form. *A Christmas Carol* demonstrates how much more skilled Dickens had become in using fairy-tale conceptions to achieve that virtuoso blending, how adept he had become in using fairy-tale elements to integrate and convey his view of life.

A Christmas Carol is the best of the Christmas books, but it is not superior to the other Christmas books in all respects, and it is not always the most technically advanced. The second Christmas book, *The Chimes,* uses a more realistic, yet at the same time more imaginative, supernatural agency to guide the fairy-tale workings of the story—no convenient *Carol* ghosts here. In *The Chimes* the vibrations of the bells slowly take on magical qualities and superintend what takes place. The transformation of the bells into allegorical forces is done most elegantly. Dickens combines compelling exactitude and wonderful fancifulness. As in *Chuzzlewit,* the story opens with a personification of the wind, this time of a winter wind moaning and wailing through a London church at night. The wind sighs through aisle, vault, and altar, and it howls dismally in the steeple belfry where dwell the chimes that are the subject of the story. The personification of the wind is masterfully done—its airy presence is elaborately evocative and eerily powerful—but each figure and trope is rooted in a most meticulous realism.

The wind buffets and engulfs the church, and near the entrance to the church, in good weather and in foul, a poverty-stricken old ticket porter, Toby (or "Trotty") Veck, takes his stand. All day long he hears the bells chime, and all night too, for he lives hard by with his daughter, Meg. From his stand at the base of the tower, he often looks up at the bells as they chime, wonders how they are lodged, how cared for, and how rung. Trotty and the bells are much alike—the narrator draws a long analogy identifying the two.[17] Indeed over the years Trotty has grown to love the bells and to commune with them. He invests them with special powers; they are his friends, sometimes they talk to him.[18] Often the chimes seem to echo his thoughts, repeating and repeating some hope or fear in concise and cadenced measure.[19] All this is developed slowly and carefully so that realism, psychology, and fancifulness blend and reinforce one another.

As Dickens creates this aura, he also unfolds the story. The story takes place on the last day of the year. Trotty, at his chill post at the entrance to the church, is visited by his daughter, Meg, and her fiancé, Richard. Owing to their poverty, Meg and Richard have postponed their marriage for three years, but life is slipping past them, and now they want to marry on New Year's Day. As the old ticket porter and the young couple stand near the church door talking, they are confronted by three gentlemen who hold three commonplace attitudes toward the poor. Alderman Cute believes in putting the poor down; a red-faced gentleman recommends forcing them back to the "good old times"; and Mr. Filer treats them as lifeless columns of charts, averages, and statistics. Later in the afternoon Trotty meets a fourth gentleman, Sir Joseph Bowley, "The Poor Man's Friend and Father." This gentleman advocates a fourth attitude toward the poor. He requires that the poor be subservient and behave like dutiful children. The statements and actions of these four gentlemen, the newspaper reports Trotty has read concerning the crimes and atrocities of the poor, and his own grinding poverty cause him to feel that the poor are born bad, that they have no useful role to play in society, that they should not marry and multiply, and that they are better off dead.

That night at home, while Trotty is reading additional newspaper accounts of the depravities of the poor, the chimes ring out. They have been talking to Trotty all the day. Now they seem to call him, and they seem to echo his despair. The bells clang and clamor. They seem to say, "Haunt and hunt him, haunt and hunt him, Drag him to us, drag him to us!"[20] The bells clash and peal, louder and louder. Trotty feels pulled toward them. Partly as a result of that pull, partly because they seem so unusually loud, Trotty decides to see whether the bell-tower door is open. When he comes to the church he is astonished to find that the tower door is indeed open. He goes in to investigate and accidentally shuts the door, locking himself in. He begins to climb the tower, going round and round, up and up, encountering mysterious objects, hearing mysterious echoes. He finally feels a freshening and then a wind as he gropes toward the belfry. Now he is in the belfry. He can see the housetops and chimneys below him; he can see the tangled quarters in which he lives; he can see the dim lights in the distance, obscured and blurred by dark mists. He accidentally touches a bell rope, and then, as though "working out the spell upon him," he feels impelled to ascend the steep ladders toward the bells.[21] Finally, he reaches them. He can just faintly make out "their great shapes in the gloom . . . Shadowy, and dark, and dumb."[22] A heavy sense of loneliness and dread falls upon him as he climbs into this "airy nest of stone and metal."[23] His head spins. He calls out, "Halloa," hears the sound mournfully protracted by the echoes, and giddy and confused, sinks into a swoon.[24] At this point the second quarter of *The Chimes* ends.

It is only with the beginning of the third quarter—more than half way through the book—that the supernatural machinery of *The Chimes* takes over, a culmination that has been carefully prepared for by the slow accumulation of enchantment and by the events of the day. Trotty's swooning consciousness is now filled with dwarf creatures— phantoms, spirits, and elves—and with the jumbled thoughts and events of the last few hours. The tiny creatures cluster about him and also swarm through the surrounding city, attending all the actions and thoughts of the teeming multitudes who live nearby. Some of the phantoms are ugly, some handsome; some large, some small; some old, some young; some beat those they attend, some comfort them with music. They swarm about all the activities of life and death, filling the air and the habitations of men with restless and untiring motion. One becomes aware after a while that these tiny forms are creatures of the bells, and that they swarm through air and earth whenever the bells begin to chime. Trotty's "charmed footsteps" brought him to the belfry, but the airy elves proclaim their own identity. There is no mistaking that identity. Dickens personifies and allegorizes the vibrating bells with wonderful skill:

> As he gazed, the Chimes stopped. Instantaneous change! The whole swarm [of tiny creatures] fainted! their forms collapsed, their speed deserted them; they sought to fly, but in the act of falling died and melted into air. No fresh supply succeeded them. One straggler leaped down pretty briskly from the surface of the Great Bell, and alighted on his feet, but he was dead and gone before he could turn round. Some few of the late company who had gambolled in the tower, remained there, spinning over and over a little longer; but these became at every turn more faint, and few, and feeble, and soon went the way of the rest. The last of all was one small hunchback, who had got into an echoing corner, where he twirled and twirled, and floated by himself a long time; showing such perseverance, that at last he dwindled to a leg and even to a foot, before he finally retired; but he vanished in the end, and then the tower was silent.[25]

At this point Trotty dimly perceives in each bell a bearded figure of the bulk and stature of the bell, at once "a figure and the Bell itself."[26] Dickens develops these bell figures with rich and evocative symbolism. Mysterious and awful, they rest on nothing, their draped and hooded heads merged in the dim roof, their muffled hands upon their goblin mouths. They are hemmed about "in a very forest of hewn timber; from the entanglements, intricacies, and depths of which, as from among the boughs of a dead wood blighted for their phantom use, they kept their darksome and unwinking watch."[27] These figures are the goblins of the bells—the subtitle of *The Chimes* is *A Goblin Story of Some Bells that Rang an Old Year Out and a New Year In*. Once the bell goblins are delineated, the masque begins. As great blasts of air come moaning through the tower and then die away, the Great Bell, its voice low and deep, but sounding with the other bells as well, begins to speak.

Trotty has come to the nest of time; the voice of the bells is the voice of time. Time now takes Trotty and shows him what the future holds in store if the pernicious doctrines he has heard that day are allowed to generate their deadly spawn. As in *A Christmas Carol,* Trotty's enlightenment is effected by being swiftly conveyed through space and time and shown vignettes that embody these lessons—vignettes that depict the harrowing destruction of Meg, Richard, and the suffering hosts of the poor, vignettes that shadow forth the final fiery death of the society that mandates such wanton perishings.

The development of *The Chimes* up to the vignettes is spare and masterful. The conception of time as the didactic agency and its embodiment in the bells is much more functional and imaginative than the three spirits of *A Christmas Carol* and is much better integrated into the realistic texture of the story. But the vignettes themselves are often feverish and overdrawn, sometimes mawkish, sometimes touched with inflated rhetoric. As a consequence, the latter portions of *The Chimes* often dwindle into tractlike preaching and excess. This tendency is not surprising. Dickens regarded the Christmas books as vehicles for social teaching. He felt that at the Christmas season men's hearts were softened and receptive. At that time, by invoking the spirit of Christmas and utilizing the magic of fairy stories, by bringing his readers through such means closer to their childhood innocence and openness, he could steal into their hearts and move them to change. In *The Chimes* he hoped to strike "a great blow for the poor"—an end he had had in mind for several years.[28] This desire to strike heavily and decisively caused him to overdraw the last two quarters of the story. He literally abandoned himself to the writing. He was seized each day by "regular, ferocious excitement," and he blazed away "wrathful and red-hot" until deep in the afternoon.[29] The story, he confessed, "has great possession of me every moment in the day; and drags me where it will."[30] It often dragged him too far. *The Chimes,* despite many sections of memorable writing, lacks the mythlike universality of *A Christmas Carol*. It is too caught up in local wrongs and local satire to speak out engrossingly to later generations. It is a tract for the times, not a fable for posterity.

In his next Christmas book, *The Cricket on the Hearth: A Fairy Tale of Home,* Dickens is neither so urgent nor so insistent, but the work sinks under other difficulties. *The Cricket* is compounded of hackneyed plot contrivances and sentimental tableaus: mysterious strangers, miserly old lechers, heart-of-oak laborers, coyly fluttering heroines, mistaken conclusions, transparent disguises, and unbelievable transformations. The story is a celebration of home—a fairy tale of home, as the subtitle has it—a celebration of trust, forbearing love, and simple domestic joys. For the most part these virtues (and the actions that convey them) are mechanically asserted and superficially manipulated; one rarely gets the feeling that Dickens' deepest energies are involved. It is not that he disbelieves in the virtues he is espousing, it is that the demonstration fails to fire his imagination. Yet there are exceptions to this generalization. The dog, Boxer, the toys created by Caleb Plummer, the antics of Tilly Slowboy—these and other touches flare into intermittent life.

There is also a more important imaginative conception that lives— and lives more steadily. This is the fairy-tale accompaniment, the magical song of the cricket. Yet this accompaniment exists primarily outside the main narrative. The magical chord sounds powerfully at the opening, reverberates strongly again when John Peerybingle sits through the night and contemplates murder, and then echoes briefly at the end. There are storybook elements elsewhere in the novelette, of course. I have already mentioned some of the folklore motifs and folklore characters that work lifelessly at the center of the story. There are occasional fairy-tale allusions and stylistic touches as well. Here, for example, is how the second section begins: "Caleb Plummer and his Blind Daughter lived all alone by themselves, as the Story-books say—and my blessing, with yours to back it I hope, on the Story-books, for saying anything in this workaday world!—Caleb Plummer and his Blind Daughter lived all alone by themselves, in a little cracked nutshell of a wooden house."[31] This entrée forms a fitting opening for the strange storybook world the toymaker and his daughter live in and for the enchanted web of illusions the toymaker has spun round his blind child.

But the primary fairy-tale energy of the story is with the cricket, and to a lesser extent, with the kettle. These two commonplace adjuncts of hearth and home open the story; their music slowly fills the cottage fireside of John Peerybingle. In a long, intricate tour de force, Dickens brilliantly animates the humble kettle and lowly cricket, until their hum and chirp embody all the attributes of a happy home. That two-voiced sound, reassuring and irresistible, transformed into the essence of home, finally beams out into the world. Eventually "the kettle and the Cricket, at one and the same moment, and by some power of amalgamation best known to themselves, sent, each, his fireside song of comfort streaming into a ray of the candle that shone out through the window, and a long way down the lane. And this light, bursting on a certain person who, on the instant, approached towards it through the gloom, expressed the whole thing to him, literally in a twinkling, and cried, 'Welcome home, old fellow! Welcome home, my boy!' "[32] The cricket soon becomes the very embodiment of the Peerybingle household, a spirit whose chirp can incorporate and summon up all the succoring powers vested in that loving home. The cricket on the hearth of John Peerybingle's house—the narrator soon tells us this outright—is the "Genius of his Hearth and Home."[33] As the cricket chirps upon the hearth, its familiar song evokes memories, reveries, and dreams in those who hear its music. Transformed by such associations, the comforting song of the cricket gradually assumes a fairy shape, enters the room in that form as well, and mingles its beneficent powers with the thoughts and yearnings of those who dwell within its circling sound. By such means (only suggested here in barest outline) Dickens translates the chirping cricket into a supernatural power while yet retaining its ordinary reality.

The cricket is much less of an active agent than the three spirits of *A Christmas Carol* or the bells of *The Chimes*. The cricket never plucks John Peerybingle out of his home and transports him bodily through space and time. The chirp of the cricket (and the spirit that chirp represents) quiets, softens, and comforts. The fairy cricket that helps John Peerybingle survive his night of anguish and fury, and the saving visions that come to him under the influence of the cricket, are less the intrusions of a supernatural force than the symbolic representation (incarnated in the cricket and its spirit) of the saving power of memory and love—this power objectified in the specific scenes and actions that John Peerybingle remembers or projects as he muses under the influence of the cricket, that is, under the influence of hearth and home. In other words, the cricket (hearth and home) helps John Peerybingle save himself. On the one hand the cricket plays much less of an interventionary role than its earlier counterparts, on the other hand its role is more domesticated and psychological.

Dickens seems to have been discontented with the overt fairy-tale machinery of his Christmas books. The intrusive ghosts and spirits of the *Carol* had given way to the carefully generated bell goblins of *The Chimes*, which in turn had yielded to the more domesticated (and limited) crickets and kettles of *The Cricket on the Hearth*. In the next Christmas book, *The Battle of Life*, he dispensed with supernatural machinery altogether. *The Battle* is not only the least typical of the Christmas books but the least successful. Dickens came close to abandoning the work, and he was several times on the verge of breakdown. In part this was owing to overwork, to concurrently beginning a twenty-part novel, but more basically it was owing to the intractability of the material.

In many respects the *donnée* of *The Battle* deserved development in a full-length novel. *The Battle of Life* focuses on an attractive wastrel, Michael Warden, who is in love with an angelic woman, Marion Jeddler, a woman he is debarred from marrying. This theme of an appealing but unworthy man longing for a seraphic woman he cannot or should not have (Dickens returned to the theme in *A Tale of Two Cities*), requires, if it is to have any depth at all, careful development and analysis—a kind of anatomy all but ruled out in a brief Christmas book, especially a Christmas book shorn of its supernatural machinery. Without the storybook machinery to manipulate and foreshorten the theme, satisfactory elaboration was impossible. Dickens soon came to see this. "I have written nearly a third of [*The Battle of Life*]," he said. "It promises to be pretty; quite a new idea in the story, I hope; but to manage it without the supernatural agency now impossible of introduction, and yet to move it naturally within the required space, or with any shorter limit than a *Vicar of Wakefield*, I find to be a difficulty so perplexing . . . that I am fearful of wearing myself out if I go on."[34] Dickens, of course, did go on. The result is a savagely reduced work that sometimes reads like a scenario, sometimes like a breathless outline, and that lacks compelling life.

With *The Haunted Man,* the last of the Christmas books, Dickens turned back to his storybook format. In some respects he also turned back to the *Carol*. Like Scrooge, the protagonist of *The Haunted Man* must learn to live with his past if he is also to live in the present and the future. But the two works show marked differences in emphasis and technique. In *The Haunted Man* Dickens set out, in a much more self-conscious way than in the *Carol,* to unite psychological, social, and allegorical truth in a single realistic fairy-tale conception.

The Haunted Man tells the story of Mr. Redlaw, a learned and benevolent professor of chemistry who is appalled by the misery he sees about him. His own life has been filled with death, betrayal, and unfulfilled love, and he longs to blot out these memories that darken his daily existence. But his mind is confused and divided. Although he yearns to escape from painful memories, he broods over the past. One Christmas Eve as he sits before his fire haunted by sad recollections, that part of his mind which desires to suppress memory takes on corporeal being as a phantom mirror image of himself. The phantom presses its arguments powerfully and wins Redlaw to its point of view. Redlaw will forget, he will have surcease from feeling, but he will retain his learning and acuteness. But the gift, as so often in fairy stories, contains an additional feature: his forgetfulness will be transmitted to those he meets. Redlaw soon discovers that his gift is a curse. For in forgetting past sorrow and feeling, he has, like Scrooge, destroyed all that is softening and human in life. Despite his learning and benevolence, he has failed to grasp a simple, oft-repeated Romantic axiom (celebrated in such different works as Keats' "Ode on Melancholy" and Emerson's "Compensation") which states that suffering and joy, decay and beauty, loss and achievement are so intertwined that banishing one banishes the other. The unhappy multitudes whose misery he had hoped to relieve by his gift are not relieved. As he goes among them he produces discord; he destroys the knot of affection and forbearance that is the saving grace of their hard lives. Only two creatures take no infection from his approach. One, a street waif, remains unchanged because his bestial life has known no human feeling and so can know no loss. The other, Milly, the wife of one of Redlaw's servants, is love and goodness incarnate, and thus proof against his curse. His experiences teach him his error, and with the help of Milly, he redeems himself and removes the blight from those he has cursed.

The debt of *The Haunted Man* to fairy tales is pervasive. The full title of the story is *The Haunted Man and the Ghost's Bargain. A Fancy for Christmas-Time*. This spectral title is reinforced by the pictorial frontispiece and the pictorial title page that stand opposite one another and introduce the volume. The frontispiece (all illustrations were suggested and approved by Dickens) features Redlaw's ghostly alter ego whispering in his ear while devils, demons, and goblins contend with radiant angels. The title page depicts a bright angel and a dark, hooded phantom leading a child in different directions. These supernatural and allegorical associations are echoed in the title of the first chapter, "The Gift Bestowed." This title awakens additional fairy-tale associations, associations underlined by the other two chapter headings: "The Gift Diffused" and "The Gift Reversed." These storybook suggestions are further reinforced by the woodcut illustration that appears on the first page and that depicts, wreathed above giant shadows and looming forms, scenes from *The Arabian Nights, The Tales of the Genii,* and *Cinderella.* These graphic allusions mirror the text, for fairy tales and childhood storybooks, and in particular some of Dickens' favorite childhood storybooks, play a role in *The Haunted Man. The Arabian Nights, The Tales of the Genii, Jack the Giant Killer,* Dr. Watts' *Divine Songs,* and *The Children in the Wood* are all worked into the story. *The Children in the Wood,* as a matter of fact, is one of the tales that helps comfort and sustain the Tetterbys. It

is also an index of their moral state. Like Scrooge, who is cold and
flinty when he has forgotten such old companions as *The Arabian
Nights, Valentine and Orson,* and *Robinson Crusoe,* and who is softened when he is made to remember them, the Tetterbys are harsh and
hostile when they cannot respond to *The Children in the Wood,* loving
and forbearing when they can.[35]

Many other allusions, graphic and literary, and many additional
touches contribute to the magical atmosphere of *The Haunted Man,*
but these features, important as they are, only serve to reinforce the
more central fairy-tale resonances of the story, the witching chords of
character and setting. Redlaw's home is a good example. It is an
enchanted castle, a group of moldering medieval college buildings
standing in the midst of the bustling city and wrapped in a gloomy
atmosphere of murky shadows and muffled shapes. His home reminds
one of a witch's castle. It was always "thundering with echoes when a
distant voice was raised or a door was shut,—echoes, not confined to
the many low passages and empty rooms, but rumbling and grumbling
till they were stifled in the heavy air."[36] With descriptions such as this,
and with scores of evocative suggestions and directive touches through
all the early pages, Dickens intensifies his ghostly mood, until he
creates an atmosphere in which the supernatural and the realistic
mingle and then combine. Here, a few lines later, is Redlaw as he sits
before the fire at the moment his Christmas Eve adventures begin:

> You should have seen him in his dwelling about twilight, in the dead
> winter time.
> When the wind was blowing, shrill and shrewd, with the going down of
> the blurred sun. When it was just so dark, as that the forms of things were
> indistinct and big—but not wholly lost. When sitters by the fire began to
> see wild faces and figures, mountains and abysses, ambuscades, and ar-
> mies, in the coals.[37]

In this thickening twilight strange things happen. Shadows close in
and gather like "mustering swarms of ghosts."[38] Then nurses turn into
ogresses, rocking horses into monsters, hearth-tongs into straddling
giants, and children, "half-scared and half-amused," into strangers to
themselves.[39] The images and the associations these suggestions
arouse are wonderfully appropriate, for they are compounded out of
childhood fears and childhood fantasies—one thinks of Dickens listening to Mary Weller—but leavened now by adult insight and knowledge.

Redlaw partakes of this ambiance. He is another metamorphosis of a
figure familiar in Dickens, the misanthropic witchlike sorcerer. Redlaw's witchlike appearance, his "hollow cheek . . . sunken brilliant eye
. . . black attired figure . . . grizzled hair hanging, like tangled seaweed, about his face"; his witchlike traffic with phantoms and the

secrets of nature (for he is a most learned chemist); and his witchlike ability to cast potent spells (he transmits as well as receives the gift)—all these mark him as the evil enchanter of fairy lore.[40] Yet like many of Dickens' witches and warlocks, like old Martin and Scrooge, for example, he is not entirely evil, he is a good human being in disguise or gone astray, he can be redeemed. And Milly, like her prototype, little Nell, in *The Old Curiosity Shop,* is the fairy princess, an embodiment of perfect goodness who will magically effect Redlaw's salvation. In *The Haunted Man* the Quilplike character who is evil incarnate (to continue the parallel with *The Old Curiosity Shop*) has undergone the greatest change. The beastlike incarnation of evil is now combined with the abandoned waif and becomes the beast-waif. Both the waif and the beast-waif are portentous characters whose origins go back to Dickens' own childhood, to his blacking-warehouse abandonment and street lounging, and both characters appear in his writings in countless permutations. In *A Christmas Carol* the chief embodiment of the waif, Tiny Tim, had appeared primarily in the image of Oliver, Smike, and little Nell, that is, as an innocent child condemned to unjust suffering. The more sinister personification of evil, the beast-waif, had emerged only in passing. This more malignant figure had been doubled in *A Christmas Carol,* but had entered the story only momentarily as the allegorical children Ignorance and Want, two demonstrations dragged into the fable as exhibits rather than actors. In *The Haunted Man* the very real beast-waif—"a baby savage, a young monster, a child who . . . would live and perish a mere beast"—has an active role in the story and becomes a central symbol not merely of nascent evil, but of society's guilt in producing evil.[41] Continuing the process begun in the other Christmas books, Dickens' recurrent fairy-tale figures—the excrescential or allegorical beast-waifs and ghosts, the more functional bell goblins and chirping crickets—are taking on an enlarged significance, and though retaining their fairy-tale origins, are becoming more closely linked with contemporary life, realistic psychology, and thematic motifs.

In *The Haunted Man* Dickens uses many additional devices commonly found in fairy stories. He uses portentous repetition, for instance, to enhance the tale's atmosphere of enchantment and to unify the work. The words of the phantom's gift-curse—"The gift that I have given, you shall give again, go where you will"—are repeated throughout the story and intensify this unity and enchantment. Redlaw soon discovers that "blowing in the wind, falling with the snow, drifting with the clouds, shining in the moonlight, and heavily looming in the darkness, were the Phantom's words, 'The gift that I have given, you shall give again, go where you will!' "[42] The repetition of the curse becomes, in storybook fashion, a magical refrain that gathers suspense until its climax and reversal when the curse-refrain is replaced by its opposite, a refrain that has been developed contrapuntally throughout the story: "Lord keep my memory green." But it is more than the fairy-tale curse, it is the imagery of Redlaw's loss associated with the curse—imagery connected with his new insensitivity to nature, time, and music—that is repeated. This repetition gradually swells into a leitmotif and sounds the knell of Redlaw's loss; the loss, in turn, through repetition and association, becomes incorporated into the curse. What Redlaw sees in nature, for example, in the blowing wind, the falling snow, the drifting clouds, the shining moonlight, is not an evocation of wildness and beauty, an experience full of associations that can quicken and comfort him, but mere physical fact. This is part of Redlaw's deprivation. He sees the curse in the blowing wind, the falling snow, and the other manifestations of nature, because the curse is an objectification of his inability to respond, an objectification of his longed-for inurement to feeling. Like Coleridge, Redlaw the analytical chemist can see, not feel, how beautiful the world is. Through such repetitions, linkings, and associations, Dickens gradually makes the curse embody Redlaw's grievous sin and loss.

There are other storybook elements in the curse. Each time the curse is transmitted, the recipient signifies his infection by a telltale action: "the wandering hand upon the forehead."[43] These and similar repetitions (which are frequently joined with one another) become increasingly magical and ritualistic, as in the following pattern of reiterations: "Three times, in their progress [Redlaw and the beast-waif] were side by side. Three times they stopped, being side by side. Three times the Chemist glanced down at [the beast-waif's] face, and shuddered as it forced upon him one reflection."[44] The dovetailing of such incantations and repetitions with their many analogues interconnects their meanings. For example, Dickens links the Redlaw–beast-waif walk and its three pauses (labeling them "first," "second," and "third") with images of memory, night, moonlight, and music—images he had been reiterating throughout the story by means of the poetic leitmotif associated with Redlaw's curse.[45] The leitmotif is coordinate with the curse, but it is more lyrical, connotative, and musical. It is another form of repetition and incantation—a linguistic extension of Dickens' fairy-tale recurrences—and it offers Dickens another means of sounding the keynote. Once this leitmotif and its many associations are established, Dickens is able, by means of the leitmotif (as well as by means of the curse), to call up Redlaw's loss with great economy and centripetal effect.

Paralleling and intermingling with the fairy-tale level of *The Haunted Man* is an allegorical level that underlines Dickens' message. Dickens was perfectly aware of the allegorical nature of what he had written. In the penultimate paragraph of *The Haunted Man* he has the narrator point to the possibility of such an interpretation: "Some people have said since, that [Redlaw] only thought what has been herein set down; others, that he read it in the fire, one winter night about the twilight time; others, that the Ghost was but the representation of his own gloomy thoughts, and Milly the embodiment of his better wisdom. *I* say nothing." Dickens, through the narrator, was suggesting various modes of interpreting his story but very properly endorsing no single mode. Yet any reader who failed to make use of each of his suggestions would miss part of what he was saying.

The allegory of *The Haunted Man* is designed to enforce the message which the other levels develop—that good and evil are intertwined, that memories and feelings associate pain and joy, and that such associations can be dissolved only at the expense of that which makes one human. Redlaw, before he is given the gift, is man in his suffering but human condition; after the gift, he is man as a mere analytical chemist, man as an arid, dehumanized husk. The phantom is that portion of Redlaw's mind which longs for surcease from feeling and tempts him to an attitude toward himself and his fellows that will produce such surcease. The gift is the symbolic result of Redlaw's assent to these promptings of his mind; it is the effect on himself and others of acquiescing in such a philosophy. Milly stands for love, and the softening, saving influence of love. The beast-waif represents two things: first, human nature bereft of feeling and sympathy, that is, human nature completely dehumanized, human nature that displays the end result of Redlaw's foolish yearnings; and second, the evil and guilt of a society that produces creatures such as the beast-waif.

The allegory of character is intensified by the allegory of setting. The worn-out leftovers of Mr. Tetterby's defunct business are ever-present tokens of his ineffectual personality; the tortuous slum Redlaw visits mirrors the twisted lives he finds within. But the chief backdrop for the action—Redlaw's college chambers—is the most revealing of the settings. The fortress in which he lives is a fitting representation of his mind. And when his mind changes, sympathetic, almost magical transformations also occur in his frost-bound home. When he allows love to reenter his heart, his dungeon and heart reawaken alike: "Some blind groping of the morning made its way down into the forgotten crypt so cold and earthy . . . and stirred the dull deep sap in the lazy vegetation hanging to the walls, and quickened the slow principle of life within the little world of wonderful and delicate creation which existed there, with some faint knowledge that the sun was up."[46]

The allegory becomes most intense toward the end of the second chapter. Redlaw visits the slums with the beast-waif. During that visit he goes through all the experiences necessary to teach him the significance of his error. Upon his return he locks himself and the beast-waif into his lonely rooms and broods despairingly. After an interval, Milly knocks on Redlaw's door. "Pray, sir, let me in!" she cries.[47] Symbolically love is knocking at the locked chambers of Redlaw's heart and asking to be let in. "No! not for the world!" is his ironic answer. The beast-waif, who has been fed and tended by Milly, cries out, "Let me go to her, will you?" (The evil that society has produced will respond to love, cries out for love.) Milly, not knowing Redlaw is the cause, tells him of the disasters his slum visit has brought. "Pray, sir, let me in," she repeats. Redlaw is horrified, contrite, anguished, but his heart is still frozen; he cannot really feel or remember, he is not yet ready to let love enter. "Pray, sir, let me in!" cries Milly, but Redlaw answers, "No! No! No!" and restrains the beast-waif "who was half-mad to pass him, and let her in." Redlaw prays to his phantom alter ego for relief, vows not to taint Milly with his curse, and, thus refusing to confront love, stands in an agony of guilt before the door he himself has locked. The phantom does not answer Redlaw's prayer. "The only reply still was, the boy struggling to get to her, while he held him back; and the cry, increasing in its energy . . . 'pray, pray, let me in!' "[48]

With these words the second chapter ends. Dickens' method is effective and sophisticated. It reminds one of Hawthorne's technique, of those portions of *The Scarlet Letter* or "Rappaccini's Daughter" in which the central allegory shades into subtle and varied suggestiveness. But that suggestiveness has other components than those so far discussed. For when Redlaw calls out to his fairy-tale phantom and hears Milly's allegorical plea, he is also acting out a psychological drama that has parallels in Dickens' life.

The third concurrent level of Redlaw's story—the psychological (and in this case the autobiographical)—appears in *The Haunted Man* from the beginning. Dickens makes it easy for the reader to regard the phantom as the representation of Redlaw's "gloomy thoughts." The phantom materializes only after many directive signs, which can be explained as natural or supernatural, have heralded its appearance. These manifestations come in conjunction with Redlaw's internal debating and self-absorption. Consequently, when the signs coalesce and then develop into the full-fledged phantom, the reader is ready to accept the apparition as another part of the storybook atmosphere, and as an appropriate representation of one portion of Redlaw's mind. Once the latter notion is established, the story becomes, like the story of murder-bent Jonas Chuzzlewit's two selves, a study of psychological strife. But here the technique is different from that used in *Chuzzlewit*. In *The Haunted Man* the conflict is depicted by utilizing the method

Tennyson used in "The Two Voices"; Redlaw's divided mind is engaged in a dialogue with itself:

> "If I could forget my sorrow and wrong, I would," the Ghost repeated.
> . . .
> "Evil spirit of myself," returned the haunted man . . . "my life is darkened by that incessant whisper."
> "It is an echo," said the Phantom.
> "If it be an echo of my thoughts . . . why should I, therefore, be tormented? . . . Who would not forget their sorrows and their wrongs?"
> "Who would not, truly, and be the happier and better for it?" said the Phantom. . . .
> "Tempter," answered Redlaw . . . "I hear again an echo of my own mind."[49]

The Haunted Man was written under special stress. In the summer of 1848, while Dickens was planning to complete his long-postponed Christmas book, his sister Fanny lay dying wretchedly of consumption. Dickens visited her often during that summer. As he looked upon her gaunt body and grieved over her early decay, his mind kept turning to the days when he and she had been children together.[50] Fanny died on 2 September, and a month or so later Dickens sat down to finish *The Haunted Man. The Haunted Man* is a dirge to memory. It probes the deep dissatisfactions that had been stirred up and intensified by his sister's death. It also shadows forth an image of Dickens. Redlaw reminds us of Dickens. Like Redlaw, Dickens worked in his "inner chamber, part library and part laboratory"; like Redlaw, he was revered and famous; like Redlaw, he was a teacher upon whose words and works "a crowd of aspiring ears and eyes hung daily"; like Redlaw, he was surrounded by "a crowd of spectral shapes"; like Redlaw, he had the power "to uncombine" those phantoms and make them "give back their component parts"; like Redlaw, he would sit in his study "moving his thin mouth as if in speech, but silent as the dead."[51]

However, it is Redlaw's confrontation with his darker self that produces the most striking parallels. Through Redlaw and Redlaw's specter, Dickens summons up the shaping events of his own past:

> "Look upon me!" said the Spectre. "I am he, neglected in my youth, and miserably poor, who strove and suffered, and still strove and suffered, until I hewed out knowledge from the mine where it was buried, and made rugged steps thereof, for my worn feet to rest and rise on."
> "I *am* that man," returned the Chemist.
> "No mother's self-denying love," pursued the Phantom, "no father's counsel, aided *me*. A stranger came into my father's place when I was but a child, and I was easily an alien from my mother's heart. My parents, at

the best, were of that sort whose care soon ends, and whose duty is soon
done; who cast their offspring loose, early, as birds do theirs; and, if they
do well, claim the merit; and, if ill, the pity."

.   .   .   .

"I had a sister" [the Phantom went on]. . . . "Such glimpses of the light of
home as I had ever known, had streamed from her. How young she was,
how fair, how loving! I took her to the first poor roof that I was master of,
and made it rich. She came into the darkness of my life, and made it
bright."[52]

But this felicity does not last. Redlaw's most trusted friend betrays
his sister and steals his fiancée. In the wake of this double catastrophe
only one thing survives, or seems to survive—jilted sister cleaves to
jilted brother.

"My sister" [continued the Phantom], "doubly dear, doubly devoted,
doubly cheerful in my home, lived on to see me famous, and my old
ambition so rewarded when its spring was broken, and then—"
"Then died," [Redlaw] interposed. "Died, gentle as ever, happy, and
with no concern but for her brother."[53]

Redlaw cannot forget. He constantly chants his litany of woe. His
words toll the knell of his (and Dickens') complaint: "Early unhappiness, a wound from a hand I loved and trusted, and a loss that nothing
can replace." These old grievances haunt and torment Redlaw.
"Thus," he continues, "I prey upon myself. Thus, memory is my
curse; and, if I could forget my sorrow and my wrong, I would!"[54]

Yet it is not the autobiography or the message that makes *The
Haunted Man* notable, it is the fairy-tale technique, or rather the
refinement and integration of a constellation of fairy-tale techniques.
These techniques help Dickens manipulate and interweave the various
strands of his story—the social, allegorical, psychological, and
fanciful—and make them part of a harmonious pattern.

The Haunted Man has other distinctions. It surpasses the earlier
Christmas books in its self-conscious use of repetition, recurrence, and
leitmotif. It also surpasses those works in its sophisticated fusion of
realism, psychology, and allegory. All these elements are used in *The
Haunted Man* to enforce the theme, and all are used to interrelate and
unify. In this centripetal movement the fairy story dominates. It serves
as subject matter, catalyst, and vehicle. The fairy tale enables Dickens
to achieve his special goal. For the mood Dickens sets at the opening,
the supernatural devices he uses to unify his plot and emphasize his
message, and the fablelike quality he gives to what he is saying prepare
the reader for the apocalyptic truth he is trying to convey—a truth in
which simple realism, ordinary events, and humdrum detail are less

important than a heightened, extrareal vision of life that quickens one's perception of the very reality it transcends.

Yet *The Haunted Man,* despite technical advances, powerful scenes, and memorable characters, fails and fades, especially in "The Gift Reversed." Milly, for one thing, is too angelic and too inanely self-congratulatory (a sort of Esther Summerson at her worst), and she is used, in the last chapter, as a mere agency for removing the curse. Furthermore, the last chapter is so clogged and tangled with melodramatic coincidences that it becomes huddled and implausible. Dickens digs up lost relations, rewards suffering fiancées, and rehabilitates suicidal derelicts. The earlier fusion of realism, psychology, and fantasy is sacrificed for the convenience of a neat winding up in the old wrenching storybook manner, and the violence done to everything but the fable reduces the effectiveness of the fable itself.

The preeminence of *A Christmas Carol* when compared to its counterparts can lead one to believe that the subsequent Christmas books represent a falling off, an effort by Dickens to repeat the *Carol* formula with imperfect success. But this is to neglect what Dickens attempted in his Christmas books and what he learned from them. After the *Carol,* Dickens tried to locate the overt fairy-tale machinery in the more ordinary surroundings and experiences of life, in chimes, crickets, kettles, and divided minds. He attempted to emphasize the reality of these agencies, and he sought to distill his supernatural effects from that carefully nurtured reality—from vibrations, chirpings, and brooding questionings. He also began to reduce the overt fairy-tale machinery, to subject less of the story to its immediate control. The supernatural machinery, though carefully prepared for, enters *The Chimes* only at the middle. The artful storybook presences of *The Cricket,* subdued now in their supernatural attributes, emerge tactfully at the beginning and tactfully at the middle. In these later works, Dickens apparently wanted to retain the unified impact and fablelike quality of the *Carol* but to do so with an ever more dominant realism, or rather with a realism that would retain its ordinary truthfulness to life while revealing life's magic and interconnectedness. With *The Battle of Life,* he dispensed with the supernatural machinery altogether, but saddled himself with a *donnée* so novelistic, so needful of expansion and development, that without the aid of magical manipulation, he barely managed to sketch the story's high points, much less develop its psychological intricacies or numinous resonances. In *The Haunted Man* he went back to the *Carol* formula, but with increased attention to an array of more subtle fantasy devices—devices more amenable to a realistic context than phantoms and goblins, though he used these as well—devices that could help him compress, combine, and enlarge.

Yet the need to depend on phantoms and magical machinery was irksome and confining. Dickens felt trapped in the Christmas-book form. In his general preface (1852) to the Christmas books, he wrote: "The narrow space within which it was necessary to confine these Christmas Stories when they were originally published, rendered their construction a matter of some difficulty, and almost necessitated what is peculiar in their machinery. I never attempted great elaboration of detail in the working out of character within such limits, believing that it could not succeed. My purpose was, in a whimsical kind of masque which the good humour of the season justified, to awaken some loving and forbearing thoughts, never out of season in a Christian land."[55] In this statement three ideas emerge clearly: Dickens felt that the narrow space of the Christmas books confined and limited him; and he believed that the fairy story could be used to solve problems of construction and to convey truth in a special way. One would assume that the sequel to such postulates would be that Dickens would turn back to the novel, and that within that larger space he would use the fairy tale, much more self-consciously and elaborately now, to help him with structure and coherence and to provide him with additional means of conveying meaning. This, in fact, is what happened.

I do not mean to imply by this that Dickens abandoned the fairy tale as fairy tale. He subsequently wrote a number of veritable fairy stories—allegories, satires, burlesques, fables, and supernatural stories that were couched in fairy-tale guise. But these pieces were scattered and intermittent; most of them were offshoots of his topical journalism. They do not have the centrality and the importance of the Christmas books. The Christmas books are at the heart of Dickens' writing and experimenting in the mid-1840s. His later redactions of fairy stories testify to his continued devotion to the genre, but his deepest and most potent storybook energies—the energies that were coeval with his power to transcend and transform, the energies that had been slowly nurtured and crucially shaped by a thousand childhood forces, by the nightmare of the blacking warehouse, by the frustrations and achievements of the apprentice novels, and now by the equivocal lessons of the Christmas books—those energies were flowing elsewhere. They were flowing, of course, into his novels.

What the Christmas books added to Dickens' fairy-tale art and what they contributed to the later novels can be quickly sketched. The Christmas books helped Dickens overcome old difficulties, and they encouraged him to introduce new techniques. Through his Christmas-book experimentation—though not exclusively by such means—Dickens learned how to make mood and atmosphere permeate every nuance of a story. He also evolved ways of making leitmotif, repetition, recurrence, and symbolism develop and integrate structure. In addition, the Christmas books helped him intensify and enrich his psychological analysis. The peculiar demands of the Christmas books encouraged him to convey states of mind through magically sympathetic objects and surroundings, to objectify internal divisions through doubles and alter egos, to depict psychological struggles through allegory and symbolism. Some of these techniques confirmed or amplified what Dickens had done earlier, others pushed him in new directions. In a similar way, his Christmas fairy tales showed him how to give the central realism of his story a consistent and thematic pattern of fancy and symbolism. What had heretofore been intermittent now became much more self-conscious, ordered, and regular. The Christmas novelettes also provided him with his first experience of completing a sizable fictional whole as a whole. They allowed him, five times over, to think and plan and write with an entirety in mind rather than a part. Dickens immediately recognized the importance of that overview. "When I see the effect of such a little *whole* as that," he wrote after finishing the *Carol,* "I have a strong sense of the immense effect I could produce with an entire book."[56]

In short, through the Christmas books and their fairy-tale potentialities, Dickens came to see more clearly how he could use fantasy to enhance character, scene, atmosphere, action, and meaning, and beyond that how he could use enchantment to bind the diverse elements of a fiction into a whole. One thing more. The Christmas books helped Dickens fuse the two dominant modes of his imagination. They helped him meld realism and fancy into rich thematic fullness. Through that new fullness, at once compellingly real and wildly fanciful, he could better convey the complexity and wonder of life.

One can see the experiments and lessons of the Christmas books reverberating in the subsequent novels. The bells and vibrations and clamor that pursue the despairing Trotty in *The Chimes* look forward to the bells and wheels and horses' feet that haunt the fleeing Carker in *Dombey.* The thematic weather that guides and unifies the *Carol* develops into the even more thematic weather that shapes and integrates *Bleak House.* The rudimentary analysis of Scrooge's childhood, its formative pressure on his adulthood, in *A Christmas Carol* turns into the more careful examination of Clennam's childhood and its consequences in *Little Dorrit.* The leitmotifs, repetitions, and incantations of *The Haunted Man* anticipate the analogous repetitions and recurrences of *A Tale of Two Cities.* The unity of mood, atmosphere, and theme that marks the *Carol* foreshadows the richer unity of tone and ambiance that pervades *Great Expectations.* The dark double that objectifies Redlaw's alienation and self-division in *The Haunted Man* evolves into the two separate selves that epitomize the alienation and self-division of such different characters as Wemmick in *Great Expectations* and Jasper in *Edwin Drood*. In each instance—the instances could easily be multiplied—it is not simply the idea that is similar but the technique of conveying it; and in each instance the technique is rooted in Dickens' Christmas-book experimentation.

I am not suggesting that Dickens went to the Christmas books, deliberately extracted these storybook devices, and then applied them to his later novels as tested ways of solving certain literary problems. I am not even suggesting that he always identified these devices with his Christmas books or with fairy stories. Nor do I doubt that many additional factors—the theater, the works of other authors, the spirit of the age, to name only three—made their contributions to these special developments. I am simply emphasizing that the Christmas books played a pivotal role in these developments. First, they forced Dickens, over a period of years, to concentrate on fairy-tale modes, a concentration that was congenial to his lifelong imaginative bent. Second, they helped him, during a crucial pause in his novel writing, to solve difficult problems of construction, integration, and transcendence. When he came to face those same problems in his subsequent novels, it was only natural that he should utilize (whether consciously or not) the methods and devices that had served him well in the Christmas books.

Yet the Christmas books themselves were unsatisfactory. They were limiting and confining. They made elaborate analysis and intricate development virtually impossible. They were dependent upon machinery that did violence to reality. Dickens was not content to convey his vision of life through phantoms and goblins. He did not wish to confine his art to ghostly allegories and whimsical masques. He wanted to present life in its density, its solid reality, but at the same time convey its shimmering strangeness and wonder.

It is not surprising, therefore, that even as the idea for his last Christmas book worked slowly through his mind, he was embarking upon a new novel, *Dombey and Son,* a novel that would display a virtuoso fusion of reality and fantasy. *Dombey* was a departure. Unlike the earlier novels, it was rooted in the present. *Pickwick, Nickleby, Barnaby,* and all the other apprentice novels had been set in the historical past, or had been hazily located in the ambiguous purlieus of a largely vanished age. *Dombey* was of the moment; it was a book about "the way we live now." It dealt with businessmen and railroads, capital and labor, the concerns and problems of the day. Yet this new book, with its new subject matter, and its up-to-date milieu, was to have the old indebtedness to fairy stories—old now in the sense of continuity, not of method. Fairy tales would appear in *Dombey* in the old ways, but they would also appear in new configurations: as elaborations and refinements of Christmas-book techniques. These techniques would help give *Dombey* a richness and unity that his earlier novels had lacked. *Dombey* would be minutely realistic, deeply social, profoundly psychological—all in ways that went beyond what Dickens had done before; but it would also vibrate intensely with fantasy and wonder— also in ways that went beyond what he had done before. *Dombey*, like the Christmas books, would be a fairy tale for the times, but a fairy tale given a surpassingly "higher form."

6 | *Dombey and Son*
The New Fairy-Tale Method

Lᵢₖₑ ᴛʜᴇ Christmas books, and in the selfsame manner as the Christmas books, *Dombey and Son* blends social, psychological, symbolic, and mythic truth. This felicitous coming together of diverse elements, a coming together that is centripetal and reinforcing, sets *Dombey* apart from the apprentice novels. In *Dombey* each component—the social, psychological, symbolic, mythic, and so on—is more consciously defined than in the earlier novels, each plays a more central role in the unfolding story, each contributes more to the controlling themes, and each blends more naturally with the overall design. But this new deftness and dovetailing is only part of the story. The use of the supernatural has changed. The magical continues, as before, to control the overarching structures of the novel, but it also contributes much more regularly now to the page-by-page texture of the story. With *Dombey,* for the first time in a Dickens novel, the fairy tale has become a consistent and pervasive force. Enchantment is now one of Dickens' chief means of integrating and deepening meaning. The fairy tale suffuses scenes, characters, and actions; it controls nuances as well as grand effects. It hovers over the book, now faintly, now forcefully, a presiding genius.

Dombey was shaped by more than Dickens' usual commerce with enchantment. When Dickens began *Dombey* he was fresh from his first three Christmas books. *Dombey and Son* exhibits the unmistakable imprint of this long concentration on ghostly fables. But this is not all. The last two Christmas books entered the picture as well. The opening chapters of *Dombey* were composed in Switzerland in the midst of planning and writing *The Battle of Life* and formulating *The Haunted Man.*[1] When Dickens sat down to write *Dombey,* therefore, he was compassed round by fairy stories. This pressure helped shape the new novel. Dickens, his mind filled with Christmas-book experiments, Christmas-book techniques, and Christmas-book plans, set out in *Dombey* to do something that he had never attempted before in a novel, but something that he had often done (and was even then doing) in his Christmas books: he set out to write a realistic story on the most up-to-date subject matter, a story, as it happened, that would be a detailed social and psychological analysis of the Victorian businessman, and at the same time he set out to make that story a magical fable of contemporary life.

How Dickens managed this integration, and how the supernatural contributed to it, can be seen very plainly if one examines the ways in which fairy tales intertwine with the controlling strands of the novel. At the center of the novel is a domestic tale, a tale that seems too real and too carefully observed to harbor any magical resonances. This pivotal tale, at once simple and realistic, focuses on the relationship of Mr. Dombey and his unloved daughter Florence. Mr. Dombey is a cold, proud, self-centered business baron. He is not a bad man, but wealth and authority have made him arrogant, and his single passion is to see the great shipping and trading firm of Dombey and Son perpetuated once more by a male heir. Mr. Dombey is certain that money can buy everything, everything, that is, but perhaps a son, and when six years after Florence's birth his wife dies in giving birth to a son, Mr. Dombey's thoughts cluster obsessively about his infant heir. The book opens with the birth of Paul and the death of Mrs. Dombey, and the huge novel that follows is designed to explore Mr. Dombey's parental sin and to humble him and shatter his money ethic. Mr. Dombey's sin is his rejection of the freely offered love of his daughter; he must come to realize that what Florence yearns to give him is a gift more valuable than anything money can buy. He must also learn that love can never be bought; that to be loved, one must love, and one must allow oneself to be loved. This theme, fresh in Dickens' day, has now become hackneyed through much imitation (one recalls celebrated nineteenth-century examples such as George Eliot's *Silas Marner* or notable twentieth-century versions such as D. H. Lawrence's "The Rocking-Horse Winner"), but Dickens' trailblazing exploration of the theme, even after more than a century of recapitulations, is moving and illuminating.

Mr. Dombey's harrowing is thorough. At first he merely neglects timid Florence, but gradually he grows envious of her, then jealous of the love she inspires in others, and finally, baffled and guilty, he hates her as the symbol of his own failure to inspire love. Dickens sets forth the father-daughter relationship at great length and with great subtlety. Mr. Dombey emerges from the book, in spite of a number of scenes that are unbearably painful, not as a villain, but as a helpless victim of his frigid personality and the new times, as a friendless, imperceptive, money-centered man, to be pitied rather than hated.

The humbling of Mr. Dombey is pointed up by a series of key episodes. The first inkling Mr. Dombey has that his money ethic may be wanting occurs when tiny Paul asks him (as Paul in "The Rocking-Horse Winner" asks his mother) what money is and what it can do. Mr. Dombey (again like the mother in "The Rocking-Horse Winner") is nonplussed by the question—he himself had always thought of money and its value as beyond examination—and he answers Paul in terms of his faith. "Money, Paul," he says, "can do anything." "Why," then asks Paul, "didn't money save me my mamma?"[2] The question is not sentimental, and it echoes through the remainder of the book. For Paul, with his strange prescient insight, intuitively perceives what his father must learn through disappointment and suffering; and when the little boy unwittingly emphasizes that money cannot buy life, he is foreshadowing his own death a few years later. That death is the first crushing lesson in Mr. Dombey's painful education, but it brings him no closer to Florence. Paul had lavished all his love on his sister, and Paul's death intensifies Mr. Dombey's jealousy of that love and his resentment that his unwanted daughter lives while his son and the plans he had centered upon him perish.

But Mr. Dombey, having failed to buy life, seeks to buy love and therewith a new son. He buys Edith, a beautiful, accomplished woman who knows she is being bought, despises the marriage contract she enters into, yet accepts it as a fair bargain freely and openly arrived at. Edith is Mr. Dombey's female counterpart; she is proud, but she is not deluded by her pride as is Mr. Dombey, and it irritates him that she makes no pretense that their marriage is anything other than a commercial arrangement. Dickens lavishes much attention on this business courtship and marriage; he shows Mr. Dombey inquiring about the widowed Edith's fertility, testing her ability as an artist and a musician, and displaying his power to command her to perform and obey. The marriage soon degenerates into a humiliating contest of wills, and Mr. Dombey watches in growing frustration as Edith, like Paul, gives Florence the love that she withholds from him. Mr. Dombey, in his pride, still cannot comprehend why this is so, and Florence's shy but still-offered love is now rejected as the cause of his misery. Florence, as he had dreaded many years before, has at last become hateful to him. He now looks upon her as a nemesis, a reminder of the insufficiency of his money and his mastery. Florence, in turn, feels guilty because her father rejects her. She has been a stranger to him since childhood, has long since become timid and inarticulate in his presence, yearns to discover the magic formula that will make him love her, and upbraids herself for not having won his love. Edith's position in the household at last becomes unbearable, and she agrees to run off with Carker, Mr. Dombey's trusted business manager. When the scandal of Edith's flight descends boltlike upon Mr. Dombey, Florence rushes to him, her timidity overcome by love and pity, but he strikes her, and, alienated at last, she flees from the home.

Mr. Dombey's proud world of money and power is now fast crumbling. Money has not saved his first wife, preserved his son, restrained his manager, bound his second wife, or secured his daughter. When the neglected firm of Dombey and Son fails also, the world wags on with clucking tongue, the showy vanities of Mr. Dombey's wealth are auctioned off as ironic reminders of what money can and cannot do, and his bought servants march out of his house in self-righteous indignation. Mr. Dombey can no longer delude himself; stripped of every defense, he must see himself as he really is. What he does see horrifies him, and tortured by the perversity of personality and values that have brought ruin to himself and those closest to him, he decides to kill himself. He is saved by the return of Florence, and after a long illness, symbolic of the death of the old Dombey and the birth of a new chastened Dombey, he is shown briefly in the humbled twilight of his life.

This domestic tale, so seemingly realistic and unadorned, is permeated, as we shall see, with magical energies. But *Dombey* is much more than a domestic novel. It is also a social tract or exemplum. The full title of the book is *Dealings with the Firm of Dombey and Son, Wholesale, Retail and for Exportation.* The title, even when interpreted ironically as intended, emphasizes the centrality of the social or business aspects of the story. These aspects are not limited to tracing the bankruptcy of Mr. Dombey's money ethic, important as this feature is. Dickens wished to underscore the pernicious tendencies in the new industrial order, and by depicting those tendencies in their multiplicity, in relation to machines, methods, and persons, show their danger and their destructiveness. The real villain of *Dombey and Son* is the soullessness of the new business world; the most condensed embodiment of that world is the manager Carker—clever, compulsive, ruthless, amoral—the first compelling portrait in the English novel of the new managerial class, of the new anonymous power breed.

The business theme, as we shall see, is wedded in Christmas-book fashion to the fairy-tale and autobiographical aspects of the story. And like these other aspects, the business theme is developed by contrast. Sol Gills' old-fashioned nautical instrument shop, small, sleepy, and human, is a perfect counterpart to the great bustling modern firm of Dombey and Son, for Sol's business, like Dombey's, takes its living from the sea. But while Dombey's impersonal and coldly efficient firm prospers, Sol sits forlornly amid his old-fashioned instruments, watching the tides of commerce flow everlastingly past his door. Sol's business is beyond repair (he is saved at the end by investments which, in storybook fashion, suddenly pour gold into his pocket), but his shop is a place of healing refuge, a succoring fairy-tale sanctuary, where the simple, the good, and the uncorrupted can congregate and take strength from one another. To it come Captain Cuttle, Toots, and Susan Nipper, and finally Florence and Walter.

Dombey's empire is flourishing, but Dickens, again using parallel construction, makes Dombey's business, in contrast to Gills', a source of infection. Walter (as originally conceived), Carker's brother, Rob the Grinder, and other characters illustrate this blighting influence. Dombey, like a deadly enchanter, freezes the blood and taints the will. Only the surpassingly pure or the irredeemably corrupt remain untouched by his baleful chill. Like Redlaw in *The Haunted Man*, Dombey transmits his gift, which is really a curse, wherever he goes. Two segments of the business theme, the Toodles (a group of minor characters), and the railroad, will demonstrate how carefully Dickens was now elaborating his Christmas-book method, and how skillfully he was using it to integrate social, symbolic, and fanciful themes.

Rob the Grinder, for instance, is a Toodle gone wrong, a Toodle touched by the Dombeian business infection. He goes to perdition, a sacrifice to Mr. Dombey's self-calculating and self-aggrandizing charitableness. But there are many other Toodles, and they also elucidate what Dickens has to say about business. The Toodles are basically good. Protected from the blighting influence of the Dombey spell, that is, protected from the soulless exploitation of the cold new business ethic, the Toodles wax and flourish. The Toodles are the new proletariat, clothed in the garb of their calling (Mr. Toodle is covered by the dirt and cinders of his railroad occupation even as Rob is branded by his Charitable Grinder uniform), taking their sustenance from the new world of business, but also contributing to that world and essential to it. Mr. Dombey in his pride refuses to recognize the latter fact; like Sir Joseph Bowley in *The Chimes*, he only acknowledges the Toodles' dependency and servitude. It is one of the defects of the new business world, and an element in Mr. Dombey's harrowing, that this relationship, in effect the relationship between capital and labor, has not been humanely established.

How Mr. Dombey regards this relationship is apparent in the domestic as well as the industrial focus of the story. At the beginning of the book, Mr. Dombey hires Rob's mother, Polly Toodle, to nurse motherless Paul. Paul, symbolically, must take his sustenance from lower-class Polly, his very life depends upon her bounty and good will;

the milk that turns into his blood and sinews emphasizes the commonality of rich and poor, their symbiotic relationship. But for Mr. Dombey, placing Paul at Polly's breast is a degrading necessity, and in order to blur that necessity, he seeks to make the arrangement a mere matter of business. He emphasizes to Polly that her milk is only a commodity; he warns her against forming any attachments to Paul; and he even buys her name, replacing the plebian "Toodle" with the businesslike "Richards."

But Mr. Dombey cannot entirely free his mind from the thought that Polly's Toodlish milk is contaminating his young son, and he has wild fears that this mixing process will go even further, that Polly may substitute her own infant for his son. And a modern redaction of a romance changeling scene, a scene that emphasizes Mr. Dombey's money-centered obtuseness, does in fact occur. Paul is taken by Polly from his great rich nursery in Portland Place, Bryanstone Square, to Staggs's Gardens, the cindery slum where the Toodles live. The slum—and here Dickens begins to work intricate counterpoint on the Toodles, the railroads, and their many larger ramifications in the story—the slum is a wasteland, a landscape made hell-like by the new railroad that is being built in its environs. In the face of this ugliness and disruption, the residents of Staggs's Gardens are resilient. They are buoyed by a fairy-tale vision. They regard their community "as a sacred grove not to be withered by railroads."[3]

The railroad, with its hints of hell and sacred groves, is doubly appropriate; it is an emblem of the new industrial order (and, as we shall see, of death) and the source of Mr. Toodle's livelihood. Paul, then, in being brought to Staggs's Gardens and the nether depths of the industrial world, is brought to the original source of his sustenance, an equivalence which is enforced whether one looks at that journey in terms of Polly's breast or of the new industrialism that undergirds his father's wealth. When Polly arrives at Staggs's Gardens and sees her infant son in her sister's arms, she rushes forward and instantly exchanges him with Paul. She clutches her son to her breast, overcome by love and joy. Dombey's dread fear, a confused fear compounded of property rights, class feelings, and vague storybook terrors, has at last come to pass. His son, like the princes in countless fairy stories and romances, is now a changeling; his rightful heir has been replaced, if only for the term of Polly's visit, by a lowly pretender. But ironically this exchange has taken place not out of envy, plot, or policy, the motives that Dombey in his pride and possessiveness feared, but out of love. Dombey's threats and interdictions, his cajoling perquisites—good wages, new clothes, rich food, commodious quarters—have not availed against mother love. Dombey's lofty position, his power and

wealth, cannot make Polly forgo her affectionate nature. The changeling episode also emphasizes the essential equality of the infants—
Polly not only loves them both but literally mothers them both—and
by implication, despite the distance and outward distinction between
Portland Place and Staggs's Gardens, and despite the fact that Polly is
later dismissed for this lapse, the equality of all Dombeys and Toodles.

   In the remainder of the book the Toodles reinforce the lessons of
their earlier appearances. Dickens continues to show that an unfeeling
ruling class sows the seeds of its own destruction. Whelplike Rob
Toodle eventually becomes Carker's tool and helps Carker run off with
Edith. Rob's Dombey-engendered delinquency thus plays a part in
Dombey's own ruin. Dombey's ruin comes at the end of the book, and
when it comes we acknowledge its justice. For Dombey rebuffs every
attempt to reach his humanity. On the industrial level of the story there
are several such attempts. These attempts parallel Florence's strivings
on the domestic level; they show that the businesslike aridity that
withers Dombey's personal life also withers all his other relationships,
and ultimately, since Dombey is representative of the new ruling class,
endangers the whole structure of Victorian society. This message is
made very clear by scenes that further interweave Dombey, the Toodles, the railroad, and Dickens' theme.

   After Paul's death, when Dombey is waiting at the railway station for
the train that will take him and Major Bagstock via Birmingham to
Leamington, he is approached by Mr. Toodle, the stoker of the train.
Dombey fails to recognize him, then treats him with frosty haughtiness,
and finally assumes that Toodle has approached him for money. Dombey can understand such an approach, but he cannot understand Toodle's real motivation. When Dombey discovers that Toodle has come to
commiserate with him, and wears mourning crepe, not for the death of
one of his own children (Toodle assures Dombey that they are flourishing in their usual apple-cheeked manner), but for Paul, Mr. Dombey is
humiliated. Mr. Toodle's act of brotherhood, which again asserts the
interdependence of Dombeys and Toodles and reawakens memories of
Paul's nursing at Polly Toodle's breast, is intolerable to Mr. Dombey.
He believes his money and position make him superior to Mr. Toodle;
sonless Dombey never stops to think that Mr. Toodle possesses something which neither his money nor his position can buy. As a matter of
fact, Mr. Dombey's train journey will emphasize this Dombeian obtuseness, for it will result in his meeting Edith, which in turn will lead
to his disastrous attempt to buy her, and through her a son.

   The symbolism here becomes extraordinarily rich. That richness is
all the more astonishing when one realizes that the railway was just
then entering everyday life. *Dombey* is the first English novel to translate the railroad into artistic vision. That Dickens was able to adapt the

railroad to his imaginative purposes so quickly and so consummately is a remarkable feat. In *Dombey* the railway is realistic artifact, industrial emblem, and wild supernatural force. This soon becomes apparent. After his colloquy with Mr. Toodle, Mr. Dombey is hurried toward his ruin on a train stoked by Mr. Toodle. Dombey's dependence on the Toodles and the new industrialism is absolute; ultimately, in generic terms, it is Toodle labor and machine power that insure Dombey's position and money. The train is an ambiguous industrial servant, rushing Dombey toward his desire, but since his industrial ethic is distorted, his desire is self-wounding, and the train hastens him toward his destruction: toward Edith and a money marriage, toward friction, scandal, and bankruptcy. For Toodle the railroad and the new industrialism mean salvation: the railroad gives him a livelihood and leads to his advancement (he becomes an engineer, sends his children to school, learns to read, and so on).

As we have seen, this dual thesis, that an industrial society is symbiotic and that an individual reaps what he sows, has already been elaborated in the nursing and changeling episodes of the novel, but it is simultaneously elaborated by the railroad imagery, imagery that enters the novel and reinforces the business theme in three major integrating episodes. First we see the railroads being built and watch them change the face of the land. Here is the new Dombeian business world constructing its vital arteries and nerves: "Everywhere were bridges that led nowhere; thoroughfares that were wholly impassable; Babel towers of chimneys, wanting half their height; temporary wooden houses and enclosures, in the most unlikely situations; carcases of ragged tenements, and fragments of unfinished walls and arches, and piles of scaffolding, and wildernesses of bricks, and giant forms of cranes, and tripods straddling above nothing. There were a hundred thousand shapes and substances of incompleteness."[4] This description of dislocation becomes more expressionistic as it goes on, until Dickens turns it into an image of hell: "Hot springs and fiery eruptions . . . lent their contributions of confusion to the scene. Boiling water hissed and heaved within dilapidated walls; whence, also, the glare and roar of flames came issuing forth; and mounds of ashes blocked up rights of way, and wholly changed the law and custom of the neighbourhood."[5]

But if the railroad building is hell, the railroad built is death—and also life. In the next great railroad episode, the one in which Mr. Dombey converses with Mr. Toodle and then travels to Edith, Dickens makes this identification with death explicit. The train forces "itself upon its iron way—its own—defiant of all paths and roads, piercing through the heart of every obstacle, and dragging living creatures of all classes, ages, and degrees behind it . . . a type of the triumphant monster, Death."[6] The last phrase, in Christmas-book fashion, is repeated with slight variations four times in the course of a two-page impressionistic description of a rapid rail journey, and becomes, along with imagery of the flowing seabound river (the latter imagery an even more persistent harbinger of death in *Dombey*), the ominous motif of Mr. Dombey's headlong journey. Yet it is Mr. Dombey and what he stands for, not the railroad, that is the villain. The slums and misery and blight that Mr. Dombey passes through existed long before the railroad. Dickens emphasizes that "as Mr. Dombey looks out of his carriage window, it is never in his thoughts that the monster who has brought him there has let the light of day in on these things: not made or caused them."[7] Dombey policy and Dombey complacency are the true culprits.

The symbolism is heightened and completed in the last great railroad episode of the book. This episode climaxes the magnificent flight chapter in which Carker, pursued by Dombey, flees through France to England, where he waits for the train that will take him to safety. The phantasmagoric flight has been punctuated—again in Christmas-book fashion—by the reiterated leitmotif of "bells and wheels, and horses' feet, and no rest," and now Carker, dazed and sick with weariness, shudders each time the ground trembles and a great train, dropping glowing coals and exhaling a deathlike breath, goes shrieking by. Confused by lack of sleep, bewildered by unearthly railroad noises, Carker suddenly sees Dombey emerge through the station door. He staggers back, loses his footing, and topples in front of a train. The wheels that rolled endlessly through his dreamlike flight now coalesce into the great avenging wheel of the locomotive "that spun him round and round and struck him limb from limb, and licked his stream of life up with its fiery heat."[8] The death is appropriate. For Carker the manager, the new industrial man par excellence, is destroyed by the iron idol, that "type of the triumphant monster, Death," he had so inhumanly served. Dombey, for his part, goes from this scene of judgment to face his own imminent ruin, while Toodle and his apple-cheeked brood roll blithely forward, propelled to felicity by the selfsame wheels that obliterate Carker and humble Dombey.

All this may seem magical enough, but the fairy-tale dimensions of the railway are much stronger and much more important than I have indicated so far. These dimensions, like the other storybook motifs of *Dombey,* unify and enrich the novel. The train that takes Dombey to Leamington and Edith is more than a realistic means of transportation, more than an emblem of "the triumphant monster, Death"; it is a supernatural creature of frightening and powerful aspect. It huffs and lumbers and churns forward; then it gathers speed; soon it is "away, with a shriek, and a roar, and a rattle."[9] The latter phrase and its many variants run through the entire passage and are repeated much more frequently than "the triumphant monster, Death." Guided by such tags and by much additional imagery, we soon come to regard the train as a creature as fabulous and frightening as any fearsome dragon. It is noisy and implacable; it fills earth and air. It flashes along with "a shrill yell of exultation, roaring, rattling, tearing on, spurning everything with its dark breath, sometimes pausing for a minute where a crowd of faces are, that in a minute more are not: sometimes lapping water greedily, and before the spout at which it drinks has ceased to drip upon the ground, shrieking, roaring, rattling through the purple distance!"[10]

Much later in the book, images from this Leamington rail journey (which Dombey made without Carker) are incorporated into Carker's flight. These images—images of trembling ground, rush and sweep, dark endless roads, and hurrying Death—look back to Dombey's Leamington rail journey and forward to Carker's railroad annihilation. Through such devices Dickens makes Carker's phantasmagoric flight involve Dombey and railways, business and industrialism, love and mastery, as well as Carker's destiny. The flight is filled with linking images. It is also filled with sick rush and hurry. Carker is haunted. He is pursued by the phantoms of those he has wronged. Ghostly specters of Edith and Dombey beset and torment him. Fear and bafflement grip him. All the while, in Christmas-book fashion, and in distant echo of the Leamington journey, the flight is permeated with directive repetition—with "smoking horses," with "the track by which he had come," with "long, long roads," and with "bells and wheels, and horses' feet, and no rest."[11]

When Carker reaches England, these portents, repetitions, and rushing presences take on the fullness of their magical meaning. Carker seeks temporary refuge in a railway inn. Ushered to his room, he sits down to eat and slake his thirst and think. Dinner comes and goes. He is dazed and disturbed. He hardly knows what he is doing. After dinner he drinks and drinks again, and all the while he muses. Time, fretted with fear and brooding, creeps slowly by. Suddenly he starts up in terror: "The ground shook, the house rattled, the fierce impetuous rush was in the air! He felt it come up, and go darting by; and even when he had hurried to the window, and saw what it was, he stood, shrinking from it, as if it were not safe to look."[12] A moment later, and terror gives way to another feeling: "A curse upon the fiery devil, thundering along so smoothly, tracked through the distant valley by a glare of light and lurid smoke, and gone! He felt as if he had been plucked out of its path, and saved from being torn asunder. It made him shrink and shudder even now, when its faintest hum was hushed, and when the lines of iron road he could trace in the moonlight, running to a point, were as empty and as silent as a desert."[13] Carker goes out to walk along that iron road, the "yet smoking cinders . . . lying in its track."[14]

He wonders when "another devil would come by."[15] He does not wonder long. "A trembling of the ground, and quick vibration in his ears; a distant shriek; a dull light advancing, quickly changed to two red eyes, and a fierce fire, dropping glowing coals; an irresistible bearing on of a great roaring and dilating mass; a high wind, and a rattle— another come and gone, and he holding to a gate, as if to save himself!"[16] The words "shriek," "roar," and "rattle," the reiterated motif of the Leamington train, sound ominously in the above passage. The Leamington train, "the triumphant monster, Death," taking on a new guise, has come again. Carker clings to the gate—he is clinging to the gate of hell, to the gate of his perdition—and thinks to save himself. But the trains that rush by will not be thwarted. They have metamorphosed into fiery demons, into veritable devils. Dickens not only describes them in these terms, he calls them by these names. The trains have become as terrible and implacable as the most frightful monsters in a blazing Boschlike inferno.

Carker is drawn to these mighty demons. Whenever a train stops at the station, he comes close to it and stares at the fearful engine. The swart monster towers over him. It stands, fierce and unappeased, like some great idol. Carker gazes with obsessed fascination at the "heavy wheels and brazen front."[17] He thinks of the brute's cruel power to crush and kill. Finally, when it is close to midnight, he returns to his room. The great trains continue to thunder by, continue to disappear into the shadowy valley, into the valley of glare and smoke. "When he felt the trembling and vibration, [he] got up and went to the window, to watch . . . the dull light changing to the two red eyes, and the fierce fire dropping glowing coals, and the rush of the giant as it fled past, and the track of glare and smoke along the valley."[18] Hours go by. Now the red glare of the monster turns into the red glare of sunrise. The burning heavens fire all the East. Soon the first beams of the sun, unsullied and resplendent, shine out as they have shone "since the beginning of the world."[19] Carker goes forth to catch the train that will take him, with glare and fire and smoke, into that distant valley. As his train—or rather as an earlier express train—approaches, Carker catches a glimpse of Dombey and staggers back onto the track. "He . . . felt the earth tremble—knew in a moment that the rush was come—uttered a shriek—looked round—[and] saw the red eyes, bleared and dim, in the daylight, close upon him."[20] The great wheels of the locomotive smash and beat him to death. The universe is appeased. The demon train has come at last and carried Carker to his infernal home.

All this is woven into a densely realistic context, a context that is rich with psychological insight and naturalistic detail. In concentrating on the most unmistakable fairy-tale elements, elements that culminate in a melodramatic climax, I have done violence to Dickens' art; I have made it seem much simpler and coarser than it is. Here as elsewhere, the supernatural, though ubiquitous, is often hardly perceptible. It is coterminous with texture and substance. It hovers subtly over image and action. It adds dimension and resonance to character and scene. It enlarges and generalizes meaning. These larger meanings are fused to the compelling realism of track and station, wheel and glowing fire. What emerges is a more profound realism, a realism that transcends the merely realistic. Through such devices, through repetitions and recurrences, through magical motifs and protean transformations, Dickens builds his storybook atmospheres and weaves his storybook spells. And by means of these spells, spells that surround locomotives, distant valleys, and guilty consciences alike, he joins iron realism with directive supernaturalism, and both with thematic meaning. We experience a sentient universe. We witness how each earthly perturbation makes the cosmos tremble. Carker's death is both earthly accident and transcendental fall. Carker, a mere railroad statistic, partakes of timeless myth. He is destroyed by the new gods he embraced (false gods, ferocious and brazen); he is felled by the old gods he scorned (true gods, omnipotent and inescapable). He is crushed by the unfeeling machine he worshiped; he is ravaged by the human spirit he flouted—a spirit as old, and in retribution as vengeful, as man's most primordial vision of demons and death.

Though the Toodles and the railroads are subordinate elements in Dickens' larger design, they serve major ends. For Dickens' design now dominates the detail as well as the grand sweep of the novel, and even minor or specialized elements (in this case primarily social or industrial elements) blend with—are actually a part of—his central conception. The blending is much richer than is suggested here, for it is compounded of the imagery of plants, plumages, clocks, jewels, rivers, and staircases, as well as railroads; it embraces characters such as Dombey, Edith, Paul, Florence, Mrs. Skewton, and Major Bagstock as well as the lowly Toodles; and it works through leitmotifs more persistent and all-embracing than the demon-train sequences. How these elements contribute to the novel and how the surreal shapes and reinforces that contribution can be quickly demonstrated by a few additional examples.

Fairy-tale touches, for instance, define many of the characters. One soon comes to recognize that Major Bagstock is a minor devil. As Dickens put it in a letter, Major Bagstock wields "a kind of comic Mephistophelean power" and has an "apoplectico-mephistophelean" air.[21] He tempts and dissembles and ogles. He is a harbinger of misfortune, and he takes pleasure in the misfortune that he brings. The very thought of mischief makes him chortle and rumble with glee. His ap-

pearance and manner betray his origins and confirm his role. He swells
and puffs himself up alarmingly, his great lobster eyes starting danger-
ously out of his head. His goblin head—Mrs. Skewton calls him a
"perfidious goblin"—turns blue and purple on the least provocation;
one momentarily expects to see flames issue from his mouth.[22] His
favorite expressions proclaim his infernal role: they are "Damme" and
"de-vilish sly!"

The storybook aura surrounds passive as well as aggressive characters, and the aura takes many forms. Captain Jack Bunsby is
mindless and inarticulate, but Dickens transforms him into a revered
supernatural oracle. This is no fanciful figure of speech but a self-
conscious strategy on Dickens' part, one that is enforced by a host of
references to oracles. The whole idea, of course, is a splendid joke, a
burlesque on seeking out and consulting oracles. When Florence
comes to Captain Cuttle and expresses fears concerning the missing
Walter Gay, Captain Cuttle offers to take her to the "oracular
Bunsby."[23] The visit is hilarious. Captain Bunsby emerges from the
bowels of his ship like some grotesque wraith, his head and then his
body rising ghostlike above the bulkhead of his cabin. He has "one
stationary eye . . . and one revolving one, on the principle of some
lighthouses."[24] After being consulted by his visitors, this nautical Cy-
clops utters such wisdom as, "Whereby . . . why not? If so, what odds?
Can any man say otherwise? No. Awast then!" then proceeds to a
series of even more gnomic declarations, and concludes with, "The
bearings of this observation lays in the application on it."[25] Captain
Cuttle is delighted with these cryptic utterances. Taking his cue from
the oracle, and following in a long tradition, he applies the windy
inanities to suit his own purposes. But Captain Bunsby's storybook
role is not confined to the gnomic and the oracular. He does battle with
a fearsome harpy, and he falls victim to a baleful spell.

The harpy is Mrs. MacStinger, Captain Cuttle's vixenish landlady, a
true ogress and man-eater. She keeps watch and ward on the amiable
Captain, and so terrorizes him with complaints and threats that he
eventually cowers meekly in his room, a helpless prisoner in a dismal
castle. When he finally manages to flee from his dragon warder, he runs
off in such panic that he leaves his most precious treasure, his sea chest
and all its contents, behind. He does not return for his sea chest. He is
too afraid of the MacStinger spell. A year later, however, the redoubtable Bunsby agrees to brave the vaunted spell and rescue the hostage
chest, and he succeeds in doing so. But in defying the spell over Cuttle,
he falls victim to the spell himself. He takes Captain Cuttle's place.
Helpless, bewitched, he becomes—to Captain Cuttle's total amazement—the new thrall in Mrs. MacStinger's wicked castle. Will-less
and supine, he follows meekly where Mrs. MacStinger leads. She

finally leads him to church and marriage. Captain Bunsby is powerless to resist. On the way to church he tells Captain Cuttle that he does not want to marry, but when Cuttle urges him to walk away, he cannot do it. Abject, dispirited, helpless, he walks weakly to the sacrificial altar. Captain Bunsby goes to his comic doom, the paralyzed victim of Mrs. MacStinger's stinglike spell.[26]

A very different case is Toots, yet he is a victim, too. Like Smike and Barnaby, he is a holy fool. But he is much better realized and much more believable than they. He is also woven more deftly into the thematic heart and the presiding enchantment of the novel. Like Paul, Toots fails under the burden of a faulty education. Forced in the great hothouse of Dr. Blimber's very expensive school, Toots blew before his time, and then, "suddenly left off blowing one day, and remained in the establishment a mere stalk."[27] As people sometimes said, when Toots "began to have whiskers he left off having brains."[28] Unlike Paul, Toots does not die under the rigors of forcing, but like Paul he demonstrates the limits of what money can do. Money cannot buy life, and it cannot produce genius. Though Toots is rich, he will not be powerful or learned or modish. He will go through life good-hearted and simpleminded, his potential withered rather than ripened by money. Inarticulate, even ludicrous, he is nevertheless understandable and believable. He is like Mr. Dick. We easily interpret his almost ritualistic actions and gestures. His innate decency and goodness shine through his most oblique utterances. He is a strange amalgam of high comedy, sad waste, and sensitive compassion. He is a far cry from Smike's sentimental helplessness or Barnaby's portentous witlessness. Yet the mantle of grace, fanciful and magical, covers Toots as totally and as miraculously as it does Smike or Barnaby. What is different is the context and the purpose. The whole nature of Dickens' presentation is changing. Shades of black and white are toning into shades of grey. Toots is one of the elect, he is one with Florence, Captain Cuttle, Sol Gills, Polly Toodle, and Walter Gay, but he is also one with Susan Nipper and Miss Tox, vessels of goodness, but hardly of perfection.

The forces of good still rally toward the end of the novel and magically defeat the forces of evil, but now the partisans of both contingents are much more ambiguous—and much more realistic. Carker, though a villain, is no mere pasteboard ranter. He is a cool and believable aggressor, a type we recognize at once, and thus all the more frightening. Though still not a thoroughly domesticated villain in the Steerforth mode, Carker is a vast improvement over the posturing and impossible Monks. What is true of Carker is even more true of Dombey. Mr. Dombey, though grievously at fault and a perpetrator of incalculable damage, is hardly a villain at all. His sins of coldness, pride, and acquisitiveness—sins that in some measure touch each one of us—are also reflexive and self-wounding. To say that Mr. Dombey is his own worst enemy, that he hurts no one more than himself, that he cuts himself off from all the satisfactions he almost pathetically yearns for, is to voice a truism that is also a simple truth. Dombey—who after all is saved in the end—belongs with the Gradgrinds of the world rather than the Quilps and Rudges. Dickens' characters, especially the more important ones, the ones that were always the most wooden and conventionalized, are becoming more believable, more ordinary and fallible. But paradoxically, at the same time, they are also becoming more richly fanciful. They are increasingly surcharged with magic and enchantment. They are also increasingly shaped to thematic purposes.

How this works can be seen quite distinctly in Paul. Paul is one of Dickens' most believable children. He has a child's frankness and freshness of vision, but also a child's naiveté. He speaks in the natural rhythms and phrases of childhood—none of Oliver's miraculous diction and copybook speeches here. His psychology is right, too. He shows jealousy and hostility as well as gratitude, irrational fear as well as sensitive insight. He is light-years away from Oliver's immaculate goodness. Increasingly, when Paul appears, we see the world through his eyes—a strange world, distorted, foreshortened, full of looming objects, vague shadows, and lurking presences. As he becomes sicker, the world becomes more scattered and chaotic, a fevered jumble of confused time and disassociated images. All this is carefully designed. In his number plans, Dickens reminded himself of his purpose: "His illness only expressed in the child's own feelings—not otherwise described."[29] The introduction of a child's consciousness into *Dombey* is one of the great innovations of the novel, a stunning advance in realistic verisimilitude and psychological portraiture.

Yet this realistic advance is the source of wildest fantasy. Paul is encompassed by divination and magic, and this supernatural influence marks him within and without. In the external world, that occult pressure is mainly associated with time and death. Paul is born with the tokens of time on him. His newborn face is "crossed and recrossed with a thousand little creases" which "deceitful Time" will smooth away in treacherous preparation for a deeper cutting.[30] We soon come to understand that Paul is an alien spirit, a brief sojourner on earth, marked for blight and failure. He has the Dombey chill of death on him. His christening is cold and frigid, his early years frosty and frozen. He cannot throw off the congealing Dombey presence. At five he is as wan and frostbitten as at the moment of his glacial christening. "The chill of Paul's christening had struck home, perhaps to some sensitive part of his nature, which could not recover itself in the cold shade of his father; . . . he was an unfortunate child from that day."[31] He is also a strange child, gnomelike and wizened. He is like a miniature Father Time, a weird childish harbinger of death. As such, he is the notable prototype of a notable literary progeny. He is, to cite only one instance, a precursor of Hardy's poor pinched "Father Time" in *Jude the Obscure*. Though youthful, Paul is old. He seems to have a sense of his mortality. He also has a childlike percipience, an almost otherworldly wisdom. He is, in fact, the changeling that his father feared he might be, but a changeling that is far beyond the grasp of Mr. Dombey's prosaic ken. Paul "looked (and talked) like one of those terrible little beings in the fairy tales, who, at a hundred and fifty or two hundred years of age, fantastically represent the children for whom they have been substituted."[32] This conception of Paul as an extrarational or mythic embodiment of time and death is conveyed by these and hundreds of similar touches.

After a while, we begin to interpret everything Paul says and does in realistic and in mythic terms. For example, when Paul grows so weak that he must be wheeled about in a little carriage, he rejects the "ruddy-faced lad" who is originally hired to pull him, and asks instead to be guided by "a weazen, old, crab-faced man, in a suit of battered oilskin, who had got tough and stringy from long pickling in salt water, and who smelt like a weedy sea-beach when the tide is out."[33] Paul feels a deep affinity for this timeworn incarnation of the sea. He is drawn to this ancient man, but he shows no interest in his youthful contemporaries: he sends all young children who approach him away.[34] Guided by this old man of the sea, pushed and pulled by him, Paul steers for the watery domain of death. By the time all this takes place, by the time we meet the old man of the sea, we know how to interpret his mythic mission. Long before he comes on the stage, the signs and portents that surround Paul have taught us to read each new signature in his mortality.

Those signs and portents are part of Paul's inner consciousness as well as his outward garniture. He asks unsettling questions; he exhales an old-fashioned air. He begins to be haunted by recurrent images, by waves and fast flowing rivers. As he grows frail, then sick, and finally dozes into death, the distorted objects of his contracting world—now concentrated into the feverish phantasmagoria of his sickroom—ebb and flow and coalesce into hallucinated visions. Faces come and go, footsteps echo, doctors, their gold watches ticking, stand beside his bed. The sense of fragmented time and deep disorder is marvelously real in these scenes, but so also is the pressure of the invisible world. The transmuting alembic is Paul's sick vision. In Paul's fevered mind, the real and the imaginary intermingle and merge. The sunlight shimmering and quivering on the wall of his room turns into golden water, the somber shadows of the encroaching night change into a dark flowing river. At the very end he hears waves, feels the motion of a boat upon the stream, and glides out into the sea.

Paul returns to the sea of death, the sea that encompassed and beckoned him throughout the book. But the sea that takes also gives; the sea of death is also the sea of immortality. In the final pages of the book a new Paul appears, the son of Florence. This new son emerges from the sea; he is born aboard a ship traveling toward Dombey from across the ocean. One Paul sails sickly away into the trackless deep, and then, much later, another Paul, different and yet somehow the same, sails out of that immensity, healthy and reborn. We last see Dombey, humbled but newly human, walking with his young grandson at the marge of the limitless sea, the sea that engulfed his changeling child, and that brought him his changeling grandson.

The water imagery in *Dombey* is sometimes too insistent and too explicit, and the actual moment of Paul's death is marred by a banal vision of heaven, but for the most part the penumbra of magic and prescience that surrounds Paul works wonderfully well. It fills Paul's outer world, it suffuses Paul's inner consciousness; it guides and gathers meaning. It intensifies the numinous, while deepening the real; it integrates the magical and the mundane.

The intricate and interconnecting way this fusion takes place can be seen in the small details of Dickens' design as well as the larger motifs. The great clock that stands in the hall of Doctor Blimber's school illustrates this process very well. The clock is an ordinary clock, very real and very loud. Its ticking sounds through all the house, even to the garrets. When Paul is brought to Doctor Blimber's school and introduced to that learned gentleman, the Doctor asks, "And how is my little friend?"[35] Paul does not answer at first, but the great clock in the hall seems to say, and to go on saying, "'How, is, my, lit, tle, friend? how, is, my, lit, tle, friend?' over and over and over again."[36] This is the beginning of the process whereby Doctor Blimber's establishment (seen through Paul's eyes) takes on a life of its own, growing more and more expressionistic and animistic, until, when Paul becomes disturbed and ill, the house turns out to be as strange and haunted—but all the while as real—as any house in fiction. But the role of the clock is not limited to initiating this metamorphosis. The clock asks its insistent question through all the scenes at Doctor Blimber's establishment: "How, is, my, lit, tle, friend? how, is, my, lit, tle, friend?" The spiritual and psychological answer to that question is, "Not good, not well." Significantly, as Paul grows ill, so does the clock. Paul comes downstairs one day to find the clock dismantled, its displaced face "ogling him," and a workman poking into its insides.[37] The clock is soon cured, but Paul continues his slow decline. Yet no one really asks the question that the clock insists on ticking out—Doctor Blimber's repeated queries are simply polite formalities—and Paul, a weak nursling roughly and rudely transplanted, is thrust willy-nilly into the forcing house of time, a hothouse that will propel him with unnatural swiftness to his premature doom.

But the question that parent and teacher neglect to ask is asked, and asked repeatedly, by the clock. Paul loves to sit on the hallway staircase and listen to the clock tick.[38] The hallway clock ticks out its question, but the voice is the voice of time. As in *The Chimes,* time, animated and personified, enforces what man neglects. For the great hall clock, ticking its loud tick, is ticking Paul's life away. Time insistently tells us that Paul is not well, that his father's care and his father's money will not save him. This lesson was foreshadowed in the first chapter, for there the fashionable doctors, called in at great expense to attend Paul's birth, consult their heavy gold watches which tick, tick, tick, as Mrs. Dombey, heedless of gold and summoned by time, drifts "out upon the dark and unknown sea that rolls round all the world."[39] Here images of gold, time, water, and death coalesce and look forward, accumulating enormous richness and power on the way, to Paul's own death. At Paul's death the fashionable doctors and their ticking gold watches again appear and go through their ineffectual rituals. Their reappearance is designed to remind the unheeding Dombey (and to convince the mindful reader) of the true provinces of money and time. Dombey is not reminded. Despite his grief over Paul's physical dissolution, he never hears and never answers the deeper inquiry, so doleful and so dusty, of the ticking watches and the inexorable clock.

All this and more, the real but also fairy-tale clock—loudly repeating its steady inquiry of, "How, is, my, lit, tle, friend?"—does or, by its intricate links and associations, helps to do. Doctor Blimber's stately clock, solemn, repetitive, and mindless, but talking eloquently to those who will listen to its prophetic voice, is one tiny magical detail in a vast storybook design. The detail, taken by itself, is circumscribed; the detail, reverberating with its many analogues, is centripetal and directive.

The central staircase in the somber Dombey mansion is another example of an ordinary object that acquires deep-toned richness through fairy-tale means. The staircase, wide and dismally grand, soon becomes associated with other details, most notably with singing and with music, and through Christmas-book techniques, through repetition, recurrence, magical enlargement, and the like, is gradually turned into a resonant leitmotif. This leitmotif operates on all levels of the story. It foreshadows the crucial progressions of the novel, and it powerfully colors our responses to the chief characters and their acts. Yet the staircase and the music always remain ordinary and realistic. Dickens accomplishes this legerdemain through his usual process of suggestion, association, and fusion. Here is his first strong sounding of the music-staircase leitmotif:

> After [Paul and Florence] had left the room together, [Mr. Dombey] thought he heard a soft voice singing; and remembering that Paul had said his sister sung to him, he had the curiosity to open the door and listen, and look after them. She was toiling up the great, wide, vacant staircase, with him in her arms; his head was lying on her shoulder, one of his arms thrown negligently round her neck. So they went, toiling up; she singing all the way, and Paul sometimes crooning out a feeble accompaniment. Mr. Dombey looked after them until they reached the top of the staircase—not without halting to rest by the way—and passed out of his sight; and then he still stood gazing upwards, until the dull rays of the moon, glimmering in a melancholy manner through the dim skylight, sent him back to his own room.[40]

The staircase, as the reader gradually comes to perceive, is the staircase upon which the characters wend their lives; one end of the staircase descends into hell, the other ascends to heaven. Drooping Paul, clasped in Florence's arms, winds his weary passage to heaven while angelic Florence helps him and sings him on his way. But the brother-sister clasp of love evokes more than their toilsome pilgrimage up the great wide stairs of life. Florence's loving embrace of Paul as he ascends those stairs toward death connects present with past and future. The clasp of love harks back to Florence holding her mother in her arms as she drifts out on the sea of death (Dombey at a distance looking on), points ahead to Florence holding Paul in her arms as he glides into eternity (Dombey again at a distance looking on), and foreshadows Florence at the end of the book holding her chastened father in her arms (he no longer remote from the circle of love) as he dies and is reborn. Angel Florence, musical and dolorous, ushers ordinary mortals from death to everlasting life.

The music-staircase leitmotif and the elements that compose it are extraordinarily effective and operate with equal beauty on the supernatural and realistic levels. After establishing the leitmotif, Dickens deepens it through accretion and association and then works intricate variations on it. In Christmas-book fashion, but in ways that go far beyond the Christmas books, Florence's singing, "a golden link between [Paul] and all his life's love and happiness,"[41] soon serves, along

with the staircase, to call up, foreshadow, and perpetuate central features of the book—Mrs. Dombey's death, Paul's death, his and Florence's unity in the face of an unloving parent, Mr. Dombey's blind
egocentricity, Florence's neglected angel-goodness, and the chief
characters' ultimate ascension or damnation. When Paul goes home to
die, he begins his journey by descending Doctor Blimber's shadowy
staircase. Florence, who has just sung a song, descends the staircase
with him. Her singing has lulled and hushed Paul; it reminds him somehow of the "mysterious murmur" of the sea.[42] That murmur, the soft
voice of death and immortality, seems to speak to him. It allies itself
with objects, thoughts, and dreams. Now brother and sister, descending the staircase, pass the place on the stairs where Paul loved to sit
and listen to the hallway clock tick time away. Then they go out into
the night.

When Paul finally reaches home, he is "carried up the well-
remembered stairs" of the Dombey mansion.[43] Paul has gone down
one staircase and up another. Now he is through toiling on those vacant
stairs. His next ascension, wound in Florence's arms, the mysterious
murmur all around him, will be direct to heaven. But the music-
staircase leitmotif does not end with Paul's death. It continues, becoming ever more magical, ever more rich. After Paul dies, Mr. Dombey, in
the dead of night, gropes tentatively up the stairs to his son's empty
room, there to mourn secretly till the break of day. Mr. Dombey's
mute, self-regarding, night-shrouded vigil is contrasted with Florence's
more heaven-bound mourning, a mourning blended with the singing
motif and with the staircase ascent of the brother and sister: "It was
not very long before, in the midst of the dismal house so wide and
dreary, her low voice in the twilight, slowly and stopping sometimes,
touched the old air to which [Paul] had so often listened, with his
drooping head upon her arm. And after that, and when it was quite
dark, a little strain of music trembled in the room: so softly played and
sung . . . and broken murmurs of the strain still trembled on the keys,
when the sweet voice was hushed in tears."[44]

Though father and daughter grieve for the same object, their grief
does not unite them. When Florence later creeps down the night-
shrouded staircase to kneel at her father's door, supplicating for love,
she finds it "ever closed, and he shut up within."[45] Again and again she
steals "lightly down the stairs through the thick gloom," seeking her
father in the dark regions where he dwells.[46] One night, after pausing in
"irresolution on the staircase," she finds the door slightly ajar.[47] She
pushes it open, and "with her hands a little raised and trembling,"
glides prayerfully into his room. She calls to her father and he leaps up,
half terrified by her unaccustomed apparition. "What is the matter?

. . . Why do you come here? What has frightened you?'' he asks. She
tries to speak, but he repels her, and she begins to cry. "Go, Florence,'' he says, and then he adds with terrible irony, "You have been
dreaming. . . . I will remain here to light you up the stairs.'' Florence
has indeed been dreaming. Her father's next words underline the separateness of their staircase-divided worlds. "The whole house,'' he
says, "is yours above there.'' Florence, sobbing, "silently ascended''—the term is wonderfully appropriate—while her father, "hard,
unresponsive, motionless,'' watched her "winding up those stairs,'' a
phrase that once more recalls the toiling and singing ascent of the
isolated brother and sister.[48]

Mr. Dombey watches, but he fails to respond. In his frigid self-love
he is unable to comprehend the significance of anything he has witnessed: Florence's singing, her ministrations to Paul, her mission to
himself, and within a few weeks he has forgotten her altogether. But
Mr. Dombey's forgetfulness helps the reader remember. After Paul's
death, Mr. Dombey courts mercenary Edith, his wife to be, and pro-
spectively the mother of a new son, and tests her worthiness to be his
wife. One episode in this testing occurs when he asks her to play and
sing. Edith obediently plays her harp, an instrument he had first heard
her play only a few moments before as he came up the staircase to her
apartment, and an instrument that simultaneously and ironically reminds the reader of Florence's angelic staircase singing. Then Edith
goes to the piano and unwittingly plays and sings the air that Florence
used to croon to Paul as they wound their way up the heavenly stairs.
But to self-centered Mr. Dombey, Edith and her singing are simply
additional acquisitions; he does not recognize the air.[49]

The music-staircase leitmotif echoes through the remainder of the
book, linking innumerable scenes, harmonizing additional characters
and actions, gathering new meaning and intensity. Carker goes down
the staircase, down to doom, after arranging his assignation with Edith;
Edith runs wretchedly down its steps as she hastens to that meeting
and her own damnation; and Florence stands at the bottom of the
terrible stairs when her father strikes her in his fury.

Toward the end of the novel, the leitmotif reaches a climax and then
a resolution. Mr. Dombey wanders ghostlike on the enchanted
staircase—wanders terrifyingly between hell and heaven—after his
ruin and during his long phantasmagoric pilgrimage to humility and
love. His most ordinary actions reverberate now with recurrent and
amplified meaning. In "the dead of night, and with a candle in his
hand,'' he leaves his dark room and goes "softly up the stairs,'' weeping as he goes.[50] Now, on the staircase, he begins to fathom the
significance of scenes he had often looked upon but never understood;
and on the staircase he finally calls up the portentous scenes he had

witnessed there so long ago, scenes radiant at last with magical meaning: "He almost saw it, going on before. He stopped, looked up towards the skylight; and a figure, childish itself, but carrying a child, and singing as it went, seemed to be there again. Anon, it was the same figure, alone, stopping for an instant, with suspended breath; the bright hair clustering loosely round its tearful face; and looking back at him."[51] Mr. Dombey's apotheosis of an ascended Paul and a dolorous angel Florence marks his submission and conversion.

But Mr. Dombey cannot give birth to his new self. In his remorse and anguish he is ready to do self-murder. At this point Florence enters and takes her father in her arms. The old embrace on the staircase, musical and life-giving, the embrace of love that transforms earthly death into heavenly life, an embrace that Dombey could not give or receive— could not even understand—is now vouchsafed him through angel Florence. "Clasped in one another's arms," Dombey at last becomes part of the magic circle of love from which he was self-excluded.[52] The scene of father and daughter locked in one another's arms is followed by Mr. Dombey's long sickness and delirium, outward signs of the death of the old Dombey and the birth pangs of the new. It is during this process of rebirth that Mr. Dombey imagines "that his heart smote him, and that he went out after her, and up the stairs to seek her."[53] Mr. Dombey's vision of ascending the stairs and seeking his daughter signalizes his rebirth. And now by a last significant sounding of the old chord, Dickens makes the leitmotif, like Mr. Dombey, come full circle. For when Mr. Dombey finally awakens from his sickness, he hears Florence, now with another Paul, with her own infant Paul in her arms, singing the old air, and he listens and understands and responds.[54]

The book ends by the vast marge of the murmuring sea. We recall that the mysterious murmur of the sea had somehow echoed in Florence's voice as she sang at Doctor Blimber's. Now, many years later, white-haired Mr. Dombey, accompanied by his two grandchildren, walks along the shore of the whispering sea. One great cycle of the novel, a cycle sweeping and stately, a cycle intricately compounded of waves and stairs and clocks and embraces and songs, has slowly turned and turned again. The end of *Dombey* is a beginning, a beginning with a fairer promise for the future. By the side of the sounding sea, hoarse-voiced incarnation of death and immortality, Mr. Dombey walks. He no longer walks alone. He walks in contradiction to his earlier path through life. He walks with a little Paul and a still smaller Florence walking by his side.

The music-staircase leitmotif is typical of many other thematic clusters that thread through the novel. Some of these clusters, such as the sea cluster, are stronger and more pervasive than the music-staircase leitmotif; some, such as the railroad, are weaker and more confined. Sometimes the clusters—the sea and the music-staircase, for example—combine for a while, then go their separate ways, though they often, even in their separateness, support the same thematic ends. For the most part these motifs undergird and direct the novel in subtle and enriching ways, but sometimes, as with the heavenly ship and glorified presences at Paul's death, or with the reiterated "Let him remember it in that room, years to come" when Mr. Dombey sends Florence back up the stairs, they become too insistent and heavy-handed.[55] What most of these leitmotifs share is an integrating effect and a numinous dimension. The reiterations, foreshadowings, and interconnections that are at the heart of the leitmotifs serve to bind the most diverse parts of the novel together; such recurrences, signaling new connections and new meanings in each new context, help show how the intricate web of existence vibrates and trembles at each distant touch.

Virtually all the leitmotifs work in this way. The sea motif illustrates the effect most centrally. The sea that ebbs and flows through the entire novel unites Mrs. Dombey, Paul, Florence, and Mr. Dombey in the mysteries of life and death. But it also unites dozens of other characters in those same mysteries, and, through Dombey's maritime business and Sol Gills' nautical shop, it encompasses virtually all the characters of the story. The leitmotif echoes and reechoes throughout the book. The flowing rivers, the tides of commerce, the whispering waves, the deeps of death—all these and much more, conceived and conveyed as images of the sea, enter the novel again and again, now soft, now loud, now hardly perceptible, focusing and enlarging meaning. Even the names of many of the characters in *Dombey* syllable the pull and swing of the sea: Cuttle, Gills, Briggs, Brogley, Glubb, Nipper, Perch, and Morfin.

The fairy-tale components of the leitmotifs—components which strengthen and gain strength from the recurrences—work in analogous ways. The demon locomotives, talking clocks, and murmuring seas direct our awareness and our judgments. They also affirm the mysterious bonds between objects and persons. In Dickens' world objects are intimately connected with their human counterparts: with lobster-eyed devils, spell-casting ogresses, and changeling children—the Bagstocks, MacStingers, and Pauls of life. By virtue of this reciprocity and sympathy, objects and characters, real and at the same time wildly fanciful, testify in concert to the singular nature of the universe. The leitmotifs are an essential part of that astonishing testimony. The fairy-tale energies of the leitmotifs inform us as clearly as the directive repetitions that the universe is interdependent and sentient, full of mysterious affinities, secret signatures, and magical correspondences.

The leitmotifs help define structure and meaning; they also mark a change. These intricate, slowly accreting, thematic clusters, consistent and recurring through hundreds of pages, these constellations of phrases, images, and associations, richly reiterated and dense with beckoning signs, are something new in Dickens. They separate the pre-*Dombey* from the post-*Dombey* novels; they proclaim their debt to Christmas-book experimentation. They help Dickens weld old usages and new conceptions into a tighter, more expressive unity. Though nurtured in the Christmas books, these magic-laden leitmotifs transcend the Christmas books. The intermittent fairy-tale scenes and devices of the early novels, the supervisory ghosts and stark incantatory repetitions of the Christmas books, have been domesticated and perfected and transformed. Out of storybook fantasy and meticulous observation, out of reverberating leitmotifs and cindery slums, out of fiery monsters and purple-faced majors, Dickens forges a deeper unity and a higher realism.

II.

The innermost design of *Dombey,* especially in relation to Florence and Walter, works changes on the *Cinderella* theme, and this familiar theme, and the fears and fulfillments it embodies, gives *Dombey* a part of its emotional appeal. The opening words of *Cinderella* recall the central situation of Dickens' business novel: "There was once a gentleman, who, having lost his wife, resolved to marry a second time. The lady he chanced to fix upon for that purpose was the proudest and most haughty woman ever known. . . . The gentleman . . . had a daughter, who, in sweetness of temper and carriage, was the exact likeness of her deceased mother, whose loss she had much deplored."[56]

Dombey, of course, contains much more. For instance, Dickens also reworks the *Cinderella* theme, more subtly and psychologically than with Florence and Walter, through Florence and her father. Florence is the dispossessed, the cinder girl, the princess in disguise, the treasure whom Dombey must learn to recognize and appreciate. Dombey combines the roles of the wicked stepmother, the proud vain stepsisters, and the searching prince: he neglects and humiliates his princess daughter, leaves her home when he goes off to the balls and fêtes of the world, and persecutes her for his own failings. Dickens gives this *Cinderella* (and poor-little-rich-girl, Lear–Cordelia) theme a mythlike power and fascination, but he also maintains the story's realism and he infuses his fairy tale with autobiographical passion. In this he was doing again what he had earlier done in *Oliver Twist, The Old Curiosity*

Shop, and *A Christmas Carol,* and what he was even then planning to do in *The Haunted Man.*

The autobiographical passion comes from the profound childhood feelings, still sore and intense, that invest this version of *Cinderella* with deep ground swells of remembered emotion, emotion heavily laden on the one hand with memories of parental rejection and neglect (in particular of hurrying in solitary isolation through hostile London streets), and on the other with memories of yearning for parental acceptance and love. Mr. Dombey's rejection of Florence recapitulates Dickens' own sense of rejection. Florence, like Dickens, feels orphaned. But unlike the many true orphans in Dickens' writings, unlike Oliver, little Nell, Pip, and others, Florence is no ordinary waif. She is an orphan (and in this she is most like Dickens) whose father is still alive. The scene in which Dickens gives this notion explicit form is accompanied by great waves of emotion and by an unusual richness of complementary imagery (imagery notably of falling flowers and flowing water) and is followed by an interpolated exemplum, a reverse father-daughter story that accentuates Dickens' horror at the rejection he is depicting. The term orphan is no critical subtlety, for Dickens himself applies the metaphor to Florence: "The flowers were scattered on the ground like dust; the empty hands were spread upon the face; and orphaned Florence, shrinking down upon the ground, wept long and bitterly."⁵⁷ The sense of being orphaned, of being a lonely waif in a great unfeeling city, runs through all of *Dombey,* though usually by implication or dramatic demonstration rather than direct statement. The idea, so simple and primal, is projected with the force and clarity of a fairy story: the neglected child, an innocent victim, is thrust by unfeeling parents into the dark threatening dangers of the trackless forest, or rather, as usual in Dickens, into the dark threatening dangers of the trackless streets. In this respect *Dombey* is an elaborate urban version of *Hop o' my Thumb* or *Hansel and Gretel* or *The Children in the Wood.*

The first strong enunciation of this theme occurs when Florence, as a child, is lost in the city of London, a scene that recalls Dickens' similar childhood experience and that also mirrors one aspect of his ambivalent childhood response to London life and London streets.⁵⁸ This crucial scene sets the pattern for what is to follow, for the orphan label and the lost-child symbolism reappear at climactic moments throughout the story. The predictability with which Dickens sounds this chord at such moments testifies to its profound meaning for him. When Dombey strikes Florence, Dickens writes: "She saw she had no father upon earth, and ran out, orphaned, from his house."⁵⁹ And when she is running through the streets, he has her think: "Where to go? . . . She thought of the only other time she had been lost in the wide wilderness of London—though not lost as now—and went that way."[60] Loss and abandonment become intertwined with rejection, and significantly, in view of Dickens' own experiences, when Florence later feels that Walter also rejects her, she summons up her childhood days, again remembers the trauma of her terrifying city experience, and recalls "when she was a lost child in the staring streets."[61]

In such recurrent nightmare scenes, scenes wild with childish horror, scenes teeming with "terror," "clash and clangour," "staring streets," and witchlike predators, fairy tale and autobiography coalesce.[62] The unreasoning fears of childhood, irrational and illimitable, filled with watching presences and lurking monsters, combine with painful memories of early rejection, "orphaning," and neglect. Poor orphaned Florence is both lost babe in the wood and outcast Cinderella. As babe, she must flee through the forest of London, all but perishing. As Cinderella, she must languish in grievous durance while her blind father-prince neglects her.

While Florence is languishing, she enacts another *Cinderella* role. In Walter she finds an aware and appreciative prince. This second *Cinderella* motif is also imbued with autobiographical overtones, overtones that cause strange discrepancies and distortions. The Walter-Florence love relationship is replete with *Cinderella* imagery and *Cinderella* analogues, but it is treated through much of the book as a brother-sister relationship. It thus parallels the other central love relationship of the novel, that of Paul and Florence. Dickens counterpoises the love that exists between Paul and Florence to the love that is lacking between the children and their father. Driven in on themselves, the "orphaned" children turn to one another. They find in their brotherly-sisterly love a substitute for the parental love they need, the love that Dombey is incapable of giving them.

The reenactment of the brother-sister love through Walter and Florence is thus thematic, but it is also strangely dissonant. It does not accord with the developing destinies of the two: with their emerging sexuality, predestined marriage, and *Cinderella* roles. In a most curious way, the sibling quality of their relationship is emphasized at the same time that the possibility of sexual love and marriage is also underscored. In this respect, Dickens is perpetuating, through Walter and Florence, little Paul's equally curious yearning for his sister. "'I mean,' said Paul, 'to put my money all together in one bank, never try to get any more, go away into the country with my darling Florence, have a beautiful garden, fields, and woods, and live there with her all my life!'"[63] Again the dream is a storybook dream, this time of a magical garden paradise safe from the encroachments of time and change. It is a dream of Eden, a soothing counterpart to the dark surrealistic nightmare of fleeing through clamorous streets. It is also a dream of eternal love, of a steadfast substitute for an inadequate parent. And after Paul has died in Florence's sisterly arms, and the Captain Cuttle–Sol Gills circle views Walter's marriage to Florence and his accession to the head of Dombey and Son as certain, Dickens goes out of his way to make Walter a surrogate of Paul, and to give the brother-sister relationship of Walter and Florence an almost legal status. The day before Walter voyages into shipwreck on the *Son and Heir,* Florence visits him and says, "If you'll be a brother to me, Walter, now that [Paul] is gone and I have none on earth, I'll be your sister all my life, and think of you like one wherever we may be!"[64] Walter accepts the offer, Florence gets into a waiting coach, says "You are my brother, dear!" and the coach drives off.[65] But Walter is to be Florence's husband, not her brother, and years later when he returns and realizes that he loves her sexually, the pledge of brotherhood becomes a torment to him, forces him to avoid her, and is dissolved only when Florence confesses her unsisterly love for him.

This strange sister-lover conjunction that Dickens idealizes in *Dombey,* and that he portrays as a saving, if transitory, substitute for neglectful parents, is similar to a pattern that appears in his own life and in many of his works. That confused pattern goes back to his earliest days. Dickens never got over his feeling that his mother had rejected and abandoned him. First she had put him aside to care for a steady procession of new infants; later she had consigned him to the blacking warehouse. In response to the initial betrayal (I adopt here the exaggerated coloring that Dickens' wounded emotions gave to these events), he turned to his sister Fanny. Fanny, one year older than Dickens, became the close, loving companion of his formative childhood years. But when the family moved to London, Fanny was sent to the Royal Academy of Music and Dickens to the blacking warehouse—another abandonment and betrayal, and one that now involved his sister as well as his mother. This early pattern of trusting love violated by sudden treason—I again adopt Dickens' aggrieved response—had lifelong consequences. His mother, his sister Fanny, and his first love, the faithless Maria Beadnell formed his image of womanhood and shaped his attitude toward love, his wife, and his heroines. What Dickens yearned for was an adoring female who would never change and never turn away, who would undo and heal his past. What he longed for were unrealities that would not betray the heart. He sought a wife who would be a companion, a sexual partner, a bearer of children, but at the same time, and unlike his unforgiven mother or the inconstant Maria, be steadfast and innocent, untouched and untouchable, the matured and idealized image of his prelapsarian sister. The very terms of his desire made it unattainable, for to find the paragon wife was to destroy the sister, and to preserve the immature sister was to have no wife at all.

Hence Dickens' curious domestic compromise, his anomalous household which from shortly after his marriage contained not only his wife, but his wife's sixteen-year-old sister, Mary Hogarth. And when Mary died in his arms at the age of seventeen, still budlike and perfect, and thus forever so, he was able to convince himself that he had redis- covered, though again in fleeting and forsaking form, the all-loving sister that he had idealized and then lost in childhood. Now more than ever, therefore, he sought to give actual form to his dream of a sister- wife fusion. Five years later he brought fifteen-year-old Georgina, another Hogarth sister, into his household. And there Georgina re- mained, unmarried and sisterly, sisterly even after her sister, Dickens' wife, moved out of his home, sisterly until his death, clinging to that portion of her brother-in-law which had need of a worshiping sister surrogate such as she.

His need and the dream that embodied it also led to a host of female characters into whom he projected, and through whom he partly vicariously realized, the confused sister-wife ideal of his emotional yearning. In his early works this projection is sometimes an idealized blending of Fanny Dickens and Mary Hogarth, a combination of the perfect but vanished childhood sister companion and the doomed sister substitute: a figure who is most notably represented by little Nell. Or more commonly, such female characters are sister-wife figures who are depicted both as perfect sisters and perfect wives. (One usually gets the feeling that the sister role is the important one, that happy wifehood is a vague status that comes late in the novel as a reward for loyal sister- hood.) In the typical case, the dutiful, loving sister, having proved her boundless devotion, is allowed to marry an impeccable but bloodless spouse: Rose Fleming, the foster-sister of Oliver, and his aunt, as it turns out, marries Harry Maylie, whose foster-sister—to compound the pattern—is the very same Rose; Kate Nickleby, the sister of Nicholas, marries Frank Cheeryble; Ruth Pinch, the sister of Tom, marries John Westlock. In each case the marriage occurs at the end of the book, and it is the sister relationship, not the lover relationship, that is important. Sometimes, as with Ruth Pinch, the sister per- petuates the brother-sister relationship after marriage by bringing the brother into, or next to, her new household; and in some cases the sister never marries, but, as with Harriet Carker, sacrifices her chance for marriage and happiness—nobly and fittingly as Dickens makes clear—in loyalty to her brother. In most of these instances the pro- tagonists are parentless, or they have parents who are incompetent or neglectful or inimical.

In later works Dickens probes the nuances of sister-lover relationships with greater subtlety; he also presents his conflicting feelings with increasing insight and sophistication. Yet he never fully resolves what are, after all, irreconcilable yearnings. Even his latter-day heroines— think, for instance, of Rosa Bud and Helena Landless in *Edwin Drood*—have a tendency to metamorphose from lovers into sisters or to waver uncertainly in the limbo of conflicting roles. But he is much more likely in his later works to make the antipodal roles of sister and lover thematic, often by separating and then counterpointing them. In *A Tale of Two Cities,* for example, through Sydney Carton and Charles Darnay (alter-ego twins, and two projections of Dickens, as Dickens himself recognized[66]), he again depicts a love that combines sexual and brother-sister qualities. The pale married love of Lucie and Charles represents an idealized husband-wife relationship; the emotional Lucie-Sydney conjunction represents a forbidden sexual love that is repressed and finally sublimated into a precarious brotherly love.[67] At the end of the book this brotherly love is purged of its remaining sexual taint when Sydney (Dickens as illicit lover-cum-brother) forgoes the possibility of marrying a widowed Lucie and saves Lucie's lawful sexual partner (Dickens as conventional lover-cum-husband) by sacrificing himself.

Permutations of this pattern appear in most of the late novels, in *David Copperfield, Hard Times, Little Dorrit, Bleak House, Great Expectations,* and *Edwin Drood,* for example. It is as though Dickens were compelled to examine this node of his emotional makeup over and over again. In his early novels he was probably only vaguely aware of the exact relationship between the loves he was depicting fictionally and his own emotional situation; yet his great urge to give creative objectivity to what he was feeling assured that the shaping pressures of his life would be projected into his fiction. His self-analysis therefore was partly unconscious and partly calculated. It was emotional and dramatic, not systematic. But it was not naive, and it was not static. *David Copperfield* and *Great Expectations* examine the sister-lover conjunction with a depth and sophistication that is beyond *Dombey* and the earlier novels. I shall have more to say about these matters in the chapters on *Copperfield* and *Great Expectations*.

Yet, fittingly, as Dickens' first psychological novel, *Dombey* is also the first novel to deal with this node of his life with anything more than the idealized and impossible brother, sister, and wife figures of his early works. In this shift, fairy tales—wild incarnations of fancy and make-believe—contribute, paradoxically, to a new realism. Among other things, *Dombey*'s storybook structure and mythic atmosphere help give aesthetic coherence to the psychological complexities of the Florence-Walter, Florence-Paul, and Florence-Dombey relationships.

The process by which this takes place is central to Dickens' art. Dickens uses Christmas-book techniques to make emotionally freighted autobiography take on the profound fears and fulfillments of fairy stories. Through such fusions he gives vent to his emotions, while at the same time distancing and containing them. The result is much more than autobiography. He now gives—or at least he now more frequently gives—his personal trials and yearnings pattern and universality; he also makes those personal impulsions fablelike and thematic. This is not to say that fairy tales resolve the distortions or the incongruities that stem from Dickens' confused feelings about parent-child and brother-sister-lover relationships. Fairy tales do, however, contribute a certain universalizing power and coherence to such feelings—they liberate, disguise, and sanction such feelings—and they make it easier to imbue objects, persons, and events with magical meaning.

Mary Hogarth's death in Dickens' arms is a case in point. That sisterly death is projected into *Dombey* more than once, but with modifications important both autobiographically (in terms of the death's larger significance for Dickens) and aesthetically (in terms of his new skill in mythifying meaning). When Paul lies dying he recalls being told that his mother held Florence in her arms as she was dying, and therefore (so he reasons) she must have loved Florence much better than her father, "for even he, her brother, who had such dear love for her, could have no greater wish than that."[68] Accordingly, Dickens has Paul in his last moments (in the Dickens-Mary Hogarth manner) clasp Florence to his breast: "Sister and brother wound their arms around each other, and the golden light came streaming in, and fell upon them, locked together."[69] Again the father is excluded from this final gesture of love (a fact that makes Mr. Dombey jealous and helps turn him against his daughter), and the love between brother and sister is made to compensate, if only haltingly and temporarily, for the inadequate love between parent and child. That Dickens connected the brother-sister love of Paul and Florence with his love for Mary Hogarth, and Mary's death with Paul's, is made even clearer a few pages earlier. In the earlier scene, Paul, already in his presageful final illness, watches Florence, and thinks how "young, and good, and beautiful" she is—the words Dickens placed on Mary Hogarth's tombstone.[70]

We are dealing here with a nexus of actions and feelings that for Dickens was surcharged with overwhelming personal emotion. But Dickens translates this nexus into the realms of ritual and fairy-tale recurrence. In the manner of the Christmas books, he turns a painful memory—Mary's deathbed embrace—into a recurrent symbolic gesture, a gesture magical in its overtones and implications. That gesture transcends its autobiographical origins and takes on mythic attributes;

it becomes the angelic embrace that ushers frail humanity from mortal
death to eternal life. The magical nature of the gesture is further emphasized when Dickens, at the end of the novel, signalizes Dombey's
salvation by that selfsame gesture and selfsame image, a gesture and
image that had earlier proclaimed Dombey's exclusion and damnation.
Father and daughter now repeat the love-death embrace of mother and
daughter, brother and sister—and, one might add, of Dickens and
Mary Hogarth. Father and daughter remain "clasped in one another's
arms," while "the glorious sunshine that had crept in with Florence"
bathes them in celestial light.[71] The painful memory has been glorified;
the darkness in Dombey has been exorcised. He too can now bask in
"golden light," in "glorious sunshine." He too can come within the
magic circle of Florence's arms. Clasped in that transcendent embrace,
he will die and be reborn.

Dickens is enlarging and consolidating his mastery. He shows this in
his fabling. He now finds it much easier to free autobiographical parallels from their outward events, probably because he is much more
adept at making such parallels true to the inward emotions of the
events. What is even more important, he is now more likely to subordinate these parallels to the larger demands of the novel, a new feature in
his writings. This new flexibility also marks his handling of fairy tales,
and fairy tales, in turn, help him mythify autobiography and extend his
fabling. The folklore structures that carry his thesis, the enchanted
atmosphere that hovers over object and scene, and the magical devices
that shadow forth the hidden messages of the invisible world are introduced more tactfully than in the past and are carefully formulated with
an eye toward the artistic whole. One sees this everywhere. Florence's
recurrent angel-embraces, part of her dolorous ministerings, are translated into myth and at the same time are merged imperceptibly into the
surrounding realism. The storybook fulfillments of the conclusion, still
unmistakably present, undergo a similar transformation. Walter, at the
conclusion, purged of his brotherliness, recapitulates the *Cinderella*
myth, but he does so in a subdued and believable fashion, a departure
from the wand-waving finales of the early novels. Mr. Dombey is an
even more striking example of this development. He too is an avatar of
Cinderella, a blind and unworthy prince. Dickens harrows and chas-
tens him, and then brings him to awareness. But Mr. Dombey is not
like his rudimentary storybook counterparts, the reformed Scrooges
and Redlaws of the Christmas books. Mr. Dombey can only enjoy his
tardily recognized princess in sadly diminished form—a switch from
the old method which would have turned the converted Mr. Dombey
into a dazzling prince and caused him to shower golden blessings on the
elect.

Dickens' use of the fairy tale has changed. The fairy story has become a more important force in his writings, but it has also become a more supple, realistic, integrated force. This shift can be seen not only in the naturalistic rendering of *Dombey*'s complex double-tiered *Cinderella* framework and the interaction of the framework with the motifs I have just been tracing, but in other areas as well. A portion of the plot is worked out through quasi-supernatural means, through the prophecy, special knowledge, portentous interference, and ultimately the astonishing blood relationship of Good Mrs. Brown. But Good Mrs. Brown, a witch out of folklore and fairy literature, is also a realistic Victorian ragpicker. This cunning camouflage—or rather fusion—is omnipresent; it enters scene and fable as well as character. The plot, for example, is unified not only by the matter-of-fact thaumaturgy of Good Mrs. Brown and the familiar fulfillments of *Cinderella*, but by a host of additional devices, and they too are deceptively dual. For Dickens many of these devices, seemingly straightforward contrivances such as recurrent gestures, repeated phrases, leitmotifs, allegorical symbolism, and so on, are profoundly entwined with fairy tales.

The Dombey mansion is a case in point. It is real and solid, but it possesses a mythlike potency and centripetal power that spring from storybook energies. The supernatural atmosphere of the mansion is composed of magical staircases, heavenly skylights, and weeping chandeliers, all wonderfully blended into the realistic fabric of the novel, but it is also composed of an intricate web of moods and spells. A wasting enchantment broods over the mansion, subtly controlling scene and action. This enchantment is always present, now hovering faintly in the background, now emerging strongly in the foreground. The scenes that wed the house most explicitly to the story's magical nimbus begin with the opening words of Chapter XXIII: "Florence lived alone in the great dreary house, and day succeeded day and still she lived alone; and the blank walls looked down upon her with a vacant stare, as if they had a Gorgon-like mind to stare her youth and beauty into stone." This introduction, with its repetition and its supernatural and fablelike elements (later, the whole sentence becomes a refrain repeated throughout the chapter) reminds one of Dickens' Christmas-book technique, a similarity strengthened when Dickens goes on in the next sentences to introduce a host of fairy-tale allusions. "No magic dwelling-place in magic story, shut up in the heart of a thick wood, was ever more solitary and deserted to the fancy, than was her father's mansion in its grim reality." Although there were not "two dragon sentries keeping ward before the gate of this abode, as in magic legend are usually found on duty over the wronged innocence imprisoned," there was a "monstrous fantasy of rusty iron"; and though there were "no talismanic characters engraven on the portal," neighborhood boys had chalked the neglected railings and pavements with ghosts.[72] The decaying mansion is bewitched: "The spell upon it was more wasting than the spell that used to set enchanted houses sleeping once upon a time, but left their waking freshness unimpaired."[73] The allusion is to *Sleeping Beauty,* but as the narrator indicates, the spell that withers Dombey's mansion is far different from that which binds Sleeping Beauty's enchanted castle. In the Dombey mansion curtains droop, mirrors grow dim, boards creak and shake, keys rust, fungus proliferates, and spiders, moths, black beetles, and rats multiply in frightening multitudes. Dickens makes the decaying house and its spell-like isolation mark the passage of time, underscore Dombey's neglect of Cinderella-Sleeping Beauty Florence, and dramatize her magical transformation into lovely womanhood. The interlude, like the interlude in Virginia Woolf's *To the Lighthouse* which describes a similar scene and achieves an identical effect, goes on for several pages without slackening in tautness or evocativeness. The house is now boldly termed "an enchanted abode," and in this supernatural mansion Florence "bloomed . . . like the king's fair daughter in the story."[74] The interlude continues, associating the staircase, flower, and lost-child imagery with the storybook atmosphere, and after further allusions to the "circle" that enabled Florence to live on while "nothing harmed her," and references to "an enchanted vision," and "a haunted house," and after an intricate juxtaposition of the mansion with Florence's solitary life and frustrated will to love, Dickens concludes by repeating the Gorgon refrain for a third time.[75]

This synthesis of prosaic detail, suprarealistic atmosphere, and fairy-tale point of view is not confined to the Dombey mansion or to interpolated interludes. Mrs. Pipchin, the dour, redoubtable teacher of little Paul, and his later overseer and nurse, combines meticulous realism, satiric humor, and artful supernaturalism. Mrs. Pipchin is the old folklore ogress-witch, but so thoroughly transformed that she bears little relationship to the one-dimensional witches and godmothers of Dickens' early writings. For Mrs. Pipchin's diablerie is more than Gothic trimming, it is a reflection of Paul's view of her. Mrs. Pipchin was modeled on two real persons, a Mrs. Roylance, a hard and unresponsive lady who took Dickens in to board during a portion of his blacking-warehouse days, and another woman, probably the keeper of a dame school he attended briefly several years earlier; but his childhood sufferings, especially those of his blacking-warehouse days, caused him to transform his flesh-and-blood models into a flesh-and-blood witch.[76] Mrs. Pipchin is a young child's image of evil—it is noteworthy that Dickens makes Paul younger than he himself was—

and her representation accentuates the child's view of the world that Dickens is depicting in this portion of the book.

Mrs. Pipchin is a "marvellous ill-favoured, ill-conditioned old lady" with a "stooping figure," "mottled face," "hook nose," and "hard grey eye."[77] Her witchlike appearance is accentuated by her "black bombazeen" clothing of a "lustreless, deep, dead, sombre shade," and by the fact that her presence is always a "quencher."[78] This "ogress and child-queller" lives in a frightening storybook "Castle."[79] The castle is cold and inimical and eerily animistic; its objects and furnishings bristle with baleful menace. Even the parlor plants are sinister and threatening: writhing cacti, lobster-claw greens, long spidery vines, creeping vegetables, and sticky-leaved exotics.[80] Paul's first conversation with Mrs. Pipchin adds to this intimidating fairy-tale ambiance:

> "Well, sir," said Mrs. Pipchin to Paul, "how do you think you shall like me?"
> "I don't think I shall like you at all," replied Paul. "I want to go away. This isn't my house."
> "No. It's mine," retorted Mrs. Pipchin.
> "It's a very nasty one," said Paul.
> "There's a worse place in it than this though," said Mrs. Pipchin, "where we shut up our bad boys."[81]

This "worse place," an empty apartment at the back devoted to correctional purposes, Dickens calls the "Castle Dungeon."[82] Paul's predicament, in his childish view, is catastrophic. He is trapped in a horrible storybook castle presided over by a merciless witch. Words such as "ogress," "castle," "black," and "dungeon" reverberate through the remainder of the passage, and harmonize with Mrs. Pipchin's "black teapot," "coiled" black cat, and "hard grey eye."[83]

Paul, who is not lacking in supernatural qualities himself, is fascinated by this horrific old lady, even as Dickens was fascinated by his own lady mentors and nursemaids and their terrifying folklore stories. Soon a strange unspoken rapport develops between Paul and Mrs. Pipchin. The two would sit before the fire and Paul would stare at his keeper "until he sometimes quite confounded [her], ogress as she was."[84] The atmosphere of the scene, despite its foundation of realism, becomes charged with an ever-increasing supernaturalism. "The good old lady," writes Dickens, "might have been—not to record it disrespectfully—a witch, and Paul and the cat her two familiars, as they all sat by the fire together. It would have been quite in keeping with the appearance of the party if they had all sprung up the chimney in a high wind one night, and never been heard of any more."[85]

"This," continues Dickens in the next sentence, "never came to pass," and with that remark, though the supernatural atmosphere continues to hover strongly over the remainder of the chapter, the emphasis shifts from the occult to the realistic. The passage is a good example of Dickens' method of combining the realistic and the fantastic, and the passage illustrates what he gained thereby: a suggestive atmosphere, an evocative point of view, a flexible suprarealism, and a unity of vision.

Dickens puts this synthesis to work throughout the novel. Another, even more important, example of how this fusion operates may be seen in the Walter-Florence-Good Mrs. Brown meeting. At this encounter, which seems at first to be a picturesque digression, some of the controlling motifs of the story—the *Cinderella*, lost child, business world, witch, and enchantment motifs—meet and intermingle. Presiding over that meeting and guiding its development are pervasive fairy-tale details and a pervasive fairy-tale aura.

The meeting occurs without warning. Florence had accompanied Polly Toodle and Susan Nipper on Paul's fateful visit to Staggs's Gardens, but in a moment of confusion on the way home had become separated from them. An old woman, horrible and witchlike, hobbles up to Florence, grasps her by the wrist, and promises to bring her back to her friends. The old woman appears as suddenly and as purposefully as a wicked fairy bent on fatal mischief. Her physical attributes and physical mannerisms confirm her baleful role. She is as ugly and frightening as any evil crone in fairy story or legend. She has "red rims round her eyes, . . . a mouth that mumbled and chattered of itself," and a "shrivelled yellow face and throat" that went through "all sorts of contortions."[86] When the old woman seeks to soothe Florence and lead her away, Florence asks, "What's your name?" "Mrs. Brown," answers the old woman, "Good Mrs. Brown."[87] We are in the realm of archetypal personages and archetypal happenings, a realm where objects and actions radiate magical meaning, where lost children fall prey to lurking monsters, where chattering evil masquerades as "Good."

Good Mrs. Brown now leads Florence through dirty lanes and muddy roads to her witch's abode, a "shabby," "closely shut up" house.[88] She unlocks the door, and pushes the child into a room with black walls, black ceiling, and no furniture. On the floor there is "a great heap of rags of different colours . . . a heap of bones, and a heap of sifted dust or cinders." "Sit upon the rags," says Good Mrs. Brown. And then Good Mrs. Brown, taking her own seat on the bones, warns, "Don't vex me. If you don't . . . I won't hurt you. But if you do, I'll kill you. I could have you killed at any time—even if you was in your own bed at home."[89]

So little Cinderella sits near her heap of identifying cinders and confronts her own Mrs. Pipchin, a witch and child-queller infinitely more terrifying than Paul's. But the episode and its fablelike implications have only begun. Good Mrs. Brown now commands Florence to take off her clothes. The command and its consequences are deeply meaningful, for in *Sartor Resartus* fashion, Florence's garments, like Rob the Grinder's, Mr. Toodle's, Mr. Toots', and those of other characters in *Dombey,* proclaim and conceal identity. Florence trembles and obeys. Off come her costly frock, bonnet, petticoats, and shoes; in their place, taken from the heap of rags, go two wretched substitutes for shoes, an old worn girl's cloak, and the "crushed remains of a bonnet that had probably been picked up from some ditch or dung-hill."[90] Florence is now clothed in an outfit that correctly represents her outcast state.

Then, suddenly, in a frightening scene, she almost undergoes a more crippling transformation. In putting on her filthy substitute bonnet, she had entangled it in her "luxuriantly" beautiful hair, and Good Mrs. Brown, watching like a great black spider, falls into a strange fit of excitement. Trembling with desire, the old woman "whip[s] out a large pair of scissors," ruffles Florence's very salable curls "with a furious pleasure," and prepares to cut them off.[91] Florence is on the verge of despoliation. Her hair, rich and luxuriant, haloing emblem of her sanctity and femininity, is about to be cropped, sold for money. In a moment she will be mutilated, a damaged cast-off thing. The great scissors hovers over her head, dramatizing her vulnerability, her mortal danger. The scene, for Dickens, is filled with nightmare horror. It haunts his imagination. A fearsome adult brandishing a deadly weapon over a helpless child occurs like a frozen delirium elsewhere in his writings, most notably in *Oliver Twist* and *David Copperfield*. It is Dickens' most intense icon of ferocious adult aggression against innocent childhood. Good Mrs. Brown, her terrible scissors poised over Florence's head, covets and ruffles her luxuriant hair. But then, remembering her distant daughter's long hair, she pauses, finally stops, and at last gives way to a "wild tossing up of her lean arms" and a passionate parental grief that "thrilled to the heart" of the unloved Florence. The old woman tells Florence to hide her curls under her bonnet and "let no trace of them escape."[92]

Mrs. Brown's passionate daughter, Alice, tossing her wild hair, will later appear in the story, a transmutation of the innocent Florence, and a foil to upper-class Edith (just as Good Mrs. Brown is a foil to Edith's mother, Mrs. Skewton); and Alice and her mother will also serve as one more study of a blighting, money-centered parent-child relationship. But the talismanic hair episode, with its frightening despoliation implications, and its many fairy-tale and legendary analogues — analogues that range from the reassuring *Rapunzel* to the dismaying Samson and Delilah — is more than a clue to a character who must

appear much later. It is part of the terrifying storybook evil that hovers
about the immature Florence, and it is part of the enchanted atmosphere of the entire story. For the whole episode is a way of objectifying
in a magical and exceptionally evocative manner, and also, from a
child's point of view, in a brilliantly appropriate manner, the mortal
peril that encompasses innocent Florence. And it follows that Florence's brief sojourn in the hell-like charnel house, a house that is
identical, emotionally, to her bleak palace home, epitomizes the hell-
ishness of her daily life. The fairy-tale significance of the episode is
carried forward when Good Mrs. Brown returns with Florence to the
London streets.

The two leave the black room of cinders, rags, and bones, but only
after Mrs. Brown has insisted that Florence not go home but find her
way "to her father's office in the City."[93] Mrs. Brown accompanies
this injunction with terrifying threats, and enjoins Florence to wait at
the street corner "until the clock [strikes] three." Florence waits in
fear and bewilderment. She looks back to see "the head of Good Mrs.
Brown peeping out of a low wooden passage . . . likewise the fist of
Good Mrs. Brown shaking towards her," but at last the witch disappears, London's many clocks toll the magic number three, and Florence ventures into the London thoroughfare, seeking her father's
offices. Of the offices she knows, fittingly and ironically, only "that
they belonged to Dombey and Son."[94]

Lost and in rags, Florence goes through the commercial heart of the
city asking the way to Dombey and Son. Symbolically, Florence has
begun the great pilgrimage of her life—she is seeking the way to her
father's heart, the way into the cold commercial citadel that is her
father's life. At last she comes to a dock where Dombey's name is
known. Walter, Dombey's office boy, is nearby, and when she hears
that he is from Dombey and Son, she runs eagerly up to him, leaving
one of her slipshod shoes upon the ground. "I am lost," she cries,
bursting into tears. At the same time her bonnet falls off, her hair
comes "tumbling down about her face," and Walter, moved to
"speechless admiration" by this magical sign, instantly falls into a
worshipful daze of love.[95] But he is not too dazed by this ragged,
glory-crowned princess to champion her and guide her through the city
labyrinth. His first act is to pick up the shoe "and put it on the little foot
as the Prince in the story might have fitted Cinderella's slipper on."[96]
This done, they walk arm in arm through the London streets, Walter
neat and prosperous and Florence dirty and neglected, in a reversal of
their social roles but in accordance with their spiritual states.

Walter brings Florence to Uncle Sol's nautical instrument shop, the
refuge she will again come to when she flees her father's house and
once more hurries dispossessed through London streets, and he calls

out to his uncle, "Here's Mr. Dombey's daughter lost in the streets, and robbed of her clothes by an old witch."[97] After dinner, Florence falls asleep and Walter goes off to tell Mr. Dombey of his strange storybook encounter. Sol remains by Florence's side, "building a great many airy castles of the most fantastic architecture; and looking, in the dim shade, and in the close vicinity of all the instruments, like a magician . . . who held the child in an enchanted sleep."[98]

Walter returns with Susan, Florence's maid, and with fresh clothing. Florence once more takes off her garments, again dons her usual clothes, and reassumes her former appearance. Walter and Florence exchange a kiss, Florence gets into the waiting coach, and the coach carries her off to her father's palace. "The entrance of the lost child," comments the narrator, "made a slight sensation, but not much," for Mr. Dombey "had never found her."[99]

This remarkable episode, so striking in its fairy-tale analogues, so momentous in its symbolism and foreshadowing, encompasses in foreshortened form much of what Dickens was trying to do in *Dombey*. The groundwork is here laid for the intricate interaction of many of *Dombey*'s central characters—Florence, Walter, Mr. Dombey, Uncle Sol, Good Mrs. Brown, and Carker Junior—and for the interplay of characters who have not yet appeared or who have not yet been entangled in the enchanted web—Edith, Mrs. Skewton, Alice, Harriet Carker, and Carker himself. But Dickens has also succeeded in casting a penumbra of magic, myth, and fairy lore over the scene, a penumbra he will maintain and enlarge as the book progresses, using it to reveal hidden connections and to unify the novel. This aura of enchantment helps convey as well as connect. It helps give events and characters an overwhelming significance. The real and the extrareal mingle and strengthen one another, and the union helps produce Dickens' special vision of life.

That vision enhances reality. Dickens' re-creation of his everyday world, even when he records it with hypnotic exactitude, possesses a numinous essence that intensifies meaning, an essence that works upon the reader even when the reader has no clear notion of what he is responding to. This is a compelling power, but it can give the reader deceptive satisfactions. Like *Gulliver's Travels, Moby-Dick,* and similar works of literature, *Dombey and Son* and the later Dickens novels can be read pleasurably on the most superficial levels. Readers accustomed to thinking of Dickens as a popular author, and remembering their youthful introduction to him, do not often look in him for the hidden meanings, ambiguities, and wordplay, the subtle recurrences and arcane signalings, that they have been taught to search for in a writer such as Joyce. Joyce demands this special attention. Portions of

A Portrait of the Artist as a Young Man, much of *Ulysses,* and most of *Finnegans Wake* are unintelligible without exegesis that pivots on hidden elements. In such instances, one must crack the code, so to speak, or remain mystified. But *Dombey* is more like *Dubliners*—or like *Gulliver* or *Moby-Dick*—for *Dombey* can be read meaningfully, and to all appearances, satisfactorily, on a casual perusal. This universal availability is a virtue and a trap: it enables the work to speak unencumbered to a huge differentiated audience, but it also leads to misinterpretation. If a reader responds to elements of a work of art without knowing they are there or why he is responding, or if he becomes so absorbed by the beguiling surface that he fails to notice the signaling depths, he will respond erratically and incompletely. If the guiding symbolism, the fairy-tale core, the recurring motifs of *Dombey* are missed, the book's meaning will be attenuated, and the novel's impact will be lessened. One can see this very quickly if one follows Good Mrs. Brown through the rest of *Dombey.* The hidden fairy-tale filaments that knot momentarily in the opening Good Mrs. Brown scene float in thousands of threadlike spinnings through the rest of the book, knotting again here and there, until they form an intricate web that binds together one whole movement of the novel.

The scene in which Good Mrs. Brown's magical associations are projected with the greatest force occurs halfway through the book. The episode takes place in Leamington. Dombey is courting Edith, testing her accomplishments, and displaying her to Carker whom he has called down from London. Carker, like most of the important characters in *Dombey,* has his share of occult qualities. He is the folklore devil who often appears disguised as an animal—in *Dombey* he is described most frequently as a cat, but notably also as a wolf and a snake. Carker, the sinister stalking cat or hypnotizing snake, affects Florence, Edith, Rob the Grinder, Diogenes the dog, and others in supernatural ways. Florence shudders whenever he comes near, and almost faints when he fixes his serpent's eyes upon her; Diogenes growls and barks ferociously when he appears; and Rob is so terrorized and hypnotized by him that he follows him trancelike through the streets, his eyes never wavering from Carker. Carker often imposes his silent will upon others and speaks to them without articulating. In his passionate interviews with Edith, his snaky malignancy, magnified by the surrounding supernatural symbolism, creates truly terrifying effects. In one interview, he looks at her—bright, caged, fluttering bird—and Dickens writes: "He saw the soft down tremble once again, and he saw her lay the plumage of the beautiful bird against her bosom for a moment; and he unfolded one more ring of the coil into which he had gathered himself."[100] The horror condensed into these words is difficult to convey, for the terror of the scene accumulates from snaky associations that have been building around Carker from the first. This aura of terror always clings to Carker. It is with him in the Leamington scene, and it adds its special appropriateness to the meaning and effect of that scene.

The scene occurs before breakfast in the countryside. Carker has strolled beyond the town, and in his return he goes by way of a "deep shade of leafy trees."[101] Once in this dark, deep, magical grove, he begins a strange serpentine ritual: "Mr. Carker threaded the great boles of the trees, and went passing in and out, before this one and behind that, weaving a chain of footsteps on the dewy ground." As this snaky Satan softly glides round the trunk of one large tree "on which the obdurate bark was knotted and overlapped like the hide of a rhinoceros or some kindred monster of the ancient days before the Flood," he sees a figure sitting on a nearby bench "about which, in another moment, he would have wound the chain he was making."[102] The figure is that of a beautiful, elegantly dressed lady who is struggling with herself. The lovely lady in distress is Edith, whom Carker has not yet met. But even as he looks at her from behind his antediluvian tree, "a withered and very ugly old woman . . . scrambled up from the ground—out of it, it almost appeared—and stood in the way."[103] The old woman—who is Good Mrs. Brown, although never so identified in this scene—disturbs Edith with her demands for silver and her threats to call out her fortune. Edith, frightened, rushes toward the hidden Carker, who snakelike is "slinking against his tree," and who seizes this moment to cross her path and assume her defense. But Good Mrs. Brown is not put down. "Give me something," she tells Carker, "or I'll call it after *you*!" Carker throws her a piece of silver, and Good Mrs. Brown, "munching," Dickens writes, paraphrasing Shakespeare, "like that sailor's wife of yore, who had chestnuts in her lap, and scowling like the witch who asked for some in vain" (Shakespeare, too, conflates realistic crone and threatening witch), Good Mrs. Brown picks up the silver coin, crouches "on the veinous root of an old tree," and utters the following gnomic spell: "One child dead, and one child living: one wife dead, and one wife coming. Go and meet her!" Carker, in spite of himself, is startled by the prescience of the old hag's utterance, and turns to look at her. Munching and mumbling, she "pointed with her finger in the direction he was going, and laughed." Carker pauses, but then hurries on. As he leaves the dark wood, however, he looks over his shoulder "at the root of the old tree." "He could yet see the finger pointing before him, and thought he heard the woman screaming, 'Go and meet her!'"[104]

The scene is dramatic and compelling; the details I have emphasized blend unobtrusively into the texture of the whole, a texture that is largely realistic. Indeed the realistic texture is so satisfying that most readers have rushed past the hints that I have underscored. Yet the scene is penetrated with suggestion and foreshadowing, and it is penetrated also by the most profound vibrations of folklore and fairy story. The enchanted grove, the predestined meeting, the chain of fate, the forbidden antediluvian, biblical tree, the serpent in the garden, the piece of silver, the gnomic prophecy, the finger pointing the way to adultery and destruction—all these signs heighten the events that are to come, underline their inevitability, and give the episode, when seen in the context of the entire novel, a cosmic significance.

That expanding and ramifying significance and the fairy-tale contributions to it are forged bit by bit. For example, much of the irony and tension of a scene that occurs several pages later is lost if the secret implications of the episode in the magic woods are missed. The new scene takes place after breakfast on the day of the meeting in the enchanted grove. The Dombey party is exploring the neighborhood of Warwick Castle, and Dombey is again testing and displaying Edith, now by requesting her to sketch for him. She asks him negligently what he would like her to sketch, and Dombey chooses a nearby view. The view is portentous: "There happened to be in the foreground, at some little distance, a grove of trees, not unlike that in which Mr. Carker had made his chain of footsteps in the morning, and with a seat under one tree, greatly resembling, in the general character of its situation, the point where his chain had broken."[105] Carker suggests that it is "an interesting—almost a curious—point of view." His statement, meaningful only to Edith, is the beginning of the skillful psychological process whereby he forces upon her a peculiarly personal and secret relationship. "Will you like that?" Edith asks Mr. Dombey. "I shall be charmed," is Dombey's unwitting reply. "Therefore," continues the narrator, "the carriage was driven to the spot where Mr. Dombey was to be charmed"; and a few moments later Carker, sharpening Edith's pencils, and then holding them while she sketches, comments upon her "extraordinary skill—especially in trees." Mr. Dombey, oblivious, looks on "like a highly respectable ghost." "Are you satisfied?" asks Edith. Mr. Dombey, charmed, thinks it is "perfection."[106]

Such ironies and directives, underlined and extended by the expressionistic atmosphere and storybook structure of *Dombey,* and linked together by innumerable fairy-tale reverberations, save scene after scene—but by no means all scenes—from having only melodramatic or coincidental significance, for episodes that would be impossibly contrived in a purely realistic novel often take on luminous meaning in so preternatural a work as *Dombey.* Good Mrs. Brown's integrating supernatural-realistic role continues (though at times too thinly) through the remainder of the book: through the Dombey wedding, the return of Alice, and the threatening of Rob. As the book progresses we begin to understand Good Mrs. Brown's unforgivable sin and its relationship to Dickens' fundamental purpose. Her sin is avarice, a willingness to sacrifice everything—she has already sacrificed her daughter—for money. A money ethic has turned her into a veritable witch; yet her sin is identical to Mrs. Skewton's and Mr. Dombey's sin and, one might add, with Dickens' conception of his parents', especially of his mother's sin in the blacking-warehouse days. Good Mrs. Brown's story is therefore another permutation of the central fable of *Dombey and Son;* she is a character who forces the reader to see that placing money before human values is witchlike and disastrous. That these characters are part of the central fable and exhibit the same evil is made explicit through a confrontation scene, with strong supernatural overtones, involving Good Mrs. Brown, Alice, Mrs. Skewton, and Edith, and by the revelation at the end of the book, in romance fashion, that Alice is Good Mrs. Brown's illegitimate daughter by Edith's father's brother, so that Edith and Alice, whose physical as well as emotional and moral resemblances have been pointed up throughout the novel, are first cousins. Finally, parallelism, poetic justice, and storybook coincidence are additionally served by Good Mrs. Brown's thaumaturgic part in the destruction of Edith, Carker, and Mr. Dombey.

This intricate interdependence and compensation, like that developed in the industrial and domestic levels of the story, the whole enwrapped in a tremulous web of magic and enchantment, points Dickens' theme of the essential unity of society, while at the same time it affirms his sense of the potency of those hidden forces that transcend the ordinary and the rational. The connections and coincidences serve Dickens' moral purpose, but they are more important than mere happenstance and moral juggling, for the atmosphere of myth and fairy story that he casts over them gives them a psychological depth and a poetic appropriateness that help universalize the novel.

As the novel progresses, Dickens develops his fairy-tale characters and folklore themes. The original *Cinderella* encounter of Florence and Walter, an encounter that evokes a reassuring fable of wish-fulfilling transformation, is associated from its outset with its dark counterpart, the antipodal fable of Good Mrs. Brown's abduction of Florence, a nightmare horror compounded out of a child's most primordial fears of loss and deprivation. Both enchantments—the bright dream and the fearful nightmare—twine and cross through all of *Dombey*. The aura of witchcraft and malign aggression that surrounds Good Mrs. Brown is

counterpointed by the *Cinderella* imagery that hovers over deprived
Florence and lowly Walter. The initial meeting of Florence and Walter,
a meeting brought about by Good Mrs. Brown, but controlled thereafter by *Cinderella* motifs—by cindery disguises, ragged clothes, lost
slippers, searching quests, and princely rescues—that first meeting,
magical and portentous, predicts the roles of Florence and Walter and
their destinies. *Cinderella* associations continue to hover over the predestined pair, reassuring and guiding the reader. Walter preserves
Florence's ragged shoes and enshrines them in his room. This act, and
Dickens' later references to it, keep our memory of the *Cinderella*
meeting alive and prepare us for what is to come. But Walter's action
also reflects his personality, and his romantic gesture links the realistic
and fantasy levels of the story. Dickens tells us that Walter has a
"strong infusion" of the "spice of romance and love of the marvellous" in his nature, and attributes to this trait Walter's "uncommon
and delightful interest" in the adventures of Florence with Good Mrs.
Brown.[107] Walter, then, is attracted to Florence by a fairy-tale episode,
but he exemplifies in his own relationship to her another fairy tale. He
not only preserves the *Cinderella* shoes, he dreams storybook dreams.
He will go to sea, come back an admiral with epaulettes of "insupportable brightness," and bear Florence off to the "blue shores of somewhere or other, triumphantly."[108] And when Walter does go to sea,
sent there for very unromantic reasons by Mr. Dombey, he takes with
him Florence's ragged shoes.

But the *Cinderella* atmosphere does not evaporate with Walter's
nautical exile. Just before he leaves for his ship, Florence comes to Sol
Gills' shop in a coach. This visitation casts a magical aura over Walter's
departure and holds his future in suspense. In depicting the atmosphere
of the scene, Dickens speaks specifically of a "fairy influence," and
that influence, which clings to Walter and shapes our lasting impression
of him (for he now disappears from the book for hundreds of pages),
hovers over Florence in all her subsequent relations with the Sol
Gills-Captain Cuttle world.[109]

Much later, for example, when Florence seeks sanctuary in Sol Gills'
shop (now in charge of Captain Cuttle, owing to Sol's wandering search
for the missing Walter), Dickens uses *Sleeping Beauty* and *Beauty and
the Beast* imagery to maintain the reader's sense of the marvelous and
to intensify Florence's aura of storybook enchantment. Florence has
fled her father's house, hurried once more through the frightening
streets, and come at last to the nautical instrument shop. She is led
through the shop to a high upstairs room and there falls asleep on a
couch. The beautiful girl, slumbering on a couch, isolated from the
bustling world, is a Sleeping Beauty who has come to an enchanted
sanctuary and who waits for the wakening kiss of her absent prince.

She even has her magical warders. Her dog, Diogenes, miraculously follows her and becomes a protective dragon who keeps guard by her side (Sleeping Beauty also had a dog who slumbered by her side); and good Captain Cuttle, sensing her fairy lineage, goes softly into her room and gazes upon the sleeping girl "with a perfect awe of her youth and beauty."[110]

When the action is resumed (for Dickens used the above scene to conclude a monthly part), the fairy-tale atmosphere is maintained, but now primarily in *Beauty and the Beast* imagery. Dickens contrasts Florence's "youth and beauty," echoing the *Sleeping Beauty* words of the month before, with Captain Cuttle's "knobby face," "great broad weather-beaten person," and "gruff voice."[111] The situation, the narrator remarks, was "an odd sort of romance, perfectly unimaginative, yet perfectly unreal."[112] And a few lines further on he tells the reader that "a wandering princess and a good monster in a story-book might have sat by the fireside, and talked as Captain Cuttle and poor Florence thought—and not have looked very much unlike them."[113] This fusion of the real, the grotesque, and the fanciful, held together and made viable by a fairy-tale essence, shapes the remaining adventures of Florence in her castle sanctuary. High up in that sanctuary, in her magical chambers, Florence lives on, safe at last from the cruelties of the commercial streets. Captain Cuttle looks upon her with wonder; she is a celestial "fairy, daintily performing . . . offices for him."[114] He guards her; he keeps watch and ward "upon the charmed ground outside her door."[115] It is while in her new home, an enchanted castle under a different and more benign spell than that which grips her father's house, that Florence finally receives and returns the love of the resurrected Walter. The imagery surrounding their castle trysts and the rapturous emotion Dickens lavishes on their romance meetings maintain the fable atmosphere: "Florence never left her high rooms but to steal downstairs to wait for him when it was his time to come, or, sheltered by his proud encircling arm, to bear him company to the door again and sometimes peep into the street."[116]

The wedding that finally unites Florence and Walter rounds out one major fairy-tale motif. The wedding is symbolic and magical: it exorcises the childhood trauma of the London streets (even in her castle sanctuary and encircled by Walter's protective arm, Florence had only dared "peep" into the terrifying streets), and it unites Cinderella with her enraptured prince. "It is very early, Walter," says Florence, on her marriage morning, "and the streets are almost empty yet. Let us walk."[117] Walter asks if walking to church will not tire her, but Florence answers, "Oh no! I was very tired the first time that we ever walked together, but I shall not be so to-day." And so "Florence and

Walter, on their bridal morning, walk through the streets together.''
"Not even in that childish walk of long ago," Dickens reminds the
reader, "were they so far removed from all the world about them as
to-day. The childish feet of long ago, did not tread such enchanted
ground as theirs do now."[118] And with this magical and cyclical ritual,
in which the symbolic and unsatisfactory walk through the terrifying
streets to Dombey and Son is replaced by the equally symbolic but
satisfactory walk through the enchanted streets to church, one great
tension of the novel is resolved.

In *Dombey*, obviously, the fairy story has become a central support
upon which Dickens relies for a wide variety of purposes and effects:
for integration, connection, connotation, emphasis, evocation,
enlargement, and much more. In *Dombey* he solved the problem that
had baffled him in the apprentice novels. With the aid of storybook
devices, storybook atmospheres, and storybook reverberations, he
made the great structuring themes of his novel, the grand and the local
actions, the auras, artifacts, settings, and characterizations cohere and
take strength from one another. The segregated use of fairy tales in
Pickwick, the erratic use of fairy tales in the other apprentice novels, in
Nicholas Nickleby or *Martin Chuzzlewit*, say, has given way in *Dombey* to a circumambient fablelike conception that imbues every cranny
of the novel with special life. That fablelike conception causes ordinary
objects, everyday scenes, familiar occasions—staircases, songs,
locomotives, clocks, embraces, seashores, scavengers, walks to
church—to take on centripetal and magical meaning. Dickens' fabling
imagination is not a new-found power; it is a heritage from his earliest
years. That transforming imagination enters his apprentice as well as
his mature writings. But it enters those writings in changing ways. In
his earlier works, it enters as a broken and intermittent energy, often as
an extrinsic power; in his later writings, it enters as an organizing and
controlling force, usually as an intrinsic power. The experiments of the
Christmas books pointed the way to this development. The Christmas
books encouraged Dickens to use fantasy in central and all-encompassing ways. But *Dombey* goes far beyond the Christmas books. *Dombey*
is not simply a fairy story raised to a higher form, but ordinary, humdrum reality, reality with its stubborn solidity, with its dark shadows
and glinting surfaces, given incomparable mythic meaning.

    Dickens, in fact, has developed a new fairy-tale method. The old
storybook wrenchings, the gross storybook manipulations worked so
unsubtly through fairy godfathers, through the brothers Cheeryble or
old Martin, for instance, have been muted or transformed. At the same
time the domesticated fairy-tale energies of the earlier novels, marvelous in themselves, but usually limited and discrete, energies that give a

fullness of meaning to many scenes in those novels—to the windblown clothes that Barnaby turns into sly gamboling conspirators, to the last walk, so ordinary yet so transfigured, that moves Ralph Nickleby to his doom, to the potent labyrinthine mysteries of Todgers's, so magically intense with the baleful pressure of things—these self-contained surreal episodes (or rather their many later analogues) are now elaborated into recurrent fantasy suggestions and motifs that cluster here and there and then recur and intertwine through an entire novel, part of a consistent pattern. In *Dombey,* Dickens weaves his complex *Cinderella* imagery and action, like his many other storybook elements—his witches, child-quellers, enchanted abodes, spells, sacred groves, and magic circles—into patterns that amplify and interconnect meaning. Taken together, experienced concurrently as they actually appear, reinforced by the other magical episodes of the book, aided by hundreds of additional fantasy touches ranging from isolated words to recurrent storybook motifs, and blended with the other major strands of the story, with the industrial, psychological, and autobiographical themes, these fairy-tale elements become a central foundation of *Dombey*'s method and meaning. Indeed one can hardly conceive of *Dombey* shorn of its mystic nimbus. Such a *Dombey* would have the lineaments but not the soul of Dickens' genius.

Dombey is the crucial breakthrough, the advance from the old to the new fairy-tale method (though one should remember that the old method is sometimes subsumed in the new). But in *Dombey* Dickens has not yet perfected his new fairy-tale technique. He has succeeded in using Christmas-book devices to unify, enhance, and make continuous, but he is still bedeviled by lapses and difficulties. At times he displays an uncertainty in managing his new method. The leitmotifs reflect this uncertainty. The enchanted Dombey mansion and the music-staircase leitmotifs echo and reverberate with softly resonating meanings; the "Let him remember it" leitmotif, on the other hand, falls of its own leaden weight. The delicately modulated sea motifs that whisper forebodingly throughout the novel usually emanate from the book's compelling realism, but occasionally they are forced upon the reader—bald and insistent contrivances. The same unevenness of touch surrounds storybook characters as well as storybook leitmotifs. Good Mrs. Brown in her early appearances is a consummate blend of real Victorian scavenger and folklore witch; in her later appearances, when she is more involved in unraveling the plot, she tends to become a storybook figure in the old mechanical juggling manner, a convenient sorceress who can be used to contravene reality. Carker, too, smooth manager and stalking devil, dwindles at times into a mere Gothic villain, a celibate Captain Murderer complete with glistening teeth. One could easily multiply these examples, but to do so would give the occasional breakdowns and uncertainties in Dickens' fairy-tale art a false prominence; Dickens' magical effects are now usually sustained and enhancing. What impresses one in *Dombey* is how definitively Dickens deploys his new fairy-tale method in his first novel-long attempt. That method, scarcely changed, becomes a central feature in all his subsequent novels.

The new fairy-tale method shapes Dickens' next novel, *David Copperfield,* powerfully and astonishingly. As we shall see, one can scarcely respond to some of the richest and most exquisite harmonies in *Copperfield* if one fails to hear the book's arcane groundnotes, groundnotes that are superbly muted and counterpointed. In *Copperfield,* the fairy tale controls great arching structures, perplexing scenes, deep probings, and delicate nuances; it gives significance to gestures, images, and actions; it interconnects and unites; it helps convey Dickens' transforming vision of life—and it does all this in virtuoso ways. The fairy story, in short, is a vital part of *Copperfield*'s innermost meaning. But *Copperfield* could not be what it is without the breakthrough of *Dombey*. In fantasy terms, *Copperfield* is simply a polished *Dombey*. Dickens' storybook method, freshly forged and tempered in *Dombey,* helps *Copperfield* fulfill—and more than fulfill—the innovative promise and magnificent achievement of Dickens' dark fairy tale of love and business.

7 | *David Copperfield*
The Fairy-Tale Method Perfected

THE FIRST five paragraphs of *David Copperfield* constitute one of the strangest openings in all Dickens' fictions. The paragraphs seem to digress and dawdle; at times they seem whimsical, at times almost pointless. Readers have accepted this odd introduction, presumably, as a bit of typical Dickensian fancy, and have rushed through it. Critics have done little more. With the exception of speculations concerning the initial sentence, in which David raises the question as to whether he will turn out to be the hero of his own life, the import of this opening has hardly been remarked upon. This is all the more surprising since Dickens regarded his openings as exceptionally important and lavished extraordinary care upon them. The results of this care are well known. The introductory passages of *Dombey and Son, Bleak House, Hard Times, Little Dorrit, A Tale of Two Cities,* and *Great Expectations*—to cite these six only—are among the most celebrated in English fiction. The initial paragraphs of *Copperfield* are also a tour de force, but their true relevance only emerges in relation to the fairy-tale aura of the entire novel. That aura is powerfully present from the outset, but it is obscured—or discounted—by a most artful strategy. Dickens toys playfully with the reader. He adopts a facetious, rambling tone in the first five paragraphs, and he concludes the paragraphs by having David remind himself "not to meander," an admonition that is followed by a resolve to go "back to my birth," that is, to go back to the opening sentences from which he has wandered. David immediately puts this resolve into practice. The sixth paragraph begins: "I was born at Blunderstone, in Suffolk, or 'thereby,' as they say in Scotland. I was a posthumous child. My father's eyes had closed upon the light of this world six months, when mine opened on it.''[1] This is businesslike enough; no meandering here.

Now, when an author celebrated for his openings and for the importance he attaches to them tells us that he has been meandering in his first five paragraphs and will get back to business in the sixth, we can assume that he is certain he has not meandered at all. As a matter of fact, the first five paragraphs introduce some of the major themes and motifs of the novel. Above all the opening paragraphs alert the reader to the fact that this is a novel in which signs, wonders, predictions, spells, and ghosts—the myriad confluences and portents of the puissant invisible world—will play their crucial roles.

The first five paragraphs raise a central question, establish a presiding ambiance, and introduce a number of all-important predictions. The question raised is whether we are to regard David as the hero of the novel. The answer is both yes and no. David is not a hero in the ordinary mid-Victorian sense of that term. He is not an active hero such as Nicholas Nickleby or Martin Chuzzlewit, nor is he a passive paragon such as Oliver Twist or little Nell or little Dorrit—or, what is more to the point, such as Agnes. In other words David is not a primary focus of righteousness who either by bold action or spiritual example defeats the forces of evil and succors the forces of good. He is in fact a deeply flawed character whose romanticism, lack of discipline, and self-deception lead him and many of his friends (all unwittingly, it is true) into disaster. Nevertheless he *is* a hero. He is a hero in the sense that Pip is a hero. His essential goodness outweighs his blindnesses and his foibles; through hard experiences and suffering he learns to chasten himself and change. All this develops slowly through the novel. As the opening sentence suggests, whether David will turn out to be the hero of his own life, ''these pages must show.''

On the other hand, the presiding atmosphere of the novel is established at once. That atmosphere is a combination of realism and storybook enchantment. Surrounding the intensely visualized streets, houses, dinners, and carriages of the novel, surrounding the almost palpable characters, events, and settings, is a suprarational aura, now delicate, now strong, now barely perceptible, now dominant, which guides and enhances meaning. That aura is composed of spells and signs and predictions and portents; it includes devils and angels, castles and dungeons, cruel stepparents and wicked princesses, knights errant and immured ladies; it draws on superstitions, folklore, dreams, and fairy stories. Dickens uses all these elements in the most artful and self-conscious ways. The first five paragraphs sound some of the keynotes and suggest what is to come.

David tells us that he was born on a Friday night as the clock began to strike twelve. The moment of birth is significant and carries with it superstitious meaning. Both his nurse and "some sage women in the neighbourhood" agree that the day and hour of David's birth are unpropitious. (Dickens himself was born "toward the small hours" on a Friday. He later came to believe, and often reiterated, that most important events in his life occurred on a Friday.) David's birth is attended by another special sign. He is born with a caul. According to folklore, those born with a caul, or those owning a caul, will be protected from drowning at sea. David's caul is advertised for sale in the newspapers at fifteen guineas, but "whether sea-going people were short of money about that time, or were short of faith and preferred cork jackets," there were no takers.[2] Ten years later the caul is raffled off and is won by an old lady who "died triumphantly in bed, at ninety-two." But David lets us know that the old lady "never had been on the water in her life, except upon a bridge."[3] The humorous deflation of old wives' tales and superstitions is typical of the opening paragraphs—I have quoted only a sampling of the possible examples—and serves to put David and the reader in a position of amused superiority when contemplating the superstitious and gullible. In other words, Dickens surrounds David's birth with special signs and portents but then laughs away their significance.

This paradoxical strategy is reiterated in the predictions made in the opening paragraphs. The same unreliable chorus—nurse and sage neighborhood women—predicts, first, that David is "destined to be unlucky in life," and second, that he will be "privileged to see ghosts and spirits."[4] David says on the first score that he will let his history speak for itself, while on the second he testifies that he has not yet come into his inheritance, and that anyone who is presently enjoying it is welcome to keep it. But despite David's typical skepticism and levity (and despite, perhaps, a modicum of ironic impercipience as well), both predictions are stunningly correct. David *is* unlucky in life. His history is a long tale of woe. Born a posthumous child to an immature and ineffectual mother, he is tormented by cruel stepparents, brutalized by a sadistic schoolmaster, orphaned, and then consigned to the endless drudgery of a laboring hind. Running away from this fate, he is victimized by a predatory adult world, and though saved by the miraculous intervention of a fairy godmother, makes a disastrous marriage, loses his inheritance, is betrayed by his closest friend, and brings death and suffering to some of those he loves best. It is only at the very end of the novel, after his first wife's death and his own symbolic death and rebirth, that he marries his predestined love and lives happily ever after. It is true that David's life contains positive elements as well (a few real friends, a good education, a successful writing career, a saving decency), but any objective observer would have to admit that the emphasis throughout the book until the very end (and concerning the end I shall have more to say later) is on a person "destined to be unlucky in life."

The prediction that David will be "privileged to see ghosts and spirits"—since David denies that he has or wishes to come into this inheritance—is an even more flagrant example of David's evasiveness or imperceptiveness, and a more striking example of Dickens' artfulness. For one of the great themes of *David Copperfield,* a theme which David (and of course Dickens) develops marvelously well, is how the ghosts and spirits and shadows of the past—and future—haunt each moment of our waking and our sleeping lives. And even more to the point is the fact that David as a writer, as a professional seer and creator of ghosts and spirits, who makes his very living out of seeing these shadows and visions, should tell us that he never came into this inheritance and hopes he never will. Since *David Copperfield* is so avowedly autobiographical, often in wish-fulfilling as well as in literal ways, it is worth noting what Dickens wrote on the subject of "ghosts and spirits" in his preface to *Copperfield,* a preface written immediately upon finishing the novel. After speaking of the regret he feels in "the separation from many companions" created in the course of a "two-years' imaginative task," he goes on to remark "how an Author feels as if he were dismissing some portion of himself into the shadowy world, when a crowd of the creatures of his brain are going from him for ever." Thus Dickens on authors and their self-created ghosts and spirits. And so much for Dickens' avatar, David, who can pretend that he has no traffic with his daily stock in trade.

The fact is that Dickens in the first five paragraphs of *Copperfield* is attempting two very different things. He is commencing a truthful story about everyday life, and he is tracing the wonder and mystery that reside in that outwardly ordinary life. He wishes to convey through the everyday, even through the sordid and the cruel, the same sense of magic, of deep half-understood connections, that fairy tales project. The novel is not to *be* a fairy tale, it is not to offend our sense of what life is, but while conveying reality, it is to help us see those hidden dimensions in life that go beyond the merely rational and mundane. And so we recognize with something of a shock that while Dickens has laughed at the superstitions surrounding a caul, he has introduced this portent at David's birth for a most serious and predictive purpose. For while David will not drown at sea, some of his closest friends will; and in a very real sense he, though immune, will help them to that fate. Furthermore, the caul, and its attendant imagery of sea and disaster, is the beginning of a motif that will run through the entire novel, engulfing half the characters of the book—little Emily, Mr. Peggotty, Rosa Dartle, Mrs. Steerforth, Mr. Barkis, the Micawbers, David, Ham, Steerforth, and more—so that the superstitions of nurses and sage neighborhood women, while laughable in themselves, suggest mysteries that reverberate in realms untouched by rational knowledge.

We overlook or discount these mysteries at our peril, for the elements evoked in the opening paragraphs multiply and accumulate throughout the novel and help form the book's central meaning. The extrarational conveys the deeper, more hermetic verities which remain buried (through the earlier portions of the book, at least) in the simple facts and actions of the story. This is Dickens' method in all his later writings. It is a way of rendering his vision of life. Life is a chaos, a seemingly random welter of experiences, which yet, upon more penetrating scrutiny and analysis, is seen to be filled with patterns and connections that are meaningful and that are usually amenable to moral interpretations. The thrust here is secular, not religious. The fairy story permits Dickens to affirm his sense of the wonder and mystery of life without committing himself to doctrine or dogma. Furthermore, Dickens uses fantasy not as a means of escaping the everyday, but as a means of reseeing and reinterpreting it. He does this by artfully including in the commonplace those dimensions, those secret consonances and reverberations of existence, that are usually overlooked or misunderstood by the ordinary observer. In Dickens' mature art the supernatural is not at war with the realistic (as it sometimes was in *Oliver Twist* and other early works) but in accord with it. The supernatural resonates with the realistic and conveys a more profound and complete realism.

In *Copperfield* the "meandering" opening begins this blending process. In the remainder of the first chapter, and then in the next two chapters (the three chapters constitute the first number), Dickens consolidates and expands what he so cunningly began in the first five paragraphs. How this process works, and then rays out into the rest of the novel, can be seen very distinctly in Betsey Trotwood. She enters the story immediately after the "meandering" opening (in the seventh paragraph, as a matter of fact) and her entrance, actions, and leave-taking, as well as her subsequent role in the story, are pervaded by portentous signs and secret meanings. Betsey Trotwood is David's fairy godmother. She appears abruptly and unexpectedly a few hours before David's birth—David's mother has never seen her before—and she appears in memorable fashion. She walks, all aglow, out of the setting sun—the image is Dickens'—and into unborn David's life.

Miss Betsey's manner is harsh and domineering, and from outward view she appears to be a witch rather than a godmother. But her forbidding exterior and eccentric mannerisms are a storybook disguise. Miss Betsey's true self is soon revealed, as the following episode, the first of a recurrent series, makes clear. "Take off your cap, child . . .

and let me see you," says Miss Betsey to David's mother. Then David continues: "My mother was too much afraid of her to refuse compliance with this odd request, if she had any disposition to do so. Therefore she did as she was told, and did it with such nervous hands that her hair (which was luxuriant and beautiful) fell all about her face."[5] Miss Betsey looks at the frightened young widow, and exclaims, "Why, bless my heart! . . . You are a very baby!" David's mother hangs her head and sobs piteously. "In a short pause which ensued, she had a fancy that she felt Miss Betsey touch her hair, and that with no ungentle hand."[6] But when she looks up, Miss Betsey has resumed her more ordinary demeanor and sits frowning at the fire with her skirts tucked up, her hands folded on one knee, and her feet upon the fender.

This revelatory scene, with its sudden glimpse of the bright wonder-working hair, and with the potent ability of that talisman to stir Miss Betsey to godmotherly response, reminds one of analogous scenes in *Dombey and Son,* of the similar effect of Florence's hair on Good Mrs. Brown and on Walter. But in *Copperfield* the hair is more than an isolated talisman; the enchanted hair, and the half-seen, half-understood gesture, will play a sustained role consonant with the theme.

The remainder of the chapter formalizes Miss Betsey's godmother-hood and rounds out the magical visitation. When David's mother is about to go upstairs and deliver David in an evening-long accouchement, Miss Betsey turns toward her and in best fairy-tale manner pronounces a prophecy and a pledge: "From the moment of this girl's birth, child, I intend to be her friend. I intend to be her godmother, and I beg you'll call her Betsey Trotwood Copperfield. There must be no mistakes in life with *this* Betsey Trotwood."[7] But Miss Betsey is wrong on two counts: the child will be a boy, and he will learn through his own painful errors.

All evening long, Miss Betsey haunts the Copperfield home, dominating the household with her grotesque imperiousness. But when David is finally born and Miss Betsey is told that the child is a boy, she is mortally affronted and vanishes from the story as abruptly as she entered. Dickens describes the scene in a significant simile: "[She] walked out, and never came back. She vanished like a discontented fairy."[8]

But despite her fairy-tale disappearance and discontent, her presence continues to hover over the book. And when David, his mother now dead, decides to run off from his Murdstone and Grinby misery, he does so in the hope of being succored by his puissant godmother. He had often heard the story of his birth from his mother. "My aunt," David recalls, "walked into that story, and walked out of it, a dread and awful personage; but there was one little trait in her behaviour which I liked to dwell on, and which gave me some faint shadow of encouragement. I could not forget how my mother had thought that she felt her touch her pretty hair with no ungentle hand; . . . I made a little picture, out of it . . . which softened the whole narrative. It is very possible that it had been in my mind a long time, and had gradually engendered my determination [to run away]."⁹

When David arrives at his aunt's house, she greets him by crying, "Go away! . . . Go along! No boys here!"—a seriocomic reminder of her role at David's nativity, of her abortive fairy-tale predictions and real fairy-tale pique.¹⁰ But despite her gruffness, she pities poor David and takes him in. And hours later, when he has been bathed and has fallen asleep on the sofa, a strange event again takes place: "It might have been a dream, originating in the fancy which had occupied my mind so long, but I awoke with the impression that my aunt had come and bent over me, and had put my hair away from my face," and said, "'Pretty fellow,' or 'Poor fellow.'"¹¹ But when he looked about him, his aunt was sitting quietly in the bow window gazing out to sea.

Years later, at another crucial moment in the story, a variation of this reiterated scene—by now richly fraught with protective and intercessionary associations—occurs once more. On the night after Miss Betsey tells David she is ruined, she appears several times in his room "like a disturbed ghost." David dozes and dreams restlessly. When he wakes he sometimes finds that his aunt, as of old, has come "to the side of the sofa on which I lay." Then, as David pretends to sleep, a further repetition occurs: "I found that she sat down near me, whispering to herself 'Poor boy!'"¹² As in a magic glass that has the power to summon up revelatory events, such recurrent scenes by their strange and unaccountable return, identify, interrelate, and then indelibly fix the chief stages of David's life: his omen-filled birth, his miraculous rescue, his precarious progress—stages presided over by the hovering presence of his powerful, but not omnipotent, godmother. All this unfolds as the novel works toward its predestined end.

In the days and hours before his boyhood rescue, however, David is at the brink of destruction. Miss Betsey saves him. And soon after that moment, soon after the bedraggled David, motivated by a storybook fancy, walks back into Miss Betsey's life (here David reverses the startling scene in which Miss Betsey walked into his life), she becomes his godmother in good earnest. She summons the wicked Murdstones and exorcises them before his eyes. This done, she christens him anew, calling him "Trotwood," thereby reinstituting one portion of her birth-visitation pledge and reaffirming the godmotherly covenant sworn at Blunderstone. "Thus," writes David, "I began my new life, in a new name, and with everything new about me."¹³

In the remainder of the book the godmother motif is elaborated in dozens of scenes and tokens. David, for example, undergoes a typical folk-tale testing. Miss Betsey comes to him bereft of her fortune (but only apparently so, as it turns out), and places herself on his charity. He does not fail the test, but gives up the easy prospect of a gentlemanly profession and its rewards in order to aid her. In storybook fashion this sacrifice is later repaid many fold. But he still has much to learn before he can receive his reward; and his reward is an adjustment to himself and to those around him, not a dazzling romance treasure. His godmother has no power to spare him what he is unable or unwilling to spare himself. Only slowly does he let himself comprehend Miss Betsey's gnomic utterances regarding Dora and Agnes; only after years of blindness, frustration, and suffering can he discipline his "undisciplined heart," understand Miss Betsey's wise counsels, and assume his proper destiny.

Hundreds of details—from the grotesque portents that surround Miss Betsey's first appearance, to the magical sanity she infuses into Mr. Dick's simplemindedness—add supernatural potency to David's succoring godmother. But Miss Betsey is no fairy-tale abstraction. She is eccentric, even grotesque, but she emerges from the book a flesh-and-blood reality. Dickens has taken one of his early godmother figures, made it even more exact in its godmotherly analogues, but at the same time concealed its storybook antecedents by a newly believable realism. And now the fairy-tale mechanisms, far from weakening the story, or being simply ancillary to it, underline and deepen it. Miss Betsey's godmotherhood serves to emphasize David's traumatic childhood trials, dramatize his struggle in a world of confusing good and evil, and enhance our sense of his painful apprenticeship to life—an apprenticeship that forms the chief substance of the book. Miss Betsey offers no escape from life; fairy-tale figure though she is, she constantly forces David back into life and helps him discover himself. Yet in this she is a fairy godmother after all, and Dickens' achievement lies in thus uniting the magical and the mundane.

This blending is all the more impressive when one realizes that much of *David Copperfield,* especially the early *Copperfield,* is an artful interweaving of autobiographical fact, solaceful wish fulfillment, and intricate novel-making. Dickens himself testifies on this score. "I . . . worked," he wrote, "many childish experiences and many young struggles, into Copperfield."[14] This blend of fact and fancy can be seen very plainly if one compares Dickens' release from Warren's blacking warehouse and its immediate aftermath with David's escape from Murdstone and Grinby's wine warehouse and its immediate aftermath. In real life, Dickens longed fruitlessly for release, and then unexpectedly, in a moment, through no initiative of his own, through a sudden

legacy and a family quarrel, found himself free—a fantasy consummation indeed. In fiction, David, inspired by a storybook vision, takes the
initiative, runs away, and finds succor with his fairy godmother. In real
life, Dickens was sent for a year or two to a marginal school (a prototype for Mr. Creakle's sadistic school), then, very early, began a
haphazard ascent from solicitor's errand boy, to court reporter, to
parliamentary reporter, to journalist, to author—all through his own
prodigious effort. In fiction, David's godmother sends him to the best
of schools, and then, when he is well educated, expensively launches
him on a lucrative career as a gentlemanly proctor. It is only when Miss
Betsey is ruined that the real and fictional careers coalesce and David
descends, or rather rises, to laborious effort, shorthand reporting, and
authorship. The differences between reality and fiction are instructive.
Dickens has David engineer his own escape, thus allowing himself to
fantasize a self-liberation untrue to life. He then provides David with
the most wish-fulfilling dream of love, care, education, sponsorship,
profession, and the like, a dream Dickens must often have dreamt in
the blacking warehouse, but a dream that was achieved in real life,
insofar as it was achieved, not through magical intercession, but
through long years of unremitting toil.

What we have here, obviously, is an intricate blending of fact and
fantasy. Dickens called it a "very complicated interweaving of truth
and fiction."[15] The raw material of reality is the given of the fiction. But
the fiction allows Dickens to triumph over reality in wish-fulfilling
ways: through managing his own escape; through imagining a fairy
godmother who saves him, defeats his enemies, satisfies his material
wants, provides him with an education, launches him in his profession,
and guides him into manhood. Yet reality combines with wish
fulfillment. Though David has the fairy godmother Dickens longed for,
she can only smooth his way. She has no power to transform the flawed
recesses of David's character. And it is from the profound depths of his
flawed character that his most grievous errors and discontents spring.
Here David must learn through painful and chastening experiences—
even as Dickens did. Thus Dickens fuses fairy-tale transcendence with
psychological realism, and both with autobiographical fact.

This fusion takes many forms in the opening number. The first crucial movement of the novel unfolds with amazing rapidity. It ends with
the conclusion of the second chapter, barely two-thirds of the way
through the first number. At this point David leaves his happy home in
Blunderstone for a fortnight's visit with the Peggottys in Yarmouth.
What David does not realize is that his mother intends to marry Mr.
Murdstone in the interval, so that David's happy home, his security,
and his mother's undivided love are about to be taken from him. In
effect, the events which end the second chapter mark the end of his

innocent childhood. David has no way of knowing this. His obliviousness compounds his later trauma. His expulsion from Eden is all the
more devastating because it comes so suddenly and seems so unaccountable and so unjust.

Dickens manages this pivotal scene with utmost economy. At his
leave-taking David and his mother, both weeping, kiss lovingly; Mr.
Murdstone looks on disapprovingly; and then the cart, which is to
transport David away from innocent childhood, moves off slowly, carrying David and Peggotty (the latter filled with button-bursting anguish)
away from home. The chapter ends with these words: "I sat looking at
Peggotty for some time, in a reverie on this supposititious case:
whether, if she were employed to lose me like the boy in the fairy tale, I
should be able to track my way home again by the buttons she would
shed."

This archetypal scene, which evokes the most devastating of primal
fears—of being abandoned by one's parents—goes back equally to
Dickens' early life and early reading. We have already seen how Dickens felt betrayed and abandoned by his parents, a feeling fed by his
mother's turning from him to his newborn brother, Alfred. (Later in
Copperfield, in a profoundly moving scene that reflects some of this
feeling, David returns from school to find his mother suckling Mr.
Murdstone's unannounced son.) We have also noted Dickens' other
complaints against his parents: that they neglected him in their financial
difficulties; that they failed to send him to school when they moved to
London; and that they consigned him to the blacking warehouse while
Fanny went to the Royal Academy of Music. We have also seen how
fairy tales, childhood reading, and storytelling became a means of
imaginative survival for Dickens (they play a similar role in David's
life), and how the fable of parents abandoning their children (Dickens
knew the fable best in such versions as *Hop o' my Thumb* and *The
Children in the Wood*) had come—as in his later controversy with
Cruikshank—to have enormous emotional meaning for him.

In the *Copperfield* leave-taking scene, these autobiographical and
emotional meanings surcharge but do not overwhelm the episode. They
are translated into effective and economical art by the way Dickens
uses the fairy story to end his chapter. For the fairy story operates
equally well on different levels of the novel. The fairy tale of the boy
whose parents abandon him is an appropriate association to enter little
David's mind. It is an association fitting to his childhood circumstances
and his childhood reading. At the same time the fairy tale works
thematically. It foreshadows for the reader, in ways that David cannot
comprehend, the fate that lies in store for him. It objectifies what David
will try to do for the remainder of the book ("track my way home
again"). And it lifts David's individual predicament to the archetypal

level. In other words, here Dickens uses the fairy story, most naturally and economically, to generalize and mythify meaning: the fairy tale of the parents who lose their child serves as a paradigm of all weak and neglectful parents and all abandoned children.

I have dwelt thus far on the centrality and variety of the storybook elements in the opening number and on the ways in which these elements radiate through the novel, underlining and integrating meaning. Most of the elements I have discussed have had to do with more or less overriding developments of plot or theme. The elements may be hidden in humor and satire (the omens and predictions surrounding David's birth) or they may blend unobtrusively into the realistic narrative (Aunt Betsey's godmotherhood), but when isolated and then examined, they predict major developments or emphasize major themes. There are, however, other, less obvious, conflations of fairy-tale elements—in the opening number and throughout the book—and these more local and often more subtle fairy-tale effects build up gradually and help give the novel its richness of meaning and intricacy of design. For example, one such conflation in the opening number helps make us sensitive to some of the central concerns and interrelationships in the novel.

The opening number concludes with David returning from his fortnight in Yarmouth and being told some momentous news by Peggotty. "What do you think?" she says. "You have got a pa!"[16] David is dumbfounded. He trembles, turns white, and then thinks of his dead father: "Something—I don't know what, or how—connected with the grave in the churchyard, and the raising of the dead, seemed to strike me like an unwholesome wind." This noxious breath of supernatural emanations from the dark grave rises up, lingers for a moment, and then subsides. But the antipathy that evocation represents does not subside. David does not want to see his new father. He finally yields, however, and goes into the best parlor where his mother and the black-haired Mr. Murdstone are waiting for him. In an atmosphere of frosty constraint he gives Mr. Murdstone his hand, kisses his mother, and then, not able to look at them, gazes out the window at some shrubs that are "drooping their heads in the cold."[17] Soon he creeps out of the room and roams into the yard. Then come the last words in the chapter and the number: "I very soon started back from there, for the empty dog-kennel was filled up with a great dog—deep-mouthed and black-haired like Him—and he was very angry at the sight of me, and sprang out to get at me."

The "Him," of course, is Mr. Murdstone; the usurping father has become the usurping dog. One might say that David has transformed his new black-haired father into an angry, aggressive, black-haired dog. But the dog is also real. The real dog simply objectifies David's feelings and predicament—as the shrubs drooping their heads in the cold also do. That the dog stands for a new and aggressive father that occupies a formerly empty place, that it objectifies David's jealousy and Oedipal conflicts—these and similar meanings we can take directly from the scene, and they are assuredly at the heart of the scene. But there are other dimensions to the scene that have been building through the first number, and these dimensions, which are connected to the storybook focus of the number and of the entire novel, are seen more clearly if viewed in their magical context.

Early in the first chapter, in the first paragraph after the five "meandering" opening paragraphs, as a matter of fact, David tells us that he has a shadowy remembrance of his first childish associations with his father's white gravestone (he can see the gravestone from his bedroom window) and those associations consist of strange feelings he had as he sat with his mother and Peggotty, all warm and bright at the fireside. At such times he would feel that the gravestone was "lying out alone there in the dark night" with "the doors of our house . . . almost cruelly, it seemed to me sometimes—bolted and locked against it." David's earliest memories thus consist of guilty feelings that he was cruelly barring his father—self-protectingly transformed here by David into his father's gravestone—from his rightful place at the family fireside. David recognizes and somehow feels responsible for the empty place; he is glad that the place is empty (he need not share his mother), but he feels guilty too, as though his good fortune is the cause of his father's cruel banishment. That Dickens was aware of and intended these meanings is quite apparent from a host of supportive associations and from an array of anagogic resonances that harmonize and magnify those meanings.

The empty place at the family fireside, for example, is reinforced and given significance by other unnatural vacancies. The yard contains an empty dog kennel, the back garden an empty pigeon house. The elm trees in the front garden are filled with old rooks' nests—all empty. Ironically, David's father, counting on the promise of the old nests, had named the house the Rookery, but no rooks ever appeared, and Aunt Betsey, when she asks about the name and is told of her nephew's trustful gesture, regards the episode as a prototypical emblem of his unrealistic romanticism. Indeed, the empty rooks' nests predict not rooks but emptiness—the elder Copperfield is gone from his nest within a year of purchasing and naming it. David, when he looks out of his bedroom window, can see the nearby churchyard and his father's white gravestone; he can also see the elm trees and their empty old rooks' nests.

As Dickens describes these objects and events he also begins to cast a magical aura about them. This is done through hints, figures of speech, comparisons, recurrences, allusions, and many similar touches. The elm trees, stirred by the enemy wind, "bent to one another, like giants who were whispering secrets."[18] Dickens quickly intensifies the aura. After a few seconds of repose, the elm trees "fell into a violent flurry, tossing their wild arms about, as if their late confidences were really too wicked for their peace of mind." And all the while, the "ragged old rooks'-nests burdening their higher branches, swung like wrecks upon a stormy sea."[19]

Dickens has evoked an occult world in which elm trees suddenly transform themselves into frightening giants who whisper wicked secrets to one another and toss about in violent discontent. In part this is David's perception, the perception of a young imaginative child who actually sees and experiences the animism he later records, but in part it is David's projection, an unconscious projection onto the outer world of his own guilty secrets and fears. In part, also, these subtle fairy-tale vibrations are Dickens' economical way of evoking a suprarational world without violating his realistic narrative. The significance of the thronging signs, so hidden and so magical, becomes apparent only as they intertwine and accumulate or as they take on meaning through the unfolding events of the novel. Thus the empty nests accumulate meaning from the other emptinesses they symbolize and reinforce, guilty and threatening emptinesses that will soon be aggressively filled.

By the same token, the larger significance of the fact that the old nests swing like "wrecks upon a stormy sea" can only be comprehended in the fullness of the novel. For wrecks upon a stormy sea and their attendant deaths by drowning will form the climax of the novel, a climax brought about (predestined, one might say) by the forces that shape David's character, forces that Dickens is disclosing to us in these opening pages. Furthermore, wrecks upon a stormy sea harks back a few pages to the meandering opening, to the fact that "unlucky" David is born with a caul and is presumably immune to stormy seas, wrecks, and drownings. At the same time, the phrase also looks forward to David's idyl with little Emily in Chapter III, an idyl filled with allusions to stormy seas, wrecks, and drownings. The point is that the empty rooks' nests, swinging like wrecks upon a stormy sea, and the giant elms, whispering their wicked secrets in dark discontent, like all the other signs running thickly through these opening pages, are part of a universe of secret suprarational significances. The fairy-tale nimbus alerts us to and confirms those significances.

As Dickens develops the story, he develops the nimbus as well. Helped by that nimbus, by those strange predictions, signs, and recurrences, we begin to see the hidden connections between objects, persons, and events. One Sunday evening, for instance, when David, his mother, and Peggotty are in the best parlor (the parlor that David has

come to associate with his father's funeral, and the parlor in which he
will later greet his new father, Mr. Murdstone), David's mother reads
to them about Lazarus being raised from the dead. David is terrified.
He is so frightened that Peggotty and his mother are "afterwards
obliged to take me out of bed, and show me the quiet churchyard out of
the bedroom window, with the dead all lying in their graves at rest,
below the solemn moon."[20] What David is shown is his father's grave;
he sees that his father is lying at rest.

But the dead are not at rest. They work their influence, baleful and
benign, throughout the novel. David does not understand this, but he
feels that potent influence. He constantly does obeisance to the sovereignty of the dead. In marrying Dora, for example, David, all unwittingly, pays homage to the dead; he seeks to recapture his incompetent
pre-Murdstone mother in an incompetent post-Murdstone wife. But
David does more than mindlessly reiterate the wounding past; he re-
makes the past in self-deluding ways. He clings unconsciously to false,
self-made images of the past. Those images comfort him, but they blind
him to the hidden realities that daily hurt him. The false images of the
past allow him to bury the real past—the unquiet past—in the deceptive quietus of death. David often relies on that treacherous burial and
quietus, and he often pays heavily for that reliance. As a child he is
soothed by the thought that his dead father will not rise again and
disturb his comfortable Eden; as a boy he will not look at his dead
mother's face—she too might rise, Lazarus-like, from her quiet bed of
death and disturb his image of her innocent love. When Peggotty brings
him into the solemn stillness that surrounds his mother's corpse and
starts to turn the cover gently back, he cried, "'Oh no! oh no!' and held
her hand."[21] After the funeral, Peggotty gives David an account of his
mother's and his baby brother's deaths. When Peggotty is done, Dickens has David end the chapter, and the third number, with the following words:

> Thus ended Peggotty's narration. From the moment of my knowing of
> the death of my mother, the idea of her as she had been of late had
> vanished from me. I remembered her, from that instant, only as the young
> mother of my earliest impressions, who had been used to wind her bright
> curls round and round her finger, and to dance with me at twilight in the
> parlour. What Peggotty had told me now, was so far from bringing me back
> to the later period, that it rooted the earlier image in my mind. It may be
> curious, but it is true. In her death she winged her way back to her calm
> untroubled youth, and cancelled all the rest.
>
> The mother who lay in the grave, was the mother of my infancy; the
> little creature in her arms, was myself, as I had once been, hushed for ever
> on her bosom.[22]

David has blotted from his mind all the suffering and pain that his mother's weakness and immaturity have brought him. He preserves in his mind the gay, prelapsarian image of a careless, youthful playmate. He replaces the usurping son of Murdstone with his own unsullied infant presence, and lies forever, unchanging and unchanged, on his mother's breast.

David is enslaved by the past, and by his distortions of the past. He will not look at the reality of his dead mother's face, but he will bow in unconscious, lifelong homage to the false image of her that he has preserved in his mind. David, despite his scoffing disclaimers, is a seer of "ghosts and spirits." He is haunted by the ghosts of the past; his story is one long evocation of passionate, tangible memory. One of the great achievements of *David Copperfield* is to make us feel and understand this ghostly imposition of the past. *David Copperfield* demonstrates the myriad ways in which the past intrudes upon the present and the future, try as one will to dominate it or block it from one's view. Dickens is here a precursor of Ibsen and Joyce.

In *Copperfield* the way in which the past rises to haunt the present is demonstrated again and again. The coming of Mr. Murdstone is a case in point. His coming is heralded by signs and premonitions rooted in the past. We recall those warning signs. We recall the empty place at the fireside, the empty dog kennel, the empty pigeon house, and the empty old rooks' nests. We think of other signs as well. We think of David, haunted by his father's white gravestone, terrified at the thought of a risen father, reassured by the sight of his absent father at rest below the solemn moon. But his father is not at rest. With the coming of Mr. Murdstone, his father rises like an "unwholesome wind" from his unquiet grave. The fairy-tale signs, fairy-tale fears, and fairy-tale predictions have been verified by an evil fairy-tale presence. The wicked whisperings of the elms have given birth to a wicked father. This dark father has usurped David's place, even as David had guiltily usurped his father's place, and the risen father now casts his evil spell—Dickens himself uses the term—on David and all his household.[23] A cruel dark shadow of David's real father, a murderous, stonelike emanation of the gravestone ("Murd-stone"), has risen from the grave. This dark shadow is a compound of fear and jealousy and guilt within, of betrayal and aggression and danger without.

In this magical context the kennel filled with a great dog, "deep-mouthed and black-haired like Him," takes on its full significance. We realize that the forces unleashed by the image are attached to fears and confusions and wild imaginings that coalesce in Mr. Murdstone but that also antedate him. We realize that the now filled kennel is filled by more than an aggressive dog, more than a surrogate for Mr. Murdstone. It is filled by the risen fears and memories of the past, of which the white tombstone, wicked elm trees, and raised dead are both emblems and harbingers.

All these strange fears and wild imaginings are appropriate to a sensitive, impressionable boy who has known loss and cruelty in his early years. The storybook atmosphere wonderfully projects the fantasies and distortions of a child's imagination. It also helps Dickens introduce and then manage the recurrences and reversals that integrate his novel.

How this process works can be seen if we examine Dickens' continued use of dog imagery. For the angry dog that springs out at David at the conclusion of the first number is not only connected to guilty fears and real dangers that have been gathering through the first three chapters, but to a series of strangely transformed and transforming recurrences that run magically—and centripetally—through the entire book. When Miss Betsey labels Mr. Murdstone a dog, she is only confirming an identification made by David years earlier.[24] David's act of identification is also an act of transformation. He turns Mr. Murdstone into a dog. In this respect, *Copperfield* is like innumerable fairy stories—like *The Six Swans* or *The Frog Prince*—in which a protagonist is transformed for a term into an animal. David effects his magical transformation when he finds "a great dog" in the once empty kennel and refers to the beast as "deep-mouthed and black-haired like Him." This favor is returned by Mr. Murdstone who first torments David into biting him and then causes David to acknowledge publicly that he has become an animal by forcing him to wear a placard that says, "*Take care of him. He bites.*" That Dickens desires David's biting to conjure up an aggressive dog, and thus to complement the deep-mouthed Murdstone-dog that David conjured up, is made clear by the scene in which David, upon his arrival at Mr. Creakle's school, discovers the placard he is to wear. When he reads the placard, he scrambles up on a desk and looks about him for "a great dog." When none appears he turns to Mr. Mell:

> "I beg your pardon, sir," says I, "if you please, I'm looking for the dog."
> "Dog?" says he. "What dog?"
> "Isn't it a dog, sir?"
> "Isn't what a dog?"
> "That's to be taken care of, sir; that bites?"
> "No, Copperfield," says he, gravely, "that's not a dog. That's a boy. My instructions are, Copperfield, to put this placard on your back. I am sorry to make such a beginning with you, but I must do it."
> With that he took me down, and tied the placard, which was neatly constructed for the purpose, on my shoulders like a knapsack; and wherever I went afterwards, I had the consolation of carrying it.[25]

It is as though a necromantic Mr. Murdstone, angered by David's hostile perception of him as a dog, revenges himself by turning David into a veritable dog. Dickens is very much aware of the implications of this transformation, and he takes pains to alert the reader to what is going on. Some months after the biting scene, for instance, he has David make the following remark about Mr. Murdstone: "He ordered me like a dog, and I obeyed like a dog."[26] Mr. Murdstone has transformed David into a beast.

These potent recurrences and transformations, filled with supernatural associations, attach themsleves to other permutations of the dog theme in *Copperfield*. When David meets Dora (Dora is a devastating parallel of his mother) he finds that she, like his mother, is guarded by a black dog. Jip, as the dog is called, is an aggressive guardian who regards David as an enemy. This guardian dog, who snarls and snaps at David, is not so dangerous as the deep-mouthed dog who guarded his mother. Dickens' presentation of Jip is part brilliant parody and part genial humor. It soon becomes clear, however, and it is confirmed by scores of incidents throughout David's and Dora's life, that Jip is much more than a comic sketch: he is a rival to David and an objectification of Dora. In this respect, Jip is an exact counterpart of the Murdstone dog. There are many signs of Jip's oneness with Dora. Dora's death, for instance, is conveyed through Jip's death, a correspondence that was extremely important to Dickens, as his number plans make clear. But most particularly, Jip objectifies Dora's childishness and intransigence. David is powerless to contend against this childishness in Jip or in Dora. He doesn't understand that the soft petulant incompetence his rational mind abhors in Dora has an obverse side—a soft femininity and dependency that he adores. He hates the spoiled Jip, but he adores the pouting Dora who created Jip in her own spoiled image. He doesn't realize that it is the irresponsible weakness and dependency in Dora, his mother in Dora, that attracts and defeats him, the same traits in his mother that attracted and defeated him as a child. The potent past again controls the present.

The entire evocation that surrounds Jip, then, in addition to being an end in itself (for Jip is a masterpiece of humorous observation), is meant to enforce comparisons and relationships that take the reader directly back to the traumatic engendering nodes that are set forth most succinctly in the opening chapters of *Copperfield*. Dickens uses dogs, as he uses empty nests, tombstones, and whispering elms, to convey and clarify meaning. The dogs in *Copperfield*, like their multitudinous counterparts, are part of the vast invisible world that signals everywhere to man. That this is true, that the correspondences I have been tracing are really there, and that Dickens expected the perceptive reader to see them, is made even clearer when Miss Murdstone suddenly turns up as Dora's mentor and keeper. This new role for Miss Murdstone is as unlikely as it is coincidental, and it strains one's credulity. But its real purpose is not rooted in the probabilities of Dora's life, but in the traumas of David's past. Miss Murdstone hovers darkly and malignly about David's beloved Dora, just as she hovered darkly and malignly about David's beloved mother. David makes nothing out of this magical recrudescence of his past, first in Jip and then in Miss Murdstone, but such magical recurrences are designed to help the reader see what David fails to understand.

Thus, in a seriocomic climax, Jip and Miss Murdstone collaborate to bring about David's downfall. For when Jip purloins David's letter from Dora's pocket, Miss Murdstone discovers the fervent note and reveals the secret correspondence to Dora's father, who immediately puts a stop to the correspondence and the lovers' clandestine meetings. David, knight-errant that he is, eventually rides triumphantly over these and other obstacles and makes his beloved Dora his bride. He pays heavily for this foolish gratification, but it is only after years of thwarted hopes and unattained fulfillments that he begins to comprehend the neglected signs and recurrences that attended his birth and accompanied him all his life; it is only at the end of the book that he begins to slough off some of the mirages and impositions of the past.

The reader, on his second or third journey through *Copperfield*, begins to grasp the intricate growth of needs and spells that fashions David's character. The storybook nimbus that surrounds this growth—a compound of the myriad suprarational effects I have been tracing—fuses the hypnotic realism and idiosyncrasy at the core of the story to the universal hopes and fears Dickens is also conveying. By this means Dickens imparts his sense of how the world we know and experience is, at one and the same time, surpassingly real and discrete, and surpassingly numinous and interrelated.

The differences, in this respect, between *Dombey and Son* and *David Copperfield* are the differences between inauguration and mastery. In *Dombey and Son* Dickens took techniques he had used intermittently in his early fiction, and more consistently and richly in his Christmas books, and made them a central means of organizing his novel and conveying his meaning. By and large he was successful in *Dombey and Son,* but he also faltered. Some of his effects were too blatant, or not sufficiently fused to the novel's realism, or not adequately supportive of major themes. Good Mrs. Brown as the realistic yet witchlike abductor of Florence is wonderfully imagined and wonderfully executed; but Good Mrs. Brown as *deus ex machina* toward the end of the novel is little more than melodramatic bluster. The wild waves are magical, but they are also artificial and overdone. Carker is a stalking catlike villain with sinister abilities to fascinate and to pounce, but his gleaming teeth and grinning stare remind one less of folklore than of chapbook illustrations. One can easily see the distance Dickens has traveled in the brief interval between *Dombey and Son* and *David Copperfield* if one compares Good Mrs. Brown to Betsey Trotwood, or the wild waves to the slowly rising Yarmouth storm, or the grinning Carker to the much more frightening (because much more malignly ordinary) Uriah Heep. I shall return to some of these matters later.

The difference, then, is not one of kind but of skill and of scope. The magical atmosphere in *Copperfield* is more domesticated, more naturally and unobtrusively fused to the central realism of the story, than is the reverberant ambiance of the ground-breaking *Dombey and Son.* The energy of enchantment in *Copperfield* is also more artfully (and less obviously) present as a cluing, guiding, and organizing force. It is inseparable, for example, from the shaping themes of the novel. Finally, and perhaps most strikingly, the invisible world is more pervasive in *Copperfield* than in *Dombey.* It enters *Copperfield* in thousands of diverse ways, from slowly accreting nuances to profound thematic keynotes.

As the first consummate example of this new mastery, *Copperfield* is worth examining in greater detail. For the storybook influence which so profoundly shapes the opening chapters of *Copperfield* runs powerfully through the entire book. Major actions, characters, scenes, settings, relationships, atmospheres, and motifs take part of their essential color, and some of their innermost meaning, from their hidden fairy-tale attributes.

How central the fairy story is to Dickens' method and how crucial it is to understanding his art may be glimpsed in the brilliant scenes which depict how David, prompted by the stories his mother had told him of his aunt's visitation at his birth, and sustained by his own desperate fantasizing of the one soft gesture in those stories, flees from Murdstone and Grinby servitude and sets out to find the fairy godmother he so longs for. When David flees, he flees into the mazes of the merciless adult world. Dickens conveys David's predicament with marvelous richness. The journey that David undertakes, a journey from London to Dover, is a pilgrimage from storybook nightmare to storybook felicity. This pivotal journey is paralleled by an earlier journey, David's first trip from Blunderstone to Mr. Creakle's London academy. The chief incident of the earlier journey serves as an important prelude to the trials that David will later undergo on his harrowing flight to Dover.

The forerunner scene, in which David is victimized by a hungry waiter who bilks him of his meal even as he serves him, shows what innocent childhood can expect at the hands of experienced adulthood. David is on his own for the very first time. The waiter soon recognizes this, and he is merciless. He exploits the child thoroughly and cynically. The scene is mitigated, however, by our knowledge that David is in no real danger. There are many signs of this. He is allowed to eat a portion of his meal; he has money in his pocket, a known destination, friends and loved ones at home. The scene is further mitigated by its presentation. The shrewd maneuverings of the waiter, his larcenous strategies and self-serving imagination, are wonderfully humorous and lovingly realized. The scene has no fairy-tale enlargements.

The scene depicts the ordinary, everyday exploitation of children by adults. Reprehensible as such exploitation is, and much as Dickens abhors it, it is not lethal, and he presents it as an instance of moral weakness rather than of mortal sin; it is a special case, aggravated because children are supposedly more innocent and defenseless than adults, of the way in which the initiates of this world prey upon the guileless. But the scene also throws into relief its companion scenes to come. The scenes on the road to Dover have a terrifying quality which the precursor scene lacks. That quality, plus the explosive aggressions and expressionistic terrors that also imbue the scenes, are signs that in the trip to Dover we are in a new realm, a realm where exploitation has become dire and transcendent. The exploiting adult can now easily destroy his innocent prey. This life-threatening danger is further conveyed by sudden revelations of horror and by glimpses of utmost savagery. All this is brought to life by Dickens' fairy-tale method.

The very structure of the Dover journey is conceived in storybook terms. It clearly follows an immemorial pattern. An outcast creature, lost in a forest or dangerous place, encounters witches, ogres, giants, and other dire monsters who lie in wait for him and almost destroy him, but, led by some enchanted influence, he makes his perilous way to a magical refuge. This is not simply an analogy, but Dickens' rendition of the journey. Yet Dickens combines this storybook structure with other elements, so that the results go far beyond the ordinary effects of a fairy tale.

At the very outset of his Dover journey, David is threatened and robbed by a long-legged young man. He is so shaken by this experience, and by the indifference of the thronging London world, that a strange transformation takes place: he feels he is a criminal rather than a victim. This disastrous beginning sounds the keynote for all that is to follow. David plods his solitary way toward Dover, trudging through villages, tramping along country lanes, sleeping in fields. Each day he grows more weary, frightened, and footsore; each day his vision of the world grows darker and more filled with fear. The persons he meets, the places he stops at, become part of a terrifying nightmare. An ordinary shopkeeper, a Mr. Dolloby, sitting in front of his shop (the shop has coats and trousers dangling from the ceiling), appears to David "like a man of a revengeful disposition, who had hung all his enemies, and was enjoying himself."[27]

In David's frightened eyes, the denizens of the countryside take on the same somber hues. Beadles glower at him as he goes by; devilish tinkers, black of hand and foul of mouth, threaten to rip his body open and knock his brains out. Everything he sees and experiences enforces the same lesson: that the vast, teeming, unknown adult world is unimaginably brutal and aggressive; that in every alley and every lane frightening monsters prey voraciously on one another; that the innocent and the weak are victims of the cunning and the strong.

What keeps David going in the midst of this callousness and brutality is the radiant picture he preserves in his mind. In that picture his mother weeps during Aunt Betsey's visitation, and his aunt relents toward her and caresses her beautiful hair. This visionary picture of his aunt with his mother, "always went before me, and I followed."[28] "It always kept me company. It was there, among the hops, when I lay down to sleep; it was with me on my waking in the morning; it went before me all day."[29]

But David's predicament and his yearning are conveyed by more than brutal incidents and comforting visions. At the heart of each episode is a fairy-tale conception that enlarges meaning. How this conception transforms each vignette may be seen in the longest and most revealing of the episodes on the way to Dover, the scene in which David attempts to sell his jacket to a secondhand clothing dealer.[30] The scene is perplexing. At first it seems merely odd and farcical: a self-indulgent interlude of Dickensian grotesquerie rather than a thematic episode of well-wrought artistry. But when viewed from a fairy-tale perspective it becomes profoundly thematic, and it takes on depth and resonance. The episode is seen through David's eyes; the evil is thus a child's notion of evil, an expressionistic nightmare of inexplicable sadism and brutality. This nightmare world is the dark counterpart of Miss Betsey's magical sanctuary.

The clothing dealer's shop stands "at the corner of a dirty lane, ending in an enclosure full of stinging-nettles." The shop contains rusty guns, and "rusty keys . . . various enough to open all the doors in the world." Dickens makes the physical characteristics of the shop suggest David's predicament. The stinging nettles are fitting tokens of David's cruel encounters with life; the guns, of his subjection to violence and coercion; and the rusty keys, of his baffled attempts to open the doors of escape. When David enters the shop, he encounters additional stings, and he unlocks no doors. The shop—Dickens calls it a "den"—is "low and small" and "darkened rather than lighted" by a tiny window. One must descend in order to enter, and when David does enter, he is snatched up by a terrifying old man. The old man, David recalls, "rushed out of a dirty den behind [the store], and seized me by the hair of my head." In a whirl of horror, David catches a glimpse of more stinging nettles, and then he hears the monster's strange cry: "Oh, my eyes and limbs, what do you want? Oh, my lungs and liver, what do you want? Oh, goroo, goroo!" David is paralyzed; instinctively he recognizes the fearful old man for what he is.

The old man is a ravening ogre; at the same time he is an unclean bird of prey who feeds on the flesh of other creatures: he has already sunk his claws—the term is Dickens'—into innocent David's hair. This cruel echo of the hair theme, this reversal of his godmother's caress of his mother's and later of his own hair, emphasizes David's alienation and danger. The dismaying words, "Oh, goroo!" are the appropriate call of the ogre, a call which is nothing more nor less than a variation of the word "ogre" itself. But the ogre identifies himself by more than his call; his fierce chant has to do with "hearts" and "eyes" and "limbs" and "lungs" and "livers"—the things upon which he feeds. Dickens choruses this cannibalistic chant throughout the episode. David describes how the old man, "still holding me by the hair," and with his eyes starting out of his head, repeated, "Oh, what do you want? Oh, my eyes and limbs, what do you want? Oh, my lungs and liver, what do you want? Oh, goroo!" When David tells him he wants to sell his jacket, the terrible old man replies, "Oh, let's see the jacket! . . . Oh, my heart on fire, show the jacket to us! Oh, my eyes and limbs, bring the jacket out!" Then the old man "took his trembling hands, which were like the claws of a great bird, out of my hair," and began to examine the jacket. Amidst many "lungs" and "livers" and "Oh, goroos," a price is fixed, but when the bargain is closed and the jacket is thrown on the shelf, the ogre cries, "Oh, my liver! . . . Get out of the shop! Oh, my lungs, get out of the shop! Oh, my eyes and limbs—goroo!" David goes out to wait for his money. Hours go by, but the ogre, who "enjoyed the reputation of having sold himself to the devil," does not stir from his den. It is only when the neighborhood boys skirmish about the shop and taunt him with his devil's compact that he rushes out of his lair in a fury of slavering frustration. "Sometimes in his rage he would take me for one of them, and come at me, mouthing as if he were going to tear me in pieces," but he would stop just in time, and dive into his shop.

David crouches outside the shop. After many hours and innumerable terrifying rushes by the devil-ogre, David wrests the promise of a grudging pittance from him. Then, faint, trembling, and alienated, he approaches the ogre, takes "the money out of his claw," and departs.

This marvelous episode says much, but it suggests even more. For the episode is doubly and trebly effective, and it is doubly and trebly linked to the novel's central meanings, to themes of orphaning, alienation, childhood helplessness, adult exploitation, and the like. The fairy-tale perspective helps compound and convey these meanings. It allows us to observe and become David. It permits us to look on dispassionately while participating fully. Dickens combines meticulous realism with wild expressionism, controlled adult insight with blind childhood terror. The scene fuses elements that should war with one another. It is simultaneously humorous and pathetic, frightening and satisfying, grotesque and matter-of-fact, personal and universal. That such a scene can—really *must*—be read in all these ways is a tribute to the ramifying subtlety of Dickens' fabling imagination, an imagination that constantly blends workaday reality with storybook transcendence in order to reach the beating heart of experience.

Dickens' fabling imagination continues to move and guide us when David reaches Dover. Upon asking some inhabitants of Dover about his aunt, David is mocked and guyed by them. One boatman tells David that "she was seen to mount a broom, in the last high wind, and make direct for Calais."[31] Stories such as these perpetuate the world's cruel rejection of David. They also reactivate the supernatural aura that surrounded Miss Betsey at the opening of the novel (she has been gone from the novel since then), but suggest, falsely, of course, that she is a witch rather than a discontented fairy. This suggestion that David is mistaken in his dream is accentuated by other reports of his aunt's harshness and grotesque behavior. His initial experience of her more than confirms these reports. When he first sets eyes on her, he is horrified to discover that she is "carrying a great knife." All his early fears and forewarnings, all his Murdstone debasements, all his wayfaring torments seem about to culminate in a final murderous aggression. His aunt is not the beneficent godmother of his fairy-tale dream, but the knife-brandishing witch of his fairy-tale nightmare. Like so many of the persons in his young life, she has been transformed as if by some sorcerer into a sadistic monster. Her first words are, "Go away! . . . Go along! No boys here!" And with that she raises her arm and makes a "chop in the air with her knife."[32]

But the world does contain goodness, and fulfilled dreams, and steadfast companionship. Miss Betsey is not what she seems. Unlike Miss Havisham, who appears to be a beneficent godmother but turns out to be a veritable witch, Miss Betsey appears to be a veritable witch but turns out to be a beneficent godmother. As David soon discovers, Miss Betsey provides a double fulfillment. She redeems the caress she gave at his birth, and she satisfies the storybook fantasies he fashioned in his servitude. Under her protection he begins a "new life, in a new name, and with everything new" about him.

Though Miss Betsey cannot protect David from himself, she can assure that he will not be the helpless victim of every predatory monster. She has money, and she has godmotherly powers. She can break the spell of the evil enchanters who held David in their thrall. She summons and exorcises the Murdstones, the diabolical guardians of David's childhood, and she presents David with two new guardians: herself and Mr. Dick. David's new guardians are as strange and grotesque as his earlier guardians were sedate and respectable: Miss Betsey is an angular, dotty, imperious eccentric; Mr. Dick is a daft simpleton transmogrified into a wisdom-speaking holy fool. But David's new guardians are as radiant and pure as his old guardians were dark and corrupt. All is reversed. The fairy-tale "monsters" who have adopted him are succoring and benign; the storybook "paragons" who have given him up are evil and depraved. A new and beneficent enchantment is replacing the old maleficent spell. The nightmare of David's childhood is giving way to the dream of David's youth.

The last scene in Chapter XIII and in David's journey takes place at dusk. Wayworn David, newly bathed and drowsy with food, is finally ushered up to bed. He climbs to the top of the house and enters his room. It is pleasant and overlooks the sea. He sits for a while at his bedroom window, gazing at the water. The sea is a track of silver shining in the brilliant moonlight. He is peaceful and relaxed; he is safe at last. He thinks solemnly of his dead mother and her dead son. Without realizing it, David is caught up in another recurrence. He is once again at a bedroom window, once again in the moonlight, once again thinking of a dead parent. He is reenacting the childhood scene of looking out his bedroom window so that he might see "the dead all lying in their graves at rest, below the solemn moon." Now the pursuing gravestone and the risen father do not disturb David's thoughts. He has escaped the risen dead, or so it seems. David slips into bed and nestles in the snow-white sheets. The chapter ends as he drifts off to sleep: "I prayed that I never might be houseless any more, and never might forget the houseless. I remember how I seemed to float, then, down the melancholy glory of that track upon the sea, away into the world of dreams."

David is falling asleep, he is falling into an interval of dreaming, but he is also floating at last into the longed-for dreamworld of his prayerful imagination: a world that he has come to through a harrowing pilgrimage, a world in which he is solitary and houseless no more, a world of succor, love, and protection. Like the outcast chimney sweep in Blake's poem, David's dream of heaven is nothing more than that which every child might reasonably expect in this life. But David is luckier than the chimney sweep. Dreaming in his snow-white bed, David's other dream, his sustaining and life-preserving fairy-tale dream, as glimmering and evanescent as the melancholy glory of moonlight on water, is finally coming to be.

The storybook quality that hovers so shapingly and so pervasively over actions—David's painful journey from Murdstone and Grinby's London warehouse to Aunt Betsey's Dover refuge is one such action—also strongly colors most of the characters in the novel. Uriah Heep is a typical example. His physical appearance and his physical surroundings proclaim his magical origins. David first glimpses him as a disembodied "cadaverous face" peering out of a small window in a "little round tower."[33] He has "hardly any eyebrows, and no eyelashes"; his eyes are "so unsheltered and unshaded, that I remember wondering how he went to sleep."[34] Indeed, we later discover that his eyes are "sleepless"; they constantly glow like "two red suns."[35] His other bodily members hint at similar derangements. His "long, lank, skeleton hand" is so dank, that when he reads, his finger, following the lines in a book, "made clammy tracks along the page (or so I fully believed) like a snail."[36] This strange, repellent creature is unable to smile; he "could only widen his mouth and make two hard creases down his cheeks, one on each side."[37] His movements are equally repellent and equally suggestive: "snaky twistings of his throat and body."[38] These sinister attributes are often reiterated and reinforced. We see Uriah "slowly fitting his long skeleton fingers into the still longer fingers of a great Guy Fawkes pair of gloves"; we observe his "shadowless red eyes, which looked as if they had scorched their lashes off"; we watch a "snaky undulation pervading his frame from his chin to his boots."[39]

Uriah's physical attributes suggest that he is more—or less—than an ordinary mortal. We soon begin to read those attributes. We come to understand that Uriah's cadaverous appearance and grotesque movements are an index of his inward reality. Dickens had long used this technique. But here, as in *Dombey* and the Christmas books, he gives the technique an added dimension. The correspondence between outward and inward reality—a correspondence that is magical enough—now suggests preternatural potencies: Uriah's sinister outward traits limn an inward depravity that is larger than life. Yet Uriah always strikes us as an ordinary drudging clerk. Indeed part of Dickens' achievement here is to make us see how common, garden-variety envy and malice partake of cosmic evil.

Dickens helps us to this insight in many ways. He always depicts Uriah as a commonplace clerk, as a grubbing, almost banal example of an unremarkable tribe. Yet he infuses this portrait with anomalous hints. The most obvious of those hints we have just examined: he emphasizes the infernal in Uriah's physical appearance. But he does

much more than this. He gives Uriah and his ordinary activities an
array of supernatural touches. Almost coincident with David's first
sight of Uriah comes a strange unnerving scene. As David enters the
Wickfield house for the first time, he catches a glimpse of Uriah, who
has been left to care for the pony chaise. The cadaverous young man is
all too busy. He is, David tells us, "breathing into the pony's nostrils,
and immediately covering them with his hand, as if he were putting
some spell upon him."[40] This terrific suggestion of the malign influence
of Uriah's potent breath is enough, when coupled with his skeleton
hands, red eyes, and snaky undulations, to alert us to the magical
import of other Heepish traits. Uriah can look intently at everything,
"yet [seem] to look at nothing," and all the while ostentatiously appear
to keep "his red eyes dutifully on his master."[41] This dissembling stare
unnerves David. He is haunted by Uriah's evil eye. He is haunted also
by his evil touch: "But oh, what a clammy hand his was! as ghostly to
the touch as to the sight! I rubbed mine afterwards, to warm it, *and to
rub his off.*"[42] The chapter and the number end with David still
haunted by that ghostly touch. David has gone up to his room to spend
his first night in the Wickfield household. He cannot erase from his
mind that "uncomfortable hand . . . cold and wet upon my memory."
The last words in the chapter reinforce the image of the evil eye and the
haunting hand: "Leaning out of window, and seeing one of the faces on
the beam-ends looking at me sideways, I fancied it was Uriah Heep got
up there somehow, and shut him out in a hurry."

Uriah has been transformed into a staring gargoyle who has somehow clambered up to the verge of David's chamber. David hurriedly
shuts him out, but the gargoyle, as we shall see, eventually appropriates the entire chamber. This symbolism and its analogues, as well as
the many supernatural touches, are artfully embedded in the strong
realistic core of Uriah's characterization. Such hints quickly establish
an aura, an added dimension, which is reinforced from time to time and
which is used, as the story progresses, to convey implications and
meanings that simultaneously confirm and transcend the realistic.
Uriah's gargoyle head, for instance, continues to haunt David's dreaming and waking consciousness. The disembodied head that loomed by
day out of the little round tower and by night out of the beam-end,
years later looms out of the fading dark. As David sits on the top of a
coach thinking of Agnes, "came struggling up the coach side, through
the mingled day and night, Uriah's head." The disembodied head,
suspended in space, begins to speak: "'Copperfield!' said he, in a
croaking whisper, as he hung by the iron on the roof"—and then he
delivers his message.[43] The scene is reminiscent of an earlier scene on
top of a coach. Agnes and Uriah are returning to Canterbury, she on
the inside, he on the roof. David, who has come to see her off, de-

scribes the vignette: "Thus it was that we parted without explanation: she waving her hand and smiling farewell from the coach-window; her evil genius writhing on the roof, as if he had her in his clutches and triumphed." David is horrified. "I could not," he writes, "get over this farewell glimpse of them for a long time."[44]

Obviously, one version of Uriah that Dickens wishes the reader to respond to is Uriah as a malign, haunting demon or gargoyle who casts a baleful spell. There are many permutations of this conception. Most are fleeting suggestions or delicate touches, but some—such as most of those I have been citing—are more explicit. There are scores of these directive clues. In yet another scene, for instance, David records the following image of Uriah and Agnes: "He reminded me of an ugly and rebellious genie watching a good spirit."[45]

Uriah's supernatural watchfulness and maleficent presence are family traits; they mark him as one of the dark tribe. He is the monster offspring of a monster dam. His mother also exhibits the family likeness. She has "an evil eye," and she knits ceaselessly a strange something that "looked like a net."[46] Like Madame Defarge (still nine years away) Mrs. Heep is an implacable fate who spins the dark destiny of those she wishes to entrap. Dickens' description of her emphasizes her fairy-tale attributes: "She showed in the firelight like an ill-looking enchantress, baulked as yet by the radiant goodness [of Agnes] opposite, but getting ready for a cast of her net by and by."[47]

The family likeness embraces another resemblance that Dickens carefully highlights in his emerging portrait. Uriah is a species of devil. This is no metaphor, but part of Uriah's menacing reality. His infernal origins are implicit in his cadaverous face, red hair, sleepless red eyes, skeleton hand, and snaky writhings. But they are also explicit in many other touches. After David's first long conversation with Uriah, David dreams of him "half the night."[48] The dream is premonitory. In the dream David identifies Uriah as piratical, death-dealing, and diabolical. In another scene, some years later, a scene filled with imagery of firelight, kindling sparks, blazes of light, and grisly hands, David is overwhelmed by "a sudden sense of being no match for him."[49] David's reaction is indicative of his intuitive perception: no one is a match for the devil.

Dickens is quite self-conscious about the Satanic implications of the scene. A few paragraphs further on David speaks of Uriah's "crafty face, with the appropriately red light of the fire upon it." The key word here is "appropriately," for the red light that flickers over Uriah's face is appropriate only if Uriah is a devil. By the same token, Uriah's other red features—his red hair and glowing red eyes—also mark him as a scion of Satan. Other details in the scene project the same image. "If I had been obliged to look at him," says David of Uriah, "with his splay foot on Mr. Wickfield's head, I think I could scarcely have hated him more." This dire Boschlike image of a devil-Uriah subduing his victim under foot, an image called up by David's loathing of Uriah, is confirmed much later in Mr. Wickfield's equally suggestive image of his tormentor. "He has always been at my elbow," says Mr. Wickfield, "whispering me."[50] No doubt Mr. Wickfield has listened to the promptings of the devil—and in Mr. Wickfield's case, the devil and Uriah are synonymous.

As the book progresses, the devil imagery that surrounds Uriah grows stronger. After David strikes Uriah, he tells him, "You may go to the devil!"; and when Uriah is brought to bay he turns blue and cries, "The Devil take you!"[51] Toward the end of the book Uriah's connection with the devil is made explicit. After Micawber becomes Uriah's employee, he says over and over again that he has "sold himself to the D."[52] Elsewhere Micawber calls Uriah "diabolical," "infernal," a "serpent," the instigator of "infernal business," and a "Demon."[53] Micawber, as always, is addicted to exaggeration and rhetorical flourish. In his unmasking of Uriah, he plays his role to the hilt, and he savors every moment of his performance. Dickens gives a comic and burlesque cast to the scene. Micawber the irate knight, brandishing a ruler instead of a broadsword, tames the demon dragon Uriah, while his devoted squires, David and Traddles, with difficulty restrain him. David calls the scene "ridiculous" and makes the broadsword comparison himself, but while the rich comedy of the confrontation cauterizes Uriah's malignancy, it does not deny that malignancy. Here again, Dickens' achievement—as well as much of the power and complexity of his art—comes from successfully fusing such seemingly warring modes as realism, burlesque, and diablerie.

How complex this fusion is may be glimpsed when one recognizes that Dickens has made Uriah not only a devil, but David's double. Here again the analogy with fairy stories is striking. In fairy tales, goodness not only contrasts with but often becomes its opposite. The parent figures in fairy tales illustrate this transformation very plainly. Little Red Ridinghood's loving grandmother suddenly becomes a ferocious wolf; Hop o' my Thumb's indulgent parents unexpectedly change into dangerous enemies; Cinderella's protective mother abruptly turns into a wicked stepmother. In such instances we have two antipodal versions of the same (or symbolically the same) personage; we have, in effect, the good and evil in an individual objectified in two separate but related identities. This, of course, is one way of depicting the disturbing complexity and changeability of individuals and of life. It is no oversubtle intellectualization to say that fairy tales function this way. Fairy stories reflect everyday experience. A child intuitively appreciates this. He responds to the wild enlargements—unshackling enlargements—of everyday hopes and fears in fairy tales. The parent figures in fairy tales, for example, allow a child to indulge his most hidden yearnings and terrors concerning parents, reinforcing the former (often through a happy ending) and purging the latter (through cathartic identification). A child (the chief audience today of fairy stories) is an expert of sorts. He has firsthand knowledge of the frightening contradictoriness and unpredictability of grandparents, parents, and stepparents—indeed of all adults who hold power over him. A parent can be loving and kind one moment, cold and cruel the next. Even a parent's benevolent actions can seem harsh and inexplicable to a child. To a child, a parent is truly two persons. Such universal ambivalences and polarities, starkly simplified and powerfully intensified, are the staple of fairy stories. In fairy tales, not surprisingly then, a good person is often depicted in close conjunction with his dark opposite, who is also, in certain crucial ways, his double. In a like manner, Dickens, especially in his later writings, presents us with similar conjunctions, though he deepens and refines their significance.

David and Uriah are an instance in point. Dickens does not insist upon the consanguinity of David and Uriah throughout the book, but he emphasizes it in a number of pivotal scenes. He also casts stray hints here and there. David early confesses to the fact that he finds himself "attracted towards Uriah" who has "a sort of fascination for me."[54] This fascination is reciprocated by Uriah who feels that David is a rival who has been brought into the Wickfield home and will one day be brought into the Wickfield business—Uriah's own dream.[55] David in fact does go into the law, but on a higher level than Uriah (who is Mr. Wickfield's clerk), so that his rivalry with Uriah, though not consummated in the terms Uriah imagined, is there nevertheless, and in a manner which accentuates—as everything always does—David's favored position and smoothed way above and beyond Uriah.

This consanguinity and rivalry become much more explicit when Uriah begins to show a special interest in Agnes. Though David regards Agnes as a sister, Uriah's hungry desire for her awakens David's slumbering sexual possessiveness and stirs profound feelings in David that he cannot comprehend. Each new hint that one day Uriah means to enjoy Agnes (no matter, or perhaps all the more matter, that Uriah intends to achieve that union through the sacrament of marriage) drives David into depression or anxiety or frenzy. When Uriah tells David that he loves Agnes ("my Agnes," he calls her), David becomes "delirious." His first thought is to seize the red-hot poker out of the fire and run Uriah through with it. David abandons this revealing impulse (the imagery is equally revealing) "with a shock, like a ball fired from a rifle'' (another revealing image), but the idea of Agnes being desecrated by ''so much as a thought of this red-headed animal's'' (yet another directive image), continues to make David giddy.[56]

David now reacts in an extraordinary way. Uriah ''seemed to swell and grow before my eyes; the room seemed full of the echoes of his voice; and the strange feeling (to which, perhaps, no one is quite a stranger) that all this had occurred before, at some indefinite time, and that I knew what he was going to say next, took possession of me.''[57] David's reaction is excessive, to put it mildly. It harks back, in part, to memories of a similar menace: to memories of his adored mother being coveted and then appropriated by a threatening rival, by the black-haired Mr. Murdstone. But it also stems from the intimate connection between David and Uriah, from the fact that in some respects Uriah is an intensification of David's most deeply repressed desires and suzerainty. There are ample reasons for insisting on such an identification. Uriah, after all, is that most hated thing: what David himself might have become without money, good birth, Miss Betsey's ministrations, and the like. David, like most of us, admires a flattering image of his best self, but abhors a dark reflection of his worst self. Uriah, unfortunately, is not only the devil, but the devil in David. David hates him as the principle of evil, but also (unconsciously) as the mirror of his own dark desires and aggressions. This helps to explain why David is delirious and giddy; why the room is full of echoes; why David feels that ''all this had occurred before''; why he knows what Uriah is going to say next.

The complicated relationship between David and Uriah is hinted at also by their names. In the Bible David covets and lies with Uriah's wife, Bathsheba, then sends Uriah to his death, and marries Bathsheba. This sequence suggests Copperfield's actions as well. David, even when married, unconsciously covets Agnes (all the more so when he knows Uriah would like to marry her), then helps send Uriah to his metaphorical death (David had often dreamed of murdering him), and marries Agnes. Given these parallels, it seems unlikely that Dickens would have chosen, in conjunction with the name David, the unusual and singularly allusive name Uriah (which he uses nowhere else in his writings), unless he wished to work changes on the David-Uriah theme. Yet the differences between the Biblical story and the novel are striking. In the Bible, David is sinful, Uriah innocent. In *Copperfield,* David is innocent, Uriah sinful. This strange reversal again suggests Uriah's role as David's darker self. For if the two are one, the reversal is not so strange. Then Uriah can personify David's most aggressive and covetous thoughts—which, in fact, he does. In the Bible, David's sinfulness is open, in *Copperfield* it is repressed and objectified in Uriah.

As I have said, Uriah is only intermittently David's double. Uriah is also a self-sustaining node of evil and malevolence operating independently of David. But the consanguinity between David and Uriah is not simply a matter of names or of one or two isolated suggestions, however powerful. Dickens underlines the consanguinity in other ways and other scenes. When David and Uriah are brought together, each is bereft of his father, each is attended by a mother or surrogate mother. Each "mother" wants her son to marry Agnes; each mother plots out her son's career and helps him on his way. Each son is good to his mother and solicitous of her welfare. Each mother is puissant. Miss Betsey is a fairy godmother who saves her protégés; Mrs. Heep is an evil enchantress who enmeshes her victims.

The special connections between David and Uriah are also accentuated by a number of striking scenes. Some of these scenes center on David's most personal sanctums, that is, on his bedrooms. There are three bedroom scenes: the first takes place in the Wickfields' house, the second in David's chambers, and the third in the Wickfields' house again. David's first night in his bedroom at the Wickfields' was disturbed by Uriah's gargoyle head. David quickly shut the window, believing he was thereby shutting Uriah out. But Uriah's ghostly intrusion into David's bedroom does not end when David closes the window. The bedroom apparition heralds Uriah's forthcoming sexual encroachment on David's bedchamber (Uriah will covet the girl who will later be David's bedpartner), and it foreshadows Uriah's actual physical presence—indeed his hegemony—in David's bedroom.

This gathering encroachment powerfully shapes the second bedroom scene. Uriah has accompanied David to his rooms for some coffee, but the hour has grown so late that David feels obliged to allow him to spend the night. Devil Uriah, seeking out his natural element, chooses to "lie down before the fire."[58] David's worried thoughts circle about Agnes and "this creature"; his restless sleep is crowded with vague terrors and images of Agnes threatened. He dozes a few minutes at a time, then turns and tumbles, then dozes again. His waking intervals are as haunted as his dreams: "When I awoke, the recollection that Uriah was lying in the next room, sat heavy on me like a waking nightmare; and oppressed me with a leaden dread, as if I had had some meaner quality of devil for a lodger."[59] David then dreams his earlier wish. He imagines that he has snatched a red-hot poker from the fire and run Uriah through.

> I was so haunted at last by the idea, though I knew there was nothing in it, that I stole into the next room to look at him. There I saw him, lying on his back, with his legs extending to I don't know where, gurglings taking place in his throat, stoppages in his nose, and his mouth open like a post-office. He was so much worse in reality than in my distempered fancy, that

afterwards I was attracted to him in very repulsion, and could not help
wandering in and out every half-hour or so, and taking another look at
him.[60]

Many of the elements I have been tracing in Uriah and David are
present in this scene: identification with the devil, murderous aggression, waking and sleeping hauntings by evil but wish-fulfilling dreams,
and helpless submission to the attraction of repulsion. These elements
evoke a suprarational, fairy-tale atmosphere. Yet the scene is also vi-
sually and psychologically realistic. At the same time it is antirealistic
in a non-fairy-tale way. A grotesque humor hovers over image and
phrase. Symbolically, of course, the scene reinforces the patterns I
have been tracing: David, both disgusted and fascinated, gazes on this
nightmare monster, devil and double, sleeping at his fireside. The gurgling monster—revenant of the past, hated rival, shocking projection
of his own most hidden desires—has somehow crept into his innermost
hearth and now slumbers maleficently there. In dreams David murders
his rival and dark self. In waking reality he gazes uncomprehendingly
at his slumbering antagonist and double, torn between attraction and
repulsion. When Uriah leaves early the next morning, it appears to
David "as if the night was going away in his person." When David goes
out a little while later, he charges his landlady "with particular directions to leave the windows open, that my sitting-room might be
aired, and purged of his presence."[61]

Uriah's lingering presence in dark corners of David's mind, and his
future presence as master of David's room, are not so easily purged. As
David's neglect of Agnes and his infatuation with Steerforth and Dora
grow, Uriah steals ever more commandingly into David's innermost
sanctums. At last he takes possession. He occupies David's old bedroom in the Wickfields' house. The premonitory signs have now been
fulfilled. The haunting gargoyle head and the gurgling fireside presence
have given way to total possession. Ironically, and symbolically,
Agnes and Mr. Wickfield still refer to the chamber as "David's room."
It is David's room in a double sense: it is haunted by the ghost of
David's childhood presence, and it is currently occupied by the malignant epitome of David's darkest instincts. David can occupy the room
physically again only after he has begun to purge himself of those
unconscious urges.

The purgation begins with Uriah's downfall and Dora's death, continues immediately with Steerforth's death, and then moves slowly
toward completion with David's symbolic death and rebirth. These
climactic events—the collapse and reconstruction of David's
world—are ushered in by Uriah's downfall. When Uriah's Satanic
power is exorcised, David is freed from one incapacitating spell—and

so is his old room. Uriah's exorcism late in the novel parallels the Murdstones' exorcism early in the novel. There can be no doubt about the symbolic significance of the second exorcism: "We passed the night at the old house, which, freed from the presence of the Heeps, seemed purged of a disease; and I lay in my old room, like a shipwrecked wanderer come home."[62]

In analyzing Uriah Heep I have concentrated on his magical aspects—his malign physical features, supernatural powers, demonism, doppelgänger effect, and the like. This treatment falsifies Uriah's true presence in the novel in two ways. First, it separates elements that are not separate in the book. Uriah's physical features, his red eyes and snaky undulations, are not divorced from—they are part of—his demonic power. I have separated his fantasy components here in order to trace each in clearer and starker outline. Yet it is the whole that is important. That whole is an intricate blend of strong motifs, delicate nuances, and complicated echoes which reinforce one another and reverberate as the portrait progresses. Second, I have neglected the realistic core of Uriah's character. This is the core about which all the other elements revolve. The core also supports the sociological implications of Uriah's characterization, implications that were central to Dickens' purpose.

From a realistic and sociological point of view Uriah is ubiquitous and damned. Like Carker, he has been spawned by the new, inhuman urban-industrial society. Along with Carker he is a prototype of an increasingly important breed in Dickens: Bitzer, Bradley Headstone, and Charley Hexam are later versions of the species. Uriah is so consumed with a sense of inferiority and injustice (a burden imposed upon him by society), and so trained to suppress any outward display of his true feelings and needs (an hypocrisy demanded of him by society), that pathology is certain. It is this society-fostered disparity between outward role and inward needs that causes Uriah to seek power and ascendency. His profoundly hypocritical 'umbleness is only a dramatization of this disparity. Uriah hates David because David is the living embodiment of what he might have been but for the unjust accidents of birth and upbringing. He thus reverses David's hatred which stems (in part) from seeing in Uriah what he might have sunk to under Murdstone tutelage. The latter conflation goes back ultimately to Dickens' own horror in contemplating what he might have become when—innocent and defenseless—he was thrust into the soul-destroying blacking warehouse. On the other hand, David's attraction to Uriah, like his attraction to Steerforth, is the loadstone attraction to evil. Both Uriah and Steerforth personify evil, and Dickens counterpoints both characters to the somber answering chord in David. David openly idolizes Steerforth. For David, Steerforth is a hero. With Uriah the

matter is different. Uriah's attraction for David is the complicated
attraction of repulsion.

Dickens' psychology is profound and convincing. It works here, as
in most of his later writings, through dramatization: through action,
analogy, and symbolism, rather than exposition. It gathers in penetration as the book unfolds. By the time Uriah enters the novel, we know
so much about David's fears and hatreds, and Dickens' fairy-tale
method, that we can make sense out of odd supercharged interactions
between David and Uriah, interactions that otherwise would be inexplicable, or at least strangely jarring. The fantasy components that
surround Uriah help us make this sense. They do this in the complicated fashion I have been tracing. The fantasy elements also enlarge
Uriah's mundane evil and the threat that evil poses to society. The
fantasy elements raise that evil and its consequences to the cosmic
level. Helped by these storybook enlargements, we see the full
significance of Uriah's commonplace pathology. Uriah is a veritable
devil, glowing-eyed, cadaverous, and death-dealing, but at the same
time, and without conflict, he is perfectly realistic. We shudder at his
banal origins. We acknowledge his ubiquitous sway. He is a devil who
has been created by society, a devil who magnifies our hidden urges
and motivations, a devil who awakens an answering response in our
breasts. He is the ordinary humdrum devil everywhere about us—all
the more frightening (and thus the fairy-tale enlargement) because he is
so familiar and so destructive. By distorting reality, Dickens helps us
grasp reality. He uses the potent alchemy of fantasy to sharpen our
dulled vision and prod our complacent awareness. Helped by such
intensifications, we see the familiar world afresh. We see Uriah as he
really is.

The fairy-tale aura that surrounds Uriah surrounds many other characters in *Copperfield*. It surrounds, for example—indeed it shapes—
that taut, passionate, binary pair, Steerforth and Rosa Dartle, and it
surrounds their circling satellites, little Emily, Mrs. Steerforth, and
Agnes.

Dickens quickly establishes Steerforth's strong magical associations.
Steerforth is attractive and charming; he is also mercurial. But these
very human traits are tinged with more than human qualities. Steerforth's manner partakes of "enchantment." He has an "inborn power
of attraction" which amounts to a kind of "spell," a spell to which it
was "a natural weakness to yield" and which "not many persons could
withstand."[63] Soon David is "entranced" by Steerforth.[64] He continues to be entranced all his life. The spell lingers even after Steerforth
has betrayed David's friendship and ruined the lives of several of his
friends; it lingers even after Steerforth's death. David is not unique in

yielding to Steerforth. Even lone, lorn Mrs. Gummidge, impervious to all blandishments, succumbs to Steerforth's charm. She admits that she has been "bewitched" by him.[65]

Steerforth's irresistible charm is coupled with his ability to adapt himself effortlessly to any person or occasion. This ability is no ordinary gift, but the preternatural power to be or become anything he wants. Steerforth displays this power most notably when he is introduced to Mr. Peggotty's household, but David often underlines Steerforth's ability to take any shape he chooses. David tells us that Steerforth became "gay and talkative in a moment, as he could become anything he liked at any moment."[66] Through these and scores of similar touches, Dickens rapidly endows Steerforth with a host of fairy-tale attributes. Magical charm, protean changefulness, and spell-like enchantment are only the most obvious of Steerforth's special powers. Steerforth is larger than life, yet he is also realistic. Dickens uses this duality (fused in practice into a unity) as a means of enriching what he has to say. The supernatural aura that surrounds Steerforth adds resonance and concision to Dickens' meanings.

In the scene in which Steerforth is introduced into the Peggottys' ship-home, for instance, David describes how Steerforth drew each member of the household into his spell, "until he brought us, by degrees, into a charmed circle."[67] In context, "charmed circle" is rich with meaning. Part of that rich meaning flows from the occult associations that surround Steerforth. In its most obvious sense "charmed circle" means the warm friendly circle of assembled family and guests. Equally obviously it means the easy circle of talk and interest created by Steerforth's self-consciously exercised charm. More covertly it suggests the potent, almost irresistible spell that Steerforth's magical charm has begun to exert on the assembled circle. And lastly it predicts, with devastating irony, that the binding circle produced by Steerforth's charm will destroy that trusting family circle. Steerforth's "charmed circle"—a storybook term—turns out to be a poisoned ring. The latter meanings are evoked by the fairy-tale associations that have been accumulating around Steerforth. Those associations make us sensitive to the storybook implications of a phrase such as "charmed circle"; they also help us see that the magical circle woven by Steerforth's charm is not protective but maleficent: the "charmed circle" is the destructive circle of Steerforth's charm.

These and multitudes of similar insights are further enforced by the arcane world that Steerforth inhabits. He is not simply larger than life, a weaver of ruinous spells and assumer of deceiving shapes, he dwells in a universe in which his actions, gestures, moods, and choices are imbued with magical meanings. Indeed the universe itself is full of signs and portents. As David walks with Steerforth across the Yarmouth sands, bringing Steerforth for the first time to Mr. Peggotty's ship-house, the wind sighs and moans mournfully. David recalls hearing the same sound the first time he "darkened" Mr. Peggotty's door. This directive setting and foreshadowing, which looks to the past and reaches out to the future, is intensified a moment later when Steerforth says, "the sea roars as if it were hungry for us"—thus predicting the manner and place of his death. A moment later the two friends see a light. Steerforth inquires whether it comes from the Peggottys' ship-house, and on being informed that it does, he says that he saw the house while walking that morning and came "straight to it, by instinct."[68]

This fateful attraction is confirmed by a fateful entrance. David and Steerforth open the door of the snug little ship-house. In an instant they bring the dark and cold of the threatening night into the light and warmth of the happy room. But their coming does more than herald the chill of encroaching night; it interrupts a portentous occasion. Emily is just about to spring from Ham's side into Mr. Peggotty's arms; it is the moment of her betrothal to Ham. David writes: "The little picture was so instantaneously dissolved by our going in, that one might have doubted whether it had ever been."[69] This vignette, which records the blighting effect of Steerforth's coming, also predicts the devastating effect of Steerforth's future actions. The episode continues with this double thread of realism and magical meaning. Mr. Peggotty calls to Emily, "Come here, my little witch!" and then says how happy he is that David and Steerforth have come to see her on "the brightest night of your uncle's life as ever was or will be."[70] The ironies and foreshadowings crowd upon one another. Later in the evening Steerforth tells the story of a dismal shipwreck, thus again predicting his own end. He tells the tale "as if he saw it all before him," and during the entire time "little Em'ly's eyes were fastened on him . . . as if she saw it too."[71]

This magical predictiveness, which goes beyond ordinary dramatic irony or foreshadowing, and approaches the occult regions of magic glasses and second sight, is not limited to the fateful scene of Steerforth's introduction into Mr. Peggotty's household. It plays over all Steerforth's comings and goings, and it is often tinged with a supernatural cast. Several days later, for example, on a "dark evening," David startles Steerforth, who is alone and musing before a fire in Mr. Peggotty's ship-house. "You come upon me," Steerforth cries, almost angrily, "like a reproachful ghost!"[72] David asks if he has called Steerforth "down from the stars." When Steerforth answers no, David asks, "Up from anywhere, then?" Steerforth does not reply directly, but taking a "piece of burning wood" from the fire, he strikes out of it "a train of red-hot sparks." After this infernal gesture, he says that he has been thinking that all the people in Mr. Peggotty's household might be "dispersed, or dead, or come to I don't know what harm." And a moment later he refers to Mr. Peggotty's house as "this devil's bark of a boat."[73] Soon after he tries to explain his mood: "At odd dull times, nursery tales come up into the memory, unrecognised for what they are. . . . What old women call the horrors, have been creeping over me from head to foot. I have been afraid of myself." Even when he attempts to shake the mood, he does so in terms that are profoundly supernatural, terms that accentuate the portentous significance of what has been occurring and what will yet occur:

> "So much for that!" he said, making as if he tossed something light into the air, with his hand.
> "'Why, being gone, I am a man again,' like Macbeth. And now for dinner! If I have not (Macbeth-like) broken up the feast with most admired disorder, Daisy."[74]

These allusions dwell on Macbeth's short-lived recoveries from his own brand of "horrors." At the same time, though more subterraneously, they call up a darker array of associations—weird sisters, death-inducing predictions, destructive ambitions, premeditated murders, invisible daggers, deep disorders, and ghostly hauntings. In Steerforth's case, the strange interlude of horrors has been brought about by an unusual moment, a moment of moral insight. For a brief interval Steerforth has had an unadorned glimpse of what he is and what he contemplates, and this glimpse unmans him. But his moral awareness is fleeting; his recovery is rapid. His recovery is a return to his usual, dazzling, charming, protean self; he becomes, once more, the bright Satanic Steerforth who has no moral scruples, who seeks only mastery and pleasure. That Steerforth is "a man again," and will continue now to rush heedless on his way, is made clear a few pages later when, "pale even to his lips," he tells David that he has bought a boat. The boat, he says, is called the *Stormy Petrel,* but he will rename it the *Little Em'ly.*[75] The names foretell a joint doom: little Emily to fly petrel-like to her destruction, Steerforth to find his death in stormy seas.

That doom is confirmed a paragraph or so later by another scene of fairy-tale prescience. David and Steerforth meet Ham and Emily walking on the sands. Emily withdraws her hand timidly from Ham's arm and gives it blushingly to Steerforth and to David. As the betrothed couple continue on, Emily does not replace her hand on Ham's arm, but, timid and constrained, walks by herself. David and Steerforth watch them fade away in the light of a young moon, when suddenly, another figure—it is a prostitute named Martha, a former friend of Emily—follows after the disappearing couple. David describes the scene most carefully: "As the dark distant level, absorbing their figures into itself, left but itself visible between us and the sea and clouds, [Martha's] figure disappeared in like manner, still no nearer to them than before." Steerforth, who is about to turn Emily into a kept woman, says, "That is a black shadow to be following the girl . . . what does it mean?" David answers that perhaps the shadowing figure is a beggar, but this does not satisfy Steerforth. "It is a strange thing," he says, "that the beggar should take that shape to-night"; and later he adds, in ironic phrase, "where the devil did it come from!" David suggests that it materialized from the shadow of a nearby wall, but Steerforth is troubled: "He looked again over his shoulder towards the sea-line glimmering afar off; and yet again"—he is looking at the place where his own death will occur—and he continued to think about the figure through the remainder of the walk.[76]

Every gesture, every image in this scene—from the withdrawn hand, to the following fate, to the figures disappearing into the sea—is magical and predictive. Steerforth is unnerved because he sees his dark design shadowed forth in a startling dumb show, a show which predicts not merely what he will do to Emily, but what will happen to him. He is troubled because a cosmic symbolism has magnified and extrapolated his infernal plan.

Steerforth is not often awed by the cosmos. He is more commonly depicted (in his nonrealistic aspects) as larger than life. He is a fallen Lucifer, still astonishingly bright and attractive, still powerful and dominating, but evil. He is David's bad angel. This is not simply a metaphor, but Dickens' conception of him. Fused to the everyday James Steerforth, scion of Highgate, man about town, is the infernal dimension of a fallen angel. Dickens makes certain aspects of this conception very explicit. When David is getting drunk during a party he is giving for Steerforth and some male friends—it is David's first dissipation—he makes a speech in Steerforth's honor and then goes over to him (breaking a glass in the process) and says, "Steerforth, you'retheguidingstarofmyexistence."[77] The young men eventually wind up at the theater, where David disgraces himself in Agnes' presence. David is now very drunk, but Agnes is able to exercise enough influence to make him go home.

The next day, shamed and remorseful, David goes to see Agnes and apologize. The latter scene takes place in a new chapter entitled "Good and Bad Angels." David immediately feels the magical influence of his good angel. "She put her hand—its touch was like no other hand—upon my arm for a moment; and I felt so befriended and comforted, that I could not help moving it to my lips, and gratefully kissing it."[78] Agnes is sympathetic and understanding, and David, in a burst of gratitude, cries, "Ah, Agnes! . . . You are my good Angel!" Agnes shakes her head, but David insists, "Yes, Agnes, my good Angel! Always my good Angel!"[79] Agnes takes advantage of the moment to warn David against what she terms his "bad Angel"—Steerforth. She condemns Steerforth's influence over David. David tells her that she is unjust, that she wrongs Steerforth. Steerforth, he says, is not "my bad Angel, or any one's!" He is "a guide, a support, and a friend to me."[80] Agnes hints that she is the instrument of some higher power, that her advice is divine: "I feel as if it were some one else speaking to you, and not I, when I caution you that you have made a dangerous friend."[81]

Though David rejects the advice that Agnes gives, a chord within him stirs to her presence, so that Steerforth "in spite of all my attachment to him, darkened in that tone." Agnes repeats her warning, and the magical effect occurs once more: "Again I looked at her, again I listened to her after she was silent, and again his image, though it was still fixed in my heart, darkened."[82] The dramatic and rhetorical repetitions, the fact that David listens to her after she is silent, and the effect itself, tell us that we are in the realm of the Christmas books, a realm that goes beyond the merely realistic. Dickens usually conveys the core of his meaning realistically. Yet he also gives us hints of a congruent storybook world. Sometimes that invisible world is presented to us directly, but more often we only see its powerful effects. We catch a glimpse of the magically patterned forces (usually accompanied by attendant signs) that pull and push us on our way. So it is here. In addition to any direct labels, the divinely beneficent power that Agnes exerts tells us that she is David's good angel; just as the infernally malign power that Steerforth exerts tells us that he is David's bad angel.

Agnes' influence in opposition to Steerforth is not limited to this scene of dissipation and remorse. Some time later we see that her power is continuing to pull David away from Steerforth. David has begun to have a lurking distrust of Steerforth; he is glad when he finds that Steerforth is out of town and cannot return to London. David's analysis of his new feelings is to the point: "I suspect the truth to be, that the influence of Agnes was upon me, undisturbed by the sight of him; and that it was the more powerful with me, because she had so large a share in my thoughts and interest."[83]

David is obviously poised between good and evil; he is being pulled by the opposing lures of his good and bad angels. The truth is, however, that he is decisively committed to neither one. Despite his avowals, he gives only superficial allegiance to his good angel; despite his lurking distrust, he often yields to the bright enchantments of his bad angel. It is only after grievous loss, only after death and rebirth, that he can cleave to the former and renounce the latter. David's moral growth is marked by his turning away from self-destruction. Dora, his first wife, Steerforth, his best friend, are profoundly destructive for him. Yet he chooses to bind himself to each; he worships each with blind infatuation. It is not difficult to understand why David is attracted to that which he should avoid. We have all felt similar attractions. In David's case, however, we need not limit ourselves to such explanations. With David we understand the shaping childhood experiences that made him what he was.

But there are other reasons for David's self-destructive errors. He inhabits a world where things are often not what they seem to be. Indeed appearance often inverts reality. Wives and friends, Doras and Steerforths, are only the most devastating demonstrations of this topsy-turvy world, a world created, in part, by David's distorted vision. There are many similar inversions. The moral Mr. Murdstone proves to be a villain; the witchlike Miss Betsey proves to be a fairy godmother; the dull-witted Ham proves to be a hero; the oaflike Mr. Peggotty proves to be a gentleman. These reversals remind one of the magical inversions of *Great Expectations*. There a topsy-turvy moral vision undergirds the entire novel; here it is a subpattern circling about David's emotional immaturity.

Dickens often uses this technique of reversal, and he often associates it with fairy-tale effects. But even more often he uses a technique of polarities, and this too he often invests with storybook effects. The former technique is subsumed by the latter. Characters who turn out to be the opposite of what they seem to be are only a special subgroup of a larger category: paired characters who are opposites. David's good and bad angels are such a pair. One sees immediately why Dickens made them godlike and invested them with supernatural—in this case "angelic"—attributes. (That Steerforth is "angelic" testifies to his status as a fallen Lucifer; he is very different from such lesser devils as the gargoyle Uriah Heep.) By touching Agnes with supernal and Steerforth with infernal powers, Dickens universalizes the contest within David and makes it cosmic. This added dimension often saves scenes and actions that teeter on the edge of banality or melodrama. David's translation from drunken posturings to sober remorse might have been simply priggish. It is saved from this reduction by a number of factors: by the compelling realism, physical and psychological, which informs every line of the scene; by the marvelous humor, which makes the episode (in its earlier sections) one of the great comic scenes of the novel; and by the mythlike aura, which helps us understand, without dull prosing or pompous inflation (Agnes sometimes descends into both), that the scene is a microcosm of a larger drama—the struggle for David's soul.

This mythic contest, and the mythic figures who preside over it, have another use. The heavenly angel, Agnes, and the fallen angel, Steerforth, help Dickens structure and organize the novel. Agnes is David's better self or higher soul (I shall return to this idea later); Steerforth is David's darker self and double. This allegorical way of putting the matter is somewhat misleading, for Dickens hints and suggests rather than allegorizes. Agnes brings out the best in David, Steerforth the worst. Yet even this overstates the case. Agnes is a soothing, softening saint, but her direct influence on David (until his rebirth) may be likened to a broken strain of music that falls faintly on the ear. She is like Milly, the beneficent principle of loving goodness in *The Haunted Man,* but less allegorical, less magical, less insistent. In the same way, Steerforth's influence on David is subtle and indirect. Steerforth is a bright masterful god that David idolizes; he does not seek to initiate David into sin. In following Steerforth, David strays only slightly from the paths of virtue. David's chief failing is to be blind to Steerforth's empty selfishness, and thus, unconsciously, to help Steerforth prey upon those who love and trust David. David is thus an unconscious accomplice in Steerforth's crimes.

But Dickens darkens and complicates the matter further. He hints now and then that Steerforth is David's double, that there is a subtle alter-ego relationship between the two. The hints are muted, but they are real, and they suggest that in some subterranean way Steerforth enacts some of David's darker fantasies, or that he gives vent to what David has repressed, or that he shadows forth what David, at his worst, might be capable of. The special relationship between the two is conveyed by David's immediate enslavement to Steerforth, by his blindness to Steerforth's selfishness and amorality, by his idolatrous worship of Steerforth, by his touchy defense (until Steerforth runs off with Emily) of Steerforth's most questionable actions, and by his inability, even after Steerforth's death, to put aside Steerforth's enchantment. This special intimacy between David and Steerforth is closely associated with Steerforth's magical powers, with his ability to cast a spell. It is also associated with a number of striking parallels in their lives. Each, for example, is "bewitched" by the "fairy" elf, little Emily. This is not a casual similarity, but central. David's early love for Emily is treated in terms which foreshadow Steerforth's repetition and parody of it. (In an extraordinary doubling and inversion of the parallel, which further confirms the alter-ego relationship, Dickens later causes David to be powerfully attracted by—indeed half in love with— Steerforth's early love, Rosa Dartle.) David's love for Emily is also treated in terms that suggest his responsibility for Steerforth's sinister recapitulation of his innocent childhood romance. Both the foreshadowing and the responsibility are enforced by fantasy and enchantment.

David's juvenile love for Emily is a fairy-tale idyl. David recalls his

declaration to her: "that I never could love another, and that I was
prepared to shed the blood of anybody who should aspire to her affections."[84] David, of course, is grievously wrong: he *will* love another,
and not only will he fail to shed the blood of a rival, he will introduce
and facilitate the rival. David continues his storybook fantasy: "What
happiness (I thought) if we were married, and were going away anywhere to live among the trees and in the fields, never growing older,
never growing wiser, children ever, rambling hand in hand through
sunshine and among flowery meadows, laying down our heads on moss
at night, in a sweet sleep of purity and peace, and buried by the birds
when we were dead!"[85] This dream of idyllic changelessness contrasts
ironically with the turmoil and change to come. Its concluding allusions
to *The Children in the Wood* are more directly predictive. Like the
earlier reference to the lost boy in the fairy story, the concluding allusions are strongly associated with Dickens' own childhood fantasies
concerning his parents (and in this instance his sister Fanny also), and
they predict abandonment and death.

David, the innocent child, continues to spin his storybook dreams.
When Ham and Mr. Peggotty leave him alone with Emily and Mrs.
Gummidge, he conceives of himself as "the protector of Em'ly" and
wishes that "a lion or a serpent, or any ill-disposed monster" might
attack them so that he might slay it and cover himself with glory. That
night he dreams of dragons until morning.[86] Obviously David's fantasies circle about undying love, loyalty, changelessness, protective-
ness, and heroism—all of which he will betray in his own person or
through his hero and surrogate, Steerforth. The point is not simply that
the fairy-tale imagery foreshadows the future—much additional imagery in the segment, most notably sea imagery, does the same—but
that for David the fairy tale casts a continuing enchantment over Emily
so that he always feels a special closeness to her.

Steerforth's cruel redaction of David's enchanted dream is thus a
double betrayal: Steerforth enacts David's fantasy (he is thus both
surrogate and usurper); he also perverts each element in that fantasy
(he is thus a diabolical projection and nemesis). He is innocent David
turned dark and vicious; he is David's nightmare double. Unconsciously David's guilt flows from seeing his surrogate fulfill his fantasy
so monstrously; consciously his guilt flows from being an accomplice
(through his sponsorship of Steerforth) in that fulfillment. At times
shadowy hints of these submerged feelings rise up from David's un-
charted depths. For instance, toward the end of the book, after Emily
has been rescued, but before the tempest engulfs Steerforth, David
pays a last visit to the old ship-house before the Peggottys depart for
Australia. The wind wails about the house, reminding David of his first
night there. On that occasion the wind, accentuating the cozy snugness

of the house and his closeness to Emily, made the whole scene "like enchantment"; but later that evening, when he went to bed, the howling wind brought visions of "the great deep rising in the night"—a premonition, in context, of Mr. Murdstone's coming, and more distantly, a premonition of the great deep rising in the night and engulfing David and Steerforth.[87]

Now David is paying his final visit to the ship-house. The wailing wind reminds him of his first night there—of the magical enchantment and the rising deep—but at the same time it reminds him directly now of what (years before) was simultaneously taking place at the Rookery: the unseen coming of his risen father, the fearful Mr. Murdstone emerging from the deep. This crucial juxtaposition—of past enchantment and nightmare fulfillment (the latter heralded by omens)—is immediately followed by an analogous juxtaposition. David thinks of his fairy-tale idyl with Emily (he again uses the word "enchanted"), and then he is overwhelmed by the fearful unseen presence of Steerforth. Though Steerforth is not there, he is present with David: "I thought of the blue-eyed child who had enchanted me. I thought of Steerforth: and a foolish, fearful fancy came upon me of his being near at hand, and liable to be met at any turn."[88]

That Steerforth's fearful presence comes unbidden into David's memory of "the blue-eyed child who had enchanted me," indicates that David's innocent idyl with Emily is tainted by Steerforth's shadow. Why David's storybook promises to Emily so long ago should be encumbered by Steerforth's latter-day betrayals and supposed fearful presence is never explained. Indeed the unaccountable thought that Steerforth is near at hand (he is—and will suddenly appear) is termed "foolish." Such insistent associations, irrational fears, and omen-filled premonitions hint at deep connections. They help us see that at times David and Steerforth share an alter-ego consanguinity.

This consanguinity is given added substance by other deep connections. David and Steerforth are shaped by similar parental constellations. Each suffers from the fact that he has a bad mother and a missing father. This not only helps to identify David and Steerforth with each other, but connects them with one of the great unifying themes of the novel—the ways in which children are shaped by the inadequacies of their parents. In *Copperfield* this shaping is usually pathological and is most frequently represented by missing or bad parents or by a combination of the two. The roll call of children in *Copperfield* who suffer from missing or bad parents is truly astonishing. It includes not only David and Steerforth, but Emily, Ham, Dora, Agnes, Annie Strong, Traddles, Rosa, and Uriah—and this list is by no means exhaustive. Dickens examines some of these parent-child relationships and their consequences in great detail (David and his mother, for example), but he juxtaposes others more sketchily to the central demonstrations in the novel. As we confront crucial (and usually flawed) parent-child relationships in perspective after perspective and permutation after permutation, we begin to grasp how various, how similar, and above all how profound, are the consequences of parental pathology.

We also begin to grasp that relationships which at first seem to exist largely for convenience in plotting—David's architectonic conjunctions with Emily, Dora, Agnes, Uriah, and Steerforth, for instance—are also deeply thematic. We see that Steerforth is more than a bad angel, more than a dark counterpart of David's good angel, Agnes. David and Steerforth are two instances of the same disease. Their bad mothers and missing fathers have encumbered them in life. David and Steerforth are alter egos: two elaborated examples of the blighting consequences of bad parenting. But this is much too simple. Though David and Steerforth are victims of the same disease, their case histories are quite different, and these differences complicate and enrich their alter-ego relationship. Both are bereft of fathers and of the strong, wise counsel a good father would provide. For David this lack is filled by an evil risen father, the dark and murderous Murdstone. For Steerforth the lack is not filled, and in the scene in which Steerforth looks briefly into his own heart as he plots his betrayal of David and the Peggottys, he tells David, "I wish to God I had had a judicious father these last twenty years! . . . I wish with all my soul I had been better guided! . . . I wish with all my soul I could guide myself better!"[89] And a little later he repeats, "I tell you, my good fellow, once more, that it would have been well for me (and for more than me) if I had had a steadfast and judicious father!"[90]

With both David and Steerforth the evil that flows from a missing father is compounded by the evil that flows from a bad mother, but here there are even greater differences within the similarities. David's mother (like his dead father) was weak, wishful, and indecisive, and David inherits some of these traits. His undisciplined heart is too soon engaged and too shallowly founded—a heritage from his pipe-dreaming father and his playful, dependent, immature mother. Steerforth's mother is obstinate and imperious. She fiercely demands first place in Steerforth's heart. At the same time she indulges and spoils him recklessly. Steerforth becomes (as Rosa Dartle frequently points out) a proud, selfish, self-indulgent, uncontrollable replica of his mother. Dickens is quite self-conscious in the way he counterpoints the many similar instances of parental dereliction here and throughout the book. This is clear not simply from the intricate design of the novel itself, but from the number plans. In the plan for Number XV, in his working plans for Chapter XLV (the chapter in which Annie Strong, another fatherless child with a bad mother, reveals how she was "very young, and had no adviser''—a lesson, along with much else, that David pointedly applies to his own case), Dickens writes: ''Shew the faults of mothers, and their consequences''; and then he adds, ''all brought to bear on David, and applied by him to himself.''

David and Steerforth are thus complementary in their needs and demands. David, owing to his parents and his early history, is innocent, loving, dependent, idealizing, self-deluding, hero-worshiping, and submissive. Steerforth, owing to his parents and his early history, is experienced, selfish, masterful, realistic, self-aware, arrogant, and aggressive. Each fulfills the other's needs; each completes the other's lacks. Together they are a whole; apart they are fragments. This is the basis of their, in some ways, strange friendship. This is especially the basis of David's worship of Steerforth. Yet Steerforth is also a completion of the evil in David. In this respect he is the mirror image of Agnes who represents, as we shall see, a completion of the good in David.

These complicated bonds and completions add substance and subtlety to the alter-ego consanguinity that exists between David and Steerforth. That consanguinity is part of David's heritage; it is part of what he inherits from his parents. Yet David also makes himself, and he is far from doomed. Steerforth represents the dark impulses in David's amorphous and evolving self, a self that is partly good and partly evil, but more good than evil. Steerforth thus differs from Uriah, who (insofar as he too is an alter ego) is the objectification of David's worst self, a projection of the most aggressive and Satanic forces in David. Yet Steerforth and Uriah, like David's better counterparts—Agnes and Traddles, say—are only enlargements of potentialities within David, and this only in an intermittent and suggestive way. There is no direct equivalence or allegory here, and Dickens is always careful to maintain simultaneously the reality and separateness of each of his characters.

This technique of doubling, counterpointing, and suggesting by analogy is central to Dickens' method. It helps him convey the diversity and complexity of experience and especially the strange contradictions and hidden impulses of character. How different is the David of straightforward narration from the David who is intricately connected by recurrences, parallels, and supernatural signs to his unconscious fears and fantasies. And how complicated is the seemingly simple David who is profoundly counterpointed to such characters as his mother, Mr. Murdstone, Steerforth, and many others. Through such juxtapositions and projections we begin to see how strange and infinitely complex is the web that composes and enmeshes each one of us. Dickens' method here is profoundly psychological, and *David Copperfield* is a deeply psychological novel. But Dickens' understanding of human psychology is conveyed by action, and by analogies, signs, and hidden connections.

Fantasy is one of Dickens' primary means of pointing up these analogies, conveying these signs, and revealing these hidden connections. The way this process works, not simply in relation to David, but in the complex counterpointing of each character to other characters, as well as to David, may be seen with Rosa Dartle. David, as I have already noted, was half in love with her. This is not surprising, for in addition to the reasons already elucidated, she is a storybook character of great power and potency. Her most obvious fairy-tale sign is the terrible scar which runs across her mouth and down her chin. The scar, put there years ago when Steerforth threw a hammer at her, is now a magical index of her inner feelings, especially her passion and her repressed (or displaced) emotions. Like the sympathetic rings, garments, and mirrors of fairy stories, which reveal the true state of some endangered person or object, Rosa's scar reveals the true state of her inner life. On first meeting Rosa, David is fascinated by the scar:

> I could not help glancing at the scar with a painful interest when we went in to tea. It was not long before I observed that it was the most susceptible part of her face, and that, when she turned pale, that mark altered first, and became a dull, lead-coloured streak, lengthening out to its full extent, like a mark in invisible ink brought to the fire. There was a little altercation between her and Steerforth about a cast of the dice at backgammon, when I thought her, for one moment, in a storm of rage; and then I saw it start forth like the old writing on the wall.[91]

The scar is a sign of Rosa's outward and inward wound. Both wounds were put there by Steerforth's self-indulgent passion: the former by throwing a hammer at her, the latter by loving and then discarding her. The scar is thus Steerforth's infernal brand on her, and it comes to life as he provokes her anger, envy, jealousy, or rage.

But if Steerforth has placed his infernal mark on Rosa, by the time we meet her she is infernal enough in her own right. She is black-haired and black-eyed like Mr. Murdstone—and like the great black-haired dog in the once empty kennel. Her "gaunt eyes" seem to reveal the "wasting fire within her."[92] David can scarcely endure her "strange eyes" and their "hungry lustre."[93] Her eyes could fix one with a "lynx-like scrutiny," and when she was aroused, they "gleamed like fire."[94] At times even Steerforth quails at the thought of her. "Confound the girl," he says to David, "I am half afraid of her. She's like a goblin to me."[95]

Rosa, however, is more than intense and aggressive, she is profoundly attractive. She has an air of "wicked grace."[96] Even when she is vindictive or destructive she has "something feminine and alluring" about her that entraps and compels.[97] David falls under her spell for a brief interval. Though he finds her unsettling, at times even frightening, he is attracted by some indefinable power in her physical demeanor. How great an impression she makes on him may be gauged by the aftereffects of their first meeting. David, who is staying at the Steerforths', goes to bed in a chamber that has a painting of Rosa above the chimney piece. It is a startling likeness, and it seems to look "eagerly" at David.[98] David is disconcerted, yet fascinated, by the painting. "The painter hadn't made the scar, but *I* made it; and there it was, coming and going: now confined to the upper lip as I had seen it at dinner, and now showing the whole extent of the wound inflicted by the hammer, as I had seen it when she was passionate."[99] David is disturbed by Rosa's haunting presence, and to get rid of her, he quickly undresses, extinguishes his light, and goes to bed. But he cannot forget that she is still there, and when he does fall asleep, his uneasy dreams are filled with her presence.

This scene ends Chapter XX. It recalls the strikingly similar scene that ends Chapter XV—a scene that takes place following David's first meeting with Uriah Heep. In the latter scene a carved beam-end coalesces into Uriah's gargoyle likeness and looks "sideways" at David. David is disturbed and quickly closes the window to "shut him out." But one can no more shut out gargoyle demons than one can shut out poison ladies. The strange luring power of each—a power strongly imbued with the attraction of repulsion—is emphasized by the uncannily identical way that each begins to haunt David's life.

Later in the book we discover who Rosa Dartle is and what powers she possesses. She is "a cruel princess in a legend."[100] Wicked, alluring, envious, and vengeful, she takes pleasure in giving pain to those who rival or thwart her. Frustrated, full of rage and grief, her last baffled words to David enforce her storybook role: "A curse upon you!" she cries. "It was in an evil hour that you ever came here! A curse upon you! Go!"[101]

I have been emphasizing so far Rosa's fablelike attributes, but she is also realistically drawn. She constitutes an acute and penetrating psychological portrait. The salient features of her early history are instructive. A distant relation of the Steerforths, motherless from birth, she was brought, still young, into the Steerforths' household after her father's death. She is dark and handsome and intelligent. She has a small income of her own which she manages frugally. She is some years older than Steerforth—about thirty when David meets her. Steerforth had thrown the hammer at her while still a young boy, and that wanton act—the self-indulgent reflex of a moment of exasperation—was a premonition of disfiguring things to come. As Steerforth grew older, he took advantage of Rosa's passionate nature. Using his great charm, he compelled her love, but then grew weary of her. Rosa was embittered and enraged by Steerforth's callousness, but she was unable to free herself from his spell. Alternately longing and loathing, she retained her passion, but lost her capacity to love. All this is in the past. We discover Rosa's history and nature in condensed bits and pieces as the novel progresses. At the center of the novel, however, is a parallel action. We see Steerforth reenacting with Emily the wounding story he had enacted with Rosa.

Rosa is passion personified. Her profound sexuality smolders hotly in all her appearances and actions. But her sexuality no longer has a natural course. By the time we meet her it has been perverted into perpetual rage. Bereft of loving parents and affectionate guidance, unable to use her intelligence productively, relegated by fate and Victorian mores to a subordinate role in a hermetic household, emotionally imprisoned by her passion for Steerforth, she is utterly stifled in every turning of her life. She is, indeed, the disfigured embodiment of the scar that slants across her mouth. Her sexuality now finds vent in hostile questionings, scornful innuendoes, towering hatreds, and flaming rages. Most of the time Rosa must repress these violent emotions, but they always burn intensely just below the surface of her speech and gestures, and they explode all the more violently when they do explode because of her tense efforts to repress them.

At the climactic moments of explosion, expression approaches frenzy. David is overwhelmed by her intensity: "Such a concentration of rage and scorn as darkened her face, and flashed in her jet-black eyes, I could not have thought compressible even into that face. The scar made by the hammer was, as usual in this excited state of her features, strongly marked. When the throbbing I had seen before, came into it as I looked at her, she absolutely lifted up her hand and struck it."[102] In this instance the symbolic act of striking her old wound is only a prelude. It is followed by a most extraordinary flood of hatred. Prodigalities of hostility burst forth in hysterical torrents. Rosa says she would like to pull down Mr. Peggotty's house, brand Emily on the face, hunt her to the grave, and much, much more. The atmosphere and rhetoric are closer to Jacobean drama than Victorian fiction. David's comment on Rosa's tirade accentuates its specialness: "The mere vehemence of her words can convey, I am sensible, but a weak impression of the passion by which she was possessed, and which made itself articulate in her whole figure, though her voice, instead of being raised, was lower than usual. No description I could give of her would do justice to my recollection of her, or to her entire deliverance of herself to her anger. I have seen passion in many forms, but I have never seen it in such a form as that."[103]

The passages I have quoted are in David's words. Such passages are more controlled than the wild rhetoric and histrionic gestures that Rosa herself uses when swept by passion. In part this is only fitting, but there is also an unmistakable strain of the ranting, evil, melodrama queen in Rosa. Her scenes of towering passion sometimes topple into stagy clichés and histrionic poses. It is as though Dickens partly visualized such scenes through the artificial conventions of Victorian melodrama.

This stagy rendition of transcendent passion is partly redeemed by the fairy-tale air which surrounds Rosa. The storybook aura provides some of the same enlargement that histrionic rhetoric was designed to provide, but it does so in a more subtle, pervasive, and convincing way. This is true not simply because the fairy-tale touches are less concentrated and heavy-handed than the melodramatic fustian, or because they color the entire novel rather than set scenes, or even because they are so wonderfully suggestive, but because they enlarge by extending or transcending the natural (we accept such effects as by definition transcendent) rather than by inflating the natural. In other words, the fairy-tale method creates a climate in which strange recurrences, titanic intensities, symbolic emphases, and the like, are not simply acceptable but enhancing. Such enhancement, of course, depends upon the art with which the method is executed. In Dickens, from *Copperfield* on, the execution is almost always consummate. The storybook effects are potent yet inconspicuous; they fade deceptively into the central realism.

The preternatural opposition between Rosa and little Emily, for example, underlines the same psychological and symbolic truths that Rosa's histrionic fury is intended to enforce, but the preternatural adds to the realistic, while the melodramatic wars with it. The "cruel princess in a legend" helps Dickens more than the evil lady in a melodrama. The cruel princess draws unobtrusively upon evocative legends of dazzling princes, fateful vows, impossible tasks, hidden castles, immured rivals, strange vanishings, and superhuman malignancies. These personages and events are larger than life, but their strange powers and magical significances also distance them from life. They mirror, enlarge, and comment on reality while still not subject to the restrictions of reality. Rosa is the cruel princess, Emily the baseborn fairy-tale rival. Their roles are confirmed not simply by their labels (Rosa is called a "cruel princess"; Emily "the prettiest and most engaging little fairy in the world"[104]), but by their histories and associations. Rosa is a disfigured creature of Steerforth's passionate violence; Emily an enchanting siren of David's romantic imagination. Each plays out a role consonant with her signs and designations. Rosa with her magical scar, dark features, hungry eyes, wicked grace, alluring ways, frustrated passion, and seething hatreds, is the poison lady of folklore. "I am of a strange nature," she tells Emily, "I can't breathe freely in the air you breathe."[105] "If I could order it to be done," she says, speaking of Emily, "I would have this girl whipped to death."[106]

Emily with her dainty ways, blue eyes, rosy beauty, provoking enchantments, and dull occupations is a lowborn elfin siren. David's adoring eyes weave a bewitching penumbra about her entire youth. That storybook aura predicts and confirms her later history. She is an aspiring and disappointed Cinderella: a poor girl who yearns to be a lady, runs off with her prince charming, but instead of becoming a princess, becomes a blighted derelict. Dickens sustains her storybook associations. Her escape from Steerforth and Littimer is fairy story pure and simple. Even the manner in which the escape is narrated is redolent of folk tales. It is called up as in a magic glass. Rosa summons Littimer into her garden—he enters through a wall of holly—and then she forces him to address his story to no one. Littimer tells how he and Steerforth tried to dispose of Emily after Steerforth grew tired of her. Steerforth caused Littimer to "shut her up close" in a villa next to the sea. But "she got out in the night," forced the lattice of a window that Littimer had nailed up, "dropped on a vine that was trailed below," and "never has been seen or heard of . . . since."[107] In classic folk-tale manner, the immured maiden escapes from her castle prison and vanishes without a trace.

During Littimer's story (the escape is only part of it), Rosa exults whenever Emily is spurned and humiliated (at one point she touches her throbbing wound "with pleasure rather than pain") and suffers whenever her rival wins some joy or recognition. Both exultation and suffering focus on Emily but relate to Steerforth. Rosa exults each time Emily is rebuffed as she was rebuffed, tormented as she was tormented, made miserable as she was made miserable. Rosa suffers whenever Emily's beauty or intelligence or resourcefulness is mentioned; or whenever Steerforth's actions show that he was deeply attracted by his blue-eyed mistress. Rosa's responses, in other words, are totally sexual; they are also totally psychological. Rosa's etiology is clear. Emily has become what Rosa briefly was, Steerforth's beloved. For years Emily has triumphantly succeeded where Rosa had weakly failed. This partly accounts for Rosa's extraordinary hatred of Emily and for her jealous revelling in Emily's downfall and degradation. But there is more to Rosa's antipathy than this. Emily must pay for every jot of her success and every iota of Rosa's pain. In order to assuage Rosa's hurt, Emily must enact Rosa's humiliation and anguish in exaggerated form. Rosa has become a prisoner of her hatred. She is driven by passion; she is gripped by an overwhelming compulsion to pursue and persecute Emily. This compulsion reveals the truth: Rosa identifies obsessively with her rival. Yet she denies any kinship to her. Indeed she turns kinship into opposition. She has convinced herself that the illicit love that degraded Emily (so she puts it) ennobled her. She cannot face her own degradation. And so, in a strange reflex of her lacerating guilt, she appoints herself the cleansing scourge of Emily's pollution. Rosa, in fact, has projected her self-loathing onto Emily; through Emily she acts out her raging self-hate. In flagellating Emily, she flagellates herself.

All this Dickens conveys with subtle insight. At the same time he translates sexuality and psychology into fairy-tale correlatives. The cruel princess, malignant and implacable in her hatred, persecutes her fairy rival, who, after being cast aside and immured by their common enchanter, is finally allowed by her rival (the enchanter being dead) to sail away to a distant land. Or put it from Emily's point of view: the blue-eyed fairy, favorite of the dark prince, incurs the jealous wrath of the wicked princess, and blasted by that nascent hatred (the dark prince being dead), barely escapes with her life. This is to reduce a masterful book-long blending of realism and fancy to a one-sentence parody. The point is that the fairy-tale engram is powerfully there. In this instance, as usual, it is one of Dickens' primary ways of conveying meaning. It helps him dramatize and comment upon the corrosive nature of thwarted passion. Dickens is saying that thwarted passion, frustrated love, sexual jealousy, repressed rage—we see the full syndrome in Rosa—scar and disfigure one inconceivably. Such emotions are transcendent in their destructiveness. They turn poor trapped human beings into enormities, into cruel monsters that are larger than life. This fairy-tale enlargement, unlike its melodramatic counterpart, Dickens brings off.

Rosa is counterpointed to Emily, but she is also counterpointed to Steerforth, and this relationship too has important storybook dimensions. One can see this very clearly if one examines a remarkable scene that takes place in Steerforth's home while David is staying there. Unaccountably, and in marked contrast to his usual behavior, Steerforth sets out with his utmost skill to charm and soften Rosa. All day long he exerts the "fascinating influence of his delightful art" on his former lover. Gradually she thaws and begins to look at him with growing admiration. "I saw her try, more and more faintly, but always angrily, as if she condemned a weakness in herself, to resist the captivating power that he possessed; and finally, I saw her sharp glance soften, and her smile become quite gentle, and I ceased to be afraid of her as I had really been all day."[108] David says that the three of them finally talked and laughed together, as they sat about the dinner table, "with as little reserve as if we had been children."

Rosa finally gets up, goes into the drawing room, and begins to play the harp—something she has not done in company for more than three years. Steerforth follows her and begs her to sing a song. She puts him off, but he continues to entreat and cajole her: "Sing us an Irish song, Rosa! and let me sit and listen as I used to do."

> He did not touch her, or the chair from which she had risen, but sat
> himself near the harp. She stood beside it for some little while, in a curious
> way, going through the motion of playing it with her right hand, but not
> sounding it. At length she sat down, and drew it to her with one sudden
> action, and played and sang.
>
> I don't know what it was, in her touch or voice, that made that song the
> most unearthly I have ever heard in my life, or can imagine. There was
> something fearful in the reality of it. It was as if it had never been written,
> or set to music, but sprung out of the passion within her; which found
> imperfect utterance in the low sounds of her voice, and crouched again
> when all was still. I was dumb when she leaned beside the harp again,
> playing it, but not sounding it, with her right hand.[109]

David is spellbound, but in a minute more, something happens which,
as David expresses it, "roused me from my trance." Steerforth gets up,
puts his arm about Rosa, and says, "Come, Rosa, for the future we will
love each other very much!" Rosa strikes him, throws him off "with
the fury of a wild cat," and bursts from the room. Mrs. Steerforth
comes in to ask what is wrong with Rosa. Steerforth replies: "She has
been an angel . . . for a little while; and has run into the opposite
extreme, since, by way of compensation."[110]

This great scene, shimmering with fairy-tale hints, helps us look
more deeply into Steerforth, Rosa, and some of the larger significances
of the book. We see that Rosa had been an angel and has become a
devil. She is thus like Steerforth. Steerforth is a fallen Lucifer, a creature of infinite potentiality, who has become Satanic. He is David's,
Rosa's, and Emily's bad angel. We think also of Agnes, David's good
angel, compare her to Rosa, and better understand the waste and torment that surround Rosa's dark descent into aridity and rage. That
descent was contrived by Steerforth, and now we see better how truly
Satanic he is. For in the present scene, he is about to leave for Yarmouth and his elopement with Emily; his attention to Rosa is simply a
means of disarming her habitual sharpness. We thus see Steerforth
cynically displaying the very wiles and graces that entrapped and destroyed Rosa—that will soon entrap and destroy Emily. The creature
of light is really a prince of darkness.

Yet the heart of this extraordinary scene is elsewhere. It is in Rosa's
"unearthly" song and the "passion within her." One clue to the full
significance of that song is in the strange mimed playing that begins and
ends the performance and seems to set it off from all the rest. This clue,
plus Steerforth's old graciousness, Rosa's returned softness, the references to the reestablishment of the openness of childhood, and to
sitting and listening as in times past, help us see that the song is a
magical summoning up of a prelapsarian state. The magical implications of the scene are enforced by Rosa's mute playing, before and

after the song, and by David's falling into a trance at the conclusion of the song. The heavenly significance of the interlude is underlined by the harp, and by David's suggestion that the song was "unearthly," was never "written, or set to music," and sprang from the "passion within" Rosa. The song, indeed, is the reawakened utterance of Rosa's prelapsarian passion. It represents the nascent energy of undefiled love that once was in her. It is the unscarred love before Steerforth threw the hammer, before he wooed and then betrayed her.

The spell of that blissful time is broken when Steerforth puts his arm about Rosa and speaks of love. This rends the trancelike return to heavenly innocence by intruding the physical and verbal tokens of Steerforth's betrayal. When Rosa strikes Steerforth and bursts from the room, she becomes once more what Steerforth made her; the passion of love has been transformed into the passion of rage. Rosa's unearthly song allows us to see what she might have been had her capacity for love not been perverted. She was an angel, she is now a devil.

The sign of her fall is the hammer. It is a sign that she shares with Steerforth. The hammer can be a useful tool; it can also be an instrument of violence and aggression, an emblem of Vulcan and the devil. For Steerforth and Rosa the hammer is the sign of violence and perversion, of love turned into anger. When Steerforth threw the hammer at Rosa he turned a tool into a weapon. He turned something good into something evil, an archetypal sin. This physical sin foreshadows his greater spiritual sin: he turns love into hate—not simply love for himself into hate for himself, but the heart's capacity to love into the heart's inability to do other than hate. The great example of this perversion, of course, is Rosa. She bears Steerforth's scar, his Satanic sign (it is her sign now as well), the mark of the hammer.

The mark of the hammer is on Steerforth too, though he wields the hammer rather than receives its blow. He is disfigured inwardly; he provokes passion, but is unable to give or long receive it. His violent temper and violent end, no less than his sadistic behavior at Salem House, and his treatment of women (mother and lover alike), proclaim his profound aggressiveness. He is as imprisoned by his willful passion to dominate as Rosa is by her thwarted passion to love. They need one another. They circle one another in their joint prisonlike home, a watchful constellation of anger and attraction. Steerforth half fears the goblin he created. He is powerless to undo what he has done. He bears the inward scar of his aggression as Rosa bears the outward brand. Like Cathy and Heathcliff, Rosa and Steerforth propel each other to their doom. Or like Orlick and Mrs. Joe, another infernal Dickensian pair united by the sign of the hammer, they mutely act out their secret consanguinity as devil and disciple.

The mark of the hammer is on Steerforth too in other ways. He has lost all capacity to love or even to feel. He seeks fresh masteries, new sensations, but victories and pleasures fail to satisfy him. He is hollow and world-weary. As he approaches his end, he embraces his death—a Byronic hero, a bad angel, a fallen Lucifer. He goes down to perdition boldly waving a red cap at the engulfing waves.

Rosa is not allowed Steerforth's defiant release. Though her sin was less than his, indeed was largely instigated and accelerated by his, she is not vouchsafed a hero's death or hero's memory. Steerforth goes to his doom still handsome, still capable, still immensely attractive. David continues to feel the pull of his noble gifts. Rosa fades from our sight in a different way. We glimpse her at the end in a garden, the prisoner of her love and hate, the brand of the hammer on her. She still tends Mrs. Steerforth, faded image of her old dead lover. She still speaks fiercely and possessively of Steerforth. Mrs. Steerforth speaks of him too, but her mind wanders. She lives in a blurred half-demented twilight world that confuses past and present. Passionate and tormented, these two charred embers of Steerforth's infernal fire wound and console one another endlessly. They need one another. The last we see of Rosa, she is kneeling at Mrs. Steerforth's feet, a "sharp, dark, withered woman, with a white scar on her lip." "Thus," writes David, "I leave them; thus I always find them; thus they wear their time away, from year to year."[111]

For some time now I have been concentrating on the fairy-tale attributes of demonic characters—on the storybook auras of Uriah, Steerforth, and Rosa—but Dickens surrounds benign characters with enchantment as well. Dora is profoundly destructive for David. For him she is an aberration that originates in his deepest childhood disorders. But she is no plotting Satan, and Dickens spins a magical web about her that is far different from those I have been examining. The web begins to take shape even before David meets her. The clerks in Mr. Spenlow's office speak of the Spenlow house—it is located in suburban Norwood and none of them has ever been there, of course—as a "sacred mystery."[112] They all agree that the house is fabulous and sumptuous, a veritable storybook palace. When David visits this miraculous place, he finds the gardens beautiful and the surroundings Edenlike. "I was quite enchanted," he says.[113] The instant he is introduced to Dora, he is in love: "All was over in a moment. I had fulfilled my destiny. I was a captive and a slave. I loved Dora Spenlow to distraction." Then he adds: "She was more than human to me. She was a Fairy, a Sylph, I don't know what she was— anything that no one ever saw, and everything that everybody ever wanted."[114] After dinner, when the ladies leave the room, David is in a daze of love. He falls into a reverie and pays no attention to the conversation about him. "I was wandering in a garden of Eden all the while, with Dora."[115] Later, he, Dora, and Jip walk through the gardens and the greenhouse. "If we were not all three in Fairyland," David writes, "certainly *I* was."[116]

In the ensuing weeks and months David continues to adore and idolize his sylphlike "Fairy," casting over her the idealized image of his adoration. "I am quite sure," he writes, "I should have scouted the notion of her being simply human, like any other young lady."[117] David recognizes that he is "moon-struck." Even Mr. Spenlow becomes "etherealised" by David's love for Dora. A "reflected radiance" seems to beam about his parental head.[118] When David goes down to Norwood for his second visit, he finds Dora appareled in "celestial" blue.[119] Jip gnashes his teeth in jealousy, a fearsome dragon guarding a storybook maiden. When the whole party rides off for a picnic, David transforms the universe into Dora: "The sun shone Dora, and the birds sang Dora. The south wind blew Dora, and the wildflowers in the hedges were all Doras, to a bud."[120] David is too enraptured to know where he is going or where he has been. "Perhaps it was near Guildford. Perhaps some Arabian-night magician opened up the place for the day, and shut it up for ever when we came away."[121]

Dickens' technique here is deceptively simple. David's infatuation is conveyed by the extravagance of his concentration on Dora. That extravagance, in turn, is lifted to transcendence by fairy-tale imagery. On the one hand, the description is profoundly realistic. Dickens depicts the obsessive rapture of romantic infatuation. He gives us a convincingly detailed instance of a universal experience. On the other hand, the description is supernatural. Dickens translates David's rapture into storybook equivalencies. The fairy tale becomes a metaphor for David's transporting love. At the same time, Dickens casts a distancing humor over all these scenes, and this too helps us accept the supernatural. We see the supernatural as a humorous reflection of David's exaggerated emotions. We say, how extravagant, how transcendent, how true; and at the same time, how delightfully funny, how charmingly foolish, how blind. We laugh, but we understand how deep and transporting was David's summer-dawn of love. Yet all the while we are being given crucial insights into David's flawed character. We see him finding in Dora his falsely idealized image of his mother, an image that will entrap and trammel him; we see him indulging himself with Dora in his usual blind, wish-fulfilling, romantic way, an indulgence that will prove his undoing.

This airy but penetrating combination of realism, humor, and magical transcendence is clearly at work in the aforementioned picnic scene. In that bucolic setting David meets Red Whisker—so David

dubs him—a harmless member of the picnic party whom David jeal-
ously inflates into a deadly rival. Dickens renders this comic scene by
skillfully blending the fairy story with the mock chivalric romance.
David feels that fate has pitted him against Red Whisker, and that one
of them "must fall."[122] But Red Whisker is a formidable opponent. He
is an "ingenious beast" who can construct a wine cellar in the "hollow
trunk of a tree." When David sees him eating a lobster at Dora's feet,
he finds the sight a "baleful object" and for a time scarcely knows what
is happening. This shocking event is followed by other equally direful
blows. David is so distressed, that he wonders whether he should
"fly—I don't know where—upon my gallant grey."[123] But his lady
finally relents and admits him back into her good graces. In his bliss,
David goes "straight up to the seventh heaven"—and stays there all
evening. "It would," thinks David, "have been a happy fate to have
been struck immortal with those foolish feelings, and have strayed
among the trees for ever!"[124] Thus ennobled, David vanquishes Red
Whisker. The picnic ends with David holding Dora's handkerchief and
gloves, the tokens of his lady, while she plays the guitar. She plays, he
feels certain, only for him. He is intoxicated with joy. "I was afraid it
was too happy to be real, and that I should wake."[125]

This storybook bliss pervades David's subsequent courtship of
Dora. Like a puissant enchantress, she transforms the mundane world.
She can turn dowdy sparrows into gorgeous tropical birds. This transmutation occurs simply because Dora and he watched some sparrows
in the leafy summer of their courtship: "I love the London sparrows to
this hour, for nothing else, and see the plumage of the tropics in their
smoky feathers!"[126] This transformation is not unique. David sees
everything through a fairy-tale haze. He pictures Dora as "the little
fairy-figure," and when he sets out to win her, he conceives his role in
storybook terms: "What I had to do, was, to take my woodman's axe
in my hand, and clear my own way through the forest of difficulty, by
cutting down the trees until I came to Dora."[127] When he is thwarted
by Dora's father, he treats the poor man as if "he had been an ogre, or
the Dragon of Wantley."[128] When Dora moves in with her aunts, David
writes: "I felt as if some grim enchanter had drawn a magic circle
round the innocent goddess of my heart."[129]

David's love distorts the real world. He sees the actions and personages associated with his love as larger than life, often as magical forces
in an intense storybook drama. But away from the distorting lens of his
emotions he is sensible enough, though his emotions cripple him in
more than love. Dora is quite different. She insulates herself in a childish romance. She bends reality to her needs or excludes it from her
vision. Weak, dependent, fearful, inadequate, she draws the magic
circle of helpless immaturity round herself. This circle insulates her

from responsibility and protects her from criticism. The shocks and woes of adult existence are banished from her life. This is a dubious victory. As in fairy stories, where gifts wrongly used exact a dire toll, the price she pays for her immunity is very great. She is a pretty plaything, a mere doll who cannot give David the solacing peace and companionship he needs, and who cannot receive from David the equality and adult sharing that she needs. She will become a child-wife, doomed to pout and plead, to scold and be scolded. David, after fruitless attempts to change her, will accept his child-wife's incapacity and his own exclusion from felicity. Their marriage will endure, unsatisfactory and incomplete.

David accepts what he has foolishly chosen. He comes to realize that Dora cannot be other than what she is. He also comes to realize that he demands of her what she cannot give him. But more important (as Dora herself points out) he has praised, cherished, and loved her for what she is and thus confirmed her in what she is. He comes, at last, to be deeply divided in his feelings about Dora. (I shall have more to say on this score when I turn to Agnes.) On the one hand, David wants Dora to be an adult companion and helpmate. On the other hand, he wants her to be just the way she is: petulant, playful, provocative, and adorably dependent. She is the old insubstantial vision of his mother come back to haunt and hurt him.

While David is courting Dora all this is dimly veiled in the distant background. But even during the bliss of courtship warning symptoms emerge now and then. When David tells Dora of his aunt's ruin and tries to make her understand their realistic prospects, she refuses to be practical. She escapes into her usual diversionary games, games that combine sexual provocativeness with childish incapacity, and deflect David from his purpose. David is both exasperated and delighted. "I did," David writes, "as she bade me—rewarding myself afterwards for my obedience [with a kiss]—and she charmed me out of my graver character for I don't know how long."[130] But when the charm wears off and David returns to the fray, she begs and prays and protests, and then sobs herself into hysteria and collapse. David is utterly routed by this behavior, and implores her forgiveness. He sums up his feelings in a telling image: "I felt like a sort of Monster who had got into a Fairy's bower, when I thought of having frightened her, and made her cry."[131] If Dora is a fairy, she is an incapable fairy: a make-believe doll who thinks life is a fairy story sans work, sans responsibility, and sans change. If David is a monster, he is a practical monster: a prince charming become monstrous through dwelling on the trials and burdens of the outside world.

These and the other storybook associations I have been tracing hover over David and Dora from their first meeting to their ultimate parting. They surround the wedding of the two and connect that event with the past and the future. There is much irony in this depiction. As David drives toward the wedding ceremony in an open carriage, he refers to "this fairy marriage" and compares it to the ordinary life and ordinary people about him.[132] The people he sees must sweep the shops, go about their occupations, and engage in all the practical tasks of life, and he pities them. He, presumably, is a magical being, exempt from such mundane impositions. The wedding itself is an "incoherent dream," a dream in which half-heard somber notes sound warning (but unheeded) premonitions. An "ancient mariner" appears behind David, and then the service begins in a "deep voice."[133] We are reminded of another ancient mariner (Dickens knew Coleridge's poem well); we think of its opening wedding, its loud bassoon, its shaken wedding guest who turned away "a sadder and a wiser man." Neither David nor Dora turns away, and the service is "gravely" got through. During the ceremony and after, Dora clasps Agnes' hand. Symbolically the gesture foreshadows David's two marriages: his doomed marriage to his fairy wife, and his future marriage to his angel wife. In another way, he is marrying his two wives at once, for in a profound sense (as we shall see later) his two wives represent the total woman he yearns for.

The somber notes persist. Dora becomes hysterical and cries for her poor dead papa. Peggotty reminds David that she was present at the marriage of his father and mother—thus reminding the reader of that earlier doomed marriage of a romantic man and an ineffectual woman, a marriage now being reenacted by its offspring. As David walks down the aisle after the ceremony, "there flutter faint airs of association with my childish church at home, so long ago."[134] The church of David's childhood is the church where his mother and father lie buried; the church of the haunting gravestone and the risen father; the church where Mr. Murdstone first saw David's mother and began to court her. These dark associations of disaster and death surround David in his "fairy marriage" as he walks lovingly down the aisle.

The associations are compounded in the illustration, "I am Married," which accompanies the chapter. (Dickens ordered, supervised, and approved each illustration.) At first glance, the plate seems joyful—a radiant David and Dora lead the wedding party down the aisle and out of the church. But the plate is crowded with emblems of inappropriateness, emptiness, misuse, and death. The pulpit, its candlesticks empty, is occupied by a broom and a bucket; a memorial statue is encumbered by a giant cobweb; two memorial tablets (the only ones readable) celebrate "Uxor" and "Spinster"; the minister nods in sleeping disassociation; and David and Dora walk demurely out of church, stepping on one gravestone, about to step on another, and surrounded by a veritable charnel house of tombs, effigies, sarcophagi, memorials, and coffins. This plate, in turn, recalls (as do David's associations) the only other plate in *Copperfield* of a scene in church—the first plate in the book, "Our Pew at Church." There a similar group of satiric and predictive emblems surround a dark, intent man—Mr. Murdstone—staring at his mild and oblivious prey—David and his mother.

All these signs and portents—those in the realistic actions and statements, those in the illustrations, and those in the magical penumbra—coalesce to warn and guide the reader. They help him see the connections between David's remote past, his blind present, and his lesson-filled future. Their message in relation to the "fairy marriage" is summed up by Betsey Trotwood (that dotty spokesman for sanity) when she says, you are "a pair of babes in the wood."[135] The phrase not only epitomizes David's and Dora's blind obliviousness in the face of a perilous world and forecasts the sad end of their marriage, it connects their condition to earlier references to the same legend. For this is the legend—the lost boy in the fairy story and the babes in the wood are analogues—that David unwittingly thought of when he was banished from his mother's sole love, and this is the legend that he again thought of when he envisioned an unchanging paradise for himself and little Emily. Both associations, innocent and pathetic on the surface, forecast disaster. In the former instance, David returns to find Mr. Murdstone in possession of his mother and his hearth; in the latter, David's idyl finds fulfillment in Steerforth's betrayal. In life, David's romantic dreams of innocence and unchanging love give way to aggression and death, just as in the legend, romantic dreams of parental love give way to parental abandonment and death. As Aunt Betsey's allusion suggests, David's marriage is no different: it is inaugurated in romantic bliss, and it will end in unfulfillment and death. Through such allusions, and through many similar devices, David's disastrous marriage is repeatedly associated with parental pathology and childhood romanticism.

As we have seen, the lost boy and the babes in the wood reflect Dickens' own sense of parental abandonment. In a similar fashion Dickens draws strongly on his own experiences in depicting the courtship and marriage of David and Dora. The courtship is deeply rooted in Dickens' perfervid (and wounding) courtship of Maria Beadnell; the marriage and its aftermath in Dickens' growing disillusionment with his own marriage. This is not surmise but Dickens' own appraisal as set forth in letters to Maria and confessions to Forster in the years following *Copperfield*.[136] There is no one-to-one relationship between fact and fiction in *Copperfield*; Dickens changes and embellishes fact to suit his fictional purposes. But emotionally he stays very close to the truth, and emotionally the marriage of David and Dora draws on an intricate blend of autobiographical fact and autobiographical wish fulfillment. This blend shapes much of *Copperfield*. From a wish-fulfilling autobiographical point of view, for example, Dickens uses *Copperfield* to consummate his courtship of Maria, put an end to his marriage with Catherine, and fantasize a union with an all-succoring angel. Significantly, Dickens' trial titles for *Copperfield* show that early in the planning of the novel, he thought of naming his protagonist "Charles."

The point is that Dickens is looking as deeply as he can into his own heart and into David's. He is trying to comprehend and transcend his life. He is trying to understand through David why he himself has come in middle age to feel that there is "one happiness I have missed in life, and one friend and companion I have never made," a phrase that David uses, but which Dickens applied to his own case a few years later.[137] Dickens is trying to fathom the sources of his yearning and discontent. He is trying to understand the hidden impulses that impel and harm him. In this doleful quest, David is his foil and surrogate. David is engaged in a similar quest. David is trying to understand his destructive impulses; he is trying to comprehend why he seeks out so self-woundingly a wife or a friend who is disastrous for him. Dickens looked steadily and profoundly at these paradoxes and at the emotional needs and psychological depths which underlay them. Critics who regard David as a superficial character who fortuitously married a ninny (to his own discomfort) and later, equally fortuitously, married a saint (to his own unconvincing blessedness) are missing the heart of Dickens' analysis. They fail to understand the needs that motivate David; they fail to comprehend his complicity in all that befalls him. David sometimes examines this cause and effect directly. In relation to his marriage, for instance, he tries to understand his own contribution to its failure. But usually the darkest shadows and the most hidden connections in these profound examinations are not conveyed through analysis. They are conveyed, as I have tried to point out, by signs and parallels and doubles and recurrences and magical hints.

Dickens, then, among many other uses, employs the fairy story as a vehicle—often as an intensifying, enlarging, or probing vehicle—to help us understand the sources and the significance of David's infatuation and romanticism. David's self-destructive yearnings and his self-deluding blindnesses are rooted in childhood, but they blossom in manhood. The thronging fairy-tale hints I have been tracing make their major contribution to this demonstration. Yet the hints are barely perceptible. It is this inconspicuous density of reference and association, plus the allusive power of the materials themselves, that allows the fairy tale to work so powerfully and yet so unobtrusively in *David Copperfield*.

It is worth glancing rapidly at a few additional characters in order to see how omnipresent this storybook influence is. Virtually every important character in *David Copperfield* is conceived, in part, as a fairy-tale figure. The Murdstones are no exception. Miss Murdstone is believed to sleep "with one eye open," and she mutters in church like "low thunder."[138] She and her brother have an influence on David "like the fascination of two snakes on a wretched young bird."[139] When the Murdstones enter a house, they bring "a cold blast of air" with them.[140] They are, in fact, devils, and they act in diabolical ways, as David explicitly states.[141] David soon finds himself "under a spell," a term he himself uses.[142] To David Mr. Murdstone is a wicked giant or evil necromancer. David quails before his blighting onslaught. But Mr. Murdstone's power extends beyond poor David. He has cast a maleficent enchantment over David's mother and has caused her to obey him rather than her son.

All this is as viewed through David's childish eyes, yet the narrator is not a child but a man, and behind the man is Dickens himself. The storybook enlargement, then, represents a complex interweaving of three points of view. The Murdstones are presented as magical and death-dealing because the child David sees them, naturally enough, as similar to the only other sadistic figures with omnipotent powers that he knows of, the wicked enchanters and monsters of fairy stories. The mature David continues to present them that way, first because he is being true to his childhood remembrance of them, and second because such a representation pointedly reflects their evil. They are stark, unloving, sadistic creatures who prey upon defenseless widows and innocent children. For Dickens, of course, the victimization of children is an unpardonable sin. For him the Murdstones represent something transcendent and cosmic in its evil, and this judgment is reflected and partly conveyed by their surreal malignancies and enlargements.

The method used in creating the threatening aura that surrounds the Murdstones is thus similar to the method used in creating the romance aura that surrounds Dora: in each instance a realistic view has been raised to transcendence by the viewer's (in these examples, David's) distorting vision. The distortion, in turn, is crucial to Dickens' purpose. It helps him convey the viewer's inner reality, while at the same time it allows him to comment through that reality. David's childish fear of the Murdstones is at the core of their supernatural malevolence; David's infatuated adoration of Dora is at the core of her supernatural enchantment. In each instance the distortion is expressive and directive. The distortion allows us to apprehend the viewer, the object viewed, and Dickens' judgment of both, with great compression, and without exposition or direct authorial intervention. The distortion, of course, need not be projected through fairy tales. That Dickens uses fairy tales so often to gain this effect probably reflects his feelings about their primacy and universality, but above all it demonstrates how congenial they were to his bent.

Though the method of projecting the Murdstones and Dora is the same, the end result, indeed the entire effect, is totally different. Dickens, quite obviously, is able to infuse the method with astonishing variety. But he also has other ways of surrounding a character with a storybook aura and other purposes in doing so.

Tommy Traddles is presented through most of *Copperfield* without fairy-tale attributes. His nearest approach to a supernatural effect is his habit of drawing skeletons whenever he has been cruelly dealt with. But toward the end of the book, when David visits the recently married Traddles in his chambers at Gray's Inn, all is changed. The entire scene, as well as an important subsequent scene (the last real scene with Traddles), is suffused with a fairy-tale glow. Dickens manages this transformation adroitly. He depicts Traddles' chambers in the law-engendered desert of Gray's Inn as an enchanted garden of richness, beauty, and warmth, a garden that blooms brightly and unexpectedly in a barren wilderness. Traddles' wife's sisters, a visiting bevy of Devonshire roses, add to this romance atmosphere—and its incongruity—by surrounding Traddles with singing and mirth. To David, Traddles' magical chambers and its mirthful company, environed on every side by dry law-stationers and dessicated solicitors and barristers, "seemed almost as pleasantly fanciful as if I had dreamed that the Sultan's famous family had been admitted on the roll of attorneys, and had brought the talking bird, the singing tree, and the golden water into Gray's Inn Hall."[143] In the remainder of the interlude Dickens continues to develop the magical wonder of Traddles' enchanted bower and enchanted life in Gray's Inn. The image that emerges and then recurs is roses. Traddles has transformed the skeletons of childhood into the roses of maturity.

Dickens' method here is to associate Traddles with transformation. Traddles' purity of heart has made the wilderness of London bloom. Like a legendary character who spins some mundane substance into gold, Traddles spins the ordinary dross of life into something wondrous strange. Our final view of him is an extended demonstration of how he takes everyday life—straitened circumstances, burdensome household tasks, frugal dining, window-shopping, daydreaming, half-price playgoing—and magically turns it into purest gold.[144] Traddles has achieved happiness. His power to transmute and ennoble comes from his inward grace. Through that power he makes Gray's Inn bloom and dull life glow. Wherever Traddles is, a magic circle of warmth and light, self-made and self-contained, encompasses him. He will travel through life blissful and blessed.

Dickens was fond of this kind of demonstration. He liked to show his readers that it was possible to pluck romance, happiness too, from the tawdry streets, grimy buildings, and tedious lives all about them. That demonstration was an anodyne for pain, an assurance to the toiling multitudes who read him that their lives, hard and humdrum as they were, could have some grace and joy. Dickens believed that his art could soften those lives. It could give his readers hours of imaginative release; it could also teach them how to find romance in their routine comings and goings. Traddles affirms Dickens' belief. His fairy-tale bower and fairy-tale happiness are built out of London's most ordinary bricks and mortar—albeit with purity of heart.

Traddles' storybook role is thus very different from Aunt Betsey's or Steerforth's or Dora's. He is no fairy godmother, no fallen angel, no heavenly sylph in celestial blue. He does not radiate his magical qualities throughout the book. He is a didactic demonstration, compressed and self-contained, at the end of the novel. Yet different as he is as a wielder of supernatural powers or as an exemplar of Dickens' usual technique of fairy-tale characterization, he participates in the larger storybook atmosphere of the novel. He is another character whose truth is partly conveyed to us by effects that are rooted in or are analogous to fairy stories. He becomes a part of the total fablelike climate of the novel. He further demonstrates the flexibility and variety of Dickens' fairy-tale technique.

I have glanced quickly at some of the storybook aspects of the Murdstones and Traddles because I wished to show that the earlier and much longer demonstrations (with Aunt Betsey, Uriah Heep, Steerforth, Rosa, Dora, and the like) were not special cases isolated from the main tendencies of the book but typical of Dickens' way with most of his characters. One could easily extend the list of characters who owe a good deal to fairy stories—Miss Mowcher, Mr. Creakle, Littimer, the Micawbers, and Mr. Dick are several more. But an analysis of these and still other characters would only confirm (in ever-new permutations and combinations) what we have already seen.

There is an important additional component in this fairy-tale nexus, however. The characters I have been examining are often embedded in storybook and folklore contexts that powerfully reinforce their supernatural attributes. We have already seen this in part. Uriah has many characteristics of the folklore devil—red hair, glowing eyes, skeleton hands, snaky movements, cadaverous face, and the like. Dora, the fair maiden, is guarded by the fearsome dragon, Jip. Little Emily is imprisoned in a remote castle, escapes through a high barred window, climbs down a vine, and disappears. One can easily multiply these examples. Emily is also an inverse Cinderella; Miss Betsey subjects David to a fairy-tale testing; David has his good and bad angels. We meet doubles, holy fools (Mr. Dick), sympathetic signs (Rosa's scar), and devil-tinkers. There are many motifs I have scarcely touched upon: premonitory dreams, magic castles (the Wickfield house), and potent superstitions (Barkis can only die as the tide goes out). There are patient Griseldas (Agnes), January-May marriages (Dr. and Annie Strong), and wicked stepparents (the Murdstones).

I do not wish to belabor the point, merely to emphasize that the characters I have been examining in the central section of this chapter not only have intricate storybook attributes but are enmeshed in a context which draws heavily on fairy stories, folklore, legends, and the like. The total effect of the novel is powerfully shaped by this rich blending of suprarational detail and suprarational motif—a blending that is always fused to the central realism of the book. The storybook aspects of Uriah Heep, for example, are strengthened and made more significant as they contrast, blend, and clash with the storybook aspects of the other characters he encounters, and as they merge with the larger fairy-tale motifs and the overall realism of which he is a fragment.

It is impossible to convey the fullness of this orchestration. It emerges out of the totality of the book, and Dickens makes it subserve many purposes. Fairy-tale touches and fairy-tale motifs help him structure, emphasize, and connect; but above all, fairy-tale magic helps him convey his innermost vision. Some sense of the importance and richness of these merging effects, and a better sense of how they work in context, may be gained if we turn away from character (which, to a large extent, must be sifted out of context as one traces it through the course of a long novel) and concentrate on a scene that combines these fairy-tale effects in intricate ascending counterpoint. I have in mind the climactic chapter entitled "Tempest."

No section of *David Copperfield* is more densely fraught with witching energies and with reverberations of the irrational than is Chapter LV, "Tempest." The only other sections of the novel that approach "Tempest" in richness of suprarational evocation are the premonitory opening and the magical conclusion. The opening (which I have already discussed) invokes the portents, spells, and predictions that shape our initial expectations and control the book. The conclusion (which I shall discuss shortly) enforces the recurrences, returns, and regenerations that resolve the tensions of the novel and give the end its profound sense of closure. "Tempest" is the climax or breaking point of the book. Dickens called it the "most powerful effect in all the Story."[145] It is the mighty storm made inevitable by all that has gone before, the vast heaving of the deep, long in coming, that purges and annihilates. It is only after this necessary purgation that a chastened David can slowly fashion a sounder life. The storm, then, is more than a formal climax, more than a way of punishing Steerforth, ennobling Ham, and ridding the book of characters who have served their purpose. The storm is deeply symbolic and profoundly psychological.

Before all else, though, the storm is a tour de force of realistic description. It is one of the great renditions of natural forces in all English literature. It utilizes meticulous, almost scientific, observation to achieve sweeping Romantic effects. Like Turner, Dickens would expose himself to the fury of a gale for hours on end, and again like Turner, he used the knowledge so gained to translate literal accuracy into experiential truth. In Dickens' notes for Chapter LV, among other details for the storm, he reminds himself to use "flakes of foam seen at Broadstairs here, last night. Flying in blotches." He works this detail into the chapter in memorable images, but he uses the flying blotches of foam for more than verisimilitude. This strange coming of the ocean onto the land, this unnerving violation of the usual boundaries between land and sea, becomes, in context, part of the breakdown that pervades all nature. The violation reflects massive violations of social and domestic codes (violations of parentage, friendship, honor, trust, and love), and it reflects grievous failures of selfhood (failures of self-knowledge, perception, sensitivity, and discipline). The flying blotches of foam that Dickens observed just before writing the chapter are thus made to serve expressive as well as naturalistic ends: they help Dickens convey (in part they are correlatives of) the violation and failure, the unnatural breakdown and encroachment, recorded throughout the novel.

This is Dickens' method throughout the chapter. He makes the storm serve his larger, often apocalyptic, purposes by carefully incorporating arcane meanings into his most naturalistic effects. Dickens alerts us to this strategy. He has David tell us at the opening of the chapter that he has seen the Yarmouth storm growing larger throughout the book, "throwing its fore-cast shadow even on the incidents of my childish days."[146] He also tells us that the event is "bound by an infinite variety of ties to all that has preceded it."[147] This is simply a direct means of stating what we have already seen illustrated in countless ways in *Copperfield,* namely that there are secret, often magical, meanings that intricately connect actions and relationships that to outward view seem to have no connection at all.

The storm is heralded by an array of ominous signs. On his way down to Yarmouth, David calls the coachman's attention to "a very remarkable sky." The coachman agrees that he has never seen its equal, and then predicts, "There'll be mischief done at sea, I expect, before long."[148] The sky itself is portentous. The clouds, pile upon pile, ascend to the loftiest heights, but they are also associated with "the bottom of the deepest hollows in the earth."[149] The "wild moon" seems to plunge through the sky as if "in a dread disturbance of the laws of nature." It is as though the moon "had lost her way and were frightened."[150] David rides through this omen-filled night and into an omen-filled day, and all the while a mighty wind blows harder and harder.

Nature is signaling to man. The wild moon, the disturbed laws, the lost way are signs that nature is out of joint. Malign forces have upset the harmony of the universe; tempest and destruction must ensue before harmony can be restored. Dickens' presentation of these forces is no simpleminded rendering of the pathetic fallacy. The forces are submerged in actions and descriptions so realistically compelling that one has no sense of manipulation. The storm carries the messages Dickens wants us to receive.

As David rides toward Yarmouth the foreboding signs increase. The wind grows louder and blows harder. People arise in the night and cluster in marketplaces for fear of falling chimneys. As in *Macbeth,* where the murder of Duncan perturbs the night with toppled chimneys and unnatural omens, so in *Copperfield,* imminent death fills the night with analogous prodigies. David is told of blocked streets and devastated fields. He hears of dire destructions. Huge sheets of lead have been ripped off a high church tower and flung into the street; great trees have been torn out of the earth.[151] As David approaches the sea near Yarmouth, he finds that the mighty wind is "blowing dead on shore"—a phrase that will soon take on a sinister meaning.

The threatening atmosphere builds and grows. "When we came within sight of the sea," David writes, "the waves on the horizon, caught at intervals above the rolling abyss, were like glimpses of another shore with towers and buildings."[152] The sea, of course, has been intricately symbolic throughout the novel. Here words like "another shore," "towers," and "abyss" subtly suggest heaven and hell—the respective destinations (presumably) of Ham and Steerforth on the morrow. There are other signs of forthcoming disaster. "Bewailing women" cry for their seaborne husbands; old salts study the ocean "as if they were surveying an enemy." Wind, rain, blotches of sea foam, flying sand, and "awful noise" are everywhere.[153] David is confounded. The turmoil increases. High watery walls roll in, seem about to engulf the town, and at their highest tumble into surf. Vast waves sweep back with a "hoarse roar" and scoop out deep caves as if their purpose were to "undermine the earth." Mighty billows shake the beach with a "booming sound." Nothing keeps its shape or form.

Undulating hills of water are changed to valleys, undulating valleys are lifted up into hills. "The ideal shore on the horizon, with its towers and buildings" rises and falls. Looking at this primordial scene, David sees "a rending and upheaving of all nature."[154]

David is finally ensconced in his Yarmouth inn. He ventures from its protection to look for Ham, but finds that his friend has gone to Lowestoft and will not be back till morning. When David returns to his inn, evening is approaching. He hears that two colliers have gone down with all hands and that other ships are laboring hard. He feels restless and depressed and solitary. Ham's absence overwhelms him with an uneasiness "disproportionate to the occasion."[155] David becomes increasingly confused. His thoughts and recollections blur into a jumbled phantasmagoria. "I had lost," David says, "the clear arrangement of time and distance."[156] But though he is agitated and disoriented, his seaside surroundings, familiar to him from childhood, awaken floods of vivid memories. Obviously Dickens is loosening David's grasp on the present and forcing him into the past. He is doing more than this. He is detaching David from a fixed time and place and bringing the innermost springs of his being to the surface in a vulnerable, responsive flux.

David now has the presentiment that Ham is lost at sea. The notion becomes so strong that he feels compelled, against all reason, to investigate and reassure himself. Yet all the while he knows that the sensation is irrational. When he does investigate and confirms his irrationality, he feels "ashamed of doing what I was nevertheless impelled to do."[157] David's irrational fears, of course, are well founded. For though Ham is safe now, David's premonition will come to pass: Ham will be lost at sea. The irrational will triumph over the rational.

The tempest increases, and now there is "a great darkness besides." This darkness invests the storm with "new terrors, real and fanciful." David assesses his state: "I could not eat, I could not sit still, I could not continue steadfast to anything. Something within me, faintly answering to the storm without, tossed up the depths of my memory, and made a tumult in them."[158] Like Pip at the moment of Magwitch's return, David is at the point of self-discovery. Again like Pip, David is about to be overwhelmed by emotional rather than rational insight. And once more like Pip, David is surrounded by warning signals from unruly nature and is beset by a profound unease. In both books scene, psychology, and import are analogous. In both instances there is a magical empathy between the world of nature without and the world of consciousness within. In *Copperfield,* David makes sure that we will not miss this connection, though he is unable to analyze its significance. When he tells us that the storm "tossed up the depths of my memory, and made a tumult in them," that "something within me" answered to the storm without, he is affirming that the storm both evokes and objectifies his shaping past and his deepest fantasies and fears. It is as though David intuitively knows and profoundly dreads what the universe is secretly telling him, what he will soon discover for himself in less hermetic terms.

What he will soon discover is the linked deaths of Ham and Steerforth, and David has a supernatural presentiment of this tragic event. But while this premonition explains David's sympathetic anxiety, it does not adequately explain the tumult and storm within. That inner tumult, that deeper and more shattering storm, is evoked by David's coincident presentiment—unformulated but profoundly felt—that he is about to confront a secret part of himself. He is now in close unconscious touch with that secret self, with that weakness and darkness within. He has recently come from Dora's death and Uriah's downfall. His harrowing and purgation have begun. With fear and trembling he intuitively feels that more is yet to come.

The tumult within intensifies. David falls into a strange intermediate consciousness halfway between sleeping and waking. For Dickens this is often a state in which the unconscious depths rise to the verge of consciousness. While David is in this twilight state, he is oppressed by a "new and indefinable horror." When he emerges from his trance, he continues to be gripped by this dark signaling from his inmost self. "My whole frame," he writes, "thrilled with objectless and unintelligible fear."[159]

Suddenly, "as if by magic," he finds himself superalert, "every sense refined." In this elevated state, he lies on his bed for hours, listening to the wind and water and imagining at intervals that he hears "shrieks out at sea," the "firing of signal guns," and the "fall of houses."[160] These horrible fancies are figments of the fear that grips him, but each fancy will soon become a reality. The invisible world is again mingling with David's psyche and signaling to him. David is so agitated by what he hears, or thinks he hears, that he gets up several times and looks out the window to see if he can distinguish what is disturbing him. At this point Dickens presents us with one of his most masterful touches. Each time David looks out the window, he can see nothing "except the reflection in the window-panes of the faint candle I had left burning, and of my own haggard face looking in at me from the black void."[161] David is now facing himself and his own black void. Seeking to look at the storm without, he is forced to look at the storm within. The two, in fact, are one.

The window image is totally realistic and profoundly symbolic. It is a good example of how Dickens enriches the simplest actions of his story. It is also a good example of the way in which he conveys psychological insight: through action, image, analogy, and portent, rather than exegesis. This is a sophisticated and dangerous method. It is sophisticated because it demands much of the reader; it is dangerous because it risks lulling him into misunderstanding, even incomprehension—the surface is so compelling that one can easily overlook the depths. Dickens' art is subtle and complex. The window scene is a case in point. For this brief and deceptively simple scene, so marvelous in its cogency and compression, has yet another dimension. Through all the latter portions of the book, a light in the window has stood for Emily's shameful flight and Mr. Peggotty's steadfast faith. As David peers haggardly into the black void of his past, he sees not only his stricken face but the faint image of the candle in the window. He is responsible for that candle in the window. He is responsible for Emily's seduction, Steerforth's villainy, Ham's suffering, and Mr. Peggotty's sad wanderings. And in a few hours he will be responsible for Steerforth's and Ham's deaths. This responsibility is innocent and unwitting on David's part, yet he feels great guilt. His guilt, as we have seen, goes far beyond mere circumstance; it is rooted in David's deep psychological complicity in the tragedy.

David's glimpse of himself in the black void—he both peers into and gazes out of the void—puts an end to his vigil in his room. It is the middle of the night, but he is unbearably restless. He dresses and goes downstairs. Predictive signs and portents continue to accompany him. When he enters the kitchen of the inn and joins a group of watchers, he is immediately confronted by a disquieting omen. A pretty girl, who had stopped her ears with her apron to shut out the noise of the storm and was looking at the door, "screamed when I appeared, supposing me to be a spirit."[162] A moment later one of the group asks David if he "thought the souls of the collier-crews who had gone down, were out in the storm."[163]

After a few hours David goes back to his room. The storm roars and cannonades wildly in his ears, but he gets into bed, and soon sinks into a deep sleep. He dreams of falling off a tower and down a precipice (fit image for the fall and breakdown he is about to suffer), of being engaged with "two dear friends" who are unknown to him (Ham and Steerforth, neither of whom has as yet appeared), and of assisting at the "siege of some town in a roar of cannonading" (the besieged citadel of his mind blended with the swelling roar of the storm). He is awakened by someone knocking at his door and telling him there is a wreck close by. As so often in Dickens, the knocking is a summons to death. David throws on his clothes—it is now broad day—and, running to the beach, "soon came facing the wild sea."[164] David gazes with horror at the wrecked ship rolling and beating in the boiling surge. A bell on board, swinging with the ship, adds its grim sound to the wind and waves, and tolls a knell for those still surviving—soon reduced to two. David, who does not know that Steerforth is on the ship or that Ham will soon appear and attempt to rescue him, frantically implores a group of sailors "not to let those two lost creatures"—the phrase is doubly ironic—"perish before our eyes."[165] When Ham does appear, David links him once more—though very briefly now—to the leitmotif that has always prefigured and marked him: "the determination in his face, and his look, out to sea."[166]

Ironically, when Ham plunges into the sea, he goes forth not to murder Steerforth (as David had thought years before when he saw that look) but to save him, though Ham is not aware that Steerforth is the person he is attempting to save. David, with his usual blindness (a human frailty here rather than a sin), fails to fathom the signs he has seen so often. For Ham's determined face, steady gaze at the darkling light over the waters, and gradual disappearance into the horizon—all on that fateful verge of Yarmouth sand—have always connoted not murder and revenge, but death and apotheosis. The reader comprehends what David records but fails to understand.

Dickens' magical signs, premonitory leitmotifs, and portentous meanings undergird and direct that comprehension. Such omens herald the unseen. They bear witness to the larger truths of the invisible world, truths that Dickens believed surround man, willy-nilly, in all his thoughts and actions. These signals from the invisible world help Dickens reveal to the reader the hidden designs that he felt lie deep in the recesses of the universe. They reinforce and enlarge the other, more direct, representations of those same truths. They help the reader look into tumultuous self-probings and ocean-depths of emotions. They bear witness to the immutable consequences of actions, the fragile inviolability of community, the corrosive power of guilt, and the mysterious geometry of recurrences.

The deaths of Ham and Steerforth confirm this fairy-tale design and end the chapter. Steerforth is now the sole survivor on the wrecked ship. He clings to the ship's mast and waves his "singular red cap" as the clamoring bell sounds his death knell. Cap in hand, he is about to disappear from David's life. Like Conrad's secret sharer, more than half a century later, who leaves the captain's life by disappearing into the ocean with the captain's self-destructiveness and the captain's redemptive hat, Steerforth sinks into the sea taking his singular cap, his great sins, and David's dimly answering darkness with him. David recognizes a stirring in his own past as he watches Steerforth (still unknown to him) go down to perdition. The gesture of Steerforth waving his cap brings to David's mind an "old remembrance . . . of a once dear friend," and the memory drives him to the verge of distraction.[167] Ham, in the meantime, is desperately striving to reach the wreck. When he finally manages to push to within a stroke of his goal, a vast hillside of water moves toward the ship. Ham "leap[s] up into it with a mighty bound,'' and, like an instant annihilation of antagonistic forces come terrifically together, Ham, ship, and Steerforth are gone.[168]

Later that day David is led to a familiar verge of the shore: ''And on that part of it where [Emily] and I had looked for shells, two children—on that part of it where some lighter fragments of the old boat, blown down last night, had been scattered by the wind—among the ruins of the home he had wronged—I saw him lying with his head upon his arm, as I had often seen him lie at school.''[169]

These words end the chapter. Rather than emphasize the grim harvest, Dickens stresses the blithe sowing. By recalling the nostalgic scenes of a seemingly innocent childhood—David and Emily gathering shells on their enchanted first day together; Mr. Peggotty's delightful ship-house; Steerforth sleeping in his characteristic way, handsome head resting on his arm—by recalling these scenes, Dickens again roots the present disaster in the past. The present disaster had its growth in David's romantic reveries, undisciplined infatuations, and blind hero worship. He is an accomplice, not simply in an indirect sense, as a link between Yarmouth and Steerforth, but in a direct sense, as the flawed personality who made those preventable events inevitable. This is true whether one sees David realistically as a too-fond friend blind to his companion's depravity, or symbolically as a good human being crippled by undisciplined sentiment and unacknowledged aggressions (the latter urges objectified by David's dark alter egos). In both cases the outward event reflects the inward complicity; the storm without testifies to the tempest within.

The fairy-tale circle has been completed; the irrational murmurings have now been fulfilled. The childish troth plighted on Yarmouth sands, the childish fealty given at Salem House Academy, each accompanied by unheeded, indeed unseen, warnings, have now worked their secret way to slow fulfillment. The howling wind and ''the great deep rising in the night'' that David remarked on during his first night in the ship-house have finally gathered to fullness and swept dream and ship-house away. The signs, the places, the portents, all have magically recurred, all have been turned back on themselves. Steerforth has sailed into eternity on a *Stormy Petrel*. Little Emily, in keeping with her foolhardy action on her first day with David, has sprung forward over the sea to her destruction. Acts, thoughts, looks, gestures are filled with secret reflexive meanings that finally reveal themselves. Ham, forever gazing out to sea, forever walking into the horizon on that one small verge of sand, has at last found the fate he so often enacted. He has walked into the sea; he has embraced his death.

David rarely understands the signs that are all about him. In the case of Steerforth, he is grievously blind. He had often seen Steerforth lying in that characteristic pose, his head upon his arm. In that pose, Steerforth's face is calm, his head, as always, noble. David looks upon that angel countenance with love and admiration. So it was at Salem House, so it used to be in youth, so it is now in manhood. For David, the handsome face resting peacefully on the arm has always been an incarnation of Steerforth's attraction and perfection. Yet now the image is transformed. The calm image of repose is the cold unfeeling image of death. Looking down on the serene body of his lifeless idol, David does not yet understand what he will gradually come to perceive. Steerforth, the fallen Lucifer, David's bad angel, is the angel of death.

In worshiping Steerforth, David has worshiped death.

It should be clear by now that the fairy tale—and under this rubric I include, as always, such allied elements as folklore, myth, the supernatural, and the like—is one of the great organizing principles in *David Copperfield*. We can better understand the versatility and centrality of the fairy tale in *Copperfield* if, as a final example of Dickens' method, we look at Agnes, especially in relation to David and to closure.

Agnes has potent supernatural attributes. Her tutelary role as David's good angel begins with her entrance in the novel: she is immediately associated with stained-glass windows and tranquil radiance. The angel motif is made explicit in the scene (already noted) in which David acknowledges her as his good angel and receives her warning that Steerforth is his bad angel. And just as Steerforth sustains his role as bad angel through the remainder of the novel, Agnes sustains her role as good angel. David confesses that when he is with her he feels ''an altered person,'' that an ''influence'' comes over him that ''alters'' him for the better. He yearns to know her ''secret.'' He feels she has a ''heavenly face'' and that her dwelling is a ''sacred place.''[170]

Like a good fairy who returns to soothe and help her protégé, Agnes reappears almost miraculously when David needs her. On the day following the news that his aunt is ruined, while David is walking disconsolately in the streets, she suddenly materializes before him. David is lifted up. He sees her face and thinks of the ''stained-glass window in the church.'' He tells her that if he owned a ''conjuror's cap'' he would have ''wished'' for her. ''How different I felt in one short minute, having Agnes at my side.''[171] On another occasion, when David is troubled and trying to read, Agnes again materializes before him: ''I heard the clocks strike twelve . . . when Agnes touched me.''[172] When David needs a job, Agnes helps him find one. ''What should I do without you!'' he says. ''You are always my good angel.''[173] When Aunt Betsey moves from Dover to London, Agnes' ''noiseless presence'' makes all the special Dover amenities (birds, chairs, fans, books) reappear miraculously in London.[174] Her benign influence shines on her father as well as on David. It does ''wonders'' for him.[175]

After Dora's death, but before David goes abroad, he begins to be more aware of her beneficent influence. He associates her more strongly with the signs of her beatitude, with (to quote from one paragraph only) a "stained-glass window," a "prophetic foreshadowing," an "upraised hand," a "sacred presence," and a "purer region nearer heaven."[176]

The many signs of her angel role and the numerous tokens of her fairy-tale powers impinge on David's consciousness but fail to penetrate his understanding. He must break down, "die," and be reborn before he can read the signs that have surrounded him all along. That death occurs when he goes abroad to Europe. Once in Europe, the burials and farewells that filled with busyness the days and nights before his departure (Dora, Ham, and Steerforth are dead, Uriah has fallen, the Micawber family and the Peggotty entourage have emigrated) recede into the distance, and left to face himself, he suffers the archetypal Romantic collapse; he falls into Carlyle's "Everlasting No."

In Europe he goes through the "long and gloomy night" of his breakdown, "haunted by the ghosts" of the past.[177] Ironically, he fails to recall that at his birth it was predicted that he would see "ghosts and spirits," and that he denied possessing the power. Now all his time is devoted to seeing ghosts and spirits. And when he recovers from that haunting, he will again summon up the shadows that walked through his life and later tormented his memory by re-creating them in fiction—his first new work will be about his experiences.

David's fate—like Dickens'—is to see ghosts and spirits forever. Dickens understands this and has David present us with the irony, but David makes no connection between his present condition and those fateful natal predictions (just as he made no connection between the watery deaths of Ham and Steerforth and his own natal caul). But David's obliviousness does not protect him; he must bend to the shaping power of those natal signs. Wandering listlessly through Europe, he fulfills the promise of those early portents, and he gives sorrowful substance to the prediction that he will be "unlucky in life." He now feels (even if he does not understand) the full force of that prediction. He knows that "the whole airy castle" of his life lies in ruins—an appropriate storybook image for an ironic storybook consummation.[178] He carries the weight of his burden everywhere, and he believes that it will never be lightened. He is listless; he has no purpose, no sustaining soul. Many months go by. In his despondency he thinks that he will die. Accumulated sadness is his portion; "brooding sorrow" is "the night that fell" on his "undisciplined heart."[179]

In this condition David descends, one evening at sunset, into a valley in the Swiss Alps. The scene is exquisitely beautiful. He hears shepherds singing in the distance, watches a bright cloud floating along the side of a mountain, and looks at the little village nestled in the bottom of the gorge. For the first time since his despondency he not only sees but feels the beauty that surrounds him, and something stirs within him. David, like Coleridge in "Dejection," has undergone the archetypal nineteenth-century collapse; now he undergoes the archetypal nineteenth-century regeneration. Like John Stuart Mill, he is helped by nature to emerge from the aridity of deepest depression. The language that David uses to describe the moment of rebirth is deeply Romantic. It echoes the Wordsworth of "Tintern Abbey" and the Arnold of "Memorial Verses": "All at once, in this serenity, great Nature spoke to me; and soothed me to lay down my weary head upon the grass, and weep as I had not wept yet, since Dora died!"[180] David has begun the slow process of recovery. The burden that has weighed him down has begun to lighten; "the night was passing from my mind, and all its shadows clearing."[181] In the ensuing months he continues to turn to nature. David's language, describing his recovery, grows even more Wordsworthian: "I sought out Nature, never sought in vain; and I admitted to my breast the human interest I had lately shrunk from."[182] Gradually he begins to write again. After many months he publishes a story based on his experiences. Three years after leaving England he returns.

David has passed through the characteristic Romantic crisis. From utter hopelessness he has emerged into the "Centre of Indifference," and from there to a positive rapprochement with life. In twentieth-century terms he has gone from breakdown and depression, to long identity crisis, to finding himself, to mental health. Dickens' version of this typical progression differs somewhat from its Romantic and modern parallels. Dickensian heroes who undergo this evolution usually "die," are reborn, and then experience a slow regeneration. Of course in *Copperfield,* as in the other novels in which this progression occurs, the actual rendition conveys much more than the simple dramatic events would indicate. In context, the crisis is usually a metaphor for profound and long-anticipated symbolic and psychological breakdown. This is especially true of the middle and later novels. In *Copperfield,* David's breakdown represents, in very complicated ways, the death of his old self: the giving up, under the shocks of death and adversity, of the rationalizations and delusions that had sustained but also trammeled him. The rebirth is the moment when a new, more enlightened self comes into existence. The regeneration is the slow process whereby that reborn self learns to deal in a clear-eyed fashion with the snares and mirages that had entrapped the old self. This process is depicted many times in Dickens, though the moment of crisis or death is usually represented as a devastating physical illness rather than a mental breakdown. Young Martin in *Martin Chuzzlewit,* Arthur

Clennam in *Little Dorrit,* Pip in *Great Expectations,* and Eugene Wrayburn in *Our Mutual Friend* are examples of characters who undergo the more usual death and rebirth through physical illness.

In *Copperfield*, David's rebirth and regeneration are most clearly depicted by his changed attitude toward Agnes. The moment of his rebirth is coincident with the moment of his transformed attitude. When he first comes down into the heavenly Swiss valley, he receives a letter from Agnes. After reading it he knows that "there was no name for the love I bore her, dearer to me, henceforward, than ever until then."[183] He has finally come to realize what Agnes has always been: the good angel, the ministering madonna, the fulfilling love of his life. His reborn eyes, no longer dazzled by Dora's enchantment or Steerforth's charm, see her for what she is. The old spell woven by his mother, father, the Murdstones, Dora, and Steerforth has been broken at last. David's acknowledgement that Agnes is his good angel now has more meaning for him than a convenient analogy, however fervently expressed.

David now apotheosizes Agnes as beneficent madonna and perfect woman. In his new lexicon she is that supernal creature, the angel in the house. David feels that by giving himself over to her, by worshiping her adoringly, he will bring her angelic influence into every aspect of his life. By being true to her, he will be true to the noblest, purest spirit within him. This spirit is his best self. Thus, in David's eyes, Agnes is both ideal woman to be worshiped and an objectification of his best self. David now acknowledges her as the magical personage who will make him whole, who will bring out the best within him. She is thus, to David's way of thinking, his good angel from a supernatural, symbolic, and psychological point of view. She is also a personage who has a special meaning for Dickens. She is his highest and most spiritualized conception of woman, a conception not of this world. Dickens' formulation is in every sense unearthly. It is a fervent and longed-for fairy-tale dream of what ethereal womanhood and complete self-realization might be.

David now knows that he loves Agnes. He also knows that his love for her, unlike his love for Dora, is "founded on a rock." Yet though he loves her, indeed, though now he sees that he has always loved her, he cannot confess his love. He must practice renunciation. David's reasons for abstaining from felicity are complicated. For one thing, he thinks that Agnes loves someone else. For another, he believes that by proclaiming his love, he would destroy their close brother-sister relationship, a relationship that he could never thereafter restore. In addition, since he turned away from her in the past, he feels that he cannot now claim her as a consolation prize on Dora's death. Finally, he realizes that he must learn to put the welfare of Agnes above his own.

He returns to England resolved to remain silent, resolved to confine himself to a brother-sister relationship with Agnes. His satisfaction will come from knowing that he has at last understood his old errors and blindnesses, that he has disciplined his undisciplined heart, that he can now achieve pleasure through promoting the happiness of others rather than selfishly seeking his own happiness. There is a paradox here. For David is unusually generous and altruistic. His difficulties stem from unconscious urges and self-destructive emotional needs, not from self-seeking egotism or self-centered aggrandizement. David's decision, then, does not fully meet his problem. Yet he is not trying to escape from his problem; he chooses a stringent solution. On the other hand, his solution, though spartan, has its compensations. David is bent on a nineteenth-century ennoblement. He will seek transcendence through self-denial. This resolve culminates in a highly contrived double renunciation scene between Agnes and David.[184] In this theatrical scene—emotionally charged for Dickens as his stagy rhetoric shows—each protagonist refuses to tell the other of his love in order to leave the loved one free to love elsewhere, as each mistakenly supposes the other desires. This is the stuff of farce as well as of tragedy. Dickens, of course, is deeply moved by the situation, and he means the reader to be moved. But whether or not a modern reader is swept along by this operatic scene, it is over in a moment. David, despite his renunciatory resolutions, confesses his love, and Agnes then confesses hers.

The long ordeal of poor Agnes, the Patient Griselda of the novel, is finished at last. Agnes has loved David faithfully and mutely, despite David's silliness, blindness, willfulness, and neglect. She has kept herself for him, waiting patiently for the day when he will finally understand and choose her. David, though oblivious of her love, has depended on her loyalty. He tells her: "I felt . . . that you could be faithfully affectionate against all discouragement, and never cease to be so, until you ceased to live."[185] Given such an attitude, it is no wonder that Agnes quickly responds to David's declaration of love. "I have loved you," she says, "all my life!"[186]

Beyond the Patient Griselda motif, there is a profound storybook fulfillment in all this. As in a fairy tale, as in *Beauty and the Beast,* for example, it is when David renounces his own happiness that he finds it. But *Copperfield* is very different from *Great Expectations*—to cite another Dickensian rendition of this theme. In *Great Expectations* the renunciation (of wealth, snobbery, pretension, and so on) is part of a moral growth that transforms longing into acceptance. In *Copperfield* the consummation is simply coincident with David's resolve to renounce. The union comes about not because David has changed (though he has), but because his declaration of love allows Agnes to confess that she has always loved him. David gets a reward that he has not earned. Agnes could have been his any time he revealed his love; he did not need to change in order to win her. The consummation is a fairy-tale consummation after all: a word from David brings him fulfillment.

This is a facile and inadequate resolution, but the chief difficulty lies with Agnes. There is something disturbing and unsatisfactory in Dickens' conception of her. At the heart of the difficulty is Dickens' separation of woman as sexual partner from woman as companion and helpmate. This separation often causes Dickens to demand of one role what he has already set forth as the prerogative of the other, or to deny to each role the womanly wholeness that he really yearns for. In other words, he defines each role in a way that makes fulfillment impossible. In Dickens' calculus of love, the temptress-lover that allures him can never be combined with the angel-madonna that comforts him. The closest he comes to uniting the two roles is to create a woman who is angel-sister to one character and bloodless lover to another, or who changes painfully from loving sister (and surrogate mother) to anemic lover. In such instances, the sister role usually predominates over the lover role, or the sister role becomes an impediment to the lover role. In the *Dombey* chapter I suggested the biographical basis for these configurations, and I sketched how central the pattern is in Dickens' writings.

In *Copperfield* the two roles are separated. Dora is an alluring, sexually provocative lover. David is entranced and enslaved by her, but he needs much more than she can give him. She is not a true helpmate, and she does not bring him fulfillment. In part this is Dora's fault, but in great measure it is David's. Dora is a reflection of David's self-wounding needs and self-deluding blindnesses. She is the unsatisfactory wife his childhood-engendered emotions demanded. She is also the innocent victim of David's romanticism, of a romantic ideality that can never be realized. Like Shelley, David looks before and after and pines for what is not. David is a true heir of the Romantics. He often feels as they did; he often expresses what they too expressed. The "old unhappy loss or want of something" that shadows David's manhood and clouds his marriage to Dora is akin to the vanished glory that darkens Wordsworth's ode on immortality. David associates his loss with Dora's incapacity, but he also connects it to his own sad yearning for a freshness that is no more. He mourns for a "boyish enchantment" that has long since vanished; he yearns for a "softened glory of the past" which nothing can restore.[187] David, like Dickens (who himself drew the parallel with his protagonist), is doomed to wander through life seeking a felicity not of this world.

But the parallel between David and Dickens holds good only until

David marries Agnes. David achieves a putative bliss with Agnes that Dickens was never vouchsafed in life. Agnes, of course, is the other half of Dickens' notion of womanhood. That conception is very Victorian. Agnes is an angel-madonna, wise and helpful and understanding. Like a loving mother or a loyal ministering sister, she is always there when David needs her, patient and serene. She brings peace and comfort and calm to David. But Agnes lacks any sexual appeal. David perceives her as an etherealized, almost as a disembodied, spirit. She is a radiant angel to be worshiped rather than enjoyed. When David at last realizes that he loves her, her status as sister and as angel are two great impediments to declaring his love.

How lacking Agnes is in sexuality may be seen at once if one compares her to Dora. Dora is all sexual appeal. Her physical attractiveness, feminine archness, and provocative flirtatiousness enchant David. Until after their marriage, he is blind to her immaturity, petulance, irrationality, and wilfulness, or if not blind to such traits, he accepts them as subordinate to—perhaps as coincident with—her irresistible appeal. When David meets Dora he is enslaved instantly. He does not, as with Agnes, require trauma, breakdown, and death to teach him love. Dora's instant physical appeal was to David's senses and to his undisciplined emotions (both functions of the shaping experiences of his childhood); Agnes' slow spiritual appeal was to David's understanding and to his disciplined heart (functions of his gradual liberation from self-wounding impositions).

Dora is a summoning up of the sexual in Dickens' life. She is a recrudescence of aspects of Catherine Hogarth, Maria Beadnell, and behind them, of the playful, alluring, inconstant traits in Dickens' mother. In fiction this polarity is represented by such characters as Dolly Varden in *Barnaby Rudge,* Estella in *Great Expectations,* and Bella Wilfer in *Our Mutual Friend.* Agnes, on the other hand, is the summoning up of the sisterly and idealized in Dickens' life. She is a recrudescence of aspects of Fanny Dickens, Mary Hogarth, Georgina Hogarth, and behind them of the protective, loving, ministering traits in Dickens' mother—the mother before the fall. In fiction this polarity is represented by such characters as Ruth Pinch in *Martin Chuzzlewit,* little Nell in *The Old Curiosity Shop,* Florence Dombey in *Dombey and Son,* Amy Dorrit in *Little Dorrit,* Biddy in *Great Expectations,* and many more.

In *Copperfield,* Dickens attempts to unify these polarities, not simply by transforming Agnes from loving sister into sexless lover (he had done this before—with Florence Dombey, for example), but by making Dora and Agnes two aspects of a single experience of womanhood for David. This notion is projected by a multitude of devices. Dora, for instance, holds Agnes' hand while she is being married to David, unites herself with Agnes in subsequent scenes, calls Agnes to her bedside at her death, uses her final breaths to leave Agnes a "last request" and a "last charge," and tells Agnes that only she should "occupy this vacant place" when she is gone. As Agnes puts it later, rather disconcertingly, recalling her deathbed colloquy with Dora, "She told me that she left me something."[188] But that the two women are somehow one is made explicit by David himself. He tells Agnes that she was involved in his love for Dora: "My love [for Dora] would have been incomplete, without your sympathy. I had it, and it was perfected."[189] David follows this strange declaration by an even more extraordinary merging of the two identities: "And O, Agnes, even out of thy true eyes, in that same time [when he told Agnes that he loved her], the spirit of my child-wife looked upon me, saying it was well; and winning me, through thee, to tenderest recollections of the Blossom that had withered in its bloom!"[190]

This supernatural merging of the two identities is all very well on a fairy-tale or even on an allegorical level, but it is not very successful in resolving the realistic dilemma confronting David. One understands what Dickens is seeking to convey: that Agnes' angelic love and angelic presence helped David accept the imperfect love Dora was able to give him. Or to project the matter in the other direction, David's ripened love for Agnes is the rounding out and fulfillment of his immature love for Dora. Realistically this does not work for several reasons. First of all, Agnes and Dora are too antipodal. Agnes is not a ripening of Dora, but an alternative to Dora. Dora is all sexuality, Agnes all spirituality. What David needs — presumably what every man needs — is a blending of the two, not a choice between the two.[191] David escapes the full consequences of his choice, and the devastating results of having to choose between two such unbalanced extremes, by being allowed to experience the two polarities serially. He has his cake and eats it too, so to speak. But a cake which is served in two long-separated installments, the one installment all rich icing, the other all dry cake, is something less than a perfect confection.

As a matter of fact, the difficulty is again mostly with Agnes. In limning Dora, Dickens is disciplined and clear-eyed. He sees all her inadequacies, and he sees all the weaknesses in David that attracted him to her. He spends much of the novel tracing the path that led David to Dora, and he depicts with wonderful economy (and wonderful humor) the failure of their union. David pays a heavy toll for his blindness and self-indulgence. But David's union with Agnes is storybook wish fulfillment pure and simple. This is evident if one compares Dickens' treatment of Agnes and Dora. Both women are incomplete, both are extremes. Yet Dickens is at pains to show that one extreme leads to perfect happiness, while the other leads to frustration and unfulfillment. There is a curious inconsistency here. For the ideal of wife as ministering angel is no less romantic, and no less unattainable, than the ideal of wife as fairy-tale sylph. David's ecstatic adoration of Agnes is simply the obverse of his ecstatic adoration of Dora and should, in truth, come to the same end. That it does not is a sign of Dickens' own romantic commitment to that wish-fulfilling ideal and a chief cause of Agnes' implausibility.

Dickens masks that implausibility with ardent language. After David and Agnes are married, David writes: "Clasped in my embrace, I held the source of every worthy aspiration I had ever had; the centre of myself, the circle of my life, my own, my wife; my love of whom was founded on a rock!"[192] This is not the language of a disciplined heart, but the outpourings of a perfervid spirit.

Agnes' mannerisms and her symbolic accoutrements are tinged with the same overripe emotion. That emotion strains for transcendence, but often evokes banality. Here is another carefully arranged glimpse of Agnes: "That face, so full of pity, and of grief, that rain of tears, that awful mute appeal . . . that solemn hand upraised towards Heaven!"[193] Such posings turn the reader away in disbelief. One grows tired of the hand upraised towards heaven, of the madonna postures, of the churchly associations. One grows tired of the trite religiosity. Agnes is always "uttering platitudes in stained-glass attitudes." Like Bunthorne, of such proclivities we are "*not* fond."

The otherworldly perfection of Agnes, her angel goodness, is a fantasy substitute for examining those qualities in David which continue to make him yearn so hopelessly for such an unattainable ideal and which cause him to delude himself into believing that he has found it. It is the great weakness of *Copperfield* that Dickens, after sustaining the examination of David's blindnesses for the entire novel, and bringing him to a chastened awareness, rewards him at the end with the same promise of romantic fulfillment that has elsewhere been his nemesis.

This is not to deny the possibility of a happy ending. Had Agnes been less of a paragon, had she combined some of Dora's human frailty and allure with her own sensitivity and competence, and had David come to see and accept that imperfect combination as sufficient fulfillment in this imperfect world, the book could have ended happily and still been true to its great theme. But such an ending would have meant creating a woman far different from the usual Dickensian heroine. Such an ending would have run counter to Dickens' lifelong yearnings and to his immediate needs. In a novel one can create a supernal angel-wife. In real life there are no Agneses. Here Dickens' fairy-tale vision (spurred by unsatisfied longing) clashes with rather than enlarges his realism and subverts a part of what he was demonstrating.

Agnes, in fact, is a fulfillment in the old fairy-tale manner. Dickens, having caused David to suffer and learn, waves his magic wand and rewards him with his heart's desire. But Agnes is also part of the newer, less arbitrary fairy-tale designs that govern so much of *Copperfield*. For towards the end of *Copperfield,* Agnes is at the center of a deep movement of recapitulation, recurrence, and closure. Agnes, as David puts it, "touched the chords of my memory . . . [and enabled me to] listen to the sorrowful, distant music, and . . . shrink from nothing it awoke."[194] *Copperfield* is coincident with the chords of memory; it is coincident with learning to look steadily at the sorrowful traumas of the past. Agnes, David's good angel and mystical protectress, helps him do this and helps him resolve the past. Agnes, speaking of David's old room, tells him: "I have found a pleasure . . . while you have been absent, in keeping everything as it used to be when we were children. For we were very happy then, I think."[195]

Agnes is helping David evoke the lost storybook happiness of his lost childhood. She is the guardian of the happiest interval of David's life, the interval after the Murdstones and before the plunge into adult knowledge and responsibility. To draw the parallel in terms of Dickens, this is the period of Chatham and Dickens' closeness to Fanny, the period before he was unaccountably sent forth into the fallen world of London. Yet the notion of stopping time and returning to an idealized past is not a possibility but a make-believe dream. Dickens knew this. He knew that he enshrined a lost innocence that had never wholly been, that could certainly never be. Yet he often felt impelled to evoke a blissful Edenlike past and to yearn for its return. His writings frequently dramatize this urge. They concentrate on protagonists who have fallen from grace (usually through no overt fault of their own) and who seek to find their way back to a vanished felicity. In his fictions he could accomplish, or partly accomplish, what he could never realize in reality. David, with the help of Agnes, achieves the fantasy resolution that Dickens often yearned for but never attained.

Agnes helps David return to a childhood that has been exorcised of its evil influences. She brings him back to a past purged of his own wandering errancy and of the evil enchantments of others. A few hours after David and Agnes reveal their love to one another they take an evening walk in the surrounding Canterbury countryside. As they walk they are filled with rapture and blessed calm. When they return to the Wickfield house they stand in an old-fashioned window, the moon beaming upon them. David had noticed that window when he first glimpsed the Wickfield house from the outside. A little later he had met Agnes for the first time in the room with that old-fashioned window. A little later still, while on a staircase in the Wickfield house, looking up at Agnes, he had first associated her with a stained-glass window. Many years later, on his return to England, he had again looked through that familiar Wickfield window, recalling details he had seen and emotions he had felt when watching through the window as a boy. Now, as he looks at Agnes in that selfsame window, her eyes raised to the moon, he follows her gaze and sees a vision: "Long miles of road then opened out before my mind; and, toiling on, I saw a ragged way-worn boy forsaken and neglected, who should come to call even the heart now beating against mine, his own."[196]

The moon-blanched window recalls yet other crucial windows in David's wayworn journey: the premonitory window of his prebirth annunciation, with his fairy godmother peering grotesquely through; the fearful window of his childhood, with David staring terror-stricken at the moonlit grave of his father; the redeeming bow window of his aunt's Dover house, with his aunt gazing out to sea after magically caressing his hair and saying, "Poor fellow"; the dream-fulfilling window of his new Dover room, with David looking out the window, thinking of his dead mother and brother, and drowsily contemplating the moon's silver track on the melancholy sea; the small ground-floor turret window of the Wickfield house, with Uriah's cadaverous face looming through; the disturbing window of David's own room there, with Uriah's gargoyle head leering from a beam-end; the comforting old-fashioned upper window of the Wickfield house, with serene-eyed Agnes standing calmly in front of its leaded panes; the beatific stained-glass window of David's imagination, with Agnes as his unrecognized good angel; the vacant window of Mr. Peggotty's ship-house, with the beacon-candle burning in the night; the terrible window of the black void, with David, tempest-tossed, confronting the dark image of himself; and the sightless windows of the mourning Steerforth mansion, with David darkening each window in the house, and finally darkening the window where Steerforth lies dead. These window images are not the chance accumulation of a long book, but the self-conscious imagistic correlatives of a magically portentous and reflexive design. That Dickens was aware of the import of these images, that he used them to reinforce and integrate what he was saying, is evident not only from the book itself, but from the number plans. In his notes for the final double number, he wrote: "The old house. / Looking out of a window how he had looked out as a boy." Dickens was reminding himself to evoke again the associations built around the Wickfield window. He was also reminding himself to show David looking back on his own life. David looking through the window is therefore an incarnation of what the book is now doing (looking back upon itself) and what Dickens wants the reader to do (look back upon the sources of David's pilgrimage) as the novel concludes.

Now, even later than that retrospective window scene, at the very end of his journey, David is once more standing in the Wickfield window. The window is moon-drenched and he feels a blessed calm. It is at this point that he has the vision of himself toiling toward Dover, ragged, wayworn, and forsaken. And it is here too that he achieves the beatific union with his good angel and best self. It is toward this resolution that he has been toiling: terrified youngster, wayworn boy, unseeing youth, and tempest-tossed man. The windows of the past with their burdens and their promises dissolve and are magically replaced by a bright moon-drenched window of fulfillment and tranquility.

Agnes is both the means and the end of that fulfillment. She mildly guides him where his best self would lead him; she is his reward when he reaches that self-knowledge. She presides mutely over the long, magical, cyclical journey that enables David to turn back and meet himself. She helps provide closure in the strong fairy-tale circling of Dickens' design. That closure is made explicit by portentously returning to old sites and old images—the recurring windows are only one element in that intricately centripetal design. Closure is also enforced by recalling the crucial past, a past that both shapes the present and is resolved by it. As the novel converges towards its conclusion, one gets a powerful sense of mythic recurrence. Events, persons, things turn back upon themselves in ways that signify a suprarational ordering and significance. There is no divine intervention in this. Though Agnes is a good angel and is associated with stained-glass windows and dim religious lights, the effect that emerges from the strong centripetal movement of the novel is not religious but magical. Dickens is depicting a fairy-tale or anagogic universe, not a theocentric one. His imagination is engaged by the strong hidden connections among things, connections that defy rational analysis, but that also defy the rigidities of dogma. These connections, so ordinary and natural on the surface, so fraught with secret meanings underneath, testify to a universe that is solid and palpable but also profoundly mysterious.

In most instances the fairy-tale elements in *Copperfield* are rooted in verisimilitude; that is, storybook motifs and portents are usually fused to the central realism of the novel and work throughout the novel as an adjunct to that realism, enlarging and deepening what Dickens has to say. This is Dickens' new or mature fairy-tale method and is the mainstay of the fairy story in *Copperfield,* as it is in all the novels from *Dombey* on. At times, however, Dickens uses the old fairy-tale method of arbitrarily transforming some character or event. These transformations usually grow out of gross exigencies of plot or theme and are handled in ways that violate our sense of reality. Dickens is more likely to turn to the old fairy-tale method toward the end of a book when he is concentrating on closing it. Sometimes these simpler fantasy devices are elemental gestures of affirmation or conclusion, ritualized ways of conveying an ending. When David tells his aunt that he and Agnes are to be married, we get an ecstatic celebration in the old Christmas-book manner, a joyous storybook finale. David concludes this episode and its wild hugging with a time-honored fairy-tale formula. "Then," he says, "we were all happy together."[197] In other instances, the storybook component is more complicated. Dickens often gives a character both an old and a new fairy-tale dimension. If Agnes provides David with perfect felicity in the old fairy-tale manner, she also draws him into recurrence and resolution in the new fairy-tale manner. Other characters at the end of *Copperfield* are given strong storybook resonances at their final appearances, some in the old, some in the new manner.

Mr. Micawber and Mr. Mell, for example, are given honors, riches, and status. Dickens bestows these gifts to satisfy poetic justice and ensure a happy conclusion. Such resolutions could have been achieved through the old or the new method, but here—by virtue of the sheer implausibility of the ending—the old fairy-tale method is brought strongly to the fore. Mr. Micawber, reversing the pattern of an entire lifetime, learns prudence and responsibility in Australia, pays all his bills, waxes prosperous, and becomes a district magistrate in Port Middlebay. How arbitrary and unlikely all this is is made even clearer with Mr. Mell. Most unbelievably, he turns up in Port Middlebay too, second only to Mr. Micawber in distinction. He is now Dr. Mell of Colonial Salem-House Grammar School, Port Middlebay. That poor Mr. Mell should turn up in Port Middlebay, of all places, is fantasy enough, but that he should turn up there a "Doctor," and name his school after the brutal Salem House from which he was humiliatingly dismissed, exceeds all belief *unless* one reads the episode as an old-style fairy-tale ending, as a totally magical attempt to lay the lingering ghost of Mr. Creakle and Salem House.

The formal conclusion of *Copperfield* takes place in "A Last Retrospect," a final chapter of four or five pages. Here Dickens continues to mix old and new fairy-tale methods. Julia Mills is wild storybook extravaganza of the purest sort. She comes sailing back into the novel from India, a female Croesus. She employs "a black man to carry cards and letters to her on a golden salver, and a copper-coloured woman in linen, with a bright handkerchief round her head, to serve her Tiffin in her dressing-room."[198] On the other hand, other characters and motifs enforce profound returns, recurrences, and renewals, or effect final resolutions of the earliest stresses and vibrations of the novel. Such fairy-tale touches in the new manner serve to recapitulate and bring to a close the deep-throated harmonies that have orchestrated the entire novel. These storybook harmonies need not be euphonious; they can include disturbing dissonances. We catch a glimpse of Rosa Dartle and Mrs. Steerforth forever in a garden, forever tormenting one another with their dead deathless passion. We are given news of the murdering Murdstones. They are still flourishing, still entrapping weak loving women, still sternly reducing them to whimpering subjection. They are part of the eternal return of evil; they warn us of victims and sufferings yet to come.

There are more benign returns as well. David's children enforce renewal as well as closure. They reawaken and resolve some of the earliest tensions of the novel. Aunt Betsey is now a godmother to a real living Betsey Trotwood Copperfield: one of the first predictions of the novel has come to pass. A little Dora, offspring of David and Agnes (offspring, therefore, of dead Dora's other half) has blossomed from the grave and lives again. A third child, the youngest, totters unsteadily from Peggotty to Miss Betsey, even as David used to totter from Peggotty to his mother. Peggotty is just the same: apple cheeks, dark eyes, nutmeg-grater finger. She still reads to the children from David's old crocodile book, and when David looks at his children thus engrossed, he sees "my own infant face, looking up at me from the crocodile stories."[199] The great wheel of the novel has turned round on itself. The fairy tale of life is about to begin again.

The ghosts and spirits that it was predicted David would be privileged to see—a prediction that he scoffed at on the first page of his history—have held him spellbound throughout the novel. That long spell now dissolves; the end magically closes what the beginning magically opened. As David writes the last words of his novel, subduing his desire to linger with his creations a little longer, "these faces fade away."[200] Peggotty, the Murdstones, Aunt Betsey, little Emily, Mr. Micawber, Dora, Traddles, Agnes, Steerforth—all vanish as if part of an insubstantial dream. The predictions and portents at David's birth; the white gravestone cruelly barred from its rightful place at the cozy hearth; the ferocious Oh-goroo man chanting fiercely of lungs and livers and hearts on fire; the gargoyle head of Uriah looming cadaverously through the Wickfield window; the hammer-wrought scar that throbs across Rosa Dartle's mouth; the howling wind and rising sea that gather slowly to tempest fullness; the strange repetitions and expressive warnings that surround David at every turning; the whole secret intelligible *Copperfield* universe—every jot and tittle of it, visible and invisible, natural and supernatural, vanishes into the realm from whence it was summoned.

David's thoughts now turn to his own death, to the time "when realities are melting from me like the shadows which I now dismiss."[201] David is voicing Dickens' own feelings upon finishing *Copperfield*. As Dickens put it in the preface, he too felt as if he were "dismissing some portion of himself into the shadowy world.''[202] He was doing just that. He was dismissing a version of his own life that he had summoned up from the shadows. He was also closing a more recent phase of his existence: he was putting an end to two years of unremitting literary effort. But he was doing more. He was consigning to the vast realms of the dead the teeming spirits conjured up by his imagination. Like David, he had seen ghosts and spirits. They had played their predicted roles, had magically started up, merged, doubled, and recurred, had worked out their sign-filled destinies, and finally, tempest-tossed and purged, had come to their appointed rest. Dickens, his two-year traffic with ghosts and spirits now at an end, could well speak, as David does in the death-haunted last sentence of *Copperfield,* of ''the shadows which I now dismiss.''

Yet in that end is a beginning, not only because the novel turns back to where it began, but for more transcendent reasons as well. For at that final moment when Dickens, Prosperolike, yields up his spell, he also extends and reconfirms it. By consigning his creations to death, he assures that they will live. By breaking his so-potent staff, he commits the final necessary act of creation. He despatches the last shadows of his fading fairy tale to the deathless stasis of art.

8 | *Great Expectations*
The Factual Matrix

Pause you who read this, and think for a moment of
the long chain of iron or gold, of thorns or flowers,
that would never have bound you, but for the formation
of the first link on one memorable day.

GREAT EXPECTATIONS

Wilkie Collins had great difficulty in naming his most famous novel, *The Woman in White*. This may strike us as strange, for the book seems to demand its title. But as Collins worked on his novel, and as the days and weeks went by, he could not find a name for it, and this not only disturbed him but also Dickens, who was his intimate friend and literary mentor. Dickens considered a book's title of utmost importance, and in this case he had a business interest in the name. The untitled work was to follow *A Tale of Two Cities* as the first non-Dickensian serial in Dickens' new magazine, *All the Year Round*. Furthermore, since *All the Year Round* used no by-lines, Collins' novel had to be announced and advertised primarily by title. But as the publication date loomed closer and closer, Collins could not settle on a title. He had long since written the unforgettable opening of his book, an opening which had sounded the major chords of his story. In that opening, drawing on his own experiences, he had described how suddenly, in the dead of night, in the middle of an empty moon-blanched road, a "solitary Woman, dressed from head to foot in white," had touched a startled stranger on the shoulder and changed his destiny. The episode was haunting, premonitory, central—Dickens thought the scene one of the two most dramatic descriptions in literature—but the days and weeks wore on and Collins could think of no name. Then, one evening, while Collins was lying on the grass and staring at the North Foreland Lighthouse, the title came into his head as swiftly and as unannounced as the real woman in white had come into his real life. He sent Dickens the name and asked for his reaction. Dickens replied immediately and settled the matter. "I have not the slightest doubt," he

279

wrote on 16 August 1859, "that The Woman in White is the name of names, and very title of titles."

Collins could hardly have known why Dickens regarded "The Woman in White" as the "name of names, and very title of titles." Dickens himself was probably only dimly aware of the depth of his response. Yet even at that moment, *Great Expectations* and its "Woman in White," Miss Havisham, were forming in his mind. Scarcely three months after Collins' novel concluded in *All the Year Round, Great Expectations* took its place in the same journal. That was the astonishing culmination: a Dickens novel that revolved, in part, around a persona similar to Collins' all-white figure, a figure that had called up very special and very different associations in Dickens' mind.

Those associations reached back to curious beginnings. The first faint premonitions of Miss Havisham had begun to take shape in Dickens' consciousness some thirty-five years earlier, and the strange unlikely history of Miss Havisham's gestation and of the genesis of *Great Expectations* is a fascinating untold tale.

Some of the crucial themes which became *Great Expectations,* and some of the everyday experiences which became Miss Havisham and ordained her fiery destruction, can be traced to the most casual happenstance of Dickens' early and late years. In the case of Miss Havisham this is surely a paradox, for she is often pointed to as a character who is totally unreal. She is too bizarre, runs the arraignment, too Dickensian; she is unbelievable. Whatever the validity of this judgment, one thing is certain: Miss Havisham is constructed out of everyday events. But there is another, still greater irony, and it is this: Dickens consciously suppressed the wilder, the more "Dickensian" aspects of the everyday reality he drew upon.

That reality—"the formation of the first link," to use Dickens' phrase—commenced with childhood. As a boy, Dickens had seen a strange lady wandering through the streets of London. The sight of this grotesque creature, and the romantic and tragic speculations he attached to her, sank into his memory and became an evocative part of his consciousness. Many years later, in 1853, in his magazine, *Household Words,* he wrote an essay about the indelible impressions of his boyhood. He called the essay "Where We Stopped Growing," and in it he described the strange lady of his youth:

> Another very different person who stopped our growth, we associate with Berners Street, Oxford Street; whether she was constantly on parade in that street only, or was ever to be seen elsewhere, we are unable to say. The White Woman is her name. She is dressed entirely in white, with a ghastly white plating round her head and face, inside her white bonnet.

She even carries (we hope) a white umbrella. With white boots, we know she picks her way through the winter dirt. She is a conceited old creature, cold and formal in manner, and evidently went simpering mad on personal grounds alone—no doubt because a wealthy Quaker wouldn't marry her. This is her bridal dress. She is always walking up here, on her way to church to marry the false Quaker. We observe in her mincing step and fishy eye that she intends to lead him a sharp life. We stopped growing when we got at the conclusion that the Quaker had had a happy escape of the White Woman.[1]

Here already are most of Miss Havisham's attributes: her externals—bridal dress, all-white accoutrements, and ever-present staff (represented for the moment by an umbrella); her personality—cold, formal, conceited, eccentric, and man-hating; and her history—jilted and thereby frozen forever (she too has stopped growing!) in the ghastly garments of her dead love. But this White Woman—the White Woman of "Where We Stopped Growing"—is not the simple figure of Dickens' boyhood. He had long since begun to surround the original image with fantasies of his own creation. What he had actually seen as a boy was an eccentric woman in weird white garments. The jilting Quaker, the walk to church, the white umbrella, the romantically provoked onset of madness—all these were added or magnified, as Dickens suggests, by his imagination.

His imagination may have embroidered or intertwined some of these motifs shortly after he turned nineteen, that is, several years after he had first seen the Berners Street White Woman. On the evening of 18 April 1831, at the Adelphi Theatre in London, Charles Mathews the elder, a great favorite of the youthful Dickens, opened in the twelfth of his annual *At Homes*. One segment of the 1831 *At Home,* a sketch entitled "Nos. 26 and 27; or, Next Door Neighbours," featured a "Miss Mildew," a character based upon the Berners Street White Woman. Miss Mildew, played by Mathews, was an eccentric old lady in white who had been jilted by her first love forty years earlier. On the day originally set for her marriage, Miss Mildew had donned her wedding garments, and every day since, in those yellowing weeds, she had made her way through London streets to a place bearing a startling name: the "London Expectoration Office." At the Expectoration Office she inquires fruitlessly after her lost love. Her next door neighbor—a character played by Frederick Yates and also based upon a real-life London eccentric later described by Dickens in "Where We Stopped Growing"—dresses all in black and constantly calls at the Expectoration Office to collect a vast fortune that never arrives: another theme central to *Great Expectations*.[2]

If Dickens saw this piece, he must have done so on opening night, for the sketch, owing to its cruel mockery of two familiar London eccentrics, offended many people, and was withdrawn after its first performance. If he was present at that first performance, there is no doubt that "Nos. 26 and 27" would have brought him instantly back to where *he* stopped growing; it would also have presented him, given the context of what he had seen as a boy, with an unforgettable linking of women in white and deluded expectations.

There is a reasonable chance that Dickens was present at that first performance. During his late teens he went to the theater almost every night, and "always," as he told Forster, "to see Mathews whenever he played."[3] During this period too he thought of becoming an actor and memorized "three or four successive years of Mathews's At Homes from sitting in the pit to hear them."[4] That Mathews had seized Dickens' youthful imagination there can be no doubt, but whether Miss Mildew and her evocative cluster of associations seized his imagination depends on whether Dickens was in the Adelphi audience on that April evening in 1831, and here the record, though suggestive, is inconclusive.

Many years later, however, another, more fantastic cluster of associations merged with Dickens' boyhood White Woman and helped shape Miss Havisham and the basic structure of *Great Expectations*. The second cluster of associations apparently entered Dickens' mind in 1850, that is nineteen years after Miss Mildew's brief life and three years before he wrote "Where We Stopped Growing." In 1850 Dickens launched a monthly supplement to the weekly *Household Words*. He called this supplement the *Household Narrative of Current Events,* gave it a departmentalized format, and sold it for twopence. In the first issue, that is, in the January 1850 *Household Narrative,* in the section entitled "Narrative of Law and Crime," appeared the following paragraph:

> An inquest was held on the 29th, on Martha Joachim, a *Wealthy and Eccentric Lady,* late of 27, York-buildings, Marylebone, aged 62. The jury proceeded to view the body, but had to beat a sudden retreat, until a bull-dog, belonging to deceased, and which savagely attacked them, was secured. It was shown in evidence that on the 1st of June, 1808, her father, an officer in the Life Guards, was murdered and robbed in the Regent's Park. A reward of 300*l.* was offered for the murderer, who was apprehended with the property upon him, and executed. In 1825, a suitor of the deceased, whom her mother rejected, shot himself while sitting on the sofa with her, and she was covered with his brains. From that instant she lost her reason. Since her mother's death, eighteen years ago, she had led the life of a recluse, dressed in white, and never going out. A charwoman occasionally brought her what supplied her wants. Her only companions were the bull-dog, which she nursed like a child, and two cats. Her

house was filled with images of soldiers in lead, which she called her "body-guards." When the collectors called for their taxes, they had to cross the garden-wall to gain admission. One morning she was found dead in her bed; and a surgeon who was called in, said she had died of bronchitis, and might have recovered with proper medical aid. The jury returned a verdict to that effect.

Reading about this eccentric white woman, Dickens must have recalled his own boyhood White Woman, and perhaps, if the association existed, Miss Mildew as well (by a strange coincidence, Miss Mildew also lived at No. 27), for when he came to write about his Berners Street White Woman three years later in *Household Words,* he seems to have overlaid his early memories with details and associations from the history of Martha Joachim—that is, he projected upon his Berners Street White Woman the Martha Joachim-Miss Mildew syndrome of rejection and ensuing madness. Miss Havisham herself, who was not conceived until 1860—that is, not until almost ten years after the *Household Narrative* paragraph, and almost eight years after "Where We Stopped Growing"—is indebted in yet other ways to the *Household Narrative* account of Martha Joachim. Miss Havisham, like Martha Joachim (but unlike the boyhood or the *Household Words* White Woman, and unlike Miss Mildew) is wealthy, is associated with crime and murder, undergoes an instantaneous breakdown caused by her suitor, becomes a recluse, surrounds herself with toylike mementos of her past, and lives in a house with a walled garden. But Dickens, softening, as he so often did, life's own outrageous brand of "Dickensian" exaggerations, left out such proto-Dickensian touches as the pampered bulldog, the lead-soldier bodyguards, and the splattering brains.

Selection and suppression, then, play a role; and yet there is also a seemingly indiscriminate absorptiveness. Can scraps and bits such as these, we wonder, help shape, perhaps even help inaugurate, a great novel? And is it not curious that these trivially encountered and swiftly scanned details should become crucial parts of an artist's consciousness, or that years later they should be reproduced so faithfully, yet so wonderfully transformed? Perhaps there is no contradiction here. Perhaps herein lies the method and the power of art. In any case, Dickens was always a snapper-up of unconsidered trifles; his genius made those trifles meaningful, and when an image or association held a special emotional charge for him—as the image of the White Woman had since boyhood—he unconsciously sifted out every scrap of consonant material scattered through his life, even as a magnet sifts out every scrap of iron scattered through a heap of dust.

That sifting was intensified by a number of reinforcing factors: by his

lifelong fascination with the grotesque and by his early introduction to
the lurid delights of Gothic literature and nightmarish fairy tales. In that
terrific literature White Women abound. There are many famous late
eighteenth- and early nineteenth-century White Women: Monk Lewis'
white-veiled Bleeding Nun, for example, and his equally popular Fair
Imogine who, "arrayed in her bridal apparel of white," danced to
damnation with the skeleton specter of her jilted lover (both ladies
were great favorites of the youthful Dickens); and the tradition of the
deadly White Woman is with us still as Faulkner's ghastly Miss Emily
and her dusty bridal chamber bear witness. At the same time, Dickens'
woman in white is part of a separate but related syndrome that fascinated Dickens. For Miss Havisham is another of his daft, obsessed,
disappointed, time-stopped females: Miss Betsey Trotwood in *David
Copperfield* and Miss Flite in *Bleak House* are two earlier versions of
this type. Given Dickens' sensibility, it is not difficult to understand
why the paragraph about Miss Martha Joachim remained in his mind.

For reasons that are quite different, other portions of the January
1850 issue of the *Household Narrative* also stuck in his mind. The
January issue deals, for example, with the transportation of convicts.
In one section, a section eerily and crazily premonitory of the
Magwitch-Pip relationship, a paragraph discussing the "loathsome
contamination"—the phrase is from the paragraph—of Australia by
transported convicts, is followed by an account of how lowly emigrants
to Australia, having buried their past, can expect to achieve wealth for
themselves and social standing for their children. This theme had impinged upon Dickens' mind several times during these months. In
March 1850, in "A Bundle of Emigrants' Letters" (an article on emigrants to Australia that Dickens wrote for the first issue of *Household
Words*), he had included one letter from a transported convict. "[My
Master]," wrote the convict to his wife, "is a rich . . . Gentleman . . .
and when you come ask for me as a emigrant and never use the word
Convict . . . never let it be once named among you, let no one know
your business."[5] The account in the January 1850 *Household Narrative*
quotes similar letters. An emigrant daughter warns her father, who is
about to join her, not to "say how you got your living at home" but to
"remember, you are to be a gentleman if you come here; that is, you
will be dressed as well as any country farmer in Scotland—you will
have the best food, a good horse to ride on, and a farm of sixty acres to
go to." Here then, in matter-of-fact compression, are some of the primary concerns and concatenations of *Great Expectations*. One is
struck by the analogies: one thinks of the crude transported convict
Magwitch, of how he hides his past, accumulates wealth in Australia,
and gives his surrogate son the trappings and prestige of a gentleman;
and one thinks also of Pip, the surrogate son, of how he buries his lowly

origins (in this he is like Dickens himself), shrinks from the returned Magwitch as from a "loathsome contamination," and hurries, when summoned, to the dress and food and appurtenances of a gentleman.

But perhaps the most extraordinary example of how happenstance and association can help shape art occurs in yet another paragraph in the January 1850 issue of the *Household Narrative*. Under the section entitled "Narrative of Accident and Disaster," just a leaf removed from the Martha Joachim history, appears the following paragraph:

> An accident, fortunately not serious in its results, occurred on the evening of the 7th at the residence of W. O. Bigg, Esq., of Abbot's Leigh. There was a large party at the house, and during the night a *"German Tree,"* about five feet high, with its branches covered with bon-bons and other Christmas presents, and lit with a number of small wax tapers, was introduced into the drawing-room for the younger members of the party. While leaning forward to take some toy from the tree, the light gauze overdress of one young lady, Miss Gordon, took fire, and blazed up in a most alarming manner. One of the lads present, whose quickness and presence of mind were far superior to his years, with much thought and decision threw down the young lady, and folding her in a rug that was luckily close by, put out the flame before it had done any serious damage beyond scorching her arms severely.

Here, in brief, close enough to become forever entangled in Dickens' mind with those other *Household Narrative* themes destined for *Great Expectations* —with made gentlemen, transported convicts, hiding one's past, jilted white-robed recluses, and his own boyhood White Woman—occur the accident, the rescue, and the wound that he will later attach to *his* burning white woman and her rescuer when he comes to write *Great Expectations*. For in *Great Expectations* Miss Havisham's gauzy white dress blazes up when she approaches too close to a fire, Pip puts out the flames by throwing her down and folding her in coats and a tablecloth that are luckily nearby, and Pip's hands and arm are severely scorched.

So much for this *Household Narrative* conflation of some of the central images and themes in *Great Expectations*. But Dickens' Woman in White teases us still. Why, we ask, did a convict and a made gentleman become entangled with the White Woman, why not some other equally available human events out of the scores recorded in that ordinary issue of the *Household Narrative?* Was the eccentric Berners Street White Woman of Dickens' boyhood somehow connected with the great secret of his early years—his apprenticeship in a blacking warehouse and his association with prisons and prisoners—and did the unexpected juxtaposition in the *Household Narrative* of a daft woman in white, convicts hiding their pasts, and made gentlemen merge with his own similar hidden associations and with his current position as a self-made gentleman? In other words, did the *Household Narrative* associations become meaningful because they reinforced vital configurations in Dickens' life?

I think this was the case. In fact, I think the key reinforcement may have been the *Household Narrative* statement that Martha Joachim had died in York Buildings. For York Buildings, strange to say, linked past and present, wild romance and grim reality. On the most elementary level, the linking was physical: 27 York Buildings, the house in which white-clad Martha Joachim dwindled into her maimed destiny, was only a few hundred yards away from 1 Devonshire Terrace, Dickens' current home and his home for the preceding eleven years. The macabre contrast of their separate yet intersecting lives would not have been lost on Dickens. He was always sensitive to such juxtapositions, and he was hypersensitive to time-stopped women in white. For eleven years he had passed and repassed York Buildings, for eleven years he had led his abundant life in nearby Devonshire Terrace, and all the while, unknown to him, blighted Martha Joachim, clad in white, had sat in the gloom of her York Buildings fortress, cut off from all the world. The *Household Narrative* had revealed this neighborhood romance to Dickens. But the stunning revelation that a woman in white had immured herself for eighteen years in nearby York Buildings was only part of what made the episode unforgettable. Stranger still, and in some ways even more significant, York Buildings had older, more potent associations for Dickens: York Buildings was also the name of a street and a region that had caused him to "stop growing."

The York Buildings I now refer to—York Buildings, Strand—was located just a few hundred feet away from the blacking warehouse in which Dickens had drudged as a boy: York Buildings and the streets surrounding York Buildings were his special haunt during that time. York Buildings was thus an inextricable part of those desolate and unforgiven days when his family was imprisoned in the Marshalsea, and he became, as he put it, a "labouring hind," a "small Cain."[6] The pain Dickens felt at this time merged with the bricks and mortar, with the streets and buildings, surrounding him. One can scarcely overestimate that identification. Until long after he was a grown man, until long after he had become the most famous writer in England, he could not reenter that region.[7]

For Dickens, therefore, the very name York Buildings was surcharged with blacking-warehouse and prison emotion. Coming on the name in the *Household Narrative* in a context that emphasized another old childhood association, the powerful association of the White Woman, he must have been strangely stirred by what he read. And when he realized that the York Buildings which hid this blighted recluse in white was the York Buildings which stood impassively only yards away from his own home in Devonshire Terrace, he must have been haunted by that unexpected melding of the old and the new, the fantastic and the familiar. York Buildings probably served, therefore, as an emotional magnet that raised the intensity and influenced the pattern of his responses. It probably helped Dickens gather and then retain one of the great formative assemblages of *Great Expectations,* an assemblage composed of the hidden past and the echoing present, an assemblage that included the January 1850 *Household Narrative,* Martha Joachim, women in white, Berners Street, Devonshire Terrace, made gentlemen, imprisonment, servitude, the blacking warehouse, and his own secret childhood.

But the "long chain" was only partly formed. In the 1850s other links of "iron or gold" were hammered into place. In 1854 or shortly thereafter Dickens read the following words:

> I am one of those individuals who are born to great expectations, and who are almost certain to be made uncomfortable at some time of their lives in consequence. I was not, however, always aware of this truth, and, when a young gentleman, was almost as proud of my expectations as of my moustaches. It was, therefore, with considerable astonishment that I woke up one morning and found that my expectations were merely one of those pantomime tricks which Miss Fortune is so fond of playing us. That elderly spinster had, indeed, dealt me a knock-down thump, against which there was no reasoning. "It really, really," as Sir Leicester Dedlock says, "gave rise to consequences which could not be mentioned in good society."

This was the opening paragraph in E. C. Grenville Murray's preface to his series of travel sketches, *The Roving Englishman.* Dickens undoubtedly read the preface because he had given permission for the book to be published (the sketches had originally appeared in *Household Words*), and because he and his works were mentioned—always in flattering terms—throughout the preface. Furthermore, the preface recounted the history of Murray's affiliation with *Household Words,* and the book was dedicated to the subeditor of that journal, Dickens' intimate associate W. H. Wills. The keynotes of the initial paragraph—the phrase "great expectations," the concern with "good society," the stress on genteel outward show, the inevitable blows of deflating reality (all conjoined with Dickens and his writings)—these keynotes were not confined to the opening paragraph; they vibrated through the entire preface. After additional references to great expectations, *Household Words,* Wills, *Bleak House, David Copperfield,* and Dickens, and after additional soundings of his original motifs, Mur-

ray went on to affirm that "our 'great expectations' are something very
far less sure than our own energies." This statement might stand as a
motto for *Great Expectations*. Given this striking association of vain
hopes and longed-for gentility with the phrase "great expectations"
and with Dickens' name and writings, it is not hard to understand how
Dickens' title—one of the best he ever chose—came rushing into his
mind when he sat down to write his own consummate version of vain
hopes, longed-for gentility, and great expectations.

The long chain of iron and gold was being formed ineluctably and bit
by bit. During this period in the 1850s, while unconsciously accumulating some of the links he would later forge into title and theme, character and incident, Dickens was also assembling other segments of his
intricate chain. During the 1850s his imagination was increasingly
haunted by the figure of a blighted woman in white, and during the
same period he increasingly associated that figure with motifs that were
to dominate *Great Expectations*. His most striking anticipation of those
tangled themes appeared in *The Lazy Tour of Two Idle Apprentices,* a
series of five travel articles that he and Wilkie Collins wrote for the five
October 1857 issues of *Household Words*. Most of *The Lazy Tour* is by
Dickens, and most of it is autobiographical; the series was designed to
give a fanciful, highly personalized account of a trip that he and Collins
had made to Carlisle, Wigton, Allonby, Lancaster, and Doncaster a
few weeks earlier. In a section of *The Lazy Tour* by Dickens, a section
set at the King's Arms Inn, Lancaster, Dickens interrupted his travel
account to introduce a wild ghost story—I shall call the story "The
Bride's Chamber"—and this story, and the circumstances that produced it, shed additional light on the origins of *Great Expectations*.

The trip itself grew out of Dickens' need to escape into activity, an
escape made necessary by one of the great emotional crises of his life.
He had just returned from the distracting excitements of touring with
his amateur theatrical company in *The Frozen Deep,* but now that he
was home again and left to himself, he felt unbearably restless. The
causes of his restlessness seemed beyond remedy. He was miserable in
his twenty-year marriage with Catherine Hogarth, and he was in love
with one of the actresses in *The Frozen Deep,* teen-aged Ellen Ternan.
Yet a remedy of sorts was close at hand, for his restlessness was the
onset of a storm of emotions that would cause him, a few weeks later,
to separate from his wife. On 29 August 1857, with the storm mounting,
he wrote to Collins in "grim despair." "I want," he said, "to . . . go
anywhere—take any tour—see anything . . . We want something for
Household Words, and I want to escape from myself." At the same
time he was confessing to Forster: "Poor Catherine and I are not made
for each other, and there is no help for it. . . . She is . . . amiable and
complying; but we are strangely ill-assorted for the bond there is be-

tween us. God knows she would have been a thousand times happier if she had married another kind of man . . . I am often cut to the heart by thinking what a pity it is, for her own sake, that I ever fell in her way."[8] To Mrs. Watson he later wrote additional confessions:

> I am the modern embodiment of the old Enchanters, whose Familiars tore them to pieces. I weary of rest, and have no satisfaction but in fatigue. Realities and idealities are always comparing themselves together before me, and I don't like the Realities except when they are unattainable—*then*, I like them of all things. I wish I had been born in the days of Ogres and Dragon-guarded Castles. I wish an Ogre with seven heads (and no particular evidence of brains in the whole lot of them) had taken the Princess whom I adore—you have no idea how intensely I love her!—to his stronghold on the top of a high series of mountains, and there tied her up by the hair. Nothing would suit me half so well this day, as climbing after her, sword in hand, and either winning her or being killed.—*There's* a state of mind for you, in 1857.[9]

With these conflicting emotions—of feeling fettered to his complying wife, of blaming himself for her unhappiness, of longing to rescue an unattainable fairy-tale princess, and of yearning to escape from everyday realities—he set out for a two-week tour of Cumberland and the Midlands with Collins.

In the wild ghost story that Dickens wrote for *The Lazy Tour*, he combined the idea of destroying an unwanted wife—now a blighted bride in white—with other motifs destined for *Great Expectations*: with a damning money nexus; with a passionate, impossible love; with a decaying, isolated and isolating mansion; with a ruined, wall-enclosed, desolating garden; and with the deadly sin of fashioning another human being to be an instrument of revenge. Obviously, a crucial transformation has occurred. Images and ideas that were originally brought together by chance juxtaposition or gross association—the Berners Street White Woman, the walled garden of Martha Joachim—have now been caught up in the gravitational field of the imagination. Early memories, later experiences, and *Household Narrative* facts, freed by time and distance, and summoned forth anew by consonant emotions, are being translated into romance.

"The Bride's Chamber," the story that exhibits this new melding, is soon told. A scheming, mercenary man, put aside by a tormenting woman for a moneyed suitor, and then, when the lady becomes a rich widow, again tormented by her and again denied her, this time owing to her sudden death, determines that since he allowed himself to be tormented for money, and since he was put aside for money, he will compensate himself with money. His plan is to rear and eventually marry the widow's daughter, Ellen, now ten, and his ward, and then do away with her. The method of destruction he chooses is slow and terrible, but within the law—through long years of isolation, indoctrination, and psychological imposition, he destroys her ego and makes her a supine instrument of his will. She soon becomes compliant and fearful, and she performs a useless litany of propitiation; she constantly begs his pardon, pledges to do anything he wishes, pleads to be forgiven. At last, on her twenty-first birthday, he marries her, causes her to sign over her property to him, and then, while she begs to be forgiven, commands her to die. The isolated girl, deprived of any will or ego, constantly pleading to be forgiven, and constantly exhorted to die, proceeds in the course of time to do just that—the mercenary guardian has committed a murder which is no murder.

But for years he has been observed by a young man who again and again has climbed a tree in the garden of the house and peered through a window into the Bride's Chamber. The young man has fallen hopelessly in love with Ellen, has received a tress of hair from her, but has felt incapable of rescuing her. Now, with Ellen dead, the young man confronts the husband and accuses him of murder. The husband, seized by a spasm of uncontrollable hate, dashes a billhook through the young man's skull, and buries the body under the garden tree. Years go by and the mercenary man, fearful of discovery, remains in his dark mansion, compounding and multiplying his purloined riches. But one night a bolt of lightning cleaves the garden tree even as the young man's skull was cleft, and scientists who later come to examine the strangely split tree and to dig around its roots discover the young man's body and the billhook in his skull. The husband is apprehended, accused, ironically, of murdering his wife as well as the young man, and hanged. But even in death the husband has no peace. Every night his unshriven ghost is haunted by his innocent victims; and periodically, in doomed attempts to disburden himself, he must tell his guilty tale to spellbound listeners—Dickens at the moment is one such listener—who sojourn in the precincts of the Bride's Chamber.

This brief summary of a Gothic fairy tale emphasizes the improbable plot and ignores the elements that make the story memorable. Dickens characterized "The Bride's Chamber" as "a very odd story, with a wild, picturesque fancy in it"; he also called it a "grim" story, "a bit of Diablerie."[10] Indeed, the power of the story, like the power of Dickens' letter describing his yearning to rescue an unattainable princess, lies in its elementality, an elementality that depends upon fairy-tale correspondences and intensifications. These fairy-tale intensifications, usually of primary emotions, are achieved by a host of familiar touches and devices: by storybook phrasings, formulas, omens, repetitions, reversals, allusions, and the like, but most of all by the cunning use of profoundly evocative folklore motifs—the immured maiden, the garden tree, the token tress of hair, the tree-climbing suitor, the revelatory thunderbolt, the spellbound listener, the repeated confession of guilt, the unshriven and unshrivable narrator.

What concerns us here, however, is the way Dickens wedded these fairy-tale elements to the associations we have been tracing and to his current emotional state. *The Lazy Tour* is intensely and avowedly autobiographic; it records both the feelings and the events of Dickens' troubled flight away from self. Yet his personal revelations—and Dickens invariably revealed and concealed himself in his writings—are curiously, perhaps designedly, offhand, even lighthearted; his day-by-day account in *The Lazy Tour* of what he did and how he felt gives little hint that he was in the midst of the supreme sexual crisis of his life. "The Bride's Chamber" is an exception to this generalization. Perhaps, in a kind of emotional economy, what he suppressed by effort of will everywhere else in *The Lazy Tour* (even the title feigns an insouciance he did not feel), he released through imaginative fabling in "The Bride's Chamber." In any case, whether consciously or unconsciously, he seems to have projected paradigms of his current emotions into his desolate little fairy story.

The white-clad bride is treated in two very different ways, both of which reflect Dickens' state. As a wife, the bride is destroyed by her husband; as the object of a forbidden love, she is secretly adored by her admirer. The husband's chief crime, the destruction of his wife's identity through the imposition of his dominating will, is a version of Dickens' current treatment of his wife, Catherine (Catherine also is a weak, self-effacing woman, soon to be put away); at the same time, the husband's crime is a version of Dickens' treatment of his adored "Princess," Ellen Ternan (Ellen Ternan, like the Ellen of the story, is an inexperienced, teen-aged girl overwhelmed by a masterful, middle-aged man). In the story this destructive domination of another's personality is accompanied by massive externalized guilt. Dickens not only makes his protagonist a murderer, but requires that the villain's ghost be haunted through all eternity by the innocent creatures he has so grievously subdued. In other words, Dickens' tormented involvement with his wife and with Ellen Ternan—he cannot forbear naming the bride "Ellen"—is partly reflected in the bride's enforced submission to the protagonist and in the protagonist's eternal contemplation of that ruinous submission. By the same token, the warring aspects of Dickens' emotional predicament are also bodied forth in the two male adversaries of the story: Dickens the restless husband gives guilty virulence to the middle-aged, unloving, wife-tormenting villain; Dickens the illicit adorer gives yearning intensity to the young, passionate, disqualified lover. And fittingly, if one looks upon these adversaries as conflicting aspects of Dickens' emotional state, it is Dickens the husband who makes impossible or "murders" Dickens the lover.

These emotional tensions underlie "The Bride's Chamber." But the emotions are wedded to images and themes that have been accumulating for years. The bride is more than a bride, more even than an autobiographical Dickensian bride, she is a version of the blighted specter in white who had seized Dickens' youthful imagination. Here, dense with fairy-tale cadences and fairy-tale repetitions, is how that white specter appears in her new, ghost-story role:

> When he came into the Bride's Chamber . . . he found her withdrawn to the furthest corner, and there standing pressed against the paneling as if she would have shrunk through it: her flaxen hair all wild about her face, and her large eyes staring at him in vague terror.
>
> .   .   .   .
>
> There were spots of ink upon the bosom of her white dress, and they made her face look whiter and her eyes look larger as she nodded her head. There were spots of ink upon the hand with which she stood before him, nervously plaiting and folding her white skirts.[11]

And here is the way his blighted, white-clad bride appears at the moment of her death: "Paler in the pale light, more colourless than ever in the leaden dawn, he saw her coming, trailing herself along the floor towards him—a white wreck of hair, and dress, and wild eyes."[12]

The blighted bride lives in a blighted house encircled by a ruined garden—a gloomy version of the isolated house and walled garden in which white-clad Martha Joachim had imprisoned herself; a remarkable premonition of the ruined mansion, ruined garden, and ruined bride's chamber in which white-clad Miss Havisham would soon be immured. Here is a glimpse of this desolate precursor of Satis House: "Eleven years she had lived in the dark house and its gloomy garden. He was jealous of the very light and air getting to her, and they kept her close. He stopped the wide chimneys, shaded the little windows, left the strong-stemmed ivy to wander where it would over the house-front, the moss to accumulate on the untrimmed fruit-trees in the red-walled garden, the weeds to over-run its green and yellow walks. He surrounded her with images of sorrow and desolation."[13]

Added to this atmosphere of decay, imprisonment, and manipulation, and superimposed upon the figure of the blighted white-clad bride, is the corrupting influence of money. As in *Great Expectations,* the sin of valuing money more than men pervades and integrates the story. But the pecuniary similarities go further. In both works the destructive forces are set in motion when a projected marriage is broken off for monetary considerations. And again in both works the injured party destroys himself and all those around him in attempts to assuage his injury by monetary means. In "The Bride's Chamber" the money motif works with fablelike simplicity. The villain, who has been denied marriage owing to lack of money, seeks recompense through a marriage that will bring him money. Dickens underlines this mercenary equation by means of a refrain that recurs throughout the story: "He wanted compensation in Money." The refrain, in turn, is elaborated and counterpointed, in Christmas-book manner, by dozens of repeated images, phrases, and episodes. The villain's awareness that the white-clad bride is dead is conveyed, for example, as follows: "He was not at first so sure it was done, but that the morning sun was hanging jewels in her hair—he saw the diamond, emerald, and ruby, glittering among it in little points, as he stood looking down at her."[14] The implication, in terms of the fable, is clear. The villain now has his longed-for "compensation in money," but his treasure, as this scene hints and as we finally see, is as illusory as the insubstantial jewels that glitter momentarily in his dead victim's hair. One is reminded of the glittering jewels that Miss Havisham hangs in Estella's hair. They too preach a message of false values and deluded longing. As poor Pip will discover to his endless dole, the fiery jewels in Estella's hair are fiery only in appearance; deprived of their reflected light, they are as hard and cold and pitiless as longed-for Estella herself.

The relationship between "The Bride's Chamber" and *Great Expectations* is profound, but it is also limited. The two works have much in common: a blighted bride in white, a decaying mansion, a ruined garden, an encircling wall, a prisonlike bride's chamber, a money nexus, a preoccupation with crime, a focus on the sin of using another human being as an instrument, a reflection of Dickens' involvement with Ellen Ternan, and a fairy-tale emphasis. Yet the two works go their separate ways; each has its own logic and its own integrity. The brief ghost story with its pervasive supernaturalism and its folklore elements is no miniature *Great Expectations*. What is of special interest here is the way Dickens enlarged and refashioned old images and motifs. The Berners Street White Woman and Martha Joachim are now associated with larger considerations: with the manipulation of other human beings and with the corrosive effects of money. Places have been similarly transformed. The walled mansion of the *Household Narrative* is now more than a walled mansion: it has become the physical correlative of isolation, repression, and imprisonment. There is rearrangement as well as elaboration. Old themes have been joined in fresh configurations: commercial ethics, hopeless passion, and murderous aggression, brought together originally in naked conjunction, now whisper of darker connections. A great centripetal force is silently working. The Berners Street eccentric, the *Household Narrative* news columns, the breakup of Dickens' marriage, and the other influences that shaped *Great Expectations* are being pulled into orbit. Pip and Magwitch, Miss Havisham and Satis House are waiting to be born.

But we are not done yet. Why—to probe still further into questions we cannot answer with certainty—did Dickens begin *Great Expectations* some ten years after that fateful issue of the *Household Narrative* and some three years after the turmoil and the synthesis of "The Bride's Chamber"?

Perhaps that commencement was shaped and heralded by the fact that the street frequented by the White Woman—Berners Street, Oxford Street—again entered Dickens' everyday life, again dramatically and unforgettably, a year or so before he began *Great Expectations*. For No. 31 Berners Street, Oxford Street was Ellen Ternan's residence in 1858 and probably in 1859, a residence that Dickens himself seems to have procured for her, and a residence that Ellen and her sister moved to when Dickens sent Ellen's mother and Fanny Ternan to Italy. In any case, by virtue of this strange Berners Street conjunction and Dickens' latter-day visits to Berners Street, those motifs of self-wounding love—versions of "The Bride's Chamber" motifs of secrecy, forbidden passion, and social prohibitions—which he would soon attach to the Estella-Pip node of *Great Expectations,* became merged still further with the cluster of associations surrounding his Berners Street White Woman and the January 1850 issue of the *Household Narrative*. In other words, in 1858 and 1859 the Estella-Pip cluster became further fused with the Magwitch-Miss Havisham cluster and with myriads of associations going back to Dickens' boyhood.

The "long chain"—to use Dickens' metaphor again—was being hammered and beaten into shape; some of the great unconscious links at the center of *Great Expectations* were now almost complete. But the process went on. The slow preliminary forging, so strange, so secret, so submerged, continued until the moment Dickens put pen to paper. It went on, for instance, during the scramble to produce the weekly issues of his new magazine, *All the Year Round*. Late in 1859, several months before beginning *Great Expectations,* Dickens had to wrestle with *The Haunted House,* the extra Christmas number of *All the Year Round* for 1859. One of the stories he solicited and then carefully edited for that Christmas issue was "The Ghost in the Garden Room" by Mrs. Gaskell. "The Ghost," as chance and design would have it, contained a host of themes and juxtapositions that propelled Dickens still more rapidly in the direction he was going. For Mrs. Gaskell's story centers on a young Piplike character, a naive provincial named Ben, who is given a superior education, turned into a gentleman, and then sent off to London for final polishing—preferments made possible through the loving sacrifices of his humble father and mother. Ben, who values outward trappings more than inward grace, develops into a snob, neglects his lowly family, and ultimately becomes a criminal.

There are many scenes in Ben's early progress that remind one of Pip. For example, before going off to the false ascendency of London, Ben is fitted out with a gentleman's wardrobe, displaying all the while the same vainglorious pomposity that Pip exhibits when he too is fitted out for translation to London gentility. The story also contains a simple Joelike character (Ben's father) who unexpectedly comes into a small fortune when a distant uncle dies. As in *Great Expectations,* the fortune produces ill rather than good; it accentuates Ben's weaknesses rather than his strengths. Finally, there is Bessy, an unappreciated Biddylike character. Bessy—the names "Bessy" and "Biddy" are cognate—is a sisterly cousin who lives modestly in the home of these simple people, and who loves Ben quietly and self-effacingly. Beyond these fundamental parallels, there is an attitude and a feeling that remind one of *Great Expectations.* There is a sense of the blessedness of a simple, steadfast life; there is a consciousness of the corrupting power of money and of city ways; there is an appreciation of the true nature of gentility. But "The Ghost," like "The Bride's Chamber," is no embryo *Great Expectations.* As "The Ghost" develops, it moves further and further away from Dickens' interests and tendencies. And beyond this, Mrs. Gaskell's tale lacks the deep resonance and profound genius of Dickens' richly reverberating fable. Yet given the nature of Dickens' long-accumulating sensitivities and his sympathetic imagination, the early portions of "The Ghost" must have spoken movingly to his innermost awareness. In any case, several months after reading "The Ghost," Dickens took up some of its primary themes and configurations, wonderfully deepening and transforming them in Pip's errant pilgrimage.

That errant pilgrimage was now about to begin. The vagrant accretions of chance and circumstance were virtually complete. By 1860, all the entangled motifs and impulses that I have been tracing—and other, less discernible, influences—were floating in Dickens' mind. The long intricate gestation of *Great Expectations* had gone on for more than thirty-five years. In the last years and months before Dickens sat down to begin his novel, the crucial associations that I have been tracking were intensifying and drawing closer together. Perhaps some stray stimulus—some chance remark or sight or sound—catalyzed this highly charged constellation at the heart of *Great Expectations.* Perhaps some other influence—the sudden appearance on Dickens' desk of Mrs. Gaskell's doleful story of rough felons and a snobbish made gentleman, or the weekly installments in *All the Year Round* of Collins' novel of a white-robed woman, criminals, and death by fire—

quickened that waiting core. If Collins' novel supplied the final impetus, Dickens was responding in large part to his own creation, or more precisely to images and associations that *The Woman in White* shared with his own creation. For Collins' novel, with its monetary motivation, imprisoning mansion, victimized woman in white, manipulated identities, and murderous aggressions, was profoundly influenced by "The Bride's Chamber," the Gothic fairy tale that Dickens had told less than two years earlier in their joint work, *The Lazy Tour.* When Dickens read *The Woman in White,* therefore, he was reading an echo of what he himself had written, a recension of scenes and subjects that had stirred his imagination since childhood.

Such strange returns and coincidences engross and provoke us. But the heart of the matter eludes us still. We can look before and after, we can come close—very close—to the mystery of creation, but then we are forced to stop. The shaping process itself—the process that ultimately created *Great Expectations,* the process that selects, adds, orders, reshapes, and then finally brings forth, the process, in short, that transforms experience into art—that process goes on, as always, in silence and obscurity. The materials the imagination works on, the brute facts, even the fateful clusters of associations, are inchoate and elemental; suggestive though they are, they are parameters, not resolutions; they convey no rich insights, no extraordinary meanings, no reverberating contexts; they tell us of the anarchy of life, not the order of art. We value *Great Expectations* not for what went into it, but for what emerged from that humdrum given. We know the given all too well; we daily see the tantalizing gulf that separates it from art. In the *Household Narrative* as in life itself, the White Woman is no avenging vessel of fate, no godmother and no witch; the rude emigrant father is no dark projection of his child's guilt, no fairy-tale instrument of his redemption; Miss Gordon's scorched arms are the result of an accident, they bear no witness to the searing consanguinity of sin; Miss Martha Joachim's white dress is a sign of her eccentricity, it is no infinitely varied, endlessly accreting reminder that she has married death in life.

These latter lessons, as they emerge in *Great Expectations,* the product of so strange and slow a genesis, are the province and the gift of art. For art allows us to see ourselves and sometimes to see into ourselves; art multiplies and magnifies, orders and clarifies. And in and through art, ever remote, yet ever powerful, the imagination works its will. The imagination need reject nothing; it can merge the huggermugger of journalism with the heart's desire and with the transient flotsam of life. It can fashion a new-old song from a weird Woman in

White, an evocative "title of titles," a would-be emigrant, a routine inquest, a York Buildings allusion, a Berners Street residence, a Christmas accident, a made gentleman, an adored "Princess," and a broken marriage—and it can make that song sing to all the busy world.

9 | *Great Expectations*
The Fairy-Tale Transformation

Great Expectations opens on Christmas Eve in a nettle-choked churchyard. The sun is setting; the evening air is raw and biting; the outlines of persons and objects are gradually growing treacherous and indistinct; the lowering atmosphere is oppressive and filled with secret signs. This chill, crepuscular Christmas Eve commencement, heavy with hidden warnings and foreboding portents, is not new. We have encountered such inductions before. We are reminded of ghost stories, nurses' tales, and eerie legends told at twilight—but then these do not all begin on Christmas Eve. The immediate model is at once more exact and closer at hand. The opening of *Great Expectations* is nothing more nor less than a redaction of the archetypal onset of Dickens' Christmas fairy stories: of "Gabriel Grub," *A Christmas Carol,* and *The Haunted Man*.

Pip's initiation is true to form. Pip stands before the graves of his father, mother, and five brothers. For the first time in his young life he is truly conscious of himself and the world about him, and at this fateful moment a terrible convict with a great iron upon his leg starts up from among the graves—out of them, it seems—seizes him, and turns him upside down. Through his inverted legs, Pip glimpses the church steeple; then the whole church revolves, and he sits trembling on a high tombstone. A few moments later the convict again tilts the giddy boy until, with a last tremendous dip and roll, the church once more jumps over its weathercock and little Pip is returned to the tall gravestone. Terrified by the convict and his fierce threats, but pitying the wretch also, Pip makes an "awful promise"; he enters into a secret compact to help the ferocious outlaw.[1] After the compact is sealed, the boy runs across the lonely marshes toward his home and the glowing forge. The marshes, intersected here and there with dykes and mounds and gates, stretch away into the distance, where a glimmering river steals silently toward the sea. From the sea a savage wind rushes, and on the horizon, tiny against a sky barred with long angry lines of red and black, stand a beacon and a chain-hung gibbet.

The secret compact, the river, the leg iron, the gates, the beacon, the chains, the mounds, the gibbet, the barred sky—all play their essential parts in *Great Expectations*. Yet this intricate harmony, so complex and distinctive, so filled in addition with other motifs—with weird women in white, made gentlemen, and the slowly accumulating associations of more than thirty-five years—this rich harmony reminds us, despite its intricacy and singularity, of its rudimentary antecedents. As in "Gabriel Grub," *A Christmas Carol,* and *The Haunted Man,* so also in *Great Expectations:* a grim Christmas Eve ghost rises terrifically out of the past to chasten and instruct the erring protagonist. And when outlawed Magwitch emerges from the graves and turns Pip's dawning consciousness topsy-turvy, the act epitomizes the inverted fairy tale that Dickens is about to tell.

That fairy tale gives order and concision to the autobiographical, factual, social, and moral complexities of *Great Expectations* and helps endow the novel with the universality of myth. The myth, an ironic myth of man's desire and reward, is compounded of Dickens' most profound experiences; for *Great Expectations* was to be another first-person novel in the manner of *David Copperfield*, with "the hero to be a boy-child, like David."[2] Accordingly, before going to work on Pip's adventures, Dickens reread *Copperfield* "to be quite sure," as he put it, that he "had fallen into no unconscious repetitions."[3] There are no obvious repetitions, yet David and Pip are alike in many ways: they are both orphaned, they are both rescued from deadening childhood drudgery, they are both "sponsored" by eccentric "single" ladies, they are both given unexpected fortunes, they are both wounded by masochistic loves, they are both bereft of their expectations, and they are both forced to make their own chastened ways in life.

The autobiographical parallels are there also. *David Copperfield* is often direct, scarcely modified autobiography. *Great Expectations* is more subterranean, less recognizable in its real-life analogues. Yet the autobiography of *Great Expectations,* sometimes hidden, sometimes cunningly altered, is frequently all the more revealing because of its displacements. Protected by those displacements, Dickens can plumb the most intricate mysteries of his secret life. To mention only the most central and most obvious autobiographical parallels, Pip, like Dickens, came from lowly origins, felt himself an outcast, yearned to rise, attained wealth, entered polite society, failed to find happiness, and all

the while hid what he considered his shaming taint: the formative
episode of his childhood. Magwitch, starting up from the graves, is, in
many ways, the personification of that taint; and Pip's self-deluding
desire to run from Magwitch when the convict has returned from exile
is similar to Dickens' own attempts to run from his past. Pip's salvation
through Magwitch then becomes Dickens' mature recognition—
expressed more than once elsewhere—that his great gift was partially
created and permanently shaped by the childhood experiences he
sought to disown.

But the Pip-Magwitch relationship is no simple duality, and it is no
exclusionary focus; other areas of Dickens' life went into Pip—and
into Dickens' complex fable. Pip's sense of secret guilt suggests Dickens' own psychological condition while he was writing *Great Expectations*. Dickens was then deeply involved in a secret love relationship, a
relationship that produced—witness "The Bride's Chamber"—a Piplike sense of hidden participation in evil, even in murder. But Dickens
is also Magwitch: guilt-ridden, crudely educated, alienated; while Pip is
a synthesis of Dickens' disappointing sons: lackadaisical, materialistic,
drifting, snobbish—made gentlemen by Dickens' laboriously accumulated wealth (as Pip was by Magwitch's), unaware of their father's
origins or his early shame (as Pip was unaware of his benefactor's
history). While writing *Great Expectations,* Dickens was much concerned with his sons and their "expectations." He had sent one son to
Eton, three others to Wimbledon, and would soon send a fifth to Wimbledon and Cambridge; and he had made or was about to make further,
and largely unsuccessful, financial and gentlemanly provisions for two
additional sons. The contrast between his own secret childhood, his
role as a "labouring hind," and his sons' positions as Eton boys and
Cambridge scholars; his anguish as the rejected suitor of Maria Beadnell, rejected owing to his inferior social position and humdrum expectations, and his sons' easy acceptance by the intellectual and social
élite—these contrasts are at the heart of *Great Expectations*.

All this and more went into the book. Pip is formed by the two
regions that molded Dickens—Chatham and London. The whole of
Great Expectations takes place in the precincts of these alternating
loadstones. In *Great Expectations* the blacking warehouse becomes
the blacksmith's forge, and Pip upon his apprenticeship to Joe feels the
same sense of imprisonment that Dickens felt when his family went to
prison and he was contracted to the warehouse. That sense of imprisonment is intimately associated with shame and unworthiness, even
with sinfulness and criminality. Dickens' hidden blacking-warehouse
initiation into prison and dark experiences is psychologically analogous, therefore, to Pip's hidden tainting by crime and criminals. But for
Pip as for Dickens, the past will not remain hidden; it constantly starts

up out of the grave, it constantly reaches into the present and trammels his everyday life. When gentleman Pip, on one occasion, goes down to his childhood home, he travels huddled together with two leg-ironed convicts being transferred to the fearsome Chatham convict hulk of Dickens' own childhood. One of these shackled prisoners, who has had early dealings with Pip and Magwitch, all through that actual and psychological journey back to childhood, breathes heavily upon the unrecognized young man, and causes him to shrink from this breath of the past and to feel as though he had been "touched in the marrow with some pungent and searching acid."[4] When Pip gets off the coach, his thoughts again wander back to childhood, to "the wicked Noah's Ark lying out on the black water"—a recurrent phrase which embodies his (and Dickens') childhood image of the convict hulk—and then he is overcome by yet another sensation that Dickens often experienced: "I could not have said what I was afraid of, for my fear was altogether undefined and vague, but there was great fear upon me. . . . I am confident that it took no distinctness of shape, and that it was the revival for a few minutes of the terror of childhood."[5]

Bit by bit, in profound and in trivial ways, Dickens adds other pieces to the autobiographical mosaic. When Pip, in the noontime of his expectations, returns to the "quiet old town" of his childhood and records how people would purposely go a little way down the street before him that "they might turn, as if they had forgotten something," and pass him face to face, he is recording what the famous Dickens often experienced when he returned to his childhood town.[6] And when Pip, after his climactic scene with Estella, decides in his frustrated love that he "could do nothing half so good for myself as tire myself out," and thereupon spends most of the night walking from Rochester to London, he is performing the same numbing thirty-mile feat that Dickens imposed upon himself in his own crisis of frustrated love.[7]

Pip's love reflects the strange, complex loves of Dickens' life. Pip in his open-eyed, self-wounding, impossible love for Estella is like Dickens in his masochistic teen-aged love for Maria Beadnell or his forbidden middle-aged love for eighteen-year-old Ellen Ternan. And in a curiously revealing, quasi-fictional, quasi-autobiographical manner, Estella is both good and bad sister and good and bad sexual object—an opposition that is developed even more elaborately than usual in *Great Expectations* by the use of two additional sister figures. Mrs. Gargery, who rears Pip, but is also his sister, is a persecuting mother-sister figure, a combination, in many ways, of Dickens' most negative feelings toward his mother and his sister Fanny. On this inimical mother-sister, Dickens calls down the retribution of massive assault, paralysis, and death. Sisterly Biddy, on the other hand, is Pip's asexual confidante: she listens while he confesses his passion for the unattain-

able Estella, and she plays a surrogate-sister role reminiscent of Mary
Hogarth and Georgina Hogarth. Significantly, when Biddy, at the end
of the book, is about to be turned by Pip—so he thinks—from loving
asexual sister and housekeeper into sexual wife, she dashes his expectations by revealing that she is already married to Pip's stepfather.

These biographical parallels have their own intrinsic significance.
They are a remembrance of things past; they are also part of Dickens'
self-exploration and self-knowledge. But they are surcharged with additional meanings, meanings that accrue from Dickens' intricate modes
of presentation and organization. By presenting his experiences in
mythic patterns, he makes them universal; by ordering them in fairy-
tale configurations, he escapes the trammels of reductive realism; by
distorting them in wish-fulfilling ways, he achieves self-catharsis. This
plurality of effects is simultaneous and mutually reinforcing.

Dickens is an author who frequently, perhaps compulsively, freighted his work with cathartic autobiography. In his early writings, in the
brilliantly satiric American scenes of *Martin Chuzzlewit*, for example,
these autobiographical materials were usually forced upon the structure, disturbing and weakening it. However, in the Christmas books,
those five experimental fairy tales of the mid-1840s, Dickens developed, along with many other technical advances, methods for wedding
autobiography unobtrusively to the more universal levels of the story;
after the Christmas books, autobiography usually increases the psychological richness of his work and strengthens his art.

One method Dickens uses to achieve this new synthesis is a method
he worked out in his Christmas books—one can see it with especial
clarity in *The Haunted Man*—the method of the psychological and
autobiographical double. As early as *Martin Chuzzlewit* (in the schizoid
state of Jonas Chuzzlewit at the time of the murder), Dickens had
experimented with the fragmented objectification of a disturbed or
warring consciousness. But it was in his Christmas fairy stories that he
first elaborated this technique, and it was with Redlaw in *The Haunted
Man*, who is an even more detailed surrogate of Dickens than the
young Scrooge, that he connected it most effectively with his own
history. For Dickens, then, the doppelgänger technique, although he
invariably interfused it with realistic and autobiographical materials, is
part of a fairy-tale conception.

In his post-Christmas-book novels, Dickens enlarges and elaborates
this and many other fairy-tale techniques. He often creates an atmosphere in which the supernatural seems plausible; or, conversely, he
takes supernatural events and creatures and gives them a factual un-
derpinning. Or, yet again, by a species of double vision, he imposes an
aura of fantasy and enchantment on everyday life: a real provincial
mansion gradually metamorphoses into a strange gloomy labyrinthine

hell, an ordinary Walworth house miraculously changes into a miniature moated castle, a veritable London recluse slowly emerges as a
frightful storybook witch, an accidental fire somehow becomes a fierce
sin-scourging flame. Such transformations build that extrarational resonance that causes the reader to suspend his disbelief. Dickens can
now safely use other nonrealistic devices and magical manipulations—spells, prophetic signs, portentous rituals, fated retributions,
hidden blood relationships—to emphasize his thesis and enforce the
demands of poetic justice.

In his later novels these transformations are handled so subtly, are
combined with the more realistic aspects of the story so skillfully, that
they become a major, though often unnoticed, part of the central design. In *Great Expectations* Dickens manages these transformations
with supreme mastery. To take, for the moment, just one example, he
controls the dispersal of identity, the doubling and tripling of the ego,
with exquisite refinement.

As with Redlaw in *The Haunted Man,* whose divided mind creates a
phantom counterimage of himself, Pip the innocent and later the "gentleman" is attended by his dark shadow, Magwitch—the criminal and
outcast. But Pip is no schizophrenic Redlaw, divided neatly in two; Pip
is attended by many other realistic characters who reflect or extend or
illuminate his personality. He is associated with Estella, who has been
distorted by the same agencies that twist him; with Biddy, who resists
those distorting forces; with Joe, who also remains uncorrupted; with
Herbert, a superior version of himself, and thus the male counterpart of
Biddy and the contemporary counterpart of Joe; with Miss Havisham,
whose sin, and punishment, are linked to his; with Drummle, who is a
degenerate version of himself, the negative image of Herbert; and with
Orlick, who is Pip's most terrifying extension, an extension of nascent,
inexplicable malignancy. Dickens frequently complicates these moral
and psychological resonances. Thus Joe is also contrasted with Orlick,
Estella with Biddy, Magwitch with Miss Havisham, Herbert with
Drummle, Estella with Clara. At the same time Magwitch is likened to
Compeyson, Compeyson to Miss Havisham, Miss Havisham to
Matthew Pocket, and on and on. Jaggers is juxtaposed not only
to Wemmick but to a hidden segment of himself; Wemmick is contrasted so schizophrenically that he leads two totally opposed lives;
and Pip, whose divided mind is partly exemplified by his chief extensions (by Magwitch, Orlick, and Herbert), also reveals his ambivalence
in his own person: in his guilty vacillations between desire and duty.

Through this intricate counterpoint Dickens gives structure and
meaning to his novel. His use of Dolge Orlick is a case in point, and one
that demonstrates how fundamental this technique had become to his
art. Orlick is a character whose sinister relationships and heightened

fairy-tale attributes accentuate rather than diminish his realism and his significance. Orlick is an objectification of Pip's darkest desires and aggressions; he is also an independent manifestation of primal evil. This ambiguity gives Orlick his special effectiveness. It also gives Pip a part of his psychological complexity.

Orlick is swarthy, truculent, and powerful. In his role as the archetypal personification of evil, he slouches in and out of the book "like Cain or the Wandering Jew."[8] Although only twenty-five, he refers to himself as "Old Orlick" — and of course he *is* old, timeless — old as evil, as the devil, as Old Nick. As a matter of fact, Orlick's name is simply a version of Old Nick: Oldnick — Orlick. Orlick's infernalism is no metaphor; Dickens, combining Christian, classical, and fairy-tale motifs, gradually builds him into a lowering version of Satan. Orlick spends his Sundays not in church, but lying on sluice gates (his home is with a sluice keeper), and later he becomes the gatekeeper of tomblike Satis House. His association with gates is appropriate, for as we finally come to perceive, he is a keeper of the infernal gates. His occupation is no less symbolic. He is a blacksmith, hammering at his Vulcan's forge, beating his sparks in Pip's direction, his eyes fixed morosely on the ground. Orlick's role is simultaneously counterpoised to Joe's and to Pip's. Joe is the harmonious blacksmith, the friend of man, the Promethean keeper of the glowing forge; Pip, the dissatisfied apprentice blacksmith, lies somewhere between Joe and Orlick — he is wayward vulnerable man poised between good and evil.

Orlick the devil is constantly lashing out, and his attacks meet with carefully graded degrees of success. Good inviolable Joe (Pip's forgiving and protecting godfather) he cannot touch. In a prototypical scene of confrontation, Orlick fights Joe, is subdued and then pardoned by him. But the devil claims his own. Pip's shrewish sister, whom Orlick himself christens "Mother Gargery," and who, in keeping with her witch's name and witch's actions, provokes a fight between Orlick and Joe, is felled savagely by Orlick. Later, paralytic and diminished, she dumbly propitiates Orlick, as a cowed Caliban-mortal might acknowledge and then propitiate a vengeful devil-god. Then she dies.

Pip barely escapes a similar death, and he does not escape being seared by Orlick's hell-fire. The antipathy between Orlick and Pip is instinctive, but it is combined with an element of fascination. The combination occurs often in Dickens. It is the attractive antipathy between frail humanity and beckoning evil, but here it has been individualized and deepened, made more psychologically complex and believable, and also more universal. Dickens realizes he is portraying an actual and an archetypal contest, and he fuses the simple details of his realistic narrative with their cosmic correlatives. "This morose journeyman," says Pip, speaking of Orlick, "had no liking for me."

And then Pip reveals Orlick's lineage and foreshadows his own double trial by fire: "When I was very small and timid, [Orlick] gave me to understand that the Devil lived in a black corner of the forge, and that he knew the fiend very well: also that it was necessary to make up the fire, once in seven years, with a live boy, and that I might consider myself fuel."[9] As so often in Dickens, evil—slightly softened in retrospect by defensive humor, but evil nevertheless—has its birth in a relationship between an adult and a child, and is conveyed through an horrific fairy-tale threat.

But Pip and Orlick are more than blacksmith helpers to blacksmith Joe, and they are more than symbols, respectively, of frailty and malignancy; they are part of the novel's psychological presentation, they are alter-ego counterparts. This alter-ego relationship penetrates scores of scenes and emerges in hundreds of touches. When Joe gives Pip a half holiday, Orlick demands one too. Orlick's manner of insisting upon his demand is heavy with meaning:

> "Why, what'll you do with a half-holiday, if you get it?" said Joe.
> "What'll *I* do with it? What'll *he* do with it? I'll do as much with it as *him*," said Orlick.
> "As to Pip, he's going up-town," said Joe.
> "Well then, as to Old Orlick, *he's* a-going up-town . . . Two can go up-town. Tain't only one wot can go up-town."[10]

Orlick's surly insistence on a twinlike mutuality, together with the many analogues and elaborations of that mutuality throughout the novel, helps turn the morose blacksmith and gatekeeper into Pip's dark shadow and aggressive extension. Orlick, after fighting Joe and being subdued by him, receives his half holiday, but that night he revenges himself upon Pip's sister by sneaking up behind her and beating her to the kitchen floor with Magwitch's discarded leg iron. Pip is not present at this outrage, but he shares in the crime, and not simply by virtue of his alter-ego relationship with Orlick. Pip's disputed half holiday was the first link in the chain of events that led to Orlick's attack; and Pip himself had supplied the stolen file that Magwitch used to file off his leg iron. Thus Pip provides the occasion and the instrument that lead to his sister's murder. But even setting aside these involvements, Pip's lifelong hostility toward his sister is enough to make him feel a guilty responsibility for her violent downfall. His guilt, therefore, is tenable and simultaneous on every level of the story. That this is so accords with Pip's—and Dickens'—abnormal sense of guilt, and with Dickens' typically ambivalent treatment, here and elsewhere, of the brother-sister relationship.

In the remainder of the book Orlick fulfills his triple role as swarthy journeyman, malignant devil, and dark alter ego. He hovers about Pip and Biddy, shadowing the former and paying demonic court to the latter—a caricature reversal of Pip's neglect of Biddy. His actions become increasingly meaningful. Here, for instance, is the way he materializes in front of Pip and Biddy as they stroll across the marshes:

> When we came near the churchyard, we had to cross an embankment, and get over a stile near a sluice gate. There started up, from the gate, or from the rushes, or from the ooze (which was quite in his stagnant way), Old Orlick.
> "Halloa!" he growled, "where are you two going?"
> "Where should we be going, but home?"
> "Well, then," said he, "I'm jiggered if I don't see you home!"[11]

Old Orlick's wraithlike emergence from the primeval slime and his association with the symbolic gate (as well as his equally significant opposition to "churchyard") are merged here with his alter-ego shadowing. Much later, when Orlick becomes the gatekeeper of Satis House, Dickens' imagery and irony take on increasingly somber overtones. These overtones reach a climax in a crucial gate scene, a scene interspersed with images of gates, locks, keys, cages, prisons, convicts, and guns, recurrent images whose meanings have been expanding and ramifying as the book progresses. In that crucial gate scene, as Orlick morosely tends the gates of Satis House, he radiates his dark devil's role with fierce aggressiveness, and he foreshadows Pip's imminent double burning. When Pip asks gatekeeper Orlick whether he should go up to Miss Havisham, Orlick responds with the premonitory words, "Burn me!" Pip then says, "I am expected, I believe?" Orlick's reply is exact and full of fearful meaning. "Burn me twice over!" he says.[12] As Orlick suggests, Pip's purification by fire will be double. First he will be burned trying to save Miss Havisham from the flames, then he will be burned by the infernal Orlick himself.

The second burning—the fulfillment and resolution of Orlick's devil role—occurs in the remarkable scene in which Pip undergoes the harrowing that prepares him for redemption and regeneration. Pip has been lured by Orlick to his lair upon the marshes. His journey to that lair—simultaneously a journey to the underworld and an encounter with the devil—is introduced by foreboding symbolism. The marshes, the sky, the moon, the stars, the clouds, the distant lights, the hulks, the old Battery, the wind—all recall the opening scenes of the novel, but now each detail is made to prefigure Pip's fateful return to his sources, his climactic confrontation with evil and himself.

As Pip crosses the marshes, he closes a series of gates behind him, and finally he approaches the region of hell itself. He passes a lime kiln, "burning with a sluggish stifling smell" (it is the hell-fire furnace in which Orlick plans to burn his body), then he descends below the level of the marshes into a small stone quarry, Orlick's new and appropriate subterranean place of work, and finally he comes to the old sluice house, the house of gates—his place of rendezvous.[13] The house is surrounded by lime-coated "mud and ooze," the primitive slime out of which Old Orlick emerged. As Pip approaches the gatekeeper's house, the "choking vapour of the kiln" creeps "in a ghostly way towards" him. For a while he stands irresolutely in the entranceway, the acrid fumes engulfing him in the burning reek of hell. Then he decides. He passes through the gate and crosses the infernal threshold. In an instant he is pinioned by Orlick. Pip's burned arm—which recalls his participation in Miss Havisham's sin, a sin and wound less than hers, not fatal as hers, but growing out of the same sources and seared by the same flame—now fittingly causes him "exquisite pain."[14]

Satan Orlick, his victim secured, fastens Pip to a ladder—"the means of ascent to the loft above." But for Pip the loft above, as the ladder and the context suggest, is as far removed as heaven. Pip's destiny seems to be elsewhere; he is trapped in the dark and vaporous pit. At the moment of pinioning, the sole light in the suffocating room had been extinguished. In the pitchy darkness, Orlick picks up flint and steel and begins to strike a new light. The flint clashes and clashes on the metal and bright sparks spurt up. The sparks shower thickly about Orlick's downturned face, and Pip, tightly bound, and immersed in darkness, strains unavailingly to see his savage assailant. Years before, blacksmith Orlick had hammered ominously, beating bright sparks in Pip's direction; now Orlick strikes and strikes again, a fearsome devil flinging bright sparks into the sulfurous blackness. The sparks continue to spurt forth. Then, as the damp tinder smolders feebly and Orlick breathes upon its dim glow, his lips—but his lips only—emerge from the choking blackness; they hover menacingly in the dark, two disembodied streaks of flickering blue. Once the light is lit, Orlick begins to torment Pip. "Now . . . I've got you," says Orlick. "Unbind me," cries Pip in allegorical phrase. "Let me go! . . . Why have you set upon me in the dark?" "Oh you enemy, you enemy!" replies Orlick.[15]

Pip is in hell, the captive of the devil; but, at this supreme moment of Orlick's Satanism, Dickens makes Orlick's alter-ego quality explicit. He does this adroitly, and he does it through a modified version of the Haunted Man's alter-ego colloquies:

> "Wolf!" [says Orlick] "Old Orlick's a-going to tell you somethink. It was you as did for your shrew sister." . . .
> "It was you, villain," said I.
> "I tell you it was your doing—I tell you it was done through you . . . I come upon her from behind, as I come upon you to-night. I giv' it her! . . . But it warn't Old Orlick as did it; it was you. You was favoured, and he

was bullied and beat. . . . Now you pays for it. You done it; now you pays for it."[16]

Pip pays for his remote complicity, both wish-fulfilling and circumstantial, in his sister's death, just as he pays for every atom of sin that touches his life. But his very human sinning is merged with its opposite; his sinning and its chastening consequences help him toward redemption, and out of the inextricable web of good and evil (*The Haunted Man* again) he slowly fashions his salvation.

That salvation can begin only after Pip has been purged by the hellish fires his sins have kindled. Orlick (here both Satan and alter ego) now takes up a candle (it was a candle, Estella's starlike candle, that led Pip into the dark mazes of Satis House) and, flaring it so close to Pip that Pip must turn his face aside "to save it from the flame," begins that terrible purification.[17] The cleansing continues to the verge of death, and Pip loses consciousness.

When he comes back to life, he lies "unbound" on the floor, his eyes "fixed on the ladder." "What night is to-night?" asks the newly seeing Pip. "How long have I been here?" "I had a strange and strong misgiving," he continues, "that I had been lying there a long time—a day and a night—two days and nights—more." But Pip's long night of labyrinthine wandering is almost over. "The time has not gone by," says Herbert, speaking of Magwitch's imminent try for freedom, but also suggesting, in the context, Pip's own struggle for salvation. "Thank God!" replies Pip. When asked what hurt he has, he replies, "I have no hurt but in this throbbing arm."[18] Pip has passed safely through hell, but his throbbing arm, throbbing from his previous burning and present trussing and symbolic of his unexpiated sin, is a reminder that he has not yet been regenerated. Some months in the future he must undergo another death and rebirth, a spiritual death and rebirth.

Orlick's significance is compressed and organic. In literal terms he is a slouching villain; in psychological terms a projection of Pip's darkest self; in cosmic terms Satan, a manifestation of nascent evil. Dickens makes Orlick's depravity convincing by fusing these elements, by making Orlick's activities, speeches, even his gestures, doubly and trebly meaningful. What we learn about Orlick the ordinary journeyman, and through him about Pip and his interior history—Pip's contamination by evil, moral cowardice, false values, dark urges, morbid guilt, frustration, suffering, and chastening—is translated by means of allusion, imagery, and parallelism into an archetypal quasi-Christian retelling of man's innocence, fall, harrowing, and redemption.

Orlick's simultaneous roles as journeyman, devil, and alter ego help extend and complicate the book; those diverse roles, especially as they impinge upon Pip, also help extend and complicate the view of human nature being conveyed through the book, a view that emphasizes the deep subterranean springs of human conduct. But what is true of Orlick is true of all the characters in *Great Expectations*—they all contribute in multiple ways, often in hidden or unexpected ways, to the novel's intricate meaning. The more central the character, the more various and interrelated the filaments that radiate from him. Magwitch, for example, is part of the great structuring nodes of the novel, part of the fairy-tale pattern, the psychological elaboration, the mythic fall and redemption. But, like the other key characters, he integrates additional themes, themes having to do with money, social responsibility, and imprisonment.

Yet Magwitch also remains Pip's extension and foil, and his relationship to Pip, similar in function though not in kind to Orlick's, is the most important aspect of his role. Magwitch shows us society's guilt in producing criminals; the tainted nature of Victorian wealth and gentility; and, by means of his social, business, or blood relationships, the intricate unity of society, the universality of guilt and responsibility. But our most complete awareness of these meanings comes through Pip. Pip is both Dickens and Everyman. Pip achieves this status because Dickens uses him to focus his own most profoundly human yearnings and failings. Pip does more than state the human lessons of *Great Expectations,* however; he batters himself against their unyielding truth, and he feels the retribution of their denying force. Only in his extremity does he submit himself, and thereupon find and accept himself.

We see Pip doing all this; we see it most dramatically in his changing relationship to Magwitch: in his first traffic with his convict-savior, in his later unawareness, denial, and ultimate acceptance of him; but we also see it in his changing relationship with Joe, Biddy, Herbert, and Miss Havisham; and we believe in Pip's submission and regeneration because the self-awareness of his narration convinces us that he no longer is what he once was.

The roles of the chief characters reveal themselves most succinctly in the fairy-tale contours of the book's structure, a cyclical structure that knits the book together and provides its chief ironic revelations. The fairy-tale influence occurs in names, images, characters, actions, settings, and resolutions—Orlick's hellish demonism is one part of that influence. However, as Magwitch's symbolic upending of Pip at the dawning moment of his consciousness suggests, *Great Expectations* is an exceedingly subtle fairy story: things are rarely what they seem; values, identities, and relationships are hidden or reversed.

Pip must take responsibility for his corruption. Yet the moment of corruption is imposed upon him: it comes from the outside, from

Magwitch the outlaw convict. This ambiguity is at the heart of *Great Expectations*. For, though Magwitch is a society-produced, society-corrupting criminal who infects everything that he touches, he is also a lawless fragment of Pip's self, and Pip must recognize and accept this before he can absolve himself. Magwitch's ambiguous role as corrupter and savior (comparable to Orlick's more sinister ambiguity) is clarified by his storybook attributes. His very name is part of Dickens' irony, for the "witch" of his surname, an appropriate designation at the opening of the novel, proves to be the reverse of what Magwitch at last becomes—a saving fairy godfather. His Christian name is a more trustworthy clue. Criminal and outcast though he is, he is named Abel; he is more sinned against than sinning.

His role as a godfather introduces a host of ironies. Pip pities and aids the hunted convict, and Magwitch, in best godfatherly tradition, redeems Pip's acts of kindness by princely recompenses. But Pip's altruistic acts are strangely and terrifyingly complex: they are also acts of sin, they involve stealing, lying, and secrecy, and this ambiguity is reflected by the blighting consequences of Magwitch's gifts. Magwitch gives Pip education, status, wealth, expectations—the fairy-tale favors Pip had yearned for. But in Pip's perilous moral state such rewards become curses. Pip, since he is Everyman, since he is frail and human, must struggle toward salvation; his imperfections and the sins they lead to, imperfections and sins enlarged by Magwitch's gifts, are the awful taskmasters which chasten him. Magwitch epitomizes the ambiguity of these gifts; his gifts are scourges. But Magwitch and his love are Pip's true gifts. As in *Beauty and the Beast,* Pip must accept Magwitch the beast *as* beast. It is the act of loving acceptance, the humility, charity, and community of the act, that turns Magwitch's and thus Pip's own beastliness into beauty, into a means of salvation.

Magwitch's slowly revealed storybook role is paralleled by Miss Havisham's. As her name ("sham," "have a sham") indicates, she too is not what she seems. At the outset, she appears to be another Dickensian godmother disguised as a witch, another old Martin Chuzzlewit or Betsey Trotwood. And Pip in his upside-down morality is certain Miss Havisham is a godmother. But white-clad Miss Havisham is no godmother, she is a veritable witch. Her sham godmotherhood is only one strand in a web of shams. She allows Pip to delude himself, to believe that she gives him the gifts he receives, and that she rears for him the greatest gift of all, a Cinderella princess. Actually, Miss Havisham's only gifts are witch's curses—the curse of frigidity and suffering for Estella, longing and torment for Pip, degradation and jealousy for the worldly Pockets (another meaningful name). Miss Havisham is witchlike in her appearance, witchlike in her isolation, witchlike in her abode, witchlike in her vengeance, and witchlike in her fiery destruction.

The Cinderella she rears is another part of her sham, and another part of Dickens' topsy-turvy fairy tale. For Estella, far from being the starlike princess that she appears to be, and that her name implies, is the siren offspring of a convict and a murderess. Pip, in his self-wounding yearning for her, is yearning, as always, for a self-projected and self-defeating mirage. Estella possesses only the externals of ladyhood; in reality she is a blighted creature who mirrors Pip's own blight. Estella is a "lady" in the same ironic sense that Pip is a "gentleman"—both have been "made"; both have been fashioned impiously as instruments of revenge; both unknowingly stem (one by birth, the other by adoption) from the déclassé Magwitch; both are further distorted by the witchlike Miss Havisham; both see their sinning shapers die for their sins; both must suffer for their own assent in those sins and must be reborn. One part of Pip's rebirth consists in recognizing and accepting Estella's true identity and then confessing to her debased father—now under sentence of death—that he loves her.

Great Expectations does contain a true Cinderella prince and princess. Characteristically, the true princess is not queenly Estella, but humble Biddy. Pip spurns Biddy until it is too late. That he fails to win her is another inversion of the fairy tale. The true prince of the fable—he is also the true gentleman—is not Pip or Drummle or Jaggers but simple Joe, whom Pip in his pseudo gentility avoids as the quintessence of ungentlemanliness. Pip's errors of vision, a result of his and society's upside-down morality, are at the core of the fable. His initial upending, his later topsy-turvy values, his weathervane vacillations between good and evil, as well as his final return to an upright position are all implicit in his name, Pip Pirrip—a name both parts of which read the same backwards as forwards.

The magical names of *Great Expectations* and the relationships they mirror or disguise—"pip" also means "seed" and "disease"—are organic portions of the novel's storybook conception. That conception controls the book again and again. Thus, though Pip fails to marry the true princess in the primary fairy story, Joe, the true prince, does win her, and so fulfills a minor fairy-tale theme. And though Pip's accrual of money proves a curse, Herbert's identical accrual of money (the fairy story within the fairy story) proves a blessing—and this not only to Herbert but to Pip. Pip's anonymous endowment of Herbert is the only good that comes of his expectations. By having the identical fairy-tale money given in the identical fairy-tale manner corrupt in one instance and save in the other, Dickens is showing that it is not money itself that corrupts but its improper use—a lesson elaborated by the money-giving of Magwitch and Miss Havisham. All this is so unobtrusively embedded in the action that it comes as something of a shock to discover that the rewards and retributions in *Great Expectations* are as carefully weighed and as magical as those in the early novels. Yet, on reflection, this is not surprising. In *Great Expectations* the fairy story is still there, even more pervasively and controllingly than before, but it has been transformed. Now the fairy-tale rewards and retributions, like the other storybook elements, emerge out of the work's innermost design: in the early novels they were superimposed on the design.

It is worth looking at one or two of these storybook configurations more closely in order to see how richly and intricately Dickens was now working his fairy-tale method. Miss Havisham is a case in point. The unadorned realities that went into this memorable character have now been transformed into consummate fairy-tale art.

We first glimpse Miss Havisham seated at her dressing table in front of her looking glass, a mirror that reflects her outward visage but not her inward truth. Like the Haunted Man, Miss Havisham is haunted; like him, she has frozen herself eternally in a distant gulf of time; and again like him, she has sinned most grievously. But her sin is the opposite of his. The Haunted Man sought to obliterate the past, to prevent the past from haunting him; Miss Havisham seeks to perpetuate the past, to assure that the past will always haunt her. She has stopped time at twenty minutes before nine on her wedding morning. At that moment she was dressing to go to church, and at that moment she received the jilting letter from her suitor. Her clocks are mute and motionless; they all do homage to twenty minutes to nine. Her dressing table, her room, her person do similar homage; they have been frozen in the disarray of that anguished instant. Trinkets, gloves, parts of her trousseau, and one of her white bridal shoes are strewn about her dressing table; dresses and half-packed trunks are scattered about the room. Across the hall is another room, a feast chamber, with a long table and a tattered tablecloth. At the center of the table a bridecake festers—a rotting heap of cobwebs and black fungus.

Miss Havisham's arrayment is incomplete. She flaunts its incompleteness. She has put on only a portion of her rich lace and jewels; she wears these scraps and baubles as an ostentatious badge of her perpetual sorrow. There are other signs of her diseased vanity, of her morbid homage to sorrow and malignant memory. She has placed a long white veil on her head, but has not yet arranged it; she has drawn only one shoe on; she has left her watch and chain and gloves and handkerchief and prayer book on her table. She is dressed all in white—or rather, she was dressed all in white, for now everything she wears, like her own gaunt body, is yellowed, withered, and decayed.

She is, as Dickens put it elsewhere, a Sleeping Ugly—she waits in deathlike immobility for a promised prince, a prince who will never come, who will never kiss and waken her. Or, yet again, with her one shoe on and one shoe off, she is a blighted Cinderella. Betrayed by her faithless prince, she has turned witchlike and infernal. She is the culmination and transformation of that long-gestating cluster of associations that I traced in the previous chapter. She is the far-off revenant, wonderfully changed and wonderfully deepened, of the White Lady, Martha Joachim, Miss Mildew, and Ellen; she is also the culmination, again wonderfully transformed, of the strange incremental meldings of chance and causality: of made gentlewomen, imprisoning mansions, and blazing death by fire.

But now these accreting elements have been fused and transmuted, and they have become part of a larger fairy-tale conception. Miss Havisham is more than a real-life eccentric, more even than a bizarre synthesis. She is, as Pip tells us, "the strangest lady I have ever seen, or shall ever see."[19] Soon we realize that this strangeness has still stranger undertones. Miss Havisham's body has "shrunk to skin and bone"; her being has "no brightness left but the brightness of her sunken eyes."[20] When Pip looks at her he is reminded of a "ghastly waxwork" or a "skeleton in the ashes of a rich dress," but with eyes that moved. Pip is stunned and horrified, but he is already held thrall by Miss Havisham's spell. "I should have cried out," he says, "if I could."[21]

After a while, Pip finds that the bridal garments look like "grave-clothes" and the long veil like a "shroud." Miss Havisham herself, weird and unearthly in her mouldering clothes, sits wan and "corpse-like."[22] Miss Havisham has stopped time, or so she thinks. She has not seen the sun since the moment she was jilted. But time has had its revenge. It has set the seal of waste and decay on her and on all her accoutrements. The clocks have stopped, but the decay goes on. The blooming bride has married ghastly death. Day by day Miss Havisham grows more hollow, brittle, and corpselike. When Pip first meets her, she already looks "as if the admission of the natural light of day would have struck her to dust."[23] As Dickens limns his portrait, he introduces additional vibrations and additional connotations. Miss Havisham, corpselike embodiment of death, is a lethal enemy of life. She has turned herself into a frightful witch. The stopped clocks have not stopped this transformation either: "Her chest had dropped, so that she stooped; and her voice had dropped, so that she spoke low, and with a dead lull upon her."[24] Witchlike Miss Havisham now broods over Satis House, intent, crouching, deadly.

Pip goes home from his first encounter with this blighted white-clad bride to tell his curious sister and his bullying Uncle Pumblechook wild

stories of what he has seen. Miss Havisham, Pip says, sits in her room
in a black velvet coach, eats cakes and wine on gold plates, and has
four immense dogs who devour veal cutlets out of a silver basket. Pip
has other revelations. According to him, Miss Havisham presides over
exotic games. The three of them—Pip, Estella, and Miss Havisham—play with swords and flags. Pip waves a red flag, Estella a blue
one, and Miss Havisham waves a dazzling banner "sprinkled all over
with little gold stars."[25] This fantastic fairy story awes Pip's worldly
listeners. Their greedy dreams of preferment make them gullible be-
lievers. They immediately begin to construct a rationale for all Pip's
gorgeous nonsense. Ironically, Pip has withheld the truth from
Pumblechook and his sister because he feels they will not believe it.
And he is right. The sealed-off mansion, the stopped clocks, the
mouldering tatters of the past, the ghastly presiding witch are too per-
verse and too fantastic to be believed. The fairy tale of life outstrips the
fairy tale of fiction.

As Dickens elaborates his portrait of Miss Havisham, he elaborates
his storybook touches as well. Most of these touches hover subtly over
scene and action, blending inconspicuously with the central realism
and softly guiding our awareness; in extricating such touches from their
realistic contexts, I do violence to Dickens' art. But Dickens sometimes labels as well as suggests, more openly directing our associations. If the reader has missed the hidden hints, he should not miss the
bolder signals. When Pip first sees Miss Havisham enter the desolate
feast chamber, he is struck by a telling simile, a simile that he purveys
but fails to take to heart. "She had a crutch-headed stick on which she
leaned," says Pip, "and she looked like the Witch of the place."[26]

In the feast chamber itself, Miss Havisham tells Pip her plans. When
she is dead, she will be laid out on the long table where the bridecake
now festers, and her relatives will come and look at her. Later, when
her mercenary relatives are all present in that room, she tells them how
to arrange themselves around the table "when you come to feast upon
me."[27] This deft cannibalistic metaphor, at once so gruesome and so
apt, goes back to Mary Weller and to the fairy tales of childhood—to
stories about such fearful corpse chewers (nightly companions of Dickens' early years) as Blunderbore, Captain Murderer, and Chips' speaking rat. That such storybook associations are strongly and consciously
present for Dickens is made clear a few moments later when Camilla,
one of Miss Havisham's relatives, registers a resentful complaint. "It's
very hard," she says, "to be told one wants to feast on one's
relations—as if one was a Giant."[28] As so often in Dickens, the cannibalistic threat is leavened by humor, but the predatory reality lingers.

Miss Havisham now inducts Pip into a strange circular ritual. She
has him walk her round and round her room, and round and round the

room across the hall, the room with the long table. As they walk, Miss Havisham's arm twitches convulsively on Pip's supporting shoulder, and her shrivelled mouth works continuously. Innocent Pip, embraced by a deceptive white-clad witch, is drawn all unwittingly into his circular prison. This circling goes on and on, week after week, month after month. When Miss Havisham grows tired of walking, she does not abate her obsessive circling. She gets into a wheeled chair, and Pip continues to push her round and round the one room, then round and round the other. Pip is a captive. The white-clad witch of Satis House has woven a magic circle about him, a circle that blights and bewilders him, a circle in which he will continue to turn until its spell is broken.

Poor, blind, self-deluded Pip rarely recognizes his thralldom. He interprets the signs of his servitude as signs of his blithe good fortune. There are innumerable indications of this. Years later, for instance, gentleman Pip arranges to spend a day at Satis House. After a while Miss Havisham orders Pip to walk with Estella in the garden; when they come back, she tells him, he can wheel her about as of yore. Pip and Estella go out into the ruined garden. As they go round and round the rank, weed-grown walks, Estella rests her exquisite hand lightly on Pip's supporting shoulder. But this dainty recrudescence of his youthful past brings Pip no glimmerings of truth. He experiences no liberating insights; he feels, instead, a strangely troubled pleasure. Pip is enthralled by his cold princess. Under her haughty guidance, he recapitulates his first day in Satis House. He circled then; he circles now. The charm of the circle holds him still. He has made no headway; he has found no exit; he goes round and round his bewildering maze. He follows Estella, as he followed Miss Havisham, into his endless circle. Pip and Estella circuit the ruined garden, Pip the dutiful "Page"—the word is Dickens'—Estella the beauteous princess.[29] Round and round they go, queenly Estella trailing her handsome dress upon the blighted ground. So they walk, deluded adorer and poison princess, orbiting the ruined garden. Pip does not decipher the hieroglyphic significance of his companions or his reiterated circling. It never occurs to him that Miss Havisham is a fatal witch, that Estella is a deadly princess. It never occurs to him that his ceaseless rounds with Miss Havisham and Estella are part of his own poor labyrinth.

The imprisoning circles and the cycling rituals grow more insistent and more entangling. Miss Havisham has stopped the clocks of Satis House, and she forbids any mention of time in her presence, but she is utterly bound by time, its slave and groveling creature. Her mind festers on a time in the past; she rules her poor circumscribed life by its cycling return. Her birthday was to be her wedding day—it is also the day on which the bridecake was brought to the long table—and now each year on that day she obsessively celebrates her birth and death, yet she banishes mention of either. Gripped by the circle of her memory and her wrong, each year on her birth-death day she summons her relatives to assemble around the long table and pay their mute respects—a grotesque fairy-tale assemblage, forming a weird fairy-tale circle, in a dismal fairy-tale setting. But Miss Havisham is not content with such timebound cycling. She hopes to die on that day, too. "When the ruin is complete," she says, "and when they lay me dead, in my bride's dress on the bride's table—which shall be done, and which will be the finished curse upon him—so much the better if it is done on this day!"[30] Pip listens to these words in the heavy air and oppressive darkness of mouldering Satis House. In that blighting atmosphere he has an "alarming fancy" that presently he and Estella will "begin to decay" as well.[31] As usual, Pip's storybook fancy hides a storybook truth: he and Estella are already decaying and will continue to decay.

Miss Havisham does blind homage in other ways to the circling sovereignty of time. One day Pip comes to visit her. He has long since been apprenticed to Joe, but it is his birthday, and he seeks to pay his respects. Miss Havisham receives Pip suspiciously at first, but later she gives him a present and tells him to come and visit her each year on his birthday. Pip willingly agrees to her request. Miss Havisham, potent witch of time, as usual has her wish. She is time's secret votary and victim. A circling slave of withering time (she spurns time's healing gifts), she seeks to enslave all who come her way in time's imprisoning orbit.

Pip is caught up in that inward and outward circling. Just as he marched round and round the room with Miss Havisham, or round and round the ruined garden with Estella, or round and round the cycling years with Miss Havisham, so he goes round and round his poor maze, never breaking loose from Miss Havisham's bewildering spell. Pip often feels the power of that spell; he seems unable to withstand its desolate pull. Long after he has become a gentleman, it holds him in its blighting grip. Sometimes he feels the benign influence of Joe and Biddy leading him toward health and natural ease, but then "some confounding remembrance of the Havisham days would fall upon me, like a destructive missile, and scatter my wits again."[32]

Pip's wits were scattered on his first visit to Satis House. He never recovers from that scattering, a scattering that is at once a potent spell and a realistic psychological development. Though Pip looks steadily at his weird white patroness and her beautiful familiar, though he sees and vividly describes the sinister outward attributes of their inner reality, he fails to make the right deductions. We make the deductions that Pip fails to make. Guided by Dickens' art, we recognize the magical spell, we grasp the dismaying truth. The fairy tale that bewilders Pip focuses our clear vision. When Pip, wearing his new gentlemanly finery, takes leave of Miss Havisham before going off to London (he believes, of course, that she is the author of his storybook gift), he presents the scene as it appeared to him. He is standing before Miss Havisham. "'This is a gay figure, Pip,' said she, making her crutch stick play round me, as if she, the fairy godmother who had changed me, were bestowing the finishing gift."[33] In this scene, as always, Miss Havisham's spell is at work; Pip's scattered wits are playing their usual tricks. His topsy-turvy vision perceives the witch of his life as his godmother; just as that upside-down vision perceives the godfather of his life as his witch. In Pip's spellbound eyes, a crooked crutch is a magic wand. Pip concludes the scene by unconsciously emphasizing these incongruities and blindnesses. He persists in seeing his spell-casting witch, even when surrounded by the blighting attributes of her maleficent sway, as a benign fairy godmother: "So I left my fairy godmother, with both her hands on her crutch stick, standing in the midst of the dimly lighted room beside the rotten bride-cake that was hidden in cobwebs."[34]

Miss Havisham's spell holds dominion over Pip again and again. The spell allows him to see, but confuses his comprehension. Again and again he reports outward events but fails to understand their inward reality. That reality is magically proclaimed by the events and their signaling attributes. There are hundreds of these signaling scenes. On one of his visits to Satis House, after he has become a gentleman, Pip complies with Miss Havisham's request and again pushes her round and round the bride-feast room: "It was like pushing the chair itself back into the past, when we began the old slow circuit round about the ashes of the bridal feast. But, in the funereal room, with that figure of the grave fallen back in the chair fixing its eyes upon her, Estella looked more bright and beautiful than before, and I was under stronger enchantment."[35] And so, with the witchlike "figure of the grave" directing him and leading him ever more deftly into his old blind circle (a magic circle far different from the one that he perceives), Pip falls ever more deeply under the spell—the "stronger enchantment," as he puts it—of his poison princess, the princess Miss Havisham has impiously created.

As the story progresses, Miss Havisham wields her spell more and more openly. Potent witch and harbinger of death, she finally commands Pip to fulfill the fate that she has prepared for him. He must do what he longs to do, what he does, and what he has always done since entering her blighted domain: he must love Estella helplessly, he must suffer endless dole. "Love her, love her, love her!" Miss Havisham now openly commands him. But though Pip obeys Miss Havisham's

vehement incantation, he is troubled by it as well: "if the often repeated word had been hate instead of love—despair—revenge—dire
death—it could not have sounded from her lips more like a curse."[36]

Miss Havisham's fairy-tale attributes now become increasingly explicit and increasingly witchlike. Pip has never seen Miss Havisham eat
or drink. Jaggers tells him that he never will. "She wanders about in the
night," says Jaggers, "and then lays hands on such food as she
takes."[37] Like some restless vampire or ghastly ghoul, Miss Havisham
feeds secretly in darkness. Such images are fitting. Miss Havisham is
obsessed by fierce predators; she focuses compulsively on dim carrion
feeding. She has somber visions (visions that revolt her) of her
vulture-relatives feasting on her dead body, but she herself feasts
ravenously on the living lives of others. She can hardly control her
unclean appetite. In her "witch-like eagerness" she "hung upon Estella's beauty, hung upon her words, hung upon her gestures, and sat
mumbling her own trembling fingers while she looked at her, as though
she were devouring the beautiful creature she had reared."[38] We get
other memorable glimpses of this devouring witch and her ravishing
lure: "When we sat by her flickering fire at night, she was most weird;
for then, keeping Estella's hand drawn through her arm and clutched in
her own hand, she extorted from her . . . the names and conditions of
the men whom she had fascinated; and as Miss Havisham dwelt upon
this roll . . . she sat with her other hand on her crutch stick, and her
chin on that, and her wan bright eyes glaring at me, a very spectre."[39]

Later still, Miss Havisham becomes a specter in truth. On the first
occasion that Pip stays in Satis House—he is now an elegant gentleman—he finds that he cannot sleep. "A thousand Miss Havishams
haunted me. She was on this side of my pillow, on that, at the head of
the bed, at the foot, behind the half-opened door of the dressing-room,
in the dressing-room, in the room overhead, in the room beneath—
everywhere." After hours of restless tossing, Pip finds this haunting
unbearable. Finally, at two in the morning, he gets up and goes to walk
in the courtyard. "But, I was no sooner in the passage than I extinguished my candle; for, I saw Miss Havisham going along it in a ghostly
manner, making a low cry. I followed her at a distance, and saw her go
up the staircase. She carried a bare candle in her hand . . . and was a
most unearthly object by its light. Standing at the bottom of the staircase, I felt the mildewed air of the feast-chamber, without seeing her
open the door, and I heard her walking there, and so across into her
own room, and so across again into that, never ceasing the low cry."
Pip watches this new permutation of his old familiar circling. He is
again a captive. In the impenetrable blackness, his candle out, he is
unable to return to his room until the break of day. "During the whole
interval, whenever I went to the bottom of the staircase, I heard her

footstep, saw her candle pass above, and heard her ceaseless low cry.''[40] Witchlike Miss Havisham, Pip's "fairy godmother," has become the veritable ghost of Satis House.

Miss Havisham haunts Satis House, but she, in turn, is haunted by her unforgivable sin. She has undertaken God's role; she has acted as creator and destroyer. As Miss Havisham herself puts it, "I stole [Estella's] heart away and put ice in its place."[41] For this sin, and for all the deadly woes that flow from it, Miss Havisham must be given to the fire. Before that burning, she is brought low. Her humbling is fitting and monitory. When this proud witch, white-clad stealer of innocent hearts, asks heartless Estella for love, she learns at last what heartlessness is. Sinking down into the debris of love scattered all about her, this blighted bride now abases herself before the cold monster that she created: "Miss Havisham had settled down, I hardly knew how, upon the floor, among the faded bridal relics with which it was strewn. . . . Miss Havisham's grey hair was all adrift upon the ground, among the other bridal wrecks, and was a miserable sight to see."[42] We have witnessed this abasement before. The scene, the images, the juxtapositions, the words, the deeds echo "The Bride's Chamber." In that earlier story, Ellen, another blighted white-clad bride, abases herself before her own cold monster and creator.

Miss Havisham's burning is heralded by signs and circling rituals. Some time after Miss Havisham has groveled before Estella, Pip has his first interview with the newly remorseful recluse. Miss Havisham once more abases herself, now before Pip. Pip is shocked and shaken. After that meeting, he leaves the ruined room and its ruined occupant and goes down into the "natural air." It is twilight. Pip has a "presentiment that I should never be [at Satis House] again," and he feels that "the dying light was suited to my last view of it."[43] He goes by the rotting casks—scene of siren visions—the casks that he had walked on, entranced by Estella, on his first day at Satis House. He circles the ruined garden that he had circled with Estella. He walks through the wasted brewery. In that ravaged building he had beheld (also on his first day there) a nightmare vision of Miss Havisham hanging from a beam. He looks back over his shoulder (a premonitory gesture for Dickens), and all at once he again sees Miss Havisham hanging from that selfsame beam. He again rushes toward the vision, but again it is gone, and he stands under the beam, shuddering from head to foot. This momentary hallucination, dread specter of the circling past, so fills him with foreboding and "indescribable awe" that he goes back to the house to assure himself that Miss Havisham is safe.[44] He mounts the old familiar staircase. Miss Havisham is in the feast chamber where he left her. As he looks at her, seated in her ragged chair before a wintry fire, he witnesses a sudden transformation. He sees "a great flaming light spring up.''[45] Miss Havisham, ashy ember of a witchlike passion, bursts—spontaneously, it would seem—into a last bright storm of self-consuming flame. In a moment she is running toward Pip, ''shrieking, with a whirl of fire blazing all about her.'' Pip throws her down, folds her in his coats, and tearing the great cloth and all its heap of rottenness from the long table, covers her with that winding-sheet as well. ''Patches of tinder yet alight were floating in the smoky air, which a moment ago had been her faded bridal dress.'' Soon the patches of tinder, no longer alight, are ''falling in a black shower.''[46] In blazing flame and black rain, the witch of Satis House meets her fiery doom.

Miss Havisham, horribly burned and soon to die, is placed upon a bed on the great long table where she had always said her body should lie. Though she has passed through the fire and suffered a searing change, though her white wedding dress has been entirely consumed, she is still a blighted white-clad bride. ''For, they had covered her to the throat with white-cotton wool,'' and they had placed a white sheet over her. As she lies on her high bier, an ashy bride of living death, ''the phantom air of something that had been and was changed was still upon her.''[47]

Satis House, too, wears a ''phantom air.'' Satis House was compounded out of a real gated Rochester mansion; a name taken from another Rochester landmark; a grim, walled-off, time-stopped London residence (York Buildings); a mélange of blacking-warehouse associations; an expressionistic nightmare (the haunted, mouldering, imprisoning house of ''The Bride's Chamber''); and other bits and pieces of life and fiction. Yet all these shaping forces are less important than the wonderful phantom vision that emerged from them. That vision, like the phantom vision that is Miss Havisham, and the fairy-tale vision that molds and undergirds the whole of *Great Expectations,* helps Dickens convey his innermost meanings.

Satis House illustrates this truth. Satis House is a real English manor house and a wild fairy-tale nightmare. It is part prison, part inimical force, and part convoluted hell. It haunts Pip and shadows his life. Pip's early impressions of Satis House suggest a prison. The great mouldering mansion is dismal, locked, barred, and gated. Its doors are chained, its windows walled up or rustily barred, its gates locked, its passages so dark they cannot be negotiated without a candle. Estella tells Pip that the name ''Satis House'' is ''Greek, or Latin, or Hebrew, or all three . . . for enough.'' Pip says ''Enough House'' is a curious name, and Estella replies that it means ''whoever had this house, could want nothing else.''[48] The name will prove to be as deceptive and as magical as the house. ''Enough'' seems to promise plenitude and satisfaction, but its real significance is far different. ''Enough'' is exactly what Pip ceases to have the moment he enters that malignant domain; and enough is what Miss Havisham has never had despite her enormous wealth. Indeed Estella's explication of the name predicts these dire consequences; her definition vibrates with treacherous meanings. "Want nothing else" defines Pip's paltry dream; he now only "wants" (grievously "lacks" and obsessively "desires") Satis House and its world. Pip, as usual, longs for what he should not have. The delusive Satis House that he sighs for to the exclusion of everything else is a corrupt storybook dwelling, a haunted house, a grim castle, presided over by a white-clad witch, featuring a poison princess, and suffering under a wasting spell. All who enter its locked and barred precincts fall under that spell: they circle round their ruined hopes, corrosively yearning for what they cannot have. This is no farfetched metaphor, but Dickens' imaginative conception of the mansion.

Satis House exists in eternal night. The blighted rooms that Miss Havisham occupies—the bridal dressing room and the bridal feast chamber—have, like the rest of the house, been sealed off from the sun. In these airless and sunless rooms, always cold and dismal, wintry candles forever burn with a weird and wintry light. That light does not light a room; it "faintly trouble[s] its darkness."[49] This zone of eternal night casts its pall on all who traffic in it. Night enters their souls, perplexing judgment and confounding time. After Pip's first session in Satis House, he says, "I had fancied, without thinking about it, that it must necessarily be night-time. The rush of the daylight [when I went out] quite confounded me, and made me feel as if I had been in the candlelight of the strange room many hours."[50]

If it is always night in Satis House, it is always winter, too. On Pip's second visit to Satis House he is required to wait in a subsidiary building at a corner of the neglected garden. "There had been some light snow, overnight, and it lay nowhere else to my knowledge; but, it had not quite melted from the cold shadow of this bit of garden, and the wind caught it up in little eddies and threw it at the window, as if it pelted me for coming there."[51] The invisible world is signaling to Pip. Eternal winter is encompassing him, cold winds are pelting him—all for "coming there." But Pip does not heed these signals. He is already caught up in the black night, in the dark intricate passages, of Satis House. He is already circling in his poor labyrinth.

Warning signals confront Pip at every turn. As in *David Copperfield,* outward signs of waste and emptiness and disuse hint at deeper voids within. Those outward signs are everywhere. All of Satis House, all its surrounding structures, everything from the brewery to the pigeon house, is empty and decaying. "There were no pigeons in the dovecot, no horses in the stable, no pigs in the sty, no malt in the store-house, no smells of grains and beer in the copper or the vat."[52] The gardens and grounds convey a similar message of waste and dire neglect. Sagging gates, rank growth, tangled weeds, and obliterated paths abound. Rust, ruin, fungus, and decay reign everywhere.

Satis House provokes as well as incorporates warnings. On his first visit there, Pip sees strange premonitory occurrences, and he has terrifying visions. Out in the ruined garden, deep in the devastated brewery, he sees Estella, always far ahead, always leading him on, disappearing down walks, passing out of sight on ascending stairs, melting round corners, and vanishing into the sky. She is a luring siren, enticing Pip into ruin and devastation, vanishing illusively, forever out of reach. Her role in the ruined garden and ruined brewery mirrors her role inside Satis House. There, candle in hand, she leads Pip into the dark tangle of passage and staircase, corridor and chamber. She enacts her name; she is a guiding star, a beckoning beacon, but she leads poor topsy-turvy Pip into hell rather than heaven. During these early scenes she is also the keeper of the keys and the keeper of the gates. Though ravishing and irresistible, she traffics in locks and bars. She is enchanting and deceptive, a dainty, enticing, deadly precursor of Old Orlick.

Pip follows where Estella leads. It is while Estella is leading Pip through the neglected garden and the desolated brewery that he has his most frightening vision of disaster to come. Suddenly, in a low nook of the brewery, he sees Miss Havisham, arrayed for her bridal, yellowed and withered, one shoe on and one shoe off, hanging from a great wooden beam. He rushes toward her, and she disappears. Pip is horrified, but he no more reads this sign than all the others that throng about Satis House. He fails to comprehend that Satis House is a spell-struck source of contagion, that Miss Havisham is a witch, and that Estella, siren princess and keeper of the keys, is her lure. He fails to understand that the spell upon him, the spell that leads him into the dark circular maze of Satis House, is the spell of disease and death.

Pip feels that spell, but he cannot penetrate its true meaning, nor can he withstand its power. Years later, after he is apprenticed to Joe, the spell still governs him: "Daylight never entered [Satis House], as to my thoughts and remembrances of it, any more than as to the actual fact. It bewildered me, and under its influence I continued at heart to hate my trade and to be ashamed of home."[53] Each time he returns to Satis House, each time he circles its rooms or its ruined garden, each time he thinks of Satis House, the poisonous blackness and the mouldering decay engulf and entrance him. While all the world outside bustles on in sunshine and in shade, somber, time-stopped Satis House holds Pip in its dark contagion.

Pip in his delusion and his upside-down vision feels these midnight influences and sees these maleficent signs but explains them all away. He has his own conception of their fairy-tale meaning. Satis House is a

Sleeping Beauty palace, Estella is a *Sleeping Beauty* princess, and Miss Havisham is the fairy godmother who has chosen him as deliverer. "[Miss Havisham] reserved it for me to restore the desolate house, admit the sunshine into the dark rooms, set the clocks a going and the cold hearths a blazing, tear down the cobwebs, destroy the vermin—in short, do all the shining deeds of the young Knight of romance, and marry the Princess."[54]

This, of course, is not to be. And when Orlick appears as the gatekeeper of Satis House, the house, instead of ascending into life, descends ever more ominously into death. The great mouldering pile, ruined prison and haunted time-stopped mansion, now darkens still more malignantly into a black involuted hell. Slowly, dimly, Pip begins to sense his woeful errors. Satis House (the name echoes Satans House and Hades House) is no longer the strange perplexing embodiment of all that he desires in life. As he sets out on one of his latter-day visits to Satis House, he can write: "I . . . went out to the memorable old house that it would have been so much the better for me never to have entered, never to have seen."[55] And later still, on his last visit to Satis House, he realizes that the house is not simply a physical place that fascinates and repels him. It is part of him, and he is part of it. Its dark labyrinthine passages are correlatives of his dark labyrinthine entanglements; its ragged, worn-out vestments of his ragged, worn-out hopes; its locks and chains and bars of his spell-like imprisonment, of his prison-engendered and prison-begirt destiny. As Pip sits for the last time on a ragged Satis House chair before an ashy Satis House fire, he feels that he too "had come to be a part of the wrecked fortunes of that house."[56] Pip can now read the grievous messages of that festering storybook house, the messages that earlier he had failed to comprehend or had turned upside down. The house is now a clairvoyant mirror or magical instrument, a doleful harbinger, that speaks to him of woe. When Pip asks Miss Havisham if Estella is married, and Miss Havisham answers, "Yes," Pip comments: "It was a needless question, for a new desolation in the desolate house had told me so."[57]

Pip goes from this ruined house of his ruined hopes to his slow harrowing, death, and rebirth. After he is reborn, after he has begun to cleanse his mind of the dark shadows and vain desires that had beckoned and enthralled him, he goes abroad. There, thousands of miles from Satis House, he continues his long journey of healing and regeneration. Eleven years go by, and then, one December (December was the month in which Pip's adventures began), he returns to England. He travels down to his tiny village and there visits Joe and Biddy. The next day he takes their little Pip to the memorable churchyard and sets him on the fateful tombstone. That evening, at twilight, he makes another pilgrimage. Alone now, he returns with loitering footsteps to the dark mansion of his poor dream. But Satis House is no longer there. "There was no house now, no brewery, no building whatever left."[58] As in a fairy tale, all has vanished—along with Pip's poor dream.

Other fairy-tale deployments also shaped the innermost meaning of *Great Expectations*. The development of the strange talismanic relationship between Magwitch and Pip, for example (and all that relationship implies), owes much of its special significance to storybook associations and storybook devices. When Pip meets Magwitch he falls under his spell, a submission accompanied by ritualistic portents. The moment of yielding occurs at the instant Magwitch upends Pip—Magwitch's hypnotic eyes bore "powerfully down" into Pip's, while Pip's innocent eyes look "most helplessly" up into the convict's.[59] In this fateful instant of weakness, Pip yields himself to evil, a yielding marked by a magical meeting of eyes, the first of many similar looks. Pip's dawning moment of individual identity is also a moment of taint and guilt. His subsequent sense of sinfulness is a realistic reflection of his contamination, a contamination which is really a part of the human condition, which is coeval with individuality and self-consciousness, but his contamination, like his induction, is also underlined by magical signs. The evil adult world impinges upon Pip in the same way that Dickens, in his own childhood, visualized a sadistic adult world impinging upon himself. The supreme imagery of evil is adapted from the imagery of fairy stories: it involves graveyard ghosts, fateful glances, solemn compacts, haunted houses, poison princesses, magic circles, witches, ogres, cannibalism, and the like; and in each world the crucial relationship is the same: it centers about a brutal adult and a waiflike child. Yet the effect of the book is neither fabulous nor self-pitying. Dickens avoids the former distortion because his basic situation is psychologically realistic, it emerges from his own experiences; he avoids the latter because, although he surrounds Pip with an expressionistic reflection of his own childhood terror, he distances that terror through adult insight and retrospective humor. For the reader, therefore, Pip's real but storybook nightmare partakes of deflating yet storybook whimsy, a combination that allows Dickens to reveal and conceal his involvement.

Magwitch, for instance, threatens to eat Pip's "fat cheeks," a threat that Pip accepts as literal.[60] Later Magwitch swears that he will have Pip's heart and liver "tore out, roasted and ate," and he tells the trembling child of a bloodthirsty cohort who can "softly creep and creep his way to him and tear him open,"[61] the exact threat Good Mrs. Brown terrified Florence with in *Dombey and Son*. This ogreish bullying is grotesque, and from a detached adult perspective, amusing—for

Dickens as well as the reader. But for Dickens, and for the empathizing reader, such terrific bullying also carries a burden of undiminished horror, a burden made explicit by Pip's reactions and their consequences. Pip finds Magwitch's ferocious threats real and endlessly ramifying. By means of those threats Pip is inducted into evil. Cannibalistic bullying propels him into the nightmare world of sin and criminality, a world that scars him permanently. Pip's fall is sealed by an oath: he enters into an indissoluble compact to aid his rough tormentor; and Pip's last glimpse of the outlaw occurs as he glances over his shoulder while racing homeward toward the forge. In that backward glance, so reminiscent of fateful backward glances in mythology and fairy lore (and foreshadowing the backward glance that will show Pip Miss Havisham hanging from the beam), Pip sees Magwitch plunging toward the river, the flowing stream that runs symbolically through all of *Great Expectations* and that will ultimately convey Magwitch and himself to death and salvation.

This premonitory opening recalls some of Dickens' earlier fairy-tale scenes. One is reminded of ragged waiflike Florence, at the outset of her pilgrimage and with the tolling bells ringing in her ears, looking back over her shoulder at Good Mrs. Brown's shaking fist; one thinks also of doomed Carker emerging from the fateful grove and looking over his shoulder at Good Mrs. Brown's pointing finger; one remembers, too, an unnerved Steerforth looking fearfully over his shoulder as the figures of Ham and Emily, followed by the prostitute, disappear into the darkling sea; and one recalls the fearsome ogre of *David Copperfield,* his terrifying "Oh-goroos," and his Magwitchian appetite for hearts and livers.

But in *Great Expectations* Dickens makes the fairy tale serve his purposes in ways that go beyond his successes in *Dombey* and *Copperfield*. For Magwitch is more than a child quelling Mrs. Pipchin, a witchlike Good Mrs. Brown, or an ogreish pawnshop keeper; like Orlick, he is part of Pip, part most particularly of the best and worst in Pip. Dickens suggests this relationship with great subtlety. When Pip, after his encounter with Magwitch, asks Joe in silent lip language, "What's a convict?" Joe returns an elaborate lip-language answer, the only word of which the boy can make out is "Pip."[62] Similarly, when Pip's "all-powerful sister" responds to his questioning about convicts and prison ships, she makes him feel "fearfully sensible" that the "hulks were handy" for him.[63] This identification with Magwitch and evil soon colors Pip's entire consciousness, a development made clear by dozens of additional touches. When, for instance, Pip returns to Magwitch in order to give him the stolen food and file, he becomes symbolically shackled like the convict. "All this time," Pip relates, "I was getting on towards the river; but however fast I went, I couldn't warm my feet, to which the damp cold seemed riveted, as the iron was riveted to the leg of the man I was running to meet."[64]

Magwitch's relationship to Pip goes even deeper. Though the convict is a tormentor and an extension of Pip, he is also, like Pip, a victim and a waif. Indeed Pip and Magwitch, though poles apart in age and circumstance, are doubles. They have a common history and share a common destiny. They are shaped by similar forces; they are bound by identical bonds. Their earliest beginnings, outwardly so different, inwardly so alike, testify to their oneness. Orphaned Pip's first act as a self-aware individual, an act that is coeval with his dawning selfhood, with his "first most vivid and broad impression of the identity of things," is to steal food.[65] In other words, Pip commences his volitional life by sinning. But paradoxically, in falling, he redeems himself—or at least in falling, he makes redemption possible: the primordial moment of sin is a primordial moment of grace. This is so because Pip's sin is also a good deed, an act of loving charity. Though initially impelled by a threat, he ultimately steals out of compassion; he steals so that a friendless, hunted human being might live. Magwitch exhibits the same double-edged contradictions in his dawning moment of self-hood. Like Pip, his first memory—the time "I first become aware of myself"—is of stealing food.[66] This striking commonality proclaims their kinship. Magwitch underlines that kinship. He sketches for us the onset of his consciousness. Orphaned, abandoned, alone, hardly more than an infant, he becomes aware of his identity while lurking warily in a turnip field, thieving turnips so that he might live. His sin is nothing more nor less than the blind biological urge to survive. For starving Magwitch, to exist is to sin. Magwitch is forced to sin; years later he forces Pip to sin, to repeat his own early trespass of stealing food. The iron chain of transgression, forged slowly link by link, binds the generations in inescapable bondage. In shackling Magwitch, society shackles itself.

Pip's equivocal sin, a sin that is imposed from without but that is also acquiesced to from within, leads to guilt, secrecy, and alienation; his sin is the initiating moment of his long reticulated history of dissatisfaction, desire, and stressful dole. It is also the crucial moment that leads to, indeed that assures, his ultimate humanity and salvation. Magwitch's equally equivocal (and even less culpable) sin has much more devastating consequences. He is arrested, jailed, and eventually released, released to starve and steal again, whereupon he is rearrested, rejailed, and rereleased, only to begin the cycle once more. He is soon branded incorrigible. He is destined for prison or the underworld, forced by society to steal or starve. All unwittingly, he eventually makes society pay for what society has exacted. His attempts to live and thrive soon engulf half the characters of the book in pain and suffering. Like some unwholesome storybook monster, his baleful presence exhales an insidious contagion. Those who breathe his tainted breath know thwarted dreams and blasted expectations.

At the same time, Magwitch is the dark magnification of Pip's milder destiny. Pip and Magwitch instruct us. They show us that we are all products of the strange unfathomable equation of will and necessity, that our earliest consciousness refracts the great broad ray of life into shifting patterns that inextricably modulate light with dark, good with evil. They also demonstrate that the criminal and pariah are only exaggerated instances (given their blighted beginnings and malignant growth) of each one of us, that, but for the accident of birth or fortune or happenstance, we too could become derelicts of life. Finally, they teach us that society, whether we like it or not, is unitary, that high and low, rich and poor, valued citizen and loathsome outcast, tremble in involuntary kinship at each distant perturbation.

These intricate lessons are often given point and fullness by fairy-tale means. *Great Expectations* throngs with storybook signs. Magical covenants and hidden correspondences testify to cosmic affinities. Pip and Magwitch—to continue with those two for the moment—illustrate this mysterious commonality. The ritual bond that gives outward expression to their common guilt and common suffering foreshadows their common salvation, and this aspect of their relationship is also projected by fairy-tale means. Under threat, Pip steals food and a file for Magwitch. Full of fear and guilt, he brings these pledges to the graveyard and his brutish threatener. But Pip's terror soon gives way to another emotion, an emotion almost magical in the transformation it produces:

> Pitying his desolation, and watching him as he gradually settled down upon the pie, I made bold to say, "I am glad you enjoy it."
> "Did you speak?"
> "I said, I was glad you enjoyed it."
> "Thankee, my boy. I do."[67]

Pip's twice-repeated avowal of sympathy and Magwitch's "thankee" and "my boy" are premonitory pledges. In the ensuing years Magwitch will shower innumerable "thankees" upon Pip, forever after "my boy" to him. And when the convict finally returns to his young and self-deceived fellow bondsman, "my boy" and "dear boy" are the loving yet ironically possessive phrases most often on his lips, first to Pip's unutterable horror, but finally to his comfort. By the same token, Pip soon begins to refer to Magwitch as "my convict," reciprocating Magwitch's "my boy" and unconsciously acknowledging their kin-

ship. This is all in the future, when Pip has obscured his saving goodness with artifice and fraud. For the moment, however, the bond of
fellow feeling is quickly enlarged, and Pip in aligning himself with the
outlawed Magwitch aligns himself with sympathy and humanity as well
as pariahlike corruption. In the few hours that intervene between Pip's
traffic with Magwitch and the outlaw's recapture, Pip makes his
choice. "I hope, Joe," he says, while accompanying the hunt, "we
shan't find them."[68] Pip speaks these words on Christmas Day, and he
speaks them in a symbolic setting: "Under the low red glare of sunset,
the beacon, and the gibbet, and the mound of the Battery, and the
opposite shore of the river, were plain, though all of a watery lead
colour."[69] Seen in the perspective of the completed story, the landscape is as portentous as Pip's self-confronting encounter with Magwitch, for it epitomizes all that Pip will undergo: the furnace-glare of
hell, the deadly enticement of the starlike beacon, the taint of prison
and sin, the journey to the brink of the grave, the glimpse of the eternal
shore beyond the eternal river—all plain, yet all discolored by Pip's
still murky vision.

When Magwitch is retaken, Pip exchanges a look with the hunted
creature that complements their earlier look. The second look is as
fleeting as the first, and as full of magical meaning:

> I looked at him eagerly when he looked at me, and slightly moved my
> hands and shook my head. I had been waiting for him to see me, that I
> might try to assure him of my innocence. It was not at all expressed to me
> that he even comprehended my intention, for he gave me a look that I did
> not understand, and it all passed in a moment. But if he had looked at me
> for an hour or for a day, I could not have remembered his face ever
> afterwards, as having been more attentive.[70]

Magwitch's look is a portent of all that Pip will receive from him. A
moment later comes the first installment of that ambiguous legacy.
Magwitch lies and magnifies his guilt in order to shield Pip. This altruistic act, the complement of Pip's similar act in Magwitch's behalf,
is followed by another humanizing sign. When Joe and Pip show Magwitch a kindness, the convict's clicking throat demonstrates that, like
the beast-waif in *The Haunted Man,* he can still be transformed by
love.

The two portentous looks that help structure the opening of *Great
Expectations,* the hypnotic look of evil and the saving look of sympathy and gratitude, linger, recur, and expand. In the remainder of the
novel similar tokens accentuate the book's meaning. When Magwitch's
convict-messenger appears before Pip and gives him money (the an-
nunciatory promise of what is to come), he identifies himself by a
secret sign—he stirs and tastes his drink with a file, the guilty instru-

ment of liberation that Pip stole for the outlawed Magwitch. The words Dickens chooses to describe Pip's reaction to this fantastic, almost surrealistic recrudescence of his criminal past are significant. "I sat gazing at him," Pip writes, "spell-bound."[71] Pip, of course, *is* "spellbound," and the spell under which he labors stems from the fairy-tale compact, to which he continues to acquiesce.

How meaningful these magical details are may be seen if one examines the great recognition chapter which marks Magwitch's return, for the chapter is filled with supernatural tokens which explicate and magnify that return. Pip greets the convict from the top of a black staircase, and he listens as Magwitch's disembodied voice rises from the depths, from the "darkness beneath." Pip holds a lamp over the stair rail, but the lamp is "shaded," and its "circle of light" is "very contracted."[72] The lamp and its circle of light embody the relationship of the two. Magwitch moves into that circle for an instant, then out—just as he had moved in and out of Pip's life. It is only when Magwitch ascends the last two steps, foreshadowing the ascension and confrontation about to take place, that Pip finds that "the light of my lamp included us both."[73] Within that circle of light Pip sees a man dressed "like a voyager by sea," a man with "long iron-grey hair"—terms that vibrate with distant echoes of transportation and leg irons, and that subtly, almost subliminally, evoke Magwitch's past—Pip sees that iron-grey voyager holding out both hands to him.[74] But the magic circle of light that unites Pip and Magwitch, and the outstretched hands that give that unity human expression, are not understood by Pip. He finds his rough visitor abhorrent and rejects his offered hands. Yet the ritual bond is still at work, and the compact sealed on the marshes by looks and oaths is carried forward by other storybook signs—by a continuing ritual of hands. When Pip sees tears of gratitude and love in Magwitch's eyes, he repents his earlier rudeness, and, when Magwitch again stretches out his hand, he gives him his own.

Pip's actions reflect his confused state. He does not recognize "his convict," much less does he recognize that he is a part of the creature. He wavers between snobbery and humanity. His desire to spurn Magwitch grows out of notions superimposed upon his true self, self-wounding notions of gentility and class-consciousness; his impulsive willingness to clasp hands with him is a reflection of his innate goodness. In other words, Pip is as Magwitch left him: self-deluded, erring, but warm-hearted—capable of being saved. And now Magwitch helps Pip save himself. He does this by forcing Pip to confront his sources and thus his true self. Pip, the made gentleman, must see himself and his maker, Magwitch, as they really are, and he must acknowledge their mutual guilt and mutual responsibility. Pip must do the opposite of what the correspondents in the *Household Narrative* and "A Bundle of Emigrants' Letters'' suggested one do. He must publicly confess his oneness with the "loathsome" convict.

That acknowledgment does not come with the first glimmerings of recognition; Pip's initial reaction to his maker and true self is terror. When Magwitch identified himself, Pip "shrank from him" as "if he had been some terrible beast." Pip is horrified by his rough counterpart; he regards Magwitch with "abhorrence," "repugnance," and "dread." But Magwitch forces the truth on Pip. "Look'ee here, Pip," he says. "I'm your second father. You're my son."[75] Pip nearly faints. In that state he allows Magwitch to draw the gold watch out of his pocket, turn the diamond and ruby ring on his finger, and kiss his hands—the latter gesture another incident in the secret ritual of hands. These ritualistic actions, which draw attention to Magwitch's fairy-tale gifts and fairy-tale consanguinity, are received by Pip with fairy-tale reactions. In his trancelike state, he "recoiled" from Magwitch's touch "as if he had been a snake," and when the convict kissed his hands, his "blood ran cold" within him.[76] Pip's terrified response to Magwitch, with its unconscious acknowledgments of shared taint and blood relationship (not yet understood by Pip), is accentuated by the continuing ceremony of hands. "He laid his hand on my shoulder," writes the uncomprehending Pip. "I shuddered at the thought," he goes on with ironic disassociation, "that for anything I knew, his hand might be stained with blood."[77]

The chapter ends with a characteristic intermingling of self-accusing guilt, alter-ego consanguinity, psychological symbolism, and supernatural portents. Magwitch lies asleep in a nearby room, but Pip, with his growing self-knowledge, is far from sleep:

> In every rage of wind and rush of rain, I heard pursuers. Twice, I could have sworn there was a knocking and whispering at the outer door. With these fears upon me, I began either to imagine or recall that I had had mysterious warnings of this man's approach. That, for weeks gone by, I had passed faces in the streets which I had thought like his. That, these likenesses had grown more numerous, as he, coming over the sea, had drawn nearer. That, his wicked spirit had somehow sent these messengers to mine, and that now on this stormy night he was as good as his word, and with me.[78]

Pip's understanding and dread grow. Close by, slumbering in the dark, now unmistakably within Pip's ken and domain, lies the violent maker and projection of himself. The fury of the night increases, Pip's wild premonitions also increase, and then, at last, come the first faint dawnings of awareness. All this is compacted in Pip's next curious impulse and the language in which he records it. Pip's coalescing memories of Magwitch impel him to take up a candle, and, with that light-giving instrument in his hand, go into the convict's room and "look at my dreadful burden."[79]

Here as elsewhere, Dickens manages the mysterious alter-ego relationship between Pip and Magwitch with marvelous skill. Through that occult relationship he makes real the stunning impact of Pip's painful discovery of his unacknowledged self. Pip's confrontation with his hidden self, like David's similar confrontation in *David Copperfield,* is accompanied by tumultuous storm and stress. The unruly world without, tempestuous and full of ominous warnings, mirrors the raging turmoil within. Pip is whirled and buffeted about. Magwitch squats like a gross monster on his gentlemanly hearth. Days go by. "Words cannot tell," Pip writes, "what a sense I had . . . of the dreadful mystery that he was to me." Pip is obsessed by his rough companion, but also baffled by him. His thoughts turn to strange, unnatural storybook relationships. He thinks of Frankenstein and his monster. Frankenstein too was hounded by deep, half-understood sympathies and antipathies, by hidden consanguinities: "The imaginary student pursued by the misshapen creature he had impiously made, was not more wretched than I, pursued by the creature who had made me." Again and again Pip contemplates his secret visitor. He gazes at him with uncomprehending revulsion, but also with deep fascination. "When he fell asleep of an evening, with his knotted hands clenching the sides of the easy-chair, and his bald head tattooed with deep wrinkles falling forward on his breast, I would sit and look at him, wondering what he had done, and loading him with all the crimes in the Calendar." Pip stares at this sleeping embodiment of his guilty past. "Every hour," he writes, "increased my abhorrence of him"; but every hour also increases his commitment. Pip lives in a state of perpetual agony; he is so "haunted"—the word is Pip's—by his secret maker, so shamed by the old stain of crime, dissembling, and coarseness that emanates from him, that he has an almost uncontrollable desire "to start up and fly from him." "I doubt," says Pip, "if a ghost could have been more terrible to me."[80]

But Magwitch *is* a ghost. He haunts and terrifies Pip every bit as much as Marley's ghost, fresh from the grave, haunted and terrified Scrooge. Yet Magwitch is much more than his distant prototypes, much more than Marley's ghost or the ghost of Christmas past. Magwitch is a real person, violent and uncouth. He is also a veritable specter: he is the dread revenant of Pip's tainted origins. Dickens enforces this double role through his intricate book-long insistence on the mutuality of Magwitch and Pip, and through his skillful book-long marshaling of the most artfully connotative images, phrases, and scenes. We respond to this insistent conditioning even when we cannot formulate the sources of our response. Dickens' art controls us.

Guided by that art, we sense that the return of Magwitch is much more than a melodramatic meeting. We know that in confronting Magwitch, Pip confronts a rough alien iron-grey convict; but we also feel, even when we cannot summon the evidence for our feelings, that in confronting Magwitch, Pip also confronts the frightening ghost, risen at last, of his dark secret self.

This unacknowledged ghost of Pip's secret self, this fairy-tale ghost, at once so fanciful and real—the selfsame ghost, terrible and fearsome, that had started up from the graves at Pip's first consciousness, that had now started up again in the noontide of his prosperity—this nightmare ghost, guilt-engendering and forever haunting, will ultimately be exorcised, but only after it has been acknowledged and embraced. The first hesitant step in that acknowledgment had occurred when Pip, candle in hand, had regarded Magwitch as "my dreadful burden." That Pip was able to identify his burden, that he was able to feel that the burden was part of himself, was *his* burden, is the beginning of his (and the continuation of Magwitch's) *Beauty and the Beast* transformation. For Pip, that transformation is slow, laborious, and fablelike; it involves purgation by fire, a sojourn in hell, symbolic illness, death, and rebirth. But it also involves the completion of the compact made in the graveyard, a completion carried forward by the evolving pattern of storybook signs—by the continuing ritual of hands, among others.

That ritual is not confined to Pip and his convict. It enmeshes many other characters in a strange fairy-tale web of correspondences. And the ritual of hands is sometimes combined with other motifs, with the magically directive motif of light and fire, for example. The latter motif moves intricately and centrally through the entire novel. It involves candles, beacons, forges, hearths, sparks, flares of gas, stage fire, and sheets of cleansing flame. It also engages virtually all the characters of the book. The blazing Christmas-tree accident in the home of W. O. Bigg, Esq., has been transformed by art into a cosmic mystery of fire.

That mystery flickers and flares through scene after scene. In one crucial intersection it combines with hand imagery to provide the specific means by which Pip uncovers Estella's lineage and criminal taint, a lineage and taint that mirror his own. Through a fiery version of the occult stigmata that appear so often in legend and romance, through firelit glimpses of Estella's delicate ladylike hands, which at last recall the fierce firelit hands of her violent mother, Pip establishes Estella's identity. His yearned-for princess, dainty and exquisite, the dazzling princess who had caused him to long for a fastidious gentility far removed from Joe's awkward loyalty or Magwitch's sordid gratitude, that fair princess has a coarse criminal past even more devastating than his own. Estella's hands, soft and delicate, the epitome of refinement, incorporate the violent hands of a murderess.

After a while we grow accustomed to such directive signaling; we realize that hand imagery, to dwell for a moment longer on it, accompanies and predicts, not only Estella's parentage, but Pip's as well. Pip's painful acknowledgment of his "second father" is signaled and then confirmed by a long intricate pantomime of hands. But this masque of hands is not confined to Pip's discovery of his origins; it surrounds his every move. Slowly, secretly, bit by bit, the invisible world becomes visible. One sees its subtle signaling everywhere; one sees it clearly in the ritual of hands. The mute language of hands, ordinary and yet hermetic, comments silently on Pip's blind stumbling progress through life. Pip, after all, has been brought up by hand (as his sister never tires of reminding him), and he has also been carefully hand-fashioned over long years by Magwitch. Pip is truly the equivocal product of a profane, lifelong laying on of hands. These central metaphors and insistent repetitions ultimately combine with the intricate web of hand imagery that surrounds Pip to give his most ordinary handshakes, hand injuries, and hand gestures the symbolic force and potency of ritual. That ritual, in turn, is part of an elaborate network of hand imagery that links half the characters of *Great Expectations* in a secret freemasonry of hands. One is constantly astonished by this magical ceremony of hands, for though plain to view, it is virtually invisible; it merges with—one might almost say it loses itself in—the book's compelling realism. This method of uniting object and thesis by modulating reiterated images until the mysterious code locked in their arcane signaling reveals itself can be seen with great clarity in the Pip-Magwitch ritual of hands.

In the daily intercourse between Pip and his returned convict, that magical ritual becomes one gauge of Pip's progression. Magwitch fre quently initiates the ritual, frequently goes "through his favourite action of holding out both his hands for mine."[81] But Pip has not yet come to terms with Magwitch or himself. Magwitch's offered hands only bewilder and dismay him; they remind him of his demeaning involvement with taint and imprisonment, an involvement he has largely forgotten or suppressed or rationalized away. The true implications of that involvement and of Pip's responsibility for it are suggested by the surrounding imagery, an imagery which is unobtrusive but powerfully directive. "I released my hands as soon as I could," says Pip. And then he continues with words that recall but do not describe Magwitch's convict past, his chains and irons, and his alter-ego relationship to himself: "What I was chained to, and how heavily, became intelligible to me, as I heard his hoarse voice, and sat looking up at his furrowed bald head with its iron-grey hair at the sides."[82]

But Pip's final surrender and reversal are not far off, and, when they occur, the book's intricate structure of magical portents culminates and is resolved. When Pip has committed himself to help Magwitch and has brought him to a secret place of safety, he takes leave of his convict in a way that reverses their earlier symbolic lamplight and stair-rail scene and that emphasizes his moral revolution. "We left him," writes Pip of Magwitch, "on the landing outside his door, holding a light over the stair-rail to light us downstairs. Looking back at him, I thought of the first night of his return when our positions were reversed, and when I little supposed my heart could ever be as heavy and anxious at parting from him as it was now."[83]

The cyclical scenes, the symbolic reversals, the double meanings, the signaling names, the fateful rituals, the magical portents continue. Herbert's nickname for Pip (a nickname that violates the name-clause of Pip's fairy-tale gift and that predicts the loss of his storybook expectations) is Handel. Like so many of the names in *Great Expectations*, and like the shamanistic names in ancient myths and tribal legends, the name that Herbert so cavalierly bestows on Pip has strange hidden potencies that gradually reveal themselves. The name Handel ("hand-el," also "handle") draws attention to Pip's early history (he was brought up by hand), to his blacksmith origins (he was christened Handel because of Handel's *Harmonious Blacksmith*), to his subsequent destiny (he was manhandled by Magwitch and then turned into a handmade gentleman by him), to his searing encounter with sin (he was burned and scorched on the hands in that encounter), and to his long spell-like involvement in the crucial ritual of hands. Slowly, little by little, as the novel unfolds, we come to realize that the name Handel is as secretly magical and as secretly meaningful as Blunderbore or Snow White or Cinderella—or as Pip, Orlick, Havisham, or Magwitch, for that matter.

As the book progresses, other predictive motifs are carried forward, repeated, and fulfilled. When Pip takes Magwitch on board his boat for their culminating journey down the river, the convict says, "Dear boy! . . . Faithful dear boy, well done. Thankye, thankye!"[84] The "dear boy" and "thankye" recall Magwitch's words in the opening scenes near the river and complete the promise of those words. For Pip is now totally committed to Magwitch. When Herbert asks Pip, "You go with him?" Pip replies, "No doubt." And when Herbert asks "Where?" Pip, with unmistakable meaning, proposes, "well down the river . . . well beyond Gravesend."[85] During that final journey, Magwitch dips his hand into the water, looks into its ever-flowing depths, and listens to the boat's head "making a sort of a Sunday tune."[86] In another moment he and Compeyson and Pip will be immersed in those life- and death-dealing waters, Compeyson to be sucked to an unshriven death,

Magwitch to emerge mortally wounded but spiritually at peace, and Pip to rise to further regeneration and ultimate rebirth.

That regeneration is now marked by clusters of culminating fairy-tale imagery, including, of course, much directive imagery of hands and looks. Magwitch has come full circle, but so has Pip; though Magwitch is once more a shackled prisoner, Pip no longer flees from him or rejects his hand:

> When I took my place by Magwitch's side, I felt that that was my place henceforth while he lived.
>
> For now my repugnance to him had all melted away, and in the hunted wounded shackled creature who held my hand in his, I only saw a man who had meant to be my benefactor.[87]

Now also the look of long ago is regiven and completed. "It happened," Pip writes, "on two or three occasions in my presence, that his desperate reputation was alluded to by one or other of the people in attendance on him. A smile crossed his face then, and he turned his eyes on me with a trustful look, as if he were confident that I had seen some small redeeming touch in him, even so long ago as when I was a little child."[88]

By the time Magwitch stands in the prisoners' dock on trial for his life, Pip has completed his *Beauty and the Beast* transformation. This is made clear by his action when Magwitch enters the prisoners' dock. "No objection was made to my getting close to the dock, on the outside of it, and holding the hand that he stretched forth to me."[89] Through this gesture, Pip publicly acknowledges his oneness with his rough counterpart. The fearsome convict, so bestial and so frightening, the convict who had emerged all hedged with fairy-tale signs at the moment of Pip's dawning consciousness, the dark creature within Pip, whom Pip had perceived for so long as an alien creature without, that fierce being, Pip now recognizes and accepts as part of himself. Dickens universalizes this scene of shared guilt and unity in society's sacrificial dock and gives the episode an apocalyptic meaning. As the thirty-two condemned men and women, including Magwitch, his hand still held by Pip, stand as a group before the judge for sentencing to death, the rays of the April sun stream through the courtroom's rain-studded windows, make the raindrops glitter and dazzle, and link the judge and the condemned in one great equality of light. In that "way of light,"[90] as Dickens cunningly puts it, a way that transcends man's laws and man's dispositions, in that way, high and low, men and women, judge and criminal, participant and spectator, old offender and "innocent" benefactor are linked by their common humanity and common complicity—a link that will be strengthened all too soon by their com-

mon sufferance of death. Magwitch and Pip affirm this shared human
lot and embrace the duty it imposes of mutuality of concern. During
and after the sentencing, Magwitch clings to Pip's freely offered hand.
"He held my hand while all the others were removed, and while the
audience got up." The spectators stare at the condemned men and
women; they point to this one and to that, but "most of all" they point
"at him and me."[91] Pip accepts this pointing without protest; he now
makes no distinction between Magwitch and himself.

Later, during Magwitch's languishing and death, Pip remains with
him and shares his suffering. Pip's selfless vigil helps him achieve the
peace that he had failed to win by his self-centered strivings—and
Magwitch, as usual, is the ambiguous touchstone both of his chastening
and his salvation. These final transformations are all reflected by the
continuing fairy-tale symbolism, by recurrences—now strikingly inverted—of the supernatural gate motif. Pip, whose concern for Magwitch had induced him to obey Orlick's summons and go to the gates of
hell, is also brought by the convict to the gates of heaven; gates which
are ironically, and in keeping with Dickens' inverted fairy story, the
gates of man's earthly prison. Pip waits at those prison gates as the
child Dickens had waited at the Marshalsea prison gates. And just as
that corrosive waiting had shaped Dickens' great gift and achievement,
Pip's faithful waiting and ministering bring him a miraculous gift, the
gift of humility and understanding, the gift that saves him. As Magwitch draws his last breaths, he turns to the self-condemned fellow-
sufferer at his side:

> "Dear boy," he said, as I sat down by his bed: "I thought you was late.
> But I knowed you couldn't be that."
> "It is just the time," said I. "I waited for it at the gate."
> "You always waits at the gate; don't you, dear boy?"
> "Yes. Not to lose a moment of the time."
> "Thank'ee, dear boy, thank'ee. God bless you! You've never deserted
> me, dear boy."
> I pressed his hand in silence, for I could not forget that I had once meant
> to desert him.[92]

A moment later, when Magwitch has spoken his last words, Pip
completes another cyclical ritual of consanguinity and acceptance.
"He smiled," writes Pip, "and I understood his touch to mean that he
wished to lift my hand, and lay it on his breast. I laid it there, and he
smiled again, and put both his hands upon it."[93] The ceremony of
hands now culminates. "With a last faint effort, which would have
been powerless but for my yielding to it, and assisting it," writes Pip,
"he raised my hand to his lips. Then he gently let it sink upon his breast
again, with his own hands lying on it." Magwitch is dead. Pip murmurs

a prayer for his rough counterpart, a prayer which is an adaptation of a line from the parable of the Pharisee and the publican. The message of that parable—"every one that exalteth himself shall be abased; and he that humbleth himself shall be exalted"—epitomizes Pip's journey from Pharisaism to understanding, and presages his salvation. But Pip's adaptation of the publican's prayer does more than recall the parable's moral. By displacing the publican's "to me" with "to him," Pip again calls attention to his alter-ego relationship to Magwitch, and he underscores his new self-awareness and self-inculpation. "O Lord," he pleads, "be merciful to him a sinner!"[94]

Pip, who is also a sinner, and who now accepts responsibility for his and his fellow man's sins, leaves this scene of death and regeneration to go to his own spiritual death and rebirth. He becomes ill, sinks into a phantasmagoric delirium, awakens weeks later, helpless, tremulous, and babylike, and in the resurrecting springtime, under the godfatherly care of Joe, gathers strength and wisdom for a chastened chance at life.

Great Expectations is more than a fairy tale grown big; it is a narrative that partakes of fairy-tale transformation, a narrative that fuses autobiographical, sociological, psychological, and mythological elements into a deeply resonant unity, a unity that is at once esoteric and realistic. Vagrant motes of life, ordinary and insignificant—Martha Joachim and Miss Gordon, Berners Street and York Buildings, an emigrant letter and a stray issue of the *Household Narrative:* inconsequential and rudimentary paradigms of deluded expectations, death in life, fiery consanguinity, and made gentlemen—have been plucked from the arid wasteland of the commonplace and translated to the realms of romance. In those realms, through the alembic of Dickens' imagination, those vagrant motes and their thronging counterparts, still retaining their original form and substance, but at the same time wonderfully modified by Dickens' fabling mind, are worked into the great central structures of the controlling design and given the richness of art. This alchemy, the alchemy of art, is part of Dickens' lifelong habit of assimilation and transformation, a habit that was coincident, on the purely cognitive level, with Dickens' nascent beginnings, but that soon took on self-conscious dimensions, underwent the special trauma of his formative years, and then grew and evolved through the remainder of his life. In *Great Expectations,* Dickens' early experiences and fantasies, his fairy-tale finales and godmother figures, his later disappointments and insights have been transmuted into a subtle, endlessly ramifying fable that concentrates reality and deepens our apprehension of life.

This achievement owes much to Dickens' reliance on fairy tales. Through that reliance he gained a whole array of motifs—the gift that proves a curse, the dissembling witch, the disguised godfather, the poisonous princess, the deadly labyrinth, the haunted house, the journey to the underworld—that helped him convey his intensely poetic vision of life. Through that reliance he also gained a large family of associated techniques—techniques ranging from recurrence, ritualism, and magical symbolism, to animism, leitmotif, and alter-ego doubling—that he found suggestive and congenial. By means of these motifs and these techniques he imbued the simplest objects and personages of the everyday world—objects such as gates, fires, and hands; personages such as recluses, convicts, and made gentlemen—with the archetypal fears and fulfillments of fairyland.

Dickens' universality, like his motifs and techniques, is also connected to his commitment to fairy tales. For that commitment helped him tap the same deep reservoir of wishes and urges that fairy stories tap, a reservoir fed by man's immemorial responses to life. Fairy tales, like myths, legends, fables, fantasies, and other correlatives of the invisible world—correlatives that overlap and reflect one another— survive because they embody deep and profoundly attractive or frightening human hopes and fears. At the same time, fairy stories also embody a sense of life's mystery and wonder, a refraction of life's strangeness and wildness; they testify to the weird signatures and correspondences, the enigmatic forces that lie buried deep in the hidden heart of things. Aided by fairy tales, aided by the soft secret murmurings of the invisible world, Dickens manages to incorporate these transcendental mysteries into all his works, at first crudely, but then more subtly and pervasively. That Dickens wrote the fables he did reflects the particularity of his time and personality—especially the influence of his early years. But the fairy-tale quality of his imagination, and the undercurrent of myth, magic, and ritual to which it gave birth, link his writings with the works of other great masters of the written word.

Sophocles' insistent oracles, blind prophets, and cosmic ironies; Shakespeare's weird sisters, portentous ghosts, and guilty hallucinations; Dostoevsky's fatal loadstones, foreboding dreams, and cyclical actions; and Dickens' dissembling witches, magic circles, and dark doubles, are all part of the same imaginative reconstruction of reality. This is true not simply because Shakespeare's theater contained elements of the Sophoclean tradition, or because Dickens had absorbed Shakespeare in hundreds of performances and scores of rereadings, or because Dostoevsky had pored over Dickens' novels in his prison exile; nor is it true simply because each author (and this applies, of course, not merely to these four) had partaken of an analogous heritage of folklore and fancy. It is true because through such suprarealistic counterpoint the artist's fabling and concentrating mind is able to impose order upon the petty welter of everyday experience. It is one of the artist's primary ways not merely of remaking experience but of communicating experience and commenting on it. In the hands of a master, this heightening and concentration are fused with realism— blind Oedipus' symbolic blinding, Lady Macbeth's bloodguilt, Pip's hell journey, Raskolnikov's self-immolating, self-freeing confessions—in ways which do not belie, but instead enhance, our understanding of the infinite complexities of life.

Abbreviations

AYR	*All the Year Round*	**HW**	*Household Words*
BH	*Bleak House*	**LD**	*Little Dorrit*
BL	*The Battle of Life*	**MC**	*Martin Chuzzlewit*
BR	*Barnaby Rudge*	**MP**	*Miscellaneous Papers*
C	*The Chimes*	**NL**	Nonesuch *Letters*
CB	*Christmas Books*	**NN**	*Nicholas Nickleby*
CC	*A Christmas Carol*	**OCS**	*The Old Curiosity Shop*
CH	*The Cricket on the Hearth*	**OMF**	*Our Mutual Friend*
CS	*Christmas Stories*	**OT**	*Oliver Twist*
DC	*David Copperfield*	**PL**	Pilgrim *Letters*
DS	*Dombey and Son*	**PP**	*The Pickwick Papers*
ED	*Edwin Drood*	**RP**	*Reprinted Pieces*
F	Forster's *Life*	**S**	*Speeches*
GE	*Great Expectations*	**SB**	*Sketches by Boz*
GSE	*George Silverman's Explanation*	**TTC**	*A Tale of Two Cities*
		UT	*The Uncommercial Traveller*
HM	*The Haunted Man*	**UW**	*Uncollected Writings*
HT	*Hard Times*		

Notes

Chapter I—Dickens, Cruikshank, and the Sanctity of Fairy Tales: A Prologue

1. *The Letters of Charles Dickens*, ed. Walter Dexter, 3 vols. Nonesuch Edition (Bloomsbury, 1938), II, 463 [June 1853]. With a few exceptions which are cited directly, all of the quotations from Dickens' letters are taken from the above edition, or, in letters through 1843, from *The Letters of Charles Dickens*, ed. Madeline House, Graham Storey, and Kathleen Tillotson, Vols. I–III. Pilgrim Edition (Oxford, 1965, 1969, 1974). In order to eliminate unnecessary documentation, I have usually incorporated the date of a letter into the text. In such instances, and in certain other instances (for example, when a piece is short and I have clearly indicated the source in the text), I do not give additional documentation.

After the initial reference, I abbreviate frequently used sources. With Dickens' works, I abbreviate from the outset. For a key to these abbreviations, see List of Abbreviations.

2. *NL*, II, 465 (18 June 1853).

3. "Dullborough Town," *UT*, 160; from an autobiographical passage in *DC*, iv, 62. Unless otherwise designated, all references to Dickens' writings are taken from *The Works of Charles Dickens*, 40 vols. National Edition (London, 1906–1908), and are cited by book, chapter, and page number, as relevant.

4. "A Preliminary Word," *MP*, I, 107, 109.

5. "A Christmas Tree," *CS*, I, 14; "Ignorance and Crime," *MP*, I, 35; *LD*, I, iii, 34; *NL*, I, 825; "Mr. Barlow," *UT*, 430.

6. *GE*, xxii, 190.

7. *OMF*, II, i, 249–250.

8. *Oliver Twist* appeared in *Bentley's Miscellany* (with interruptions) from February 1837 through April 1839. The novel was completed, however, several months before its concluding serial installments in the *Miscellany*, and the book version was published in November 1838.

9. *PL*, I, 450–451.

10. Frederic G. Kitton, *Dickens and His Illustrators* (London, 1899), 17.

11. *PL*, I, 589; II, 213.

12. Blanchard Jerrold, *The Life of George Cruikshank*, new ed. (London, 1898), 221–222.

13. Mrs. E. M. Ward, *Memories of Ninety Years*, 2nd ed., ed. Isabel G. McAllister (New York, n. d.), 85–86.

14. *NL*, II, 51–52.

15. "Cruikshank's 'The Drunkard's Children,'" *MP*, I, 39–43.

16. *MP*, I, 272–278.

17. For the text of *Hop-o'-my-Thumb* and the other tales in the Fairy Library, I have used a collected edition which seems to have been made up by binding together the four original editions. For a more readily available text, see George Cruikshank, *The Cruikshank Fairy Book* (New York, 1897).

18. *MP*, I, 361–368.

19. "A Reminiscence of George Cruik-shank and His 'Magazine,'" *Notes and Queries*, 5th ser., IX (13 April 1878), 281.

20. *Letters from Charles Dickens to Angela Burdett-Coutts, 1841–1865*, ed. Edgar Johnson (London, 1953), 235.

21. *HT*, I, vii, 55.

22. Delivered to the Royal General Theatrical Fund, 6 April 1857. *The Speeches of Charles Dickens*, ed. K. J. Fielding (Oxford, 1960), 230.

23. Delivered to the Prize-Giving of the Institutional Association of Lancashire and Cheshire: Manchester, 3 December 1858. *S*, 284.

Chapter II—The Fairy-Tale Heritage: "All . . . as of Yore . . . Infinite Delights"

1. F. J. Harvey Darton, *Children's Books in England: Five Centuries of Social Life*, 2nd ed. (Cambridge, 1960), 47. My discussion of the history of English children's literature in the first section of this chapter draws upon Darton and upon the following sources: Percy Muir, *English Children's Books, 1600–1900* (London, 1954); Bettina Hürlimann, *Three Centuries of Children's Books in Europe*, trans. B. W. Alderson (London, 1967); Gillian Avery and Angela Bull, *Nineteenth Century Children: Heroes and Heroines in English Children's Stories, 1780–1900* (London, 1965); Roger Lancelyn Green, *Tellers of Tales: Children's Books and their Authors from 1800 to 1964*, rev. ed. (London, 1965); Andrew W. Tuer, *Pages and Pictures from Forgotten Children's Books* (London, 1898–1899); William Targ, ed. *Bibliophile in the Nursery* (Cleveland, 1957); Iona and Peter Opie, *The Classic Fairy Tales* (London, 1974); Victor E. Neuburg, *Chapbooks* (London, 1964); Judith St. John, *The Osborne Collection of Early Children's Books, 1566–1910* (Toronto, 1966); Judith St. John, Dana Tenny, Hazel I. Mactaggart, *The Osborne Collection of Early Children's Books, 1476–1910*, Vol. II (Toronto, 1975).

2. "Mr. Barlow," *UT*, 431–432.

3. *GE*, xiii, 111.

4. *LD*, iii, 34.

5. "Out of the Season," *RP*, 292–293.

6. "Preface to the Original Edition," *German Popular Stories* (London, 1868), xvi.

7. Ibid.

8. Dickens knew and respected Cole, but objected to some of the doctrines espoused by the Department of Practical Art, and quite unfairly, in view of Cole's ideas in general and his notions about imagination and children's literature in particular, classified him as a fact-mongering enemy of fancy, and satirized him in *Hard Times* (1854).

9. Darton, 79.

10. *OCS*, lxxi, 343; *HT*, III, vii, 325; *NL*, II, 602–603.

11. "Preface to the Third Edition," *OT*, xii.

12. Earl Leslie Griggs. ed., *Collected Letters of Samuel Taylor Coleridge* (Oxford, 1956), I, 354.

13. E. V. Lucas, ed., *The Letters of Charles and Mary Lamb* (London, 1905), I, 252–253.

Chapter III—Dickens' Fabling Mind: "A Mist of Fancy over Well-Remembered Facts"

1. H. C. Dent, *The Life and Characters of Charles Dickens* (London, n.d.), 27, quoting Sir Wemyss Reid.

2. Robert Langton, *The Childhood and Youth of Charles Dickens* (London, 1912), 29, 44, 224; "Nurse's Stories," *UT*, 191.

3. Langton, 25, 29, 58; John Forster, *The Life of Charles Dickens,* ed. J. W. T. Ley (London, 1928), 2.

4. "Nurse's Stories," *UT,* 188–202; "Dullborough Town," *UT,* 150; "The Holly-Tree," *CS,* I, 130–132. The account that follows is based, for the most part, on these essays, especially the first and last.

5. "Nurse's Stories," *UT,* 194–195.

6. "Nurse's Stories," *UT,* 200–201.

7. "Nurse's Stories," *UT,* 201; "The Holly-Tree," *CS,* I, 130–132.

8. "Nurse's Stories," *UT,* 191.

9. "A Christmas Tree," *CS,* I, 8.

10. "A Christmas Tree," *CS,* I, 8–9.

11. *NL,* III, 58.

12. "An Idea of Mine," *MP,* II, 161; *BH,* ii, 8.

13. *Mrs. Lirriper's Lodgings, CS,* II, 20.

14. "First Fruits," *UW,* II, 413–415.

15. "First Fruits," *UW,* II, 415.

16. F, 12; "Where We Stopped Growing," *MP,* I, 313.

17. *DS,* lvi, 405; *GE,* xx, 179.

18. "Travelling Abroad," *UT,* 91.

19. *The Perils of Certain English Prisoners, CS,* I, 251; "New Year's Day," *MP,* II, 175; F, 12.

20. *LD,* xxiii, 312.

21. "The Child's Story," *CS,* I, 52.

22. "A Christmas Tree," *CS,* I, 8.

23. F, 4.

24. *NL,* I, 316.

25. "Autobiographical Fragment," F, 35.

26. Langton, 25–26.

27. "The Holly-Tree," *CS,* I, 147.

28. Langton, 34–35.

29. Langton, 34–35.

30. A School-Fellow and Friend, "Recollections of Charles Dickens," *Dickensian,* VII (September 1911), 229; C. E. Bechhofer Roberts, "The Huffams, the Barrows, and the Admiralty," *Dickensian,* XXIV (September 1928), 264.

31. John T. Page, "Dickens and Guy Fawkes," *Dickensian,* VIII (October 1912), 278–279.

32. F, 6.

33. Langton, 25; F, 8.

34. *PL,* I, 382.

35. F, 6–7.

36. "Dullborough Town," *UT,* 152.

37. Ibid., 153.

38. Ibid., 152–153.

39. "A Christmas Tree," *CS,* I, 12–13.

40. My discussion of the history and vogue of the toy theater draws upon the following works, especially the first: George Speaight, *Juvenile Drama: The History of the English Toy Theatre* (London, 1946) and A. E. Wilson, *Penny Plain, Two Pence Coloured: A History of the Juvenile Drama* (London, 1932).

41. F, 3, 11, 13.

42. F, 3.

43. F, 6.

44. V & A MS, Carlyle to Forster, 16 February 1874.

45. *HT and Other Stories,* 453.

46. F, 5.

47. *DC,* iv, 62–63.

48. *DC,* iv, 63.

49. F, 8.

50. F, 8–9.

51. "Preface to the Third Edition," *OT,* xv.

52. *DC,* iv, 63; "Dullborough Town," *UT,* 152; "Preface to the First Cheap Edition," *PP,* xviii–xix.

53. *NL,* II, 773; "A Plated Article," *RP,* 171.

54. *NL,* II, 773.

55. *NL,* II, 231.

56. *NL,* II, 231.

57. "Frauds on the Fairies," *MP,* I, 361.

58. *CS,* I, 10.

59. *CS,* I, 11.

60. "Dullborough Town, *UT,* 152.

61. "Gone Astray," *MP,* I, 355.

62. "Autobiographical Fragment," F, 10.

63. *DC,* x, 170.

64. F, 8.

65. "Dullborough Town," *UT,* 160; F, 8.

66. F, 12–13.

67. F, 12.

68. "Autobiographical Fragment," F, 27; *DC,* xi, 174.

69. F, 6.
70. "Autobiographical Fragment," F, 29.
71. F, 26.
72. F, 30.
73. *DC*, vii, 103–104.
74. *DC*, vii, 104.
75. *DC*, vii, 105.
76. *DC*, vii, 106.
77. *DC*, vii, 106.
78. *DC*, xiii, 205.
79. F, 27.
80. F, 43–44.
81. F, 43–44.
82. *DC*, xi, 190.
83. F, 30.

84. F, 32–33.
85. "Autobiographical Fragment," F, 33.
86. F, 32–33.
87. "Autobiographical Fragment," F, 29.
88. "Autobiographical Fragment," F, 28, 31.
89. "Autobiographical Fragment," F, 28.
90. "Autobiographical Fragment," F, 34.
91. *DC*, xi, 192.
92. "Autobiographical Fragment," F, 35.

Chapter IV—From *Pickwick* to *Chuzzlewit:* Fairy Tales and the Apprentice Novels

1. *PP*, xlii, 252.
2. *PP*, lvii, 514.
3. *PP*, lvii, 511–512.
4. *PP*, lvii, 512.
5. *PP*, xlv, 308.
6. *PP*, iii, 45.
7. *PP*, iii, 51, 50.
8. *PP*, iii, 47.
9. *PP*, iii, 52–53.
10. *PP*, vi, 106.
11. *PP*, xvii, 297.
12. *PP*, xiv, 242.
13. *PP*, xiv, 247.
14. *PP*, xlviii, 357.
15. *PP*, xlix, 380.
16. *PP*, xxxvi, 138.
17. *PP*, xxxvi, 138.
18. *PP*, xi, 185.
19. *PP*, xi, 193.
20. *PP*, xi, 187.
21. *PP*, xxix, 515.
22. *PP*, xxix, 516.
23. *PP*, xxix, 525.
24. *PP*, xxix, 525–526.
25. *PP*, xxix, 526.
26. *OT*, xvii, 153–154.
27. *PP*, xi, 195.
28. *NN*, lxiv, 488–490.
29. *NN*, "Preface to the First Edition," xv.

30. *NN*, "Preface to the First Cheap Edition," xxi–xxii.
31. *NN*, lxii, 460–467.
32. *NN*, lxii, 460–465.
33. *BR*, iii, 39–40.
34. *BR*, x, 111.
35. *BR*, x, 111–112.
36. *BR*, vi, 70.
37. *BR*, lxxxii, 422.
38. *BR*, lvi, 146.
39. *BR*, lxii, 198.
40. *BR*, lxii, 196–197.
41. *BR*, lxii, 199.
42. *BR*, lxii, 200.
43. *BR*, lxii, 206.
44. *BR*, i, 2.
45. *BR*, i, 4.
46. *BR*, i, 16–21; xxxiii, 342–348.
47. *BR*, xxxi, 314–315.
48. *BR*, lxxxii, 418.
49. *MC*, l, 427.
50. *MC*, liii, 488.
51. *MC*, liv, 498–500.
52. *MC*, ii, 16.
53. *MC*, li, 446.
54. *MC*, iv, 55.
55. *MC*, ii, 10–12.
56. *MC*, ix, 158.
57. *MC*, ix, 159.
58. *MC*, ix, 159.

59. *MC*, ix, 160–161.
60. *MC*, ix, 162.
61. *MC*, ix, 163.
62. *MC*, xlii.
63. *MC*, xlvi, 362.
64. *MC*, xlvi, 362–363.
65. *MC*, xlvii, 364.
66. *MC*, xlvii, 364–365.
67. *MC*, xlvii, 369.
68. *MC*, xlvii, 372.
69. *MC*, xlvii, 373.
70. *OT*, viii, 75.
71. *OT*, viii, 74.
72. *OT*, viii, 74.
73. *OT*, viii, 74.
74. *OT*, viii, 75.
75. *OT*, ix, 77.
76. *OT*, li, 507.
77. *OT*, xlviii, 465.
78. *OT*, l, 493.
79. "Autobiographical Fragment," F, 25.
80. "Autobiographical Fragment," F, 28.
81. *OT*, xii.
82. *OT*, liii, 528.
83. *OT*, xxxii, 298–300.
84. *OT*, xxxii, 300.
85. *OT*, xxxiv, 328–330.
86. *OT*, xxxiv, 330.
87. *OT*, xxxiv, 330.
88. *OT*, xxxv, 330–333.
89. *OT*, li, 508.
90. F, 146.
91. *OCS*, xv, 150, 154.
92. *OCS*, i, 18.
93. *OCS*, iii, 27.
94. *OCS*, iii, 27.
95. *OCS*, iii, 27.
96. *OCS*, iii, 27, 31.

97. *OCS*, v, 51.
98. *OCS*, v, 51–52.
99. *OCS*, iv, 36.
100. *OCS*, lxvii, 297; iv, 47.
101. *OCS*, iv, 36.
102. *OCS*, lxii, 238–240.
103. *OCS*, lxii, 240–241.
104. *OCS*, lxii, 243.
105. *OCS*, l, 127.
106. *OCS*, iv, 40.
107. *OCS*, vi, 58–59; ix, 98; xi, 115.
108. *OCS*, iv, 37; lxvii, 296.
109. *OCS*, lxvii, 303.
110. *OCS*, lxvii, 304.
111. *OCS*, lxvii, 304.
112. *OCS*, lxvii, 304.
113. *OCS*, lxvii, 304–306.
114. *OCS*, lxxiii, 358–359.
115. *OCS*, i, 7, 17.
116. *OCS*, i, 13.
117. *OCS*, xlvii, 99.
118. *OCS*, xxii, 224.
119. *OCS*, xxii, 224.
120. F, 30.
121. *OCS*, lxxiii, 362.
122. *OCS*, lxxiii, 363.
123. *OCS*, lxiv, 259.
124. *OCS*, xxxiv, 344.
125. *OCS*, xii.
126. *OCS*, xix, 190.
127. *OCS*, xliv, 63–72.
128. *PL*, II, 144.
129. *PL*, II, 181–182.
130. *OCS*, liv, 168.
131. *PP*, "Preface to the First Cheap Edition," xvi.
132. *PL*, I, 540.
133. *MC*, "Preface to the First Edition," xiv.

Chapter V—The Christmas Books: "Giving Nursery Tales a Higher Form"

1. The dates given here refer to actual publication; the second and third books, though issued in December 1844 and December 1845 respectively, were dated the following year.
2. F, 422–423, 466–467.

3. F, 317.
4. *CC*, 3.
5. *CC*, i, 6.
6. *CC*, i, 7.
7. *CC*, i, 7.
8. *CC*, i, 14.

9. *CC*, i, 14.
10. *CC*, i, 15.
11. *CC*, i, 17–19.
12. *CC*, i, 20.
13. *CC*, ii, 30.
14. *CC*, ii, 30–31.
15. *CC*, ii, 32.
16. *CC*, v, 83.
17. *C*, i, 99.
18. *C*, i, 99–100.
19. *C*, i, 118.
20. *C*, ii, 139.
21. *C*, ii, 141.
22. *C*, ii, 141.
23. *C*, ii, 141.
24. *C*, ii, 141.
25. *C*, iii, 144.
26. *C*, iii, 144.
27. *C*, iii, 145.
28. *NL*, I, 627.
29. *NL*, I, 631.
30. *NL*, I, 630.
31. *CH*, ii, 220.
32. *CH*, i 196.
33. *CH*, i, 218.
34. F, 426.
35. *HM*, iii, 469.
36. *HM*, i, 389.

37. *HM*, i, 389.
38. *HM*, i, 391.
39. *HM*, i, 391.
40. *HM*, i, 387–388.
41. *HM*, i, 412.
42. *HM*, ii, 442.
43. *HM*, ii, 454.
44. *HM*, ii, 446.
45. *HM*, ii, 446–447.
46. *HM*, iii, 465.
47. *HM*, ii, 458.
48. *HM*, ii, 458–459.
49. *HM*, i, 409.
50. F, 521.
51. *HM*, i, 388.
52. *HM*, i, 406–407.
53. *HM*, i, 408.
54. *HM*, i, 408.
55. *CB*, xi. In the Preface (1868) to the Charles Dickens Edition of the Christmas books, Dickens amended the second sentence as follows: "I could not attempt great elaboration of detail, in the working out of character within such limits." In the next sentence he changed "My purpose" to "My chief purpose"—xi.
56. *NL*, I, 549.

Chapter VI—*Dombey and Son:* The New Fairy-Tale Method

1. F, 422–428, 431–432, 466–467.
2. *DS*, viii, 108.
3. vi, 75.
4. vi, 73.
5. vi, 74.
6. xx, 323.
7. xx, 325.
8. lv, 390.
9. xx, 323.
10. xx, 324–325.
11. lv, 379–385.
12. lv, 387.
13. lv, 387.
14. lv, 387.
15. lv, 388.
16. lv, 388.
17. lv, 388.
18. lv, 388.

19. lv, 390.
20. lv, 390.
21. *NL*, II, 17–18.
22. *DS*, xx, 330.
23. xxiii, 382.
24. xxiii, 384.
25. xxiii, 388–389.
26. lx, 476–480.
27. xi, 164.
28. xi, 164.
29. Number Plan V.
30. *DS*, i, 1.
31. viii, 104.
32. viii, 106.
33. viii, 125.
34. viii, 126.
35. xi, 167.
36. xi, 168.

37. xiv, 222–223.
38. xii, 192.
39. i, 12.
40. vii, 110–111.
41. xiv, 233.
42. xiv, 234.
43. xiv, 235–237.
44. xviii, 285.
45. xviii, 287.
46. xviii, 294.
47. xviii, 294.
48. xviii, 294–296.
49. xxi, 337, 341.
50. lix, 460.
51. lix, 460.
52. lix, 465.
53. lxi, 483.
54. lxi, 484.
55. For examples of the latter leitmotif, see xvii, 296; lix, 457, 458.
56. *The Child's Fairy Library* (London, c. 1835). Dickens reread *Cinderella* in this version while crossing the Atlantic on his way to America in 1842—four years before beginning *Dombey* (*NL,* II, 231).
57. *DS,* xxiv, 398.
58. See, for example, "Gone Astray," *MP,* I, 350–360.
59. *DS,* xlvii, 262.
60. xlviii, 263.
61. l, 310.
62. vi, 81, 86.
63. xiv, 220.
64. xix, 304.
65. xix, 307.
66. *TTC,* "Preface," xiii.
67. *TTC,* II, xiii.
68. *DS,* xvi, 258.
69. xvi, 260–261.
70. xiv, 233.
71. lix, 465.
72. xxiii, 365.
73. xxiii, 366.
74. xxiii, 366, 367.

75. xxiii, 368, 369, 370, 371.
76. F, 27; *NL,* I, 807.
77. *DS,* viii, 115.
78. viii, 115.
79. viii, 115.
80. viii, 116.
81. viii, 117.
82. viii, 117.
83. viii, 115–121.
84. viii, 120.
85. viii, 121.
86. vi, 81.
87. vi, 81.
88. vi, 82.
89. vi, 82.
90. vi, 83.
91. vi, 83–84.
92. vi, 84.
93. vi, 84.
94. vi, 84–85.
95. vi, 87.
96. vi, 88.
97. vi, 91.
98. vi, 93.
99. vi, 95.
100. xlv, 220.
101. xxvii, 436.
102. xxvii, 436.
103. xxvii, 437.
104. xxvii, 437–439.
105. xxvii, 448.
106. xxvii, 448–449.
107. ix, 127.
108. ix, 129.
109. xix, 305.
110. xlviii, 275.
111. xlix, 282.
112. xlix, 282.
113. xlix, 283.
114. xlix, 281.
115. xlix, 296.
116. lvi, 400.
117. lvii, 420.
118. lvii, 420.

Chapter VII—*David Copperfield:*
The Fairy-Tale Method Perfected

1. *DC,* i, 2–3.
2. i, 2.
3. i, 2.

4. i, 1.
5. i, 5.
6. i, 5–6.

7. i, 8.
8. i, 14.
9. xii, 199–200.
10. xiii, 216.
11. xiii, 221.
12. xxxv, 77.
13. xiv, 243.
14. *NL,* III, 122.
15. *NL,* II, 160.
16. *DC,* iii, 47.
17. iii, 47–48.
18. i, 6.
19. i, 6.
20. ii, 16.
21. ix, 146.
22. ix, 150.
23. iv, 61.
24. xiii, 222.
25. v, 88.
26. viii, 135.
27. xiii, 204.
28. xiii, 206.
29. xiii, 212.
30. xiii, 207–210.
31. xiii, 213.
32. xiii, 216.
33. xv, 247.
34. xv, 247.
35. xv, 250.
36. xv, 247; xvi, 264.
37. xvi, 265.
38. xvi, 266.
39. xxv, 425, 427.
40. xv, 248.
41. xvi, 260.
42. xv, 254–255.
43. xxxix, 163.
44. xxvi, 435.
45. lii, 353.
46. xxxix, 153.
47. xxxix, 153.
48. xvi, 268.
49. xxv, 428.
50. xxxix, 162.
51. xlii, 209; lii, 358.
52. xlix, 304.
53. xlix, 308, 313; lii, 359, 365.
54. xvi, 264.
55. xvi, 267.
56. xxv, 431.
57. xxv, 431.

58. xxv, 432.
59. xxv, 433.
60. xxv, 433–434.
61. xxv, 434.
62. liv, 394.
63. vii, 117.
64. xxi, 340.
65. xxi, 358.
66. xxiii, 387.
67. xxi, 357.
68. xxi, 351.
69. xxi, 352.
70. xxi, 353.
71. xxi, 357–358.
72. xxii, 362–363.
73. xxii, 363.
74. xxii, 364.
75. xxii, 366–367.
76. xxii, 368.
77. xxiv, 407.
78. xxv, 414.
79. xxv, 414.
80. xxv, 414.
81. xxv, 415.
82. xxv, 415.
83. xxvi, 436.
84. x, 165.
85. x, 166.
86. x, 167.
87. iii, 35, 38.
88. li, 345.
89. xxii, 363.
90. xxii, 364.
91. xx, 334.
92. xx, 330.
93. xxix, 486.
94. xxix, 486; lvi, 413.
95. xxi, 341.
96. xlvi, 262.
97. xlvi, 262.
98. xx, 337.
99. xx, 337.
100. xlvi, 262.
101. lvi, 416.
102. xxxii, 39.
103. xxxii, 40.
104. xlvi, 262; xxii, 377.
105. l, 325.
106. l, 324.
107. xlvi, 265.
108. xxix, 491.

109. xxix, 492.
110. xxix, 492.
111. lxiv, 498–499.
112. xxvi, 437.
113. xxvi, 440.
114. xxvi, 440.
115. xxvi, 442.
116. xxvi, 447.
117. xxxiii, 42.
118. xxxiii, 43.
119. xxxiii, 51.
120. xxxiii, 53.
121. xxxiii, 53.
122. xxxiii, 53.
123. xxxiii, 53–54.
124. xxxiii, 55.
125. xxxiii, 55.
126. xxxiii, 60.
127. xxxv, 94; xxxvi, 94.
128. xxxviii, 134.
129. xxxviii, 142.
130. xxxvii, 119.
131. xxxvii, 122.
132. xliii, 221.
133. xliii, 222.
134. xliii, 222.
135. xliv, 230.
136. *NL,* II, 626–627, 628–629; F, 638–639.
137. F, 639.
138. *DC,* iv, 54, 58.
139. iv, 61.
140. viii, 130.
141. iv, 55; ix, 145.
142. iv, 61.
143. lix, 448.
144. lxi, 466–468.
145. *NL,* II, 234.
146. *DC,* lv, 397.
147. lv, 397.
148. lv, 399.
149. lv, 400.
150. lv, 400.
151. lv, 400.
152. lv, 401.
153. lv, 401.
154. lv, 401–402.
155. lv, 402.
156. lv, 402–403.
157. lv, 403.
158. lv, 403.
159. lv, 404.
160. lv, 404.
161. lv, 404.
162. lv, 404.
163. lv, 405.
164. lv, 405.
165. lv, 407.
166. lv, 407.
167. lv, 408.
168. lv, 409.
169. lv, 410.
170. xxxix, 148–149.
171. xxxv, 82–83.
172. xxxix, 162.
173. xxxv, 88.
174. xxxv, 88–89.
175. xxxv, 93.
176. liv, 380.
177. lviii, 429.
178. lviii, 429.
179. lviii, 430.
180. lviii, 432.
181. lviii, 433.
182. lviii, 433.
183. lviii, 433.
184. lxii, 484–486.
185. lx, 464.
186. lxii, 486.
187. xliv, 238–239.
188. lxii, 488.
189. lxii, 485.
190. lxii, 485–486.
191. This is to say nothing of the conception of womanhood imparted by the two characters. Both characters epitomize male-oriented fantasies of female subordination. Dora is an alluring but helpless ninny. Agnes is an adored angel whose chief role is to serve and comfort the man who worships her.
192. lxii, 488.
193. liii, 379.
194. lx, 459.
195. lx, 460.
196. lxii, 486.
197. lxii, 487.
198. lxiv, 499.
199. lxiv, 498.
200. lxix, 501.
201. lxix, 501.
202. xiii.

Chapter VIII—*Great Expectations:*
The Factual Matrix

1. *MP,* I, 315.
2. Mrs. Mathews, *Memoirs of Charles Mathews, Comedian,* 4 vols. (London, 1839), IV, 74–79.
3. F, 380.
4. *NL,* I, 680.
5. *UW,* I, 96.
6. "Autobiographical Fragment," F, 23, 27.

7. "Autobiographical Fragment," F, 35.
8. F, 640.
9. 7 December 1857, *Dickensian,* XXXVIII (1942), 190.
10. *NL,* II, 888, 890.
11. *CS,* II, iv, 484–485.
12. *CS,* II, iv, 486.
13. *CS,* II, iv, 482–483.
14. *CS,* II, iv, 487.

Chapter IX—*Great Expectations:*
The Fairy-Tale Transformation

1. *GE,* ii, 14; i, 5.
2. F, 734.
3. F, 734.
4. *GE,* xxviii, 244.
5. xxviii, 246; F, 35.
6. xxx, 262–263.
7. xliv, 391; letter to Mrs. Watson, 7 December 1857, *Dickensian,* XXXVIII (1942), 191.
8. *GE,* xv, 120.
9. xv, 120.
10. xv, 121.
11. xvii, 140.
12. xxix, 250.
13. liii, 453.
14. liii, 453–454.
15. liii, 455.
16. liii, 458.
17. liii, 460.
18. liii, 461–462.
19. viii, 60.
20. viii, 60.
21. viii, 60–61.
22. viii, 63.
23. viii, 63.
24. viii, 64.
25. ix, 71–72.
26. xi, 90.
27. xi, 93.
28. xi, 93.
29. xxix, 256.
30. xi, 94–95.
31. xi, 95.
32. xvii, 142.

33. xix, 169.
34. xix, 170.
35. xxix, 256.
36. xxix, 257.
37. xxix, 259.
38. xxxviii, 324–325.
39. xxxviii, 325.
40. xxxviii, 330.
41. xlix, 429.
42. xxxviii, 329.
43. xlix, 430.
44. xlix, 431.
45. xlix, 431.
46. xlix, 431–432.
47. xlix, 432.
48. viii, 59.
49. xi, 89.
50. viii, 65.
51. xi, 85.
52. viii, 67.
53. xvii, 133–134.
54. xxix, 248.
55. xliii, 383.
56. xlix, 424.
57. xlix, 428.
58. lix, 519.
59. i, 3.
60. i, 3.
61. i, 4.
62. ii, 13.
63. ii, 14.
64. iii, 16–17.
65. i, 1.
66. xlii, 370.

67. iii, 19.
68. v, 34–35.
69. v, 35.
70. v, 39.
71. x, 82.
72. xxxix, 338.
73. xxxix, 338.
74. xxxix, 338.
75. xxxix, 344.
76. xxxix, 344.
77. xxxix, 346.
78. xxxix, 348.
79. xxxix, 348.
80. xl, 362.

81. xl, 354.
82. xl, 354.
83. xlvi, 406–407.
84. liv, 468.
85. lii, 448.
86. liv, 470.
87. liv, 480.
88. lvi, 490–491.
89. lvi, 491.
90. lvi, 492.
91. lvi, 493.
92. lvi, 494.
93. lvi, 495.
94. lvi, 495.

Selected Bibliography

Abrams, M. H. *The Mirror and the Lamp: Romantic Theory and the Critical Tradition* (New York: Norton, 1958).

Altick, Richard D. *The English Common Reader; A Social History of the Mass Reading Public, 1800–1900* (Chicago: University of Chicago Press, 1957).

Ashton, John. *Chapbooks of the Eighteenth Century* (London: Chatto and Windus, 1882).

Auerbach, Erich. *Mimesis: The Representation of Reality in Western Literature,* trans. Willard Trask (New York: Doubleday, 1957).

Avery, Gillian, with the assistance of Angela Bull. *Nineteenth Century Children: Heroes and Heroines in English Children's Stories, 1780–1900* (London: Hodder and Stoughton, 1965).

Axton, William F. *Circle of Fire: Dickens' Vision and Style and the Popular Victorian Theater* (Lexington: University of Kentucky Press, 1966).

Bayley, John. *"Oliver Twist:* 'Things as They Really Are,'" *Dickens and the Twentieth Century,* ed. John Gross and Gabriel Pearson (London: Routledge and Kegan Paul, 1962).

Bede, Cuthbert. "A Reminiscence of George Cruikshank and His 'Magazine,'" *Notes and Queries,* 5th ser., IX (1878), 281.

Bennett, Rachel. "Punch versus Christian in *The Old Curiosity Shop,"* *Review of English Studies,* New Series, XXII (1971), 423–434.

Bettelheim, Bruno. *The Uses of Enchantment: The Meaning and Importance of Fairy Tales* (New York: Knopf, 1976).

Blackmur, R. P. "Notes on Four Categories in Criticism," *Sewanee Review,* LIV (1946), 576–590.

Bredsdorff, Elias. *Hans Andersen and Charles Dickens: A Friendship and Its Dissolution* (Cambridge: Heffer, 1956).

Briggs, Katharine M. "The Folklore of Charles Dickens," *Journal of the Folklore Institute,* VII (1970), 3–20.

Brogunier, Joseph. "The Dreams of Montague Tigg and Jonas Chuzzlewit," *Dickensian,* LVIII (1962), 165–170.

Brown, E. K. *"David Copperfield,"* *Yale Review,* XXXVII (1948), 650–666.

Buchan, John. *The Novel and the Fairy Tale* (Oxford: Oxford University Press, 1931).

Buchanan, Robert. "The 'Good Genie' of Fiction: Thoughts While Reading Forster's *Life of Charles Dickens,"* *St. Paul's Magazine,* X (1872), 130–148.

Buckley, Jerome Hamilton. "Dickens, David and Pip," *Season of Youth: The Bildungsroman from Dickens to Golding* (Cambridge: Harvard University Press, 1974).

Butt, John. "Dickens's Christmas Books," *Pope, Dickens, and Others: Essays and Addresses* (Edinburgh: University of Edinburgh Press, 1969).

Butt, John, and Kathleen Tillotson. *Dickens at Work* (London: Methuen, 1957).

Campbell, Joseph. *The Hero with a Thousand Faces* (New York: Pantheon Books, 1953).

Carey, John. *The Violent Effigy: A Study of Dickens' Imagination* (London: Faber and Faber, 1973).

Cassirer, Ernst. *Language and Myth,* trans. Susanne K. Langer (New York: Harper, 1946).

Chartier, Emile ["Alain"]. "Le fantastique et le réel d'après les 'Contes de Nöel' de Dickens," *Nouvelle Revue Française,* LIII (1939), 817–823.

The Child's Fairy Library (London: Joseph Thomas, Tegg and Son, and Simpkin and Marshall, c. 1835).

Clayborough, Arthur. *The Grotesque in English Literature* (Oxford: Clarendon Press, 1965).

Cohen, Jane Rabb. "'All-of-a-Twist': the Relationship of George Cruikshank and Charles Dickens," *Harvard Library Bulletin,* XVII (1969), 169–194, 320–342.

Coleridge, Samuel Taylor. *Collected Letters of Samuel Taylor Coleridge,* ed. Earl Leslie Griggs. 6 vols. (Oxford: Clarendon Press, 1956–1971).

Collins, Philip. "Queen Mab's Chariot Among the Steam Engines: Dickens and 'Fancy,'" *English Studies,* XLII (1961), 78–90.

Coveney, Peter. *Poor Monkey: The Child in Literature* (London: Rockliff, 1957).

Cox, C. B. "Realism and Fantasy in *David Copperfield,*" *Bulletin of the John Rylands Library,* XLII (1970), 267–283.

Cruikshank, George. *The Cruikshank Fairy-Book: Four Famous Stories* (New York: Putnam's, 1897).

Darton, F. J. Harvey. *Children's Books in England: Five Centuries of Social Life,* 2nd ed. (Cambridge: Cambridge University Press, 1960).

Davis, Earle. *The Flint and the Flame: The Artistry of Charles Dickens* (Columbia: University of Missouri Press, 1963).

Dent, H. C. *The Life and Characters of Charles Dickens* (London: Odhams Press, n. d.).

Dessner, Lawrence Jay. "*Great Expectations:* 'the ghost of a man's own father,'" *PMLA,* XCI (1976), 436–449.

Dickens, Charles. *Charles Dickens as Editor: Being Letters Written by Him to William Henry Wills His Sub-editor,* ed. Rudolph C. Lehmann (New York: Sturgis and Walton, 1912).

———. *Charles Dickens' Uncollected Writings from "Household Words,"* *1850–1859,* ed. Harry Stone. 2 vols. (Bloomington: Indiana University Press, 1968).

———, ed. *The Household Narrative of Current Events, (For the Year 1850,)*

Being a Monthly Supplement to Household Words (London: Office, 16 Wellington Street North, 1850).

————. *The Letters of Charles Dickens,* ed. Walter Dexter. 3 vols. The Nonesuch Edition (Bloomsbury: Nonesuch Press, 1938).

————. *The Letters of Charles Dickens. Vols. I–III,* ed. Madeline House, Graham Storey, and Kathleen Tillotson. The Pilgrim Edition (Oxford: Clarendon Press, 1965, 1969, 1974).

————. *Letters from Charles Dickens to Angela Burdett-Coutts, 1841–1865,* ed. Edgar Johnson (London: Jonathan Cape, 1953).

————. *Mr. and Mrs. Charles Dickens, His Letters to Her,* ed. Walter Dexter (London: Constable, 1935).

————. *The Speeches of Charles Dickens,* ed. K. J. Fielding (Oxford: Clarendon Press, 1960).

————. *The Works of Charles Dickens,* ed. B. W. Matz. 40 vols. The National Edition (London: Chapman and Hall, 1906–1908).

Du Soir, A. P. "The Elfin Quality in Dickens," *Dickensian,* XXIII (1927), 47–51.

Dunn, Richard J. "Dickens' Mastery of the Macabre," *Dickens Studies,* I (1965), 33–39.

————. "Drummle and Startop: Doubling in *Great Expectations,*" *Dickensian,* LXIII (1967), 125–127.

Engel, Monroe. "A Kind of Allegory: *The Old Curiosity Shop,*" *The Interpretation of Narrative: Theory and Practice,* ed. Morton W. Bloomfield (Cambridge: Harvard University Press, 1970).

Fanger, D. *Dostoevsky and Romantic Realism: A Study of Dostoevsky in Relation to Balzac, Dickens, and Gogol* (Cambridge: Harvard University Press, 1965).

Fiedler, Leslie A. "Archetype and Signature," *Art and Psychoanalysis,* ed. William Phillips (Cleveland: World Publishing, 1963).

Fielding, K. J. *Charles Dickens: A Critical Introduction* (Boston: Houghton Mifflin, 1965).

Flibbert, Joseph T. "*Bleak House* and the Brothers Grimm," *Victorian Newsletter,* XXXVI (1969), 1–5.

"Folklore in Literature: A Symposium," *Journal of American Folklore,* LXX (1957), 1–24.

Folland, Harold F. "The Doer and the Deed: Theme and Pattern in *Barnaby Rudge,*" *PMLA,* LXXIV (1959), 406–417.

Ford, George H. *Dickens and His Readers: Aspects of Novel-Criticism Since 1836* (Princeton: Princeton University Press, 1955).

————. "Dickens and the Voices of Time," *Dickens Centennial Essays,* ed. Ada Nisbet and Blake Nevius (Berkeley: University of California Press, 1971).

Forster, John. *The Life of Charles Dickens,* ed. J. W. T. Ley (London: Cecil Palmer, 1928).

Frank, Lawrence. "The Intelligibility of Madness in *Our Mutual Friend* and *The Mystery of Edwin Drood,*" *Dickens Studies Annual,* V (1976), 150–195.

Friedman, Norman. "Versions of Form in Fiction—*Great Expectations* and *The Great Gatsby,*" *Accent,* XIV (1954), 246–264.

Fromm, Erich. *The Forgotten Language: An Introduction to the Understanding of Dreams, Fairy Tales, and Myths* (New York: Grove Press, 1957).

Frye, Northrop. *Anatomy of Criticism: Four Essays* (Princeton: Princeton University Press, 1957).

———. "Dickens and the Comedy of Humors," *Experience in the Novel*, ed. Roy Harvey Pearce (New York: Columbia University Press, 1968).

———. *The Secular Scripture: A Study of the Structure of Romance* (Cambridge: Harvard University Press, 1976).

———. *Spiritus Mundi: Essays on Literature, Myth, and Society* (Bloomington: Indiana University Press, 1976).

Gibson, Priscilla. "Dickens's Uses of Animism," *Nineteenth-Century Fiction*, VII (1953), 283–291.

Glicksberg, Charles I. "The Numinous in Fiction," *Arizona Quarterly*, XV (1959), 305–313.

Gose, Elliott B. *Imagination Indulged: The Irrational in the Nineteenth-Century Novel* (Montreal: McGill-Queen's University Press, 1972).

Green, Roger Lancelyn. *Tellers of Tales: Children's Books and their Authors from 1800–1964* (London: Edmund Ward, 1965).

Greene, Graham. "The Young Dickens," *The Lost Childhood and Other Essays* (London: Eyre and Spottiswoode, 1951).

[Grimm, Jakob and Wilhelm]. *German Popular Stories, Translated from the Kinder und Haus-Marchen, Collected by M. M. Grimm, From Oral Tradition* (London: Vol. I, C. Baldwyn, 1823; Vol. II, James Robins, 1826). For a more readily available edition, see *German Popular Stories* (London: John Camden Hotten, 1868).

Grob, Shirley. "Dickens and Some Motifs of the Fairy Tale," *Texas Studies in Literature and Language*, V (1964), 567–579.

Guerard, Albert J. *The Triumph of the Novel: Dickens, Dostoevsky, and Faulkner* (London: Oxford University Press, 1977).

Hannaford, Richard. "Fairy-tale Fantasy in *Nicholas Nickleby*," *Criticism*, XVI (1974), 247–259.

Hardy, Barbara. "Food and Ceremony in *Great Expectations*," *Essays in Criticism*, XIII (1963), 351–363.

Holland, Norman. *The Dynamics of Literary Response* (New York: Oxford University Press, 1968).

Hornback, Bert G. *"Noah's Arkitecture": A Study of Dickens's Mythology* (Athens: Ohio University Press, 1972).

Hürlimann, Bettina. *Three Centuries of Children's Books in Europe*, trans. Brian W. Alderson (London: Oxford University Press, 1967).

Hutter, Albert D. "Crime and Fantasy in *Great Expectations*," *Psychoanalysis and Literary Process*, ed. Frederick Crews (Cambridge: Winthrop, 1970).

———. "Reconstructive Autobiography: The Experience at Warren's Blacking," *Dickens Studies Annual*, VI (1977), 1–14.

Jerrold, Blanchard. *The Life of George Cruikshank: In Two Epochs*, new ed. (London: Chatto and Windus, 1898).

Johnson, Edgar. *Charles Dickens, His Tragedy and Triumph*. 2 vols. (New York: Simon and Schuster, 1952).

Johnson, William C. "Dickens and Demons: A Comparative Approach," *English Record,* XXII (1972), 33–40.

Kaplan, Fred. *Dickens and Mesmerism: The Hidden Springs of Fiction* (Princeton: Princeton University Press, 1975).

Kayser, Wolfgang. *The Grotesque in Art and Literature,* trans. Ulrich Weisstein (Bloomington: Indiana University Press, 1963).

Kirkpatrick, Larry. "The Gothic Flame of Charles Dickens," *Victorian Newsletter,* XXXI (1967), 20–24.

Kitton, Frederic G. *Dickens and His Illustrators* (London: George Redway, 1899).

Kotzin, Michael C. *Dickens and the Fairy Tale* (Bowling Green: Bowling Green University Popular Press, 1972).

Lamb, Charles and Mary. *The Letters of Charles and Mary Lamb,* ed. E. V. Lucas. 3 vols. (London: Methuen, 1935).

Lane, Lauriat, Jr. "The Devil in *Oliver Twist,*" *Dickensian,* LII (1956), 132–136.

———. "Dickens and the Double," *Dickensian,* LV (1959), 47–55.

Langer, Susanne K. *Philosophy in a New Key: A Study in the Symbolism of Reason, Rite, and Art,* 3rd. ed. (Cambridge: Harvard University Press, 1963).

Langton, Robert. *The Childhood and Youth of Charles Dickens* (London: Hutchinson, 1912).

Law, M. H. "The Indebtedness of *Oliver Twist* to Defoe's *History of the Devil,*" *PMLA,* XL (1925), 892–897.

Leavis, F. R. and Q. D. *Dickens the Novelist* (London: Chatto and Windus, 1970).

Lecker, Barbara. "Walter Gay and the Theme of Fancy in *Dombey and Son,*" *Dickensian,* LXVII (1971), 21–30.

Lesser, Simon O. *Fiction and the Unconscious* (New York: Vintage Books, 1962).

Levin, Harry. "The Uncles of Dickens," *The Worlds of Victorian Fiction,* ed. Jerome H. Buckley (Cambridge: Harvard University Press, 1975).

Lévi-Strauss, Claude. "The Structural Study of Myth," *European Literary Theory and Practice,* ed. Vernon W. Gras (New York: Dell, 1973).

Lewes, George Henry. "Dickens in Relation to Criticism," *Fortnightly Review,* XVII (1872), 141–154.

Lindsay, Jack. *Charles Dickens: A Biographical and Critical Study* (London: Andrew Dakers, 1950).

Longmate, Norman. *The Waterdrinkers: A History of Temperance* (London: Hamilton, 1968).

Lukács, Georg. *The Theory of the Novel* (Cambridge: M.I.T. Press, 1971).

Lüthi, Max. *Once Upon a Time: On the Nature of Fairy Tales,* trans. Lee Chadeayne and Paul Gottwald (Bloomington: Indiana University Press, 1976).

McLean, Robert Simpson. "Putting Quilp to Rest," *Victorian Newsletter,* XXXIV (1968), 29–33.

McMaster, R. D. "Dickens and the Horrific," *Dalhousie Review,* XXXVIII (1958), 18–28.

————. "Man into Beast in Dickensian Caricature," *University of Toronto Quarterly*, XXXI (1962), 354–361.

Manheim, Leonard F. "The Personal History of David Copperfield," *American Imago*, IX (1952), 21–43.

Marcus, Steven. *Dickens: From Pickwick to Dombey* (London: Chatto and Windus, 1965).

Marlow, James E. "Memory, Romance, and the Expressive Symbol in Dickens," *Nineteenth-Century Fiction*, XXX (1975), 20–32.

Marshall, William H. "The Conclusion of *Great Expectations* as the Fulfillment of Myth," *The Personalist*, XLIV (1963), 337–347.

Mathews, Mrs. *Memoirs of Charles Mathews, Comedian*, 4 vols. (London: Richard Bentley, 1839).

Meckier, Jerome. "Dickens and *King Lear*: A Myth for Victorian England," *South Atlantic Quarterly*, LXXI (1972), 75–90.

Meisel, Martin. "Miss Havisham Brought to Book," *PMLA*, LXXXI (1966), 278–285.

Miyoshi, Masao. *The Divided Self* (New York: New York University Press, 1969).

Monod, Sylvère. *Dickens Romancier* (Paris: Hachette, 1953).

————. "James Steerforth ou le problème du mal dans *David Copperfield*," *Annales de l'Université de Paris*, XXXVII (1967), 166–176.

Moynahan, Julian. "The Hero's Guilt: The Case of *Great Expectations*," *Essays in Criticism*, X (1960), 60–79.

Muir, Percy, *English Children's Books, 1600–1900* (London: Batsford, 1954).

Mulvey, Christopher. "*David Copperfield*: The Folk-Story Structure," *Dickens Studies Annual*, V (1976), 74–94.

[Murray, E. C. Grenville]. *The Roving Englishman* (London: Routledge, 1854).

Murray, Henry A., ed. *Myth and Mythmaking* (New York: Braziller, 1960).

Needham, Gwendolyn B. "The Undisciplined Heart of David Copperfield," *Nineteenth-Century Fiction*, IX (1954), 81–107.

Neuburg, Victor E. *Chapbooks: A Bibliography of References to English and American Chapbook Literature of the Eighteenth and Nineteenth Centuries* (London: Vine Press, 1964).

Ohmann, Richard M., ed. *The Making of Myth* (New York: Putnam's, 1962).

Olshin, Toby A. "'The Yellow Dwarf' and *The Old Curiosity Shop*," *Nineteenth-Century Fiction*, XXV (1970), 96–99.

Opie, Iona and Peter, eds. *The Classic Fairy Tales* (London: Oxford University Press, 1974).

Page, John T. "Dickens and Guy Fawkes," *Dickensian*, VIII (1912), 278–279.

Patten, Robert L. "The Art of *Pickwick*'s Interpolated Tales," *ELH*, XXXIV (1967), 349–366.

————. "Dickens Time and Again," *Dickens Studies Annual*, II (1972), 163–196.

Pearlman, E. "David Copperfield Dreams of Drowning," *American Imago*, XXVIII (1971), 391–403.

Penzoldt, Peter. *The Supernatural in Fiction* (New York: Humanities Press, 1965).

Phillips, Walter C. *Dickens, Reade, and Collins: Sensation Novelists. A Study of the Conditions and Theories of Novel Writing in Victorian England* (New York: Columbia University Press, 1919).

Praz, Mario. "Charles Dickens," *The Hero in Eclipse in Victorian Fiction,* trans. Angus Davidson (London: Oxford University Press, 1956).

Rabkin, Eric S. *The Fantastic in Literature* (Princeton: Princeton University Press, 1976).

Reid, J. C. *The Hidden World of Charles Dickens* (Auckland: University of Auckland, 1962).

Roberts, C. E. Bechhofer. "The Huffams, the Barrows, and the Admiralty," *Dickensian,* XXIV (1928), 263–266.

Rudwin, Maxmilian. *The Devil in Legend and Literature* (New York: AMS Press, 1970).

St. John, Judith, compiler. *The Osborne Collection of Early Children's Books, 1476–1910.* 2 vols. (Toronto: Toronto Public Library, 1966, 1975).

Scarborough, Dorothy. *The Supernatural in Modern English Fiction* (New York: Octagon Books, 1967).

A School-Fellow and Friend. "Recollections of Charles Dickens," *Dickensian,* VII (1911), 229–231.

Shumaker, Wayne. *Literature and the Irrational: A Study in Anthropological Backgrounds* (Englewood Cliffs: Prentice-Hall, 1960).

Sipe, Samuel. "The Intentional World of Dickens's Fiction," *Nineteenth-Century Fiction,* XXX (1975), 1–19.

Slater, Michael. "Dickens (and Forster) at Work on *The Chimes,*" *Dickens Studies,* II (1966), 106–140.

Speaight, George. *Juvenile Drama: The History of the English Toy Theatre* (London: Macdonald, 1946).

Spilka, Mark. *Dickens and Kafka: A Mutual Interpretation* (Bloomington: Indiana University Press, 1963).

Stange, G. Robert. "Expectations Well Lost: Dickens' Fable for His Time," *College English,* XVI (1954), 9–17.

Stoehr, Taylor. *Dickens: The Dreamer's Stance* (Ithaca: Cornell University Press, 1965).

Stone, Harry. "An Added Note on Dickens and Miss Havisham," *Nineteenth-Century Fiction,* X (1955), 85–86.

———. "Dark Corners of the Mind: Dickens' Childhood Reading," *Horn Book Magazine,* XXXIX (1963), 306–321.

———. "Dickens' Artistry and *The Haunted Man,*" *South Atlantic Quarterly,* LXI (1962), 492–505.

———. "Dickens, Cruikshank, and Fairy Tales," *George Cruikshank: A Revaluation,* ed. Robert L. Patten (Princeton: Princeton University Library, 1974).

———. "Dickens and Leitmotif: Music-Staircase Imagery in *Dombey and Son,*" *College English,* XXV (1963), 217–220.

———. "Fairy Tales and Ogres: Dickens' Imagination and *David Copperfield,*" *Criticism,* VI (1964), 324–330.

———. "Fire, Hand, and Gate: Dickens' *Great Expectations,*" *Kenyon Review,* XXIV (1962), 662–691.

————. "The Genesis of a Novel: *Great Expectations*," *Charles Dickens, 1812–1870*, ed. E. W. F. Tomlin (London: Weidenfeld and Nicolson, 1969).

————. "The Love Pattern in Dickens' Novels," *Dickens the Craftsman: Strategies of Presentation*, ed. Robert B. Partlow, Jr. (Carbondale: Southern Illinois University Press, 1970).

————. "The Novel as Fairy Tale: Dickens' *Dombey and Son*," *English Studies*, XLVII (1966), 1–27.

Sucksmith, Harvey Peter. *The Narrative Art of Charles Dickens: The Rhetoric of Sympathy and Irony in His Novels* (Oxford: Clarendon Press, 1970).

Targ, William, ed. *Bibliophile in the Nursery: A Bookman's Treasury of Collectors' Lore on Old and Rare Children's Books* (Cleveland: World Publishing, 1957).

Thalmann, Marianne. *The Romantic Fairy Tale: Seeds of Surrealism*, trans. Mary B. Corcoran (Ann Arbor: University of Michigan Press, 1964).

Thomas, Gillian. "Dickens and *The Portfolio*," *Dickensian*, LXVIII (1972), 167–172.

Thurley, Geoffrey. *The Dickens Myth: Its Genesis and Structure* (London: Routledge and Kegan Paul, 1976).

Tillotson, Kathleen. "The Middle Years: From the *Carol* to *Copperfield*," *Dickens Memorial Lectures* (London: The Dickens Fellowship, 1970).

————. *Novels of the Eighteen-Forties* (Oxford: Clarendon Press, 1956).

Todorov, Tzvetan. *The Fantastic*, trans. Richard Howard (Ithaca: Cornell University Press, 1975).

Tolkien, J. R. R. "On Fairy-Stories," *Essays Presented to Charles Williams* (Oxford: Oxford University Press, 1947).

Tuer, Andrew W. *Forgotten Children's Books* (London: Leadenhall Press, 1898–1899).

Tymms, Ralph. *Doubles in Literary Psychology* (Cambridge: Bowes and Bowes, 1949).

Van Ghent, Dorothy. "The Dickens World: A View from Todgers's," *Sewanee Review*, LVIII (1950), 419–438.

————. "On *Great Expectations*," *The English Novel: Form and Function* (New York: Rinehart, 1953).

Varma, Devendra P. *The Gothic Flame: Being a History of the Gothic Novel in England: Its Origins, Efflorescence, Disintegration, and Residuary Influences* (New York: Russell and Russell, 1966).

Victoria and Albert Museum Manuscript. Carlyle to Forster, 16 February 1874.

Ward, Mrs. E. M. *Memories of Ninety Years*, 2nd ed., ed. Isabel G. McAllister (New York: Holt, [1925]).

Welsh, Alexander. *The City of Dickens* (Oxford: Clarendon Press, 1971).

Williamson, Colin. "Two Missing Links in *Oliver Twist*," *Nineteenth-Century Fiction*, XXII (1967), 225–234.

Wilson, A. E. *Penny Plain, Two Pence Coloured: A History of the Juvenile Drama* (London: Harrap, 1932).

————. *The Story of Pantomime* (London: Home and Van Thal, 1949).

Wilson, Angus. "Dickens on Children and Childhood," *Dickens 1970: Centenary Essays*, ed. Michael Slater (London: Chapman and Hall, 1970).

Wilson, Edmund. "Dickens: The Two Scrooges," *The Wound and the Bow: Seven Studies in Literature* (London: W. H. Allen, 1952).

Winters, Warrington. "Dickens and the Psychology of Dreams," *PMLA,* LXIII (1948), 984–1006.

Index